UNDERSTANDING
ARGUMENTS
AN INTRODUCTION TO INFORMAL LOGIC

UNDERSTANDING
ARGUMENTS
AN INTRODUCTION TO INFORMAL LOGIC

Robert J. Fogelin
Yale University

HARCOURT BRACE JOVANOVICH, INC.
New York San Diego Chicago San Francisco Atlanta

ISBN: 0-15-592860-0
Library of Congress Catalog Card Number: 78-50684

Printed in the United States of America

Illustrations by Eric G. Hieber, eh Technical Services

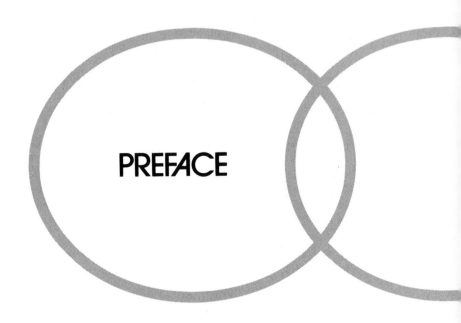

PREFACE

This book is about arguments. It considers arguments not in the narrow sense of quarrels or squabbles but in the broader, logician's sense of giving reasons in behalf of some claim. Viewing arguments in this way, we see that they are a common feature of daily life, for we are often involved in giving reasons or evaluating reasons given by others. These are not only common but important activities. Deciding what to believe, how to act, how to judge others, and the like are all, in the end, questions to be settled by weighing reasons. Traditionally, logic has been considered the most general science dealing with arguments.

For certain purposes, arguments are best studied as abstract patterns. Logic is not concerned with particular arguments—for example, your attempt to prove that the bank, not you, has made a mistake. The task of logic is to discover the fundamental principles for distinguishing good arguments from bad ones. The study of those general principles that make certain patterns of argument reasonable (or valid) and other patterns of argument unreasonable (or invalid) is called formal logic.

A different, but complementary, way of viewing an argument is to treat it as *a particular use of language*: arguing is one of the things that we do with words. This approach places stress upon arguing as a linguistic activity. Instead of studying arguments as abstract patterns, it takes them "in the rough," as they occur in actual argumentation. It raises questions of the following kind: What is the place of argument within language as a whole? In a given language (say, our own), what words or phrases are characteristic of arguments? What task or tasks are arguments supposed to perform? When an approach to arguments has this form, the study is called informal logic. As its subtitle indicates, *Understanding Arguments* is primarily a text in informal logic.

The methods of informal analysis are developed in the first five chapters of this book. Chapter 1 gives a general account of the nature of language, relying heavily upon the works of J. L. Austin and H. P. Grice. The ideas of Austin and Grice will give the student a much better idea of the complexity, richness, and diversity of linguistic activity. They also provide the conceptual tools for dealing with language in an intelligent and subtle manner. These ideas have immediate application to the language we use in everyday life and can help us make better sense of it.

Chapters 2 through 5 apply the general approach of Chapter 1 specifically to arguments. Beginning with an account of the way in which arguments are formulated, these chapters develop what we shall call *the art of close analysis of arguments.* The study involves a careful and systematic examination of the various roles that words and expressions play in the presentation of an argument. This study of the fine details of arguments lays the basis for assessing our own arguments and those of others. Close analysis is a valuable tool for both critical reading and intelligent writing.

Chapters 6 and 7 consider topics in formal logic. The emphasis here is theoretical rather than practical. In the informal analysis of an argument, the notion that a conclusion "follows from" given premises (or that an argument is *valid*) is taken as primitive. In this book, the role assigned to formal logic is to elucidate this concept of logical validity. There is, however, very little attempt to show how these formal techniques can be applied directly to arguments that arise in everday life. There are systematic reasons for this omission. The logic that underlies even simple arguments is often very complex and quite beyond the scope of a general introductory course in logic. Armed only with the introductory methods of modern symbolic logic, the general student is almost always disappointed when he or she tries to analyze concrete specimens of arguments. The material so laboriously learned is soon forgotten. On the other hand, only the methods of formal logic are adequate for a systematic investigation of such concepts as logical consequence, validity, and logical form. For the general student, the study of formal logic stands to the understanding of arguments roughly as the study of music theory stands to the appreciation of music.

The material that makes up Part Two of this book has two purposes. First, it presents extended examples of arguments on controversial topics of contemporary interest. These include discussions of the safety of atomic power plants, the legitimacy of minority quotas, and the moral issues concerning abortion. The second purpose of Part Two is to study the character of argument and reasoning as they arise in particular fields, including law, science, theology, and philosophy. We cannot understand the statements made in a given field in isolation from the reasoning that lies behind them. Understanding law, for example, cannot be separated from understanding legal reasoning. In our complex world, it is impossible for a person to be expert in many fields. But an educated person can develop a better understanding and appreciation of the way people in different fields think by concentrating on *how* they think rather than simply on *what* they think.

It has been my experience that students find Austin's theory of speech acts and Grice's theory of conversational implication both eye-opening and immediately relevant to their other concerns. This led to the idea of constructing an introductory logic course around these ideas, and this book was written to supply materials for such a course. In taking over ideas from Austin and Grice, I have sometimes simplified, even changed, them for my own purposes. To make these relationships clear, and, more importantly, to acknowledge the extent of my indebtedness, Austin's essay, "Performative Utterances," and Grice's essay, "Logic and Conversation," are reprinted in the appendix to this book. Students should be encouraged to read them.

Several people have made extensive comments on the text and corrected many minor and not a few major errors. Here I wish to thank Monroe Beardsley, William Forgie, and Thomas Pinney. In this respect I wish to acknowledge a particular debt to my friend and former colleague W. T. Jones, who gave a great deal of his valuable and scarce time to commenting both in detail and at large on this book-in-the-making.

There are also a great many other people who have contributed, either wittingly or unwittingly, to the book. They include Russell Abrams, Laurie Adams, Morton Beckner, James Bogan, Guido Calabresi, Harry Frankfurt, John Freccero, John Gleason, Richard Ketchum, Arthur Leff, Leon Lipson, Sidney Morgenbesser, Oskar Morgenstern, John Noonan, William A. Pullin, Paul A. Samuelson, and my students in Yale's Philosophy 15C. Patti O'Hara of Santa Barbara typed most of the manuscript, and I received invaluable editorial help from Claire Rubin of Harcourt Brace Jovanovich, Inc. and my wife, Florence Fogelin.

R. J. F.

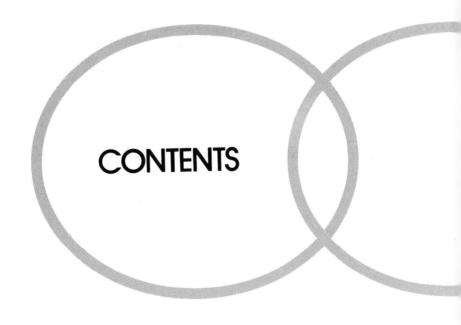

CONTENTS

PART TWO
SPECIMENS OF ARGUMENTS

For Eric, John, and Lars

An argument isn't just contradiction.

Can be.

No it can't. An argument is a connected series of statements intended to establish a proposition.

No it isn't.

Yes it is.

Argument Clinic,
from MONTY PYTHON'S PREVIOUS RECORD

PART ONE

THE ANALYSIS OF ARGUMENT

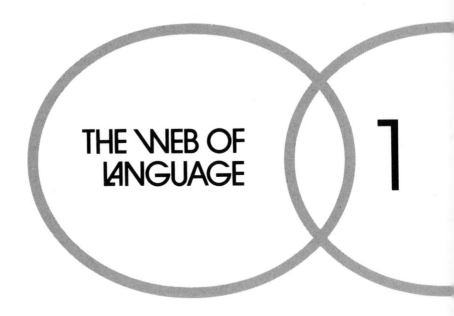

THE WEB OF
LANGUAGE

1

This chapter prepares the reader for the study of informal logic by surveying the general nature of language. It stresses three main ideas. First, language is <u>conventional</u>. Words take on their meanings within a rich system of linguistic customs. In order to understand the character of language, we must go beyond the spoken and written symbols to examine the conventions that give them meaning. Second, language is <u>diverse</u>. We sometimes use it to communicate information, but we also use it to ask questions, issue orders, write poetry, keep score, and perform an almost endless number of functions. Methods are presented here for discovering and analyzing these different uses of language. Finally, language allows us to express ourselves through <u>conversational implication</u> rather than explicit statement. The idea of conversational implication is an important guide for understanding why people speak (and act) as they do.

Language and Convention

Language is conventional: it is governed by a complicated network of conventions. Some of the conventions of language are obvious at first glance. There seems to be no reason why we, as English speakers, use the word "dog" to refer to dogs rather than to cats, trees, or anything at all. Any word might have been used to stand for anything. Beyond this, there seems to be no reason why we put words together in the way that we do. In English we put adjectives before the nouns they modify. We thus speak of a *green salad.* In French adjectives usually follow the noun, and so instead of saying *verte salade* the French say *salade verte.* The conventions of our own language are so much with us that it strikes us as odd when we discover that other languages have different conventions. A French diplomat once praised his own language because, as he said, it followed the natural order of thought. This strikes us English speakers as silly, but in seeing what is silly about it, we see that the word order in our own language is conventional as well.

It is important to realize that our language is conventional, but it is also important not to misunderstand this fact. From the idea that language is conventional, it is easy to conclude that language is *arbitrary,* so that it really doesn't matter which words we use. It takes only a little thought to see that this is not true. If I wish to communicate with others I must follow the system of conventions that others use. To put matters simply, conventions do not destroy meaning by making it arbitrary; conventions bring meaning into existence.

A misunderstanding of the conventions of language can lead to pointless disputes. Sometimes, in the middle of a discussion, someone will declare that "the whole thing is just a matter of definition." Now there are times when definitions are important and arguments turn upon them, but in general this is not true. Suppose someone has fallen off a cliff and is heading toward certain death on the rocks below. Of course, it is a matter of definition (of convention) that we use the word "death" to describe the result of the sudden stop at the end of the fall. We might have used some other word—perhaps "birth"—instead. But it certainly will not help the person who is falling to change the meaning of the word "death" in the middle of his plunge. It will do no good for him to yell out, "By death I mean birth." It will not help even if *everyone* agrees to change the meaning of the words in this way. If we all decided to adopt this new convention, we would then say, "He fell from the cliff to his birth" instead of "He fell from the cliff to his death." But speaking in this way will not change the facts. It will not, for example, make those who care for him feel better.

The upshot of this simple example is that the truth of what we say is rarely just a matter of definition. The words we use are governed by conventions, and in the process of learning our language we learn to follow these conventions in speaking. (Only later do we develop some understanding of these conventions.) We then go on to make certain claims about the world. Others can understand what we say because we follow the ordinary conventions that give meaning to our words. Whether what I have said is true or not will depend, for the most part, on how things stand in the world. For example, if a German wishes to say that snow is black, then he will use the words "Schnee ist schwartz." Other Germans will *understand* his words, but unless snow is different in Germany than every place else, they will also think that he has said something false, and may wonder how he could make such a mistake. In general, then, the truth of what we say is not merely a matter of definition or convention, and when someone uses this ploy in the middle of an argument we can usually assume that he or she is in desperate shape.

In the last sentence I have used two qualifying phrases: "in general" and "usually." To say that something holds in general, or usually, is to admit that there may be exceptions. Such a qualification is needed in this case because *sometimes* the truth of what we say is simply a matter of definition. Take a simple example. The claim that a triangle has three sides is true by definition, because a triangle is defined as "a three-sided closed plane figure." Again, if someone says that sin is wrong, he has said something that is true by definition, for a sin is defined as, among other things, "something that is wrong."

Consider a more complicated case. Suppose someone argues that the only true democracies exist in communist states. He admits that in such states there are no general elections where a large portion of the population is allowed to choose between competing parties, but he goes on to say that a genuine democracy exists only when the party in power reflects the interests of the masses. Here we might challenge the definition of a democracy that he is using and then be met by the following reply: Why should everyone in the world be bound by the capitalist definition of a democracy? Alternatively, we can accept his definition and argue that communist parties do not reflect the interests of the masses. We might then be told that no democracy is perfect, especially those in newly emerging nations. Here the only way to stop our heads from swimming is to return to common sense and reject both the definition and the facts. Historically, in a democracy the people *choose* the policies that govern them, or at least the representatives who formulate these policies. When this choice is absent, democracy does not exist. A despotism, however benevolent, is not a democracy. We should advise our opponent to be candid enough to admit that he is against a democracy and, if he is in favor of another form of government, to give it another name and defend it on its own terms. If he is misrepresenting the facts, we can say that too. In short, we need not be driven to silence by a person who distorts the meaning of words and tampers with the facts. We can simply point out that he is distorting and tampering.

Sometimes, then, it is important to ask a person to define his terms.

We should do this whenever we think that someone is distorting the meaning of words to win an argumentative point. We can also ask for a definition in order to clarify, if we think that someone is speaking in a vague and loose way. But it makes no sense to ask that *every* word be defined. This would prove an endless task and we would never get around to saying anything in particular. Beyond this, asking for definitions is often just silly. If someone says "Pass the butter," it does not usually cross our minds to ask him to define "butter."

In sum, people are able to communicate with each other because they share certain linguistic conventions. These conventions could have been very different and in this sense they are arbitrary. But it does not follow from this that the truth of what we say is also merely arbitrary. In general, the truth of what we say is settled not by an appeal to definition, but by a look at the facts. Sometimes, however, the conventions of our language are misused or even abused. Here it makes sense to call for definition in order to restore mutual understanding. It would be absurd to ask that every word be defined.

Kinds of Conventions

In the previous section we saw that a language is a system of shared conventions that allows us to communicate with one another. If we pause to look at language, we see that it contains many different kinds of conventions. We have seen that words have meanings conventionally attached to them. The word "dog" is used conventionally to talk about dogs. Proper names are also conventionally assigned, for Harry Jones could have been named Wilbur Jones. (There are, of course, social limits involved in giving meanings to words. You cannot name your son John D. Rockefeller unless you happen to be named Rockefeller. But setting aside limitations of this kind and others the assignment of meanings to words is conventional.)

Other conventions concern the way in which words can be put together to form sentences. These are often called *grammatical* rules. Using the three words, "John," "hit," and "Harry," we can formulate sentences with very different meanings. For example, "John hit Harry" and "Harry hit John." We recognize that these sentences have different meanings because we understand the grammar of our language. This grammatical understanding also allows us to see that the sentence "Hit John Harry" does not mean anything at all—even though the individual words possess meaning. (Notice that "Hit John, Harry!" does mean something: it is a way of telling Harry to hit John.) Grammatical rules are very important, for they play a part in giving a meaning to a sentence as a whole. Admittedly, some of our grammatical rules play only a small role in this important task because they are largely stylistic. If I say "Hopefully he will be here tomorrow," I have uttered an ugly and ungrammatical sentence, yet I still make sense. If I violate deeper and more fundamental grammatical rules, I speak nonsense. It is worth noting, however, that some grammatical rules which seem only stylistic at first sight do make important contributions to the meaning of a sentence. The subjunctive mood is an example.

There are, then, at least two kinds of conventions that give meaning to what we say. The ones that assign meanings to individual words are commonly called *semantic* conventions. The conventions that lay down rules for combining words into meaningful wholes are called grammatical or *syntactical* conventions. The study of semantic conventions and syntactical conventions is largely the job of linguistics. Although important advances have been made in this field, every linguist will acknowledge that the amount unknown far outweighs the amount known. For this reason, linguistics is one of the most exciting fields of scientific investigation.

Later on we shall look more closely at semantic and syntactical conventions, for at times they are a source of fallacies and other confusions. In particular, we shall see how these conventions can generate *fallacies of ambiguity*. But before we examine the defects of our language, we should first appreciate that language is a powerful and subtle tool. We will next examine the wide variety of jobs that language can perform.

Speech Acts

When asked about the function of language, it is natural to reply that we use language to communicate our ideas. But this is only *one* of its uses. This becomes obvious as soon as we set aside our prejudices and take a look at the way our language actually works. Adding up a column of figures is a linguistic activity, but it does not communicate any ideas to others. When I add the figures I am not even trying to communicate anything to myself; I am trying to figure something out.

Writing a poem is a more interesting example. Sometimes poems convey factual information, and at other times they express philosophical truths. Poems also express emotions. Yet often the most important fact about a poem is that it is an artistic creation in the same way that a painting or a sculpture is an artistic creation. A poem is a linguistic artifact. We get a bad theory of poetry, and may even lessen our appreciation of poetry, if we think of a poem as a mere device for conveying the poet's thoughts and emotions to others. Consider one example:

Upon Julia's Clothes
ROBERT HERRICK

Whenas in silks my Julia goes,
Then, then, methinks, how sweetly flows
The liquefaction of her clothes.

> Next when I cast mine eyes, and see
> That brave vibration each way free,
> O, how that glittering taketh me!

Using a modern idiom, Herrick might have said "Julia's terrific figure turns me on." This second way of speaking leaves little doubt about what Herrick thinks and how he feels about Julia. The poem, by comparison, may fail to some extent in communication, but the chief difference lies elsewhere. Herrick's emotions are, after all, fairly common. His mode of expressing them, however, produces one of the most perfect poems in the English language. A poem is not simply a news broadcast with fancy frills.

Poetry provides an example of language used for purposes other than communication, but beyond that it is a complicated linguistic phenomenon that defies easy analysis. A look at our everyday conversations produces a host of other examples of language being used for different purposes. Grammarians, for example, have divided sentences into various moods:

(1) Indicative

(2) Interrogative

(3) Imperative

(4) Expressive (and some others)

For example:

(1) He is in England now that spring is here.

(2) Is he in England now that spring is here?

(3) Go to England now that spring is here!

(4) Oh to be in England, now that spring is here!!

The first sentence states a fact; we can use it to communicate information about a person's location. If we use it in this way, what we say will be either true or false. Notice that none of the other sentences can be called either true or false.

People who insist that language is always used to communicate information might try to defend their position in the following way: In asking a question, a person communicates a desire to know something. This explanation is often just wrong. When teachers ask questions on examinations, they are not communicating the desire to know the answers; presumably they know the answers already. An attempt might be made to patch up the argument by saying that the teacher is communicating the desire to know whether the *students* know the answers to the questions. This, however, is *not* what he is asking. An examination question looks like this: "Did Lincoln rely heavily on his cabinet in formulating war policy?" not like this: "Do you know whether Lincoln relied heavily on his cabinet in formulating war policy?" It would be hard to fail an examination made up of questions of the second kind.

Someone might try other ways of showing that asking a question is really a way of communicating information, but the arguments will become more and more complicated and arbitrary. This itself is a sign that one is looking at things in the wrong way. The philosopher J. L. Austin has introduced the notion of what he called the *descriptive fallacy*,[1] the mistake of taking the simple indicative sentences used to state facts as the model for all uses of language. Stating facts is one of the important things we do with language, but it is not the only thing—nor even the only important thing—that we do with language. When pointed out, this idea may seem pretty obvious—hardly worth making a fuss over—but its consequences for the philosophy of language have been profound.

Performatives

We have already noticed that grammarians have traditionally classified sentences into different moods (indicative, interrogative, imperative, expressive, etc.) and thereby recognized that sentences can perform different jobs. This classification, though helpful, gives only a slight indication of the vast number of things done with words. Even sentences in the indicative are a mixed batch, for not every sentence in the indicative is used to state a fact. This was emphasized by Austin, who noticed that some indicatives express what he called *performatives.* Two examples, verdicts and promises, will help explain this notion.

Verdicts At the close of a hearing, the appellate judge announces: "The judgment of the superior court is affirmed." This is an important announcement for the parties involved, but it does not state a fact. One party may think that the verdict is incorrect, but he cannot say that it is false. It would make no sense for him to stand up and say, "Your honor, you are not telling the truth; you do *not* affirm the judgment of the superior court." The judge may be thought wrong to have rendered this decision, but there is no question that he has rendered it. Furthermore, and this is important, he renders the verdict by saying the words, "The judgment of the superior court is affirmed." It is this *speech act* on the part of the judge that *makes* this so.

Baseball umpires also pass verdicts. The following story is told of the old-time umpire Bill Klem. On a close play, a runner came sliding

[1] J. L. Austin, "Performative Utterances," in J. O. Urmson and G. J. Warnock, eds., *Philosophical Papers,* 2nd ed. (Oxford: Clarendon Press, 1970), p. 234. Reprinted in the Appendix to this book, page 317.

into second base. For a moment Klem said nothing. When the runner asked whether he was safe or out, Klem replied, "You ain't nothin' 'til I say so." Klem was right. Whether the runner is safe or out awaits the decision of the umpire. Of course, the umpire is guided by certain complicated rules in calling a runner safe or out. If the runner is tagged before he reaches the base (and the ball is not dropped, etc.), then the umpire is *supposed* to call him out. Yet if the umpire calls him safe (and doesn't change his mind), the runner *is* safe. He becomes safe when the umpire utters the words "You're safe" (and doesn't take this back). The runner "ain't nothin' " till the umpire says so and then he is what the umpire says he is.

These two cases of verdicts show some obvious features of performatives. Although they are formulated in the indicative, they do not *describe* the situation at hand and thus cannot misdescribe it either. When the umpire makes a bad call, he does not say something that is false, even if his call is based upon a false belief—for example, that the second baseman missed the tag. Beyond this, the performative utterance brings about a change in the game. If the player is called safe, he may remain on second base; if he is called out, he is obliged to leave the field and an out is chalked up against his team.

Promises If I say to someone, "I promise to help you if you get in trouble," I place myself in a new relationship to that person. I now have an *obligation* to help him if, in fact, he does get in trouble. In many cases I would have no obligation at all had I not spoken these words. If I had said instead, "Look, if you get into trouble, don't come around asking for my help," then I would have indicated that I would take no responsibility for helping him. In contrast, the promise binds, for if I break my promise he has a *right* to blame me. Again, when I promise, I am not describing anything—not even my own intentions. I can make a promise with no intention of keeping it, although then I will have been dishonest. All the same, I will have made a promise. If I break a promise it does not help to say, "It seems that I have made a bad guess about what I was going to do." In promising, I am not just predicting what I will do; I am committing myself to doing it. The commitment comes about through uttering certain words *in certain contexts*.

The reference to *context* introduces another important theme: the effect of settings on performatives. If someone forces me to make a promise by twisting my arm nearly to the breaking point, the promise is not binding. I am under no obligation to keep this promise because it was given under duress. I haven't really promised at all. But not all performatives are void when exacted from us. In a schoolyard brawl, pounding my head on the ground, my opponent demands that I *give up*. Or, somewhat strangely, he demands that I say "Uncle." Saying "I give up" or "Uncle" is a way of surrendering or acknowledging defeat and it is a performative utterance that is typically forced out of us. Notice that if I say "I give up," I am not supposed to resume the fight when my opponent lets me up, nor—in civilized schoolyards at least—has my opponent the right to go on pummelling me. By saying "I give up," I change the relationship between us.

Other Kinds of Performatives Performative utterances are interesting first because they help to break the spell of the descriptive fallacy; they help us to see that we do a great many other important things with language besides reporting facts. Beyond this, they draw attention to a whole range of linguistic conventions which, until recent years, have largely gone unnoticed. A whole new world opens up when we ask how many kinds of performative utterances there are and what the *conventions* are that govern them. This is an area that you can explore on your own, and it's fun.

How many kinds of performative utterance are there? We can use what I shall call the *thereby test* as a rough and ready way of finding performative utterances. It works best for statements in the first person. Here are some examples of this test:

If I say "I promise to meet you tomorrow," I thereby promise to meet you tomorrow.

If I say "I bid five clubs," I thereby bid five clubs.

If I say "I surrender," I thereby surrender.

If I say "I apologize," I thereby apologize.

If I (as a minister) say "I pronounce you man and wife," I thereby pronounce the couple man and wife.

Here it seems that *saying* something amounts to *doing* it. The situation is quite different with statements of fact. If I say "I am six feet tall," I am not thereby six feet tall. If I say "Munich is the capital of Germany," Munich is not thereby the capital of Germany. (On the other hand, an absolute monarch might declare that Munich is the capital of Germany, thereby making it so.) The thereby test will turn up a great number of performative utterances, especially if we imagine ourselves playing various roles.

But now we must remind ourselves that performatives take place only in special contextual settings. We have already noticed that if a person is *forced* to say "I promise," he is not usually said to have really promised. A more obvious example is the person who "promises" to do something when talking in his sleep. Again, if a person is led to promise something on the basis of fraudulent information, he will probably not be held to the promise. (Issues of this kind arise in the Law of Contracts, for signing a contract is another example of a performative act.) Promising is an act governed by conventions, and if we want to know the nature of promising we must look to the conventions that govern it.

We can use baseball to make some obvious points. Going back to the previous example, suppose the *shortstop* shouted "You're out!" This would be a very odd thing for him to say, unless perhaps he were trying to confuse the runner. Sometimes, then, only a certain *official* can make a performative utterance and if it is made by someone else, it has no effect. The average citizen cannot pronounce a couple man and wife. A spectator cannot raise objections in a courtroom. A janitor cannot pronounce a body dead on arrival at the hospital even if he can tell, as well as anyone else, that the body is dead. The *first* thing we might ask about a particular performative, then, is whether the right to use the performative is assigned only to a particular official—for example, a judge, minister, justice of the peace, umpire, or coronor. Sometimes such a convention exists; sometimes it does not. I do not have to have an official position to make a promise or offer apologies—although there is such a thing as offering *official* apologies, which cannot be done by just anyone.

In trying to discover the conventions that govern our language, it helps to give the imagination free play and really think of lunatic examples. There is a good reason for this. Our conventions are so much with us that it often takes extreme measures to bring them to the surface. As the runner slides into second base, the umpire shouts out "Strike two!" Here the right person makes the call, but there simply is no convention for calling strikes on anyone but a batter. If an umpire speaks in this way, we might think that he is making a joke, has gone mad, or is seeking early retirement. The example brings out another important point. The umpire is in charge, but *his powers are limited by the conventions that define his role.* More strongly, his actions make sense only in terms of these conventions that define his role. An umpire can call a strike on a batter, but *there is no such thing* as calling a strike on a base runner.

Of course, most departures from convention are not this extreme, for we rarely invoke conventions that do not exist. (It can happen, though. A person may attempt to plead justifiable homicide in a court where such a plea is not allowed.) Usually our departures from convention are less extreme. They involve what Austin called *hitches* and *flaws.* In a hitch, things have not been carried out completely; a loophole has been left open. With a flaw, things are not done quite correctly. With contracts, a hitch or a flaw can make the contract *void* —that is, not legally binding. Some contracts are void if they are not properly notarized and witnessed. (But the law is complicated on these matters and is not as narrowly legalistic as many lay persons suppose.) Hitches and flaws also arise in everyday life. If someone uses the performative utterance, "I bet five dollars that the Yankees win today," I cannot remain silent and then expect to collect the bet if the Yankees lose. The bet is not completed unless I say "Done," or "You're on," or shake hands. The bet may also be off if the terms are not spelled out clearly. People do not make bets of the following kind: "I bet five dollars that the Yankees don't do too badly today." Such a bet would leave open too many possibilities for disagreement on who has won. Acceptance of the wager and spelling out its terms are among many features that form the conventional background of making a bet.

Most performative utterances also presuppose a background of accepted *facts*. It would be senseless for me to walk in and surrender myself to the police, if no one supposes that I have committed a crime. The police would not know what to make of my "surrender." They might lock me up, but for quite a different reason. Apologizing is an interesting case. I cannot apologize for something unless it is generally believed that I have done something wrong, for in apologizing I *acknowledge* that I have done something wrong. Beyond this, I am expected to feel sorry for what I have done and to have no intention of doing it again. Imagine an apology of the following kind: "I don't think I have done anything wrong, I do not feel a bit sorry for what I have done, and given half a chance I'd do it again, but I apologize." Such an apology is quite *empty*, and would not be treated as an apology at all. Apologizing is a complicated linguistic act, governed by conventions and presupposing certain facts. In order to understand this underlying structure, it is best to think of cases where an apology fails for one reason or another.

As a simple model for analyzing performative utterances, we can ask the following questions:

(1) Does a person have to have some official position in order to perform the speech act?

(2) Are there any special words or formulas associated with the speech act?

(3) What facts are presupposed in the use of the speech act?

(4) What feelings (if any) are assumed?

(5) Is any response or uptake needed to complete the speech act?

(6) More generally, what social function does this performative serve?

Answers to these questions might be: (1) In order to pronounce a couple married, one must be a minister, a justice of the peace, a ship's captain, etc. (2) In bidding five clubs, you are expected to use the words "Five clubs." (3) Surrendering to the police presupposes that you have violated some law—or at least are *thought* to have done so. (4) When you congratulate someone, you are assumed to be pleased with his or her success. (5) A bet has not been made unless someone has accepted it. (6) The institution of promise making exists because, in order for cooperation to exist, one human being must be able to rely on another to do what he says he will do. Through making a promise, a person not only expresses an intention to do something, but also accepts an *obligation* to do it. Either through a fear of criticism or a desire to be moral, this obligation will help insure that the person will do what he says he will do. The question of social function is not always easy to answer.

So far we have noticed that a performative utterance can *do* something in the sense of bringing about a new relationship in a context. When an umpire calls a runner out, the runner's position in the game is thereby changed. When someone makes a promise, he thereby undertakes an obligation to do something. Sometimes it is important that some exact formula is used; the exact wording of a judge's verdict is often crucial. In some cases, the use of a performative utterance is the *only* way to do a certain thing. This, however, is not always true. Sometimes what I say will amount to a promise even if I do not use the words "I promise." This leads to another important feature of performative utterances. In some contexts it is not clear what I am trying to do with the words I use. It may, for example, be unclear whether I am promising that I will do something, or merely stating that in all likelihood I will do it. Here I can use the explicit formula "I promise . . ." in order to *clarify* the force of my remarks. After I say "I promise . . . ," it is no longer in doubt that I have, in fact, promised.

Authoritative Performatives The notion that performatives make our linguistic moves more *explicit* comes out also in another area of everyday life. Consider the naked imperative, "Close the door." In using this imperative I may be doing a number of things—issuing an order, making a command, making a request, offering advice, asking a favor, giving a suggestion, begging a favor. People are very sensitive about being told what to do—being bossed around—and for this reason we rarely use simple imperatives in polite conversation. We often put a "please" in front of our imperatives. More interestingly, we sometimes drop the imperative mood altogether and speak in the form of questions: "Could you close the door?" or "Do you mind closing the door?" Later on we shall see why it is often appropriate to use a question in place of an imperative, but first we can examine how performatives function in this area.

Although the name is far from perfect, we shall here speak of *authoritative performatives.* An authoritative performative clarifies the authoritative relationship between the person issuing an imperative and one who is subject to it. It is a sign of our sensitivity in this area that we have so many such performatives marking out very subtle distinctions. The most obvious example of a performative in this field is a command:

If I say "I command you to go," I thereby command you to go.

But not everyone can issue a command. I cannot command a passerby to give me change for a dollar. Commands typically involve a relationship between a *superior* and a *subordinate.* A general can issue commands. Traditionally, God has been said to issue commands. Of course, a general does not have to use the formula "I command . . ." in order to issue a command. If he shouts "Charge!" that will count as a command and those soldiers who do not charge will be disobeying his command. Yet even generals sometimes direct people's actions without commanding them to do things. Sometimes clarification is necessary. This comes out in the following contrasting remarks:

"Young man, I am not ordering you to end your investigations, I am simply giving you a piece of good advice."

"Young man, I am not advising you to stop your investigation, I am ordering you to do so."

Obviously, these two remarks have a very different force.

In the last example, we have shifted from talking about commands to talking about orders. A superior cannot only command a subordinate to do something, he can also order him to do something. Still, the notions are different. I can *order* a person off my land, but it would sound odd if I said that I *commanded* him to leave my land. I can order him to leave my land because I have a *right* to keep people off my land, but they are really not my subordinates. In fact, however, we rarely go around issuing orders. Instead, we *ask* people to do things. Suppose we ask someone to leave our land and he doesn't. We can imagine how the conversation might continue:

Look, I've asked you nicely to leave my land; now I'm ordering you to leave. If you don't leave, I shall call the police and have you charged with trespassing.

That I am in a position to call the police explains, in part at least, why I am in a position to issue an order.

Asking is weaker than ordering, but there are certain things that we do not even have a right to ask. (Think of some contexts where people say, "You have no right to ask that.") It would be very odd for me to ask someone to leave *his* land. I might *advise* someone to leave his land, perhaps because it is about to be overwhelmed by an avalanche. Weaker still, I might *suggest* that he leave his land, thereby minimizing the extent that I am butting into his business and telling him what to do. There are other examples: I can also *beg* someone to do something, and here the authoritative relationship is completely reversed.

We have thus discovered a broad spectrum of authoritative performatives present in our language. (Other languages contain such expressions as well, although the match is not always exact.) Spread out on a printed page this way, these distinctions may seem trivial, but in everyday life we respond to them, sometimes quite violently. We have all heard remarks of the following kind:

I do not mind helping you, but I won't be ordered around.

What right do *you* have to tell *me* what to do?

I think that I have had enough of your advice for one day.

Authoritative performatives provide subtle mechanisms for making adjustments in a sensitive area.

It is time to introduce some important qualifications. The force of a performative comes under many contextual influences. Performatives are highly sensitive to context. A "suggestion" uttered in a sinister tone of voice can have the force of an order—especially if the person making the suggestion is carrying a machine gun. A piece of "friendly advice" can be a threat. Social relations make an obvious difference. It matters who is speaking and to whom. Beyond this, our everyday talk often involves a subtle play upon these background conventions. This often comes out as irony and understatement. We shall come back to these devices when we examine actual arguments later on, for they often make a great deal of difference. For the moment, we will set these features of language aside in order not to consider too many things at once. There is still more to say about performatives.

Argumentative Performatives The performatives we have examined thus far concern either interpersonal relations or the relationships between persons and institutions. We can now look at a different kind of performative, which Austin called *expositives*.[2] We will call them *argumentative performatives.* Here are some examples, using the *thereby test:*

If I say, "I deny the charge," I thereby deny the charge.

If I say, "I claim he's lying," I thereby claim he is lying.

If I say, "I concede the point," I thereby concede the point.

If I say, "I allow such and such," I thereby allow such and such.

If I say, "I conclude that such and such," I thereby conclude that such and such.

If I say, "I stipulate that such and such," I thereby stipulate that such and such.

These performatives are obviously concerned with arguments. In particular, they are used to *make moves* in arguments. Furthermore, they are not statements about arguments, since they are not even statements. If the lawyer finishes his speech to the jury by saying, "I conclude that the

[2] J. L. Austin, *How to Do Things with Words* (New York: Oxford University Press, 1965), pp. 160 ff.

evidence merits acquittal," it makes no sense for someone to say, "No you don't!" We may disagree that the evidence merits acquittal and go on to challenge this, but we cannot disagree that the lawyer has drawn this conclusion.

There are other argumentative moves that are not expressed as performatives. I can challenge someone's claim by saying "I doubt that," but "I doubt that" does *not* express a performative. This is shown by applying the thereby test. If I say "I doubt that" I do not thereby doubt it. Whether I doubt something or not is a fact about me. There are some interesting intermediate cases that change with contexts. Sometimes if I say that I agree I do not *thereby* agree, for again, whether I agree or not is typically considered a fact about me. But in other contexts, saying that I agree amounts to entering into or making an agreement. Here the utterance is performative. Usually "I agree to . . ." is a performative, whereas "I agree that . . ." is not. In a court of law, however, saying "I agree that . . ." is often performative. It is one way of stipulating facts that will not be contested, and by it I waive my right to contest certain facts later on.

Why does our language contain argumentative performatives? What useful purpose do they serve? We have already noticed that argumentative performatives allow us to make moves *in* an argument. By saying "I conclude . . . ," I draw a conclusion. By saying "I disagree with what has been said," I thereby disagree with what has been said. Yet our language provides other means for making argumentative moves. We can mark a conclusion by using a word like "therefore." I can say something like this: "It has been shown that my client was in Detroit on the night in question, therefore he could not have committed this crime." Here I draw a conclusion without using the phrase "I conclude." Again, I can disagree with someone by saying "That's not so" or by saying the opposite of what he has said. In fact, we can imagine a society where arguments are carried out *without* the use of argumentative performatives. They would simply use words like "therefore" instead of phrases like "I conclude."

So the question remains: Why do we have argumentative performatives at all? Part of the answer is that argumentative performatives make our argumentative moves explicit. If I want to make it perfectly clear that I am concluding something, I can signal this by saying "I conclude. . . ." I will probably reserve this expression for the *final* conclusion, thus leaving little doubt what the argument is intended to show. At other times during an argument it is important not only to disagree, but also to make it clear that we are disagreeing. In this way we point explicitly to the part of our opponent's argument we wish to reject. We usually reserve argumentative performatives for the *important* parts of his arguments.

Performatives also allow *subtle* moves to be made in the course of an argument. Sometimes an arguer will say, "I grant the point for the sake of argument" (thereby granting the point for the sake of argument). This is a powerful move if it can be carried off, for nothing is better than refuting an opponent on his own grounds. This device also contains an escape hatch, for if our efforts go badly, we can still challenge the statement previously granted just for the sake of argument. Somewhat differently, we can say, "I reserve comment" (thereby reserving comment). Here we neither reject a claim nor accept it (even for the sake of argument); we let it pass until we see what is made of it. This is a useful tactical device. If we are arguing from a strong position, it is a good idea to keep the line of the argument clean. By reserving comment we can avoid being drawn into irrelevant discussions that will cloud the issue. At other times we do not know what we want to say in response to a particular point or we are not quite sure what the person is going to make of it. Reserving comment is a way of not sticking our necks out prematurely. Argumentative performatives are, then, powerful and subtle tools for making moves in an argument.

Explicit Performatives To give our discussion more order, I shall single out one kind of performative for special consideration. Austin called them *explicit performatives*. Explicit performatives are always in the first person, present tense, and they satisfy the thereby test *exactly:*

> If I say, "I promise...," I thereby promise....
>
> If I say, "I resign," I thereby resign.

This is a useful form because the verb that appears first inside the quotation marks, then outside of them gives us a name for a kind of speech act, here *promising* and *resigning.* We assume that all the background conditions are in order, and where necessary we play the role of the required official. I cannot marry couples, yet assuming the role of a minister I can still use the thereby test:

> If I say, "I pronounce you man and wife," I thereby pronounce you man and wife.

In contrast to these last examples, the umpire does not utter an *explicit* performative when he says, "You're out." Assuming the role of an umpire, I apply the thereby test in this way:

> If I say, "You're out," you are thereby out.

This passes the thereby test, but the expression "You're out" is not in the first person, and no verb appears that will serve as the name for the speech act. In contrast, "I call you out," though a bit odd sounding, is an explicit performative. We turn to explicit performatives because they serve an important theoretical purpose: they are a useful tool in discovering different kinds of speech acts.[3]

Exercise 1: Using a good-sized college dictionary as your source, use the thereby test to discover ten verbs that can be used to formulate explicit performatives.

Exercise 2: Consider the following performative utterances:
  (a) "I give you permission to leave."
  (b) "I claim this land in the name of Queen Victoria."
  (c) "I confer upon you the degree of Bachelor of Arts with all the rights and privileges appertaining thereto."

For each example, answer the six basic questions about performatives given on page 13. It is important to start with the most obvious facts and then trace things out in detail.

Exercise 3: Repeat Exercise 2 for five performative utterances you have discovered in doing Exercise 1.

Exercise 4: Speech acts that are superficially similar often reveal important differences when examined in detail. To see this, give a speech act analysis of the following performatives and then point out any underlying differences that distinguish them:
  (a) "I quit."
  (b) "I resign."
  (c) "I surrender."

Statements

Since we have dwelled on the fact that language is used for a great many purposes besides asserting something that is either true or false, we can

---

[3] This definition for explicit performatives is not perfect. It lets in things we want to exclude. Here is one curious example:
  If I say, "I speak English," I thereby speak English.
Although it is hard to get clear about this, *speaking English* does not seem to be a speech act in the same way that making a promise is. They are not on the same *level*. We will come back to the idea of levels in a moment. At this point we face a choice that comes up in every investigation. We can make our definition of an explicit performative more precise and thus pile up complications, or we can keep our definition simple and put up with some bad results. Where to strike the balance between simplicity and accuracy is always a difficult problem that must be settled by practical considerations. For our present purposes, clarity and simplicity seem most important, so we shall accept a definition of an explicit performative that we know is not quite right.

now discuss this use of language without suggesting that it is the sole use or even the most important use of language. When we use language to assert something that is either true or false, we are making a *statement*. It is in saying something that is either true or false that statements differ from imperatives, questions, performatives, exclamations, and other uses of language.

First we should notice that there is a whole family of activities included in "saying something that is either true or false." *Describing* is one such activity, and it has special features of its own. I can describe a building by giving a list of its most important features. Descriptions are not only true or false, but good or bad, rough or accurate, detailed or sketchy, etc. These special terms used in criticizing a description give us a good idea of the nature of this kind of speech act.

Another use of a statement is to give an *example:*

Seven is a prime number.

Here I do not start with the number seven and go on to describe it, for I could have picked some other number, say, three, as my example.

We can get a feel for the many functions performed by statements by noticing that they can be used to answer different kinds of questions. Here are some examples:

Describing:

What is the sparrow like?

He's a little bird who owned a golden arrow and killed cock robin with it.

Ascribing:

Who killed cock robin?

The sparrow killed cock robin.

Giving an example:

Give me an example of a murderer.

The sparrow who killed cock robin.

Classifying:

What crime did the sparrow commit?

The sparrow committed first-degree murder.

If you think of more questions, you will uncover more speech acts that make a statement. Statements are, then, a whole family of speech acts.[4]

---

[4] This issue is explored in detail in J. L. Austin, "How to Talk: Some Simple Ways," in Urmson and Warnock, *Philosophical Papers,* pp. 134–53.

We also make statements to achieve different purposes. In a court of law, we make a statement to get something on the record (for example, "My name is Irving Trombley and I live in Littleton, New Hampshire."). We make statements to exhibit or show off our knowledge ("That is a piece of Late Ming porcelain."). We make statements just to keep a conversation going ("It's rather chilly for this time of year."). We make statements to remind people of things they already know ("Your uncle has money to spare."). Finally, we use statements to convey information.

Without forgetting that the notion of a statement covers a variety of speech acts that can be used to achieve a variety of purposes, we can look for a moment at cases where statements are used for the purpose of conveying information. This activity is governed by a set of rules or conventions that have been explored by the philosopher Paul Grice.[5]

Grice first speaks of a very general principle that he calls the Cooperative Principle (CP):

> Make your conversational contribution such as is required, at the stage at which it occurs, by the accepted purpose or direction of the talk exchange in which you are engaged.

This, of course, is *very* general. It considers a standard case where conversation is a cooperative venture—that is, where all parties have some common goal in talking to each other. (A witness being cross-examined does not accept this principle.) The principle states, quite simply, that in such a context, what we say should contribute toward achieving this goal. This general principle gets more content when we examine other principles that fall under it. One such principle is the rule of *Quantity* or the rule of *Strength*. Grice states it in these words:

> (1) Make your contribution as informative as is required (for the current purposes of the exchange).

and possibly

> (2) Do not make your contribution more informative than is required.

Here is an application of this rule: A person comes rushing up to you and asks, "Where is a fire extinguisher?" You know that there is a fire extinguisher five floors away in the basement, and you also know that there is a fire extinguisher just down the hall. Suppose you say that there is a fire extinguisher in the basement. Here you have said something that is *true*, but you have violated the rule of Quantity. You have held back an important piece of information that, under the rule of

---

[5] H. P. Grice, "Logic and Conversation," in Donald Davidson and Gilbert Harman, eds., *The Logic of Grammar* (Encino, California: Dickenson Publishing Company, 1975), p. 67. Reprinted in the Appendix to this book, page 329.

Quantity, you should have produced. A violation of the second version of the rule would look like this: Starting with the basement, you say where a fire extinguisher is located on each floor.

There is another cluster of rules that Grice calls rules of *Quality*. In general:

Try to make your contribution one that is true. More specifically:

(1) Do not say what you believe to be false.

(2) Do not say that for which you lack adequate evidence.

In a cooperative activity, you are expected not to tell lies. Beyond this, you are expected not to talk off the top of your head either. When we make a statement, we can be challenged in the following ways:

Do you really believe that?

Why do you believe that?

How do you know that?

Are you sure?

That a person has the right to ask such questions shows that statement making is governed by this rule of *Quality*. (In a court of law, we are expected to tell the truth, the whole truth, and nothing but the truth. The demand for the *truth* and *nothing but the truth* reflects the rule of Quality; the demand for the *whole truth* reflects the rule of Quantity.)

The next rule is called the rule of *Relevance*. Simply stated, it says: Be relevant! Though easy to state, the rule is not easy to explain, because relevance itself is a difficult notion. It is, however, easy to illustrate. If someone asks me where he can find a fire extinguisher, I might reply, among other things, that there is a fire alarm box just down the hall. Though not a direct answer to his question, it is obviously relevant to this person's concerns. Perhaps a violation of the second version of the rule of Quantity, i.e., giving too much information, should be treated as a violation of the rule of Relevance. But the clear-cut violations of this principle are stronger than this. They involve *changing the subject*. Interruptions are typically violations of the rule of Relevance.

Another rule concerns the *Manner* of our conversation. We are expected to be clear. Under this general rule come various special rules:

(1) Avoid obscurity of expression.

(2) Avoid ambiguity.

(3) Be brief.

(4) Be orderly.

In obvious ways, all these rules contribute to the business of conveying information.

There are probably many other rules that should govern our conversations. *Be polite!* might be one of them. *Be charitable!* is another. That is, we should put the best construction on what others say and our replies should reflect this. We should avoid quibbling and unnecessary challenges. There are also rules that govern linguistic performance. Speak clearly, loudly enough to be heard, in a language the other person understands, etc. For the most part, however, we will not worry about rules of this kind.

If we look at these rules we notice that they sometimes overlap. The rule against offering too much information, as we have seen, could be treated as part of the Relevance rule. The rule against speaking ambiguously could be treated as a rule governing the linguistic rather than the speech act, and so on. More important, these rules sometimes clash, or at least push us in different directions. The rule of Quantity encourages us to give as much information as possible, but this is constrained by the rule of Quality, which restricts our claims to things we believe to be true and can back with good reasons. The demands of the rule of Quantity can also conflict with the demand for brevity. Again, in order to be brief, we must sometimes simplify and even falsify, and this can come into conflict with the Quality rule that we have good reasons to support the truth of what we have said. An ongoing conversation is a constant series of adjustments to this background system of rules.

Conversational Implication[6]

We have seen that speech acts are governed by a system of conventions. These conventions vary according to the kind of speech act in question. We have just seen, for example, that statement making is governed by conventions concerning quantity, quality, relevance, and manner. Of course, when people make statements they do not always follow these conventions. People withhold information, they lie, they talk off the tops of their heads, they wander off the subject, they talk vaguely and obscurely. Yet in a normal setting where cooperating toward a shared goal, people conform quite closely to these rules. If, on the whole, people did not do this, we could not have the linguistic practices we do. If we thought, for example, that people very often lied (even about the most trivial matters), the business of communicating would be badly damaged.

[6] The notion of conversational implication was also developed by Paul Grice. What follows borrows heavily from his discussion but there are some important modifications as well. These differences become obvious by comparing this section with his essay "Logic and Conversation" which is reprinted in the Appendix of this text. Most of the changes are simplifications rather than attempted improvements on his original work.

But not only do we follow these conventions, we also (1) realize that we are following them, and (2) expect others to assume that we are following them. These points are obvious. If I say that there is a fire extinguisher down the hall, I realize that I am supposed to believe what I say. This explains why it would be odd to say this: "There is a fire extinguisher down the hall, but I do not believe it." This statement, after all, could be true. I might not believe that there is a fire extinguisher down the hall, and there might actually be one there (one, perhaps, that I never noticed). Even so, I am not supposed to state that there is a fire extinguisher down the hall unless I believe it. The person I speak to is *entitled* to assume that I believe it. He too understands these conventions, and, unless he doubts my integrity, he *expects* that I will follow them.

Here, we have to be careful. If I am a pathological liar and my listener knows this, he may doubt that I believe what I say. He has a right to criticize me for abusing linguistic conventions, but since he knows that I lie he is not trapped into believing that I am, in fact, following them. Yet in normal cooperative situations people make assumptions like these:

People follow conventions.

People realize that they are following conventions.

People realize that others assume that they are following conventions.

This leads to the following important result: *In a standard cooperative context, the performance of a speech act conversationally implies that all the conventions governing that speech act are satisfied.*

A series of examples will bring home this obvious point:

Stating:

A person states that there is a fire extinguisher in the lobby.

This conversationally implies:

(1) That this is the nearest or most accessible fire extinguisher.

(2) That the speaker believes this to be true.

(3) That the speaker has good reason for believing this, and is not merely guessing.

(4) That this information is relevant to the listener's interests.

(5) That the remark is intelligible to the listener.

Bequeathing:

A person states in a will that he bequeaths his Stutz Bearcat to a nephew.

Among other things, this conversationally implies:

(1) That he owns the Stutz Bearcat.

(2) That he is not about to sell it.

(3) That he believes that the nephew has some interest in receiving it.

(4) That he is sane.

Such conversational implications are carried by all of the speech acts we have examined, for all speech acts are governed by conventions and in performing a speech act we conversationally imply that these conventions are satisfied.

We can now turn to a different matter. Sometimes the main point of a speech act is to convey a conversational implication. *We sometimes say one thing for the purpose of implying another.* This can go in two directions:

(1) I perform a speech act in order to indicate that one of the conventions is satisfied.

(2) I state something to indicate that some speech act is in order.

(1) We sometimes make statements just to make known our beliefs. I say that so and so will win the election in order to indicate my own belief on the matter or, perhaps, my loyalty. Or I promise to do something primarily to indicate my strong resolve to do it. This explains, in part at least, such odd remarks as "I promise to give you a good beating if you do that again." This isn't really a promise, but the point is clear. Again, I can ask a question in order to indicate that I am in possession of certain facts. (2) Going in the other direction, a statement can conversationally imply quite a different speech act. I say, "It's cold in here" and (in effect) ask someone to close the window. Stating this fact carries this implied request because its being cold in here is a good reason for making the request. I ask someone if he is color blind and (in effect) accuse him of bad taste. We thus find that conversational implications run in two directions: from the speech act down to the underlying conventions and from the conventions up to the speech act.

We can next look at a set of conversational implications that attracted Grice's attention. Sometimes our speech acts *seem* to violate certain conventions. On the assumption that the conversation is good-willed and cooperative, the listener will then attempt to make sense of this in a way that overcomes this appearance. Here is one of Grice's examples:

A: Where does C live?

B: Somewhere in Southern France.

If A is interested in visiting C, then B's reply is not adequate and thus seems to violate the rule of Quantity. We can explain this departure on the assumption that B does not know exactly where C lives and would thus violate the rule of Quality if he said anything more specific. In this case, B's reply conversationally implies that he does not know exactly where C lives.

In a more extreme case, a person may even flout one of these conventions—that is, obviously violate it. Here is Grice's example and his explanation of it:[7]

> A is writing a testimonial about a pupil who is a candidate for a philosophy job, and the letter reads as follows: "Dear Sir, Mr. X's command of English is excellent, and his attendance at tutorials has been regular, Yours, etc." (Gloss: A cannot be opting out, since if he wished to be uncooperative, why write at all? He cannot be unable, through ignorance, to say more, since the man is his pupil; moreover, he knows that more information is wanted. He must, therefore, be wishing to impart information he is reluctant to write down. This supposition is only tenable on the assumption that he thinks that Mr. X is no good at philosophy. This, then, is what he is implicating.)

This is called "damning with faint praise."

We can intentionally violate the rule of Relevance by pointedly changing the subject. Grice again:

> At a genteel tea party A says "Mrs. X is an old bag." There is a moment of appalled silence, then B says "The weather has been quite delightful this summer, hasn't it?"

The conversational implication here needs no explanation. We can also violate the demand for brevity and thereby *not* say something that could be said briefly. Here is one final example from Grice:

> Miss X produced a series of sounds which corresponded closely with the score of 'Home Sweet Home.'

---

[7] Grice, "Logic and Conversation," pp. 71 ff. (p. 329 in this book).

By not saying simply that Miss X *sang* "Home Sweet Home," the speaker indicates, through a conversational implication, that he is not willing to call what she did singing.

Examples of this kind can be produced indefinitely. Rhetorical devices depend upon conversational implications. Overstatement and understatement are obvious examples, and so is irony. If I say something so blatantly false that my listener assumes I cannot possibly mean it, he concludes by a conversational implication that I mean the opposite. Many jokes depend on conversational implications to set up the punch line. The buildup points in one direction, and then the standard implications are reversed at the end. The more we examine phenomena of this kind, the more we become impressed with the richness of the conventions that underly the language we speak. Furthermore, we do not simply *follow* these conventions, we manipulate them, play with them, and play off them. Here the tired metaphor of the iceberg has its place. The explicitly spoken language is merely the tip—the visible surface—of a vast underlying structure.

Pragmatics

To sum up: We have laid down the following principle: *In a standard cooperative context the performance of a speech act conversationally implies that all the conventions governing that speech act are satisfied.* We have also pointed out that people sometimes deliberately flout conventions for special effects. Overstatement, understatement, and irony are examples of this. Without a standard background of conventions which most people follow most of the time, these special devices would not work. In the correct sense of this phrase, these exceptions *prove* the rule.

So far, so good. But the idea of conversational implication is unclear in an important respect and so needs clarification. In particular, we have not distinguished between *speech act conventions* and what I shall call *pragmatic conventions*. When a speech act convention is not satisfied, the speech act does not come off—it is void. A bid made under duress is not a bid at all, for it is one of the conventions governing this speech act that the bid be made (more or less) freely. In the same way, I cannot bequeath a watch I do not own, or appoint someone to an office when I lack the authority to make such appointments.

We can contrast these failures (where the speech act is void) with failures to satisfy Grice's conversational rules. If, for example, I make a statement carrying less information than the context demands, I have, nonetheless, *made a statement.* Again, if, violating the rule of Quality, I say something that I believe to be false, I have, once more, made a statement. In short, violating these Gricean conversational rules does not vitiate or destroy the speech in the same way that violating a speech act rule does. If we think for a moment, we can see why this is so. All of Grice's principles were specifications of the Cooperative Principle—generally speaking, the rule that we should make contributions that further the *goal* of a particular linguistic exchange. This principle concerns the outcome of a speech act, the end to be achieved, or its purposes. It concerns the practical outcome of the activity or, as philosophers say, its pragmatic significance.

Grice himself talks mainly about the use of statements to convey information, but he is careful to note that his principles have a much wider application. To illustrate this, consider the activity of offering advice. All of Grice's rules, with only minor changes, apply again:

Quantity:

(1) We should not hold back relevant advice.

(2) We should not be excessive in giving advice.

Quality:

(1) We should believe that our advice will be useful to the other person.

(2) We should have good reasons for the advice we offer.

Relevance:

(1) Obviously, our advice should be relevant to the person's concerns.

Manner:

(1) Our advice should be clear, brief, orderly, etc.

In obvious ways, these rules further the activity of advising. It is also obvious that advising will carry conversational implications in virtue of these background rules. Once more, a speech act of advising carries the conversational implication that all these rules are satisfied. I can also explicitly flout these rules to achieve a special effect. I can advise someone to go jump in the lake.

These reflections suggest that we should distinguish between speech acts and what I shall call *pragmatic* acts. Sometimes this distinction is reflected in the words we use to describe a linguistic performance. For example:

I warned him of the danger.

I alerted him to the danger.

In the first case I describe the kind of speech act I performed; the effect upon the other person is left open. He may, for example, have ignored my warning. In the second case I indicated the effect my speech act had upon him: I alerted him. Here is another example:

I advised him to leave.

I persuaded him to leave.

Again the second, but not the first, utterance includes a reference to the effects of my speech act.

But now a problem arises. Speech acts have all sorts of effects. By describing my trip to Europe I may bore someone out of his mind. This may even be my intention, because I want him to go home. I can also engage someone in conversation so that I distract his attention while I pick his pocket. There is obviously no end to the kinds of effects that speech acts can have. In order to place some limits on this discussion, we must speak about the *standard* goals that are achieved by different kinds of speech acts. A standard goal—but not the only goal—of making a statement is to convey information. Grice's maxims specify rules that help us to achieve this standard goal. The standard goal—though again not the only goal—of issuing an order is to get someone to do something. Rules similar to those developed by Grice for statements hold here as well. Rules or conventions that serve to help us achieve standard goals we shall call *pragmatic rules* or *pragmatic conventions*. Grice's rules are pragmatic conventions. Grice, of course, did not *invent* them; he found them at work in our everyday language. He called our attention to things that, in a way, we knew all along.

Levels of Language

We can now return to the idea that language contains rules or conventions operating at various levels. We can summarize the discussion as follows:

Linguistic Acts and Linguistic Conventions
(saying something meaningful in a particular language)

Speech Acts and Speech Act Conventions
(doing certain kinds of things with words)

Pragmatic Acts and Pragmatic Conventions
(achieving a certain standard result by performing a speech act)

This is oversimplified, but it gives at least a rough idea of the levels of convention that govern our language.[8] To take a simple example, if I

---

[8] It corresponds to Austin's distinctions between locutionary, illocutionary, and perlocutionary acts. See *How to Do Things with Words*, pp. 94 ff.

say, "I'll see you tomorrow," first of all, I have performed a *linguistic act:* I have uttered a meaningful expression in the English language. I have also referred to certain things in the world—myself and some other person—and indicated some relationship between them. The character of the *speech act* will depend upon context. I may, for example, merely be making a statement of fact. If I expect to see someone's tightrope act tomorrow, I might tell him this. It is more likely, however, that I use this sentence to express an intention. Here we might say that the expression of intention is conversationally implied by the statement of fact. It is also easy to think of contexts where the use of these words can amount to a promise. Finally, if I am an extortionist and you are my victim, this remark can have all the force of a threat. As we know, the *pragmatic act* (which concerns the *effect* of the speech act) is much more loosely determined and depends heavily on the kind of speech act performed and the context in which it is used. Perhaps the speech act of stating that I will see you tomorrow merely conveys a piece of information and informs you of it. It is more likely that I am expressing an intention, and the point of doing so is to allow us to coordinate our activity. By expressing this intention, I make it much more likely that we will see each other tomorrow. You rely on what I say and I rely on your relying on it. I may use a promise to get you to take me quite seriously. Finally, using this remark can have the force of a threat, and here the point or purpose of the remark is to scare you silly so that you will cough up the money that I am trying to extort from you. Here the purpose is achieved by conversational implication, but, as we know, in many contexts a conversational implication is the heart of the matter.

Exercise 5: Explain what is going on in the following exchange by tracing out the conversational implications that are challenged:

A: Did you know that the Secretary of Commerce will resign within six months?

B: Are you sure of your sources?

A: Well it's pretty obvious, after all.

B: It's not obvious to me; it sounds like just another rumor.

A: Well, he wasn't at Senator Snard's big bash last month, and Snard is the head of the Senate Commerce Committee.

B: Oh come on.

A: There are other things.

B: What other things?

A: You can't be very well informed.

B: I read the same papers that everyone else does.

A: Yeah, but papers aren't the only source of information—you have to know people.

B: What people?

A: I'm sorry, I am not free to reveal that.
B: That's just great.
A: I was right about Watergate, wasn't I?
B: You were lucky.

Exercise 6: Perform the same task as in Exercise 5 with a rich piece of dialogue written by an author with literary talent.

Exercise 7: Decide whether each of the verbs below concerns a linguistic act, a speech act, or a pragmatic act.

informed	advised	shouted
misspelled	soothed	warned
convinced	whispered	amused
pledged	enlightened	abbreviated
confused	concluded	dissolved
frightened	challenged	astonished

THE LANGUAGE OF ARGUMENT

2

Using the general discussion of Chapter 1 as a background, this chapter examines the use of language to formulate arguments. It provides methods for analyzing genuine arguments in all their richness and complexity. The first stage in analyzing an argument is to discover its basic <u>structure</u>. This involves studying those words, phrases, and special constructions that mark out the premises and conclusion. The second stage involves a study of those techniques used to <u>strengthen</u> an argument. This involves, among other things, guarding (or hedging) premises so that they are less subject to criticism, offering assurances concerning debatable claims, and discounting possible criticisms in advance. Finally, this chapter considers various <u>substitutes</u> for arguments. These are devices that give the appearance of being arguments without actually producing reasons for the claims that are made.

In the first chapter we saw that language is used for a great many purposes beyond making statements, or saying things that are either true or false. When we make a promise or make a bet, we are not stating a fact. Turning now to arguments, we see that they, like promises and bets, are not used to make statements. Although an argument is (typically) constructed from statements, the argument itself, taken as a whole, is not a statement. A single example will illustrate this:

> Socrates is older than Plato; Plato is older than Aristotle; therefore, Socrates is older than Aristotle.

Taken as a whole, this sentence does not express anything that is either true or false.

This does not mean that we have no way of rejecting a bad argument. Here is an example of a bad argument:

> Socrates is older than Plato, therefore Plato is older than Socrates.

(This argument is so bad that it is hard to imagine anyone actually using it, but bad arguments often serve as good examples.) What would we say to a person who produced such an argument? In ordinary words, we would say that his conclusion does not *follow from* what he has said. The basic point is that we never call arguments true or false. If you are tempted to do so, you are off on the wrong track. Statements are true or false; arguments are not.

The Basic Structure of Arguments

Arguments are not statements, yet they are constructed out of statements. Now let's ask a very simple question: What *words* turn a batch of statements into an argument? Suppose we start with a simple list of statements:

> Socrates is mortal.
>
> All men are mortal.
>
> Socrates is a man.

This is not an argument, but we can turn it into an argument by the use of the single word "therefore":

> Socrates is mortal.
>
> All men are mortal.
>
> Therefore Socrates is a man.

We now have an argument—again, a bad argument, since the conclusion does not follow from the reasons offered in its behalf, but it is an argument nonetheless. It should be obvious how the word "therefore" works: it signals that the statement following it is a *conclusion* and that the statement (or statements) that come before it are the *reasons* offered in support of the conclusion. Here is another way of turning the list into an argument.

Socrates is mortal,

since all men are mortal

and Socrates is a man.

This produces a new argument—this time, a good argument, for the conclusion does follow from the reasons offered in its behalf. "Since" operates *roughly* in the opposite way from "therefore." The word "since" indicates that the statement or statements that follow it are reasons and that the statement (if any) that comes before it is the conclusion. There is a variation, however, where the conclusion is tacked onto the end of a since-sentence:

Since all men are mortal and Socrates is a man,
Socrates is mortal.

"Since" flags reasons; the remaining connected statement is then taken to be the conclusion, whether it appears at the beginning or at the end of the sentence.

Here is a partial list of connecting terms that introduce an argumentative structure into language by marking out reasons for a conclusion:

accordingly	thus	since
for	hence	then
because	so	therefore

We shall call all these terms *warranting connectives*. In various ways, they all present one or more statements as the warrant or backing for some other statement.

Sometimes a single sentence will contain more than one of these warranting connectives. Here is an example:

Since all men are mortal, Socrates is mortal,
for Socrates is a man.

Both the words "since" and "for" signal the appearance of a reason: the conclusion itself appears in the *middle* of the sentence. This is an interesting example. Together with the other examples, it drives home the point that a conclusion can appear anywhere in a sentence formulating an argument: at the beginning, in the middle, or at the end. Our ability to locate the conclusion of an argument depends upon our understanding of warranting connectives.

Arguments in Standard Form

It will be helpful to have a standard way of writing out arguments: For centuries, logicians have used the following scheme:

All men are mortal.

Socrates is a man.
_____

∴ Socrates is mortal.

The reasons are listed above the line; the conclusion is placed below the line; and the symbol "∴" is read "therefore." Logicians refer to the reasons stated above the line as *premises*. (For now we will not worry about the order of the premises.) This notion of a *standard form* is useful because it helps us to see that the same argument can be expressed in different ways. For example, it is not hard to see that the following two sentences express the same argument, i.e., the argument stated in standard form above:

Socrates is mortal, since all men are mortal and Socrates is a man.

All men are mortal, so Socrates is mortal, since he is a man.

By putting arguments in standard form, it becomes easier to compare them and to test their validity.

Validity, Truth, and Soundness

To have an argument at all, some statement must be marked out as a conclusion and other statements must be marked out as reasons or premises for this conclusion. Of course, merely connecting sentences together with words like "since" or "therefore" will not always produce a good or acceptable argument. As we have already noticed, an argument is no good if the conclusion does not follow from the premises. When the conclusion does follow from the premises, logicians say that the argument is *valid*. Validity is a central notion in logic and it is important to understand it clearly.

Validity is a technical notion, but it matches the commonsense idea of one thing following from another. Later on in this book we shall examine the idea of validity with some care; for now, we will rely upon the commonsense understanding of it. But we must be careful not to confuse *validity* with *truth*. Arguments are valid or invalid, but, as we have already seen, they are never either true or false. We can bring out this difference by noticing that an argument can be valid even though all the statements it contains are false:

All fishes have wings.

Whales are fishes.
_____

∴ Whales have wings.

It is not hard to see that the conclusion does *follow from* the premises. Here is another example:

All fishes have lungs.

Whales are fishes.
_____

∴ Whales have lungs.

Again we have a valid argument since the conclusion does follow from the premises, yet this time the premises are both false and the conclusion is true.

Although the notions of truth and validity are different, there is one important relationship between them. Something false never follows from something true. More technically, there are no valid arguments that start from true premises and lead to a false conclusion. This too should square with your commonsense ideas about reasoning. If you reason correctly, you should not be led from truth into error. Until we discuss the notion of validity more carefully later on, in Chapter 6, we will rely upon common sense in seeing whether a conclusion validly follows from a set of premises. Unless the argument is very complicated or tricky in some way, most people are quite good at this.

It should already be clear that an argument can be valid but still unacceptable. A valid argument with false premises will be rejected just because the premises are false. Obviously, you cannot prove something by offering a premise that is false. We thus make *two* demands upon an argument that is offered as a proof:

(1) The argument must be *valid*.

(2) The premises must be *true*.

When an argument meets both of these demands, it is said to be *sound*. If it fails to meet either one, the argument is said to be *unsound*. Thus an argument is *unsound* if it is invalid; it is also unsound if *at least one* of its premises is false. The following chart shows these relationships:

	Premises True	*At Least One False Premise*
Valid	Sound	Unsound
Invalid	Unsound	Unsound

The goal of a proof is a sound argument, not just a valid argument.

Exercise 1: Relying on your natural sense of what follows from various statements and upon your commonsense knowledge of the world, analyze the following arguments, indicating:

   a) Whether the premises are true or false.
   b) Whether the argument is valid or invalid.
   c) Whether the argument is sound or unsound.

Examples:

Munich is in Germany or Austria.	True
Munich is not in Austria.	True
∴ Munich is in Germany.	True

The argument is both valid and sound.

Munich is in France or Austria.	False
Munich is not in France.	True
∴ Munich is in Austria.	False

The argument is valid, but not sound.

1. General Motors has plants in America and Europe.
   _____
   ∴ General Motors has plants in America.

2. The Giants will win the pennant.
   _____
   ∴ Either the Giants or the Reds will win the pennant.

3. If the Giants win the pennant, then the Dodgers will not.
   _____
   ∴ If the Dodgers win the pennant, the Giants will not.

4. Canada is bigger than Spain.
   Spain is bigger than Portugal.
   _____
   ∴ Canada is bigger than Portugal.

5. If the Giants win the pennant, the Dodgers will not.
   The Giants will not win the pennant.

   ∴ The Dodgers will win the pennant.

6. Nobody is completely lacking in a sense of humor.

   ∴ General Grant was not completely lacking in a sense of humor.

7. Nobody completely lacks a sense of humor.
   Grant completely lacked a sense of humor.

   ∴ Grant was nobody.

8. Anyone religious believes in God.
   Some Buddhists do not believe in God.

   ∴ Some Buddhists are not religious.

9. Anyone religious believes in God.
   Some Buddhists believe in God.

   ∴ Some Buddhists believe in God.

10. Greeks come from the Mediterranean area.

   ∴ Rich Greeks come from the Mediterranean area.

Exercise 2:
   (1) All squares are rectangles.
   (2) All squares are triangles.
   (3) All squares have four sides.
   (4) All squares have three sides.
   (5) All triangles have four sides.
   (6) All rectangles have four sides.
   (7) All triangles have three sides.
   (8) All triangles have two sides.
   (9) All squares have two sides.
   (10) All rectangles are squares.

Using the above statements, construct arguments with two premises and a conclusion such that:
   (a) The argument is valid, but all statements are false.
   (b) The argument is valid, the premises false, and the conclusion true.
   (c) The argument is invalid, but all the premises are true and so is the conclusion.

(d) The argument is valid, one premise true, one premise false, and
the conclusion is true.
(e) The argument is valid, one premise true, one premise false, and
the conclusion is false.

Exercise 3: Why can't you construct an argument that is valid having
true premises and a false conclusion?

Now that you are accustomed to analyzing arguments in terms of
their validity and soundness, you may be struck by the fact that everyday talk is not this elaborate. We seem to be drawing more distinctions
than are found in everyday life. There is a reason for this that is connected with what we called the rule of Quantity in Chapter 1. Recall
that if we call an argument *unsound*, we can have two criticisms in
mind: that the argument is invalid *or* that one of the premises is false.
We have no right to call the argument unsound if we cannot show one
of these two things. If we do have this additional information, the rule
of Quantity demands that we bring it forth. If we think the argument
is unsound because it is invalid, we should make the stronger claim that
it is invalid. If we think that the argument is unsound because one of
the premises is false, we should come right out and say that one of the
premises is false. For this reason, we do not often say that an argument
is unsound or no good and let the matter stand there. We actually point
out what is wrong with the argument, since this makes the criticism
more pointed and informative. Again, we rarely stop with saying that an
argument is valid, for when arguments are used to prove something, validity is not enough. A proof should be *sound* as well as valid. Simply
saying that an argument is valid leaves open an important question: Are
the premises true? Thus our *summary* judgments of arguments tend to
maximize information.

(1) In accepting an argument, we say that it is sound rather than
merely valid.

(2) In rejecting an argument, we say that it is invalid or has a
false premise, rather than just saying that it is unsound.

In this way, we avoid saying less than we are in a position to say. Sound
is a stronger notion than valid, and invalid and false are stronger notions
than unsound.

It is important to note facts of this kind as we go along in order to
see the connection between logical theory and everyday argumentation.
Our everyday talk is governed by a variety of principles at the same
time, and what we actually say is the result of all these principles work-

ing simultaneously. Thus, though our arguments are guided by logical principles, to see them clearly we must look through a very tangled thicket.

Assuring, Hedging, and Discounting

The notion of soundness draws our attention to the importance of having true premises in our arguments. We cannot justify or explain something by citing things that are themselves false. This, however, presents a problem in argumentation. In order to justify one statement, I cite some others in their behalf. The question naturally arises why you should accept these new statements. Shouldn't I present an argument for them as well? If I do this, the problem comes up again: in proving the premises, I will just introduce further premises that are also in need of proof, and so on indefinitely. It now looks as if every argument will be infinitely long.

The answer to this ancient problem depends upon an obvious fact. The activity of arguing or presenting proofs depends upon a shared set of beliefs and upon a certain amount of trust. When I present reasons, I try to cite these shared beliefs—things that will not be challenged. Beyond this, I expect people to believe me when I cite information that only I possess. But there are limits to this. People do lie, and the range of shared beliefs is not firmly fixed. This presents a practical problem. How can I present my reasons in a way that does not produce just another demand for an argument? Here we use three main techniques:

(1) Assuring: indicating that we have back-up reasons without actually stating them.

(2) Hedging: weakening our claims so that they are less subject to attack.

(3) Discounting: anticipating criticisms and rejecting them.

In this way we build a defensive perimeter around our premises.

Assuring When will we want to give assurances about some statement we have made? If we state something that we know everyone believes, assurances are not necessary. For that matter, if everyone believes something, we may not even state it at all; we let others "fill in" this step in the argument. We offer assurances when we think that someone *might* challenge what we say. In giving assurances we sometimes cite authorities:

Doctors agree . . .

Recent studies have shown . . .

It has been established that . . .

I can assure you that . . .

An unimpeachable source close to the White House says . . .

Here we do not actually cite reasons; we merely indicate that they can be produced on demand. In a context of trust, this is often sufficient.

On the other hand, we as critics should view assuring remarks with some suspicion. Following the rule of Relevance, we should expect a person to give assurances only when he has a good reason to do so. Yet in point of fact, assuring remarks often mark the *weakest* parts of the argument, not the strongest parts. If someone says "I hardly need argue that . . . ," it is often useful to ask why he has gone to the trouble of saying it. In particular, when we distrust an argument—as we sometimes do—this is precisely the place to look for weakness. You should develop a keen eye for phrases of the following kind:

It's certain that . . .

Everyone agrees that . . .

Of course, no one will deny that . . .

It is just common sense that . . .

There is no question that . . .

If these phrases are used, they are used for some reason. Sometimes the reason is a good one; sometimes, however, it is a bad one. In honest argumentation, they save time and simplify discussion. In a dishonest argument, they are used to paper over cracks.[1]

Hedging *Hedging* represents a different strategy for protecting premises from attack. We reduce our claim to something less strong. Thus instead of saying *all*, we say *most*. Instead of saying something straight out, we use a qualifying phrase like "it is almost certain that," "it is very likely that," etc. Law school professors like the phrase "it is arguable that. . . ." This is wonderfully noncommittal, for it really doesn't indicate how strong the argument is, yet it does get the statement into the argument.

Broadly speaking, there are two ways of hedging what we have said:

(1) Weakening the extent of what has been said: retreating from "all" to "most," from "most" to "some," etc.

(2) Using probability phrases like "it is likely that," "virtually certain that," etc.

[1] This topic will be discussed more fully in Chapter 4.

If we weaken a claim sufficiently, we can make it completely immune to criticism. What can be said against a remark of the following kind: "There is some small chance that perhaps a few politicians are honest on at least some occasions." You would have to have a *very* low opinion of politicians to deny this statement. On the other hand, if we weaken our premises in this way to avoid criticism, we must pay a price. The premise no longer gives strong support to the conclusion. The general strategy is this: We should weaken our premises sufficiently to avoid criticism, but not weaken them so much that they no longer provide strong evidence for the conclusion. Balancing these two facts is one of the most important strategies in constructing and criticizing arguments.

Just as it was useful to zero in on *assuring* terms, it is useful to keep track of *hedging* terms. Hedging terms are easily corrupted. They can be used to insinuate things that cannot be stated explicitly into a conversation. Consider the effect of the following remark: "Perhaps the Secretary of State has not been candid with the Congress." This doesn't actually *say* that the Secretary has been less than candid with the Congress, but it suggests it. Furthermore, it suggests it in a way that is hard to combat. A more subtle device for corrupting hedging terms is to introduce a statement in a guarded form and then go on to speak as if it were not guarded at all. After a while, the word "perhaps" disappears.

> Perhaps the Secretary of State has not been candid with the Congress. Of course, he has a right to his own views and I am sure that he is acting honestly. All the same, this is a democracy where officials, even in the Administration, are accountable to Congress.

Discounting The general pattern of discounting is to cite a possible criticism in order to reject it or counter it. Notice how different the following statements sound:

> The ring is beautiful, but expensive.

> The ring is expensive, but beautiful.

Both statements express the very same facts—that the ring is beautiful and that the ring is expensive. Yet they operate in different ways. We might use the first as a reason for *not* buying the ring; we can use the second as a reason *for* buying it. The first sentence acknowledges that the ring is beautiful, but overrides this by pointing out that it is expensive. In reverse fashion, the second statement acknowledges that the ring is expensive, but overrides this by pointing out that it is beautiful. The word "but" discounts the statement that comes before it in favor of the statement that follows it.

"Although" is also a discounting connective, but it operates in reverse fashion from the word "but." We can see this using the same example:

Although the ring is expensive, it is beautiful.

Although the ring is beautiful, it is expensive.

Here the statement following the word "although" is discounted in favor of the connected statement. A partial list of terms that function as discounting connectives includes the following conjunctions:

although	nonetheless
but	still
however	yet
nevertheless	though

Exercise 4: Give examples of statements using the discounting connectives above, and then indicate which statement is discounted when two are conjoined by each connective.

The clearest cases of discounting occur when we are dealing with facts that point in different directions: that the ring is beautiful is a reason for buying it, that it is expensive is a reason for not buying it. We discount the fact that goes against the position we wish to take. Discounting is, however, often more subtle than this. We sometimes use discounting to block certain conversational implications of what we have said. This comes out in examples of the following kind:

Jones is an aggressive player, but he is not dirty.

The situation is difficult, but not hopeless.

The Democrats have the upper hand in Congress, but only for the time being.

A truce has been declared, but who knows for how long?

Take just the last example. The claim that a truce has been declared naturally suggests that peace has been restored. The but-clause cancels out this suggestion. The nuances of discounting terms can be very subtle, and a correct analysis is not always easy. All the same, the role of discounting terms is often very important in capturing the force of an argument. These terms anticipate criticisms, control conversational implications, and, in general, point to structures within an argument that are not actually stated. Once more, it is often useful to ask yourself why a term occurs in an argument—what would the argument be like without it?

Parentheticals

The philosopher J. O. Urmson has noticed the importance of parenthetical expressions in our language.[2] Sometimes parenthetical remarks are just asides—we put things in parentheses because of the rule of Relevance—but sometimes they play an important role in adjusting our remarks to the background rules that govern them. They allow us to comment on what we are saying at the very same time that we are saying it. Here is an example:

That, if you do not mind my saying so, is a pretty ugly hat.

Notice that with this remark I *do* say that the hat is pretty ugly. Telling someone that he is wearing an ugly hat is not exactly polite. The parenthetical remark acknowledges this and, to some extent, neutralizes it. (Of course, tone of voice will also make a difference here.)

The word "parenthetically" can also be used parenthetically. In writing a graduate school recommendation, a professor says:

Gilbert is a first-rate mathematician and, parenthetically, a world class swimmer.

It is not hard to see what is going on here: the parenthetical expression is connected to a rule of relevance. Being a world class swimmer is not relevant in any obvious way to future success in a graduate school, but it is to some extent an indication of a generally good character. Words like "incidentally" and "by the way" can also be used in this way. They get the fact in, but in a way that does not give it too much weight.

There seems to be no limit to the jobs that parentheticals can do. They can be used to give assurances:

Jones, as you will soon discover, cannot keep off the bottle.

Jones, unless I am sadly mistaken, has run out of ideas.

They can be used for guarding:

Daniels, rumor has it, is about to get married.

Daniels, as far as I know, is not coming East.

They can be used in discounting:

I don't care what you have heard; Chrysler will not fold.

[2] J. O. Urmson, "Parenthetical Verbs," *Mind*, LXI (1952), pp. 480–96.

And so on.

It is a good idea to pay close attention to parentheticals, for they are often surprisingly helpful in revealing the underlying structure of an argument.

Argumentative Performatives

In the previous chapter, we saw that our language contains a rich system of argumentative performatives that actually give our conversations an argumentative structure. We saw that expository performatives not only introduce an argumentative structure, but do so in a *clear* and *explicit* way. If someone says, "I conclude such and such . . ." there is no doubt that he or she is concluding. When people say, "I admit such and such" there is no doubt that they are admitting something. We also saw that argumentative performatives allow us to make very subtle and complicated argumentative moves, like "I shall reserve comment until my opponent says something worth answering."

Along with parentheticals, argumentative performatives deserve close attention. Used correctly, they are powerful and subtle devices for constructing a clear, forceful argument. They can also be used incorrectly and dishonestly.

> **Exercise 5:**
> (a) Construct three interesting examples of statements containing assuring terms.
> (b) Do the same for hedging terms.
> (c) Finally, do the same for discounting terms.
>
> **Exercise 6:** In Part Two of this book there is a collection of arguments of some complexity. Take one of these arguments and label all the warranting connectives, assuring terms, discounting terms, and hedging terms.
>
> **Exercise 7:** Perform Exercise 6 with an argument taken from the editorial pages of a newspaper.

Substitutes for Arguments

So far we have seen that the basic categories of the language of argument are *warranting connectives, assuring terms, hedging terms,* and *discounting terms.* We have also noticed that other devices show the structure of an argument, in particular, *performatives* and *parentheti-cals*. The first task in assessing an argument is to look for these terms, for they reveal the basic structure of the argument. Once the bare bones of the argument have been exposed, still other questions remain, for it is not always easy to assess the exact force of an argument. In particular, we are sometimes misled by devices that are mere substitutes for genuine arguments. Here we shall examine a common device of this kind. It is called *slanting*.

Slanting Although some words in our language are relatively neutral, others carry a strong positive or negative connotation. That is, in using many words in our language we are not only describing something, but also evaluating it, expressing our feelings toward it, or in various other ways indicating our attitudes concerning it. Ethnic and racial slurs are obvious examples of this. To say that a person is a Jew is to comment upon his or her ethnic origin: to call someone a kike conveys the same information, but combines it with an expression of contempt. Actually, in this area, connotations are so prevalent that we have to look to scientific language to find more or less neutral language. For example, "white" is a positive term, whereas "whitey" (and "honkey") are negative. "Caucasian" is more or less scientific and neutral. Here we must use the guarding expression "more or less" because all the language in this area is highly charged. For many, "Black" is a positive term, and "nigger" is a term of contempt, but "Negro" is not really neutral in the way, for example, that "Mongolian" is. These tensions in the language reflect deeper tensions in our society.

When we stop to think about it, it is surprising how many words appear in our language that are intended to express contempt. Beyond racial and ethnic slurs, our language contains a vast system of words charged with negative connotations. Our language contains a rich system of obscenities. When we describe something using obscene language, we are usually (though not always) condemning it. There seems to be no end to the ways in which we can describe things in demeaning, degrading, and insulting ways. New forms of insult are constantly invented as the old ones lose their sting.

We should also notice that the connotations of a word vary with context; they depend upon who is saying what to whom. An irresponsible conservative will accuse his liberal opponents of being communists, thereby associating them with an organization generally held in contempt in this country. On the other hand, it wouldn't have made sense to *accuse* Joseph Stalin of having been a communist. That's not something that Stalin would want to deny—he was proud of it. In the reverse fashion, radicals sometimes call their more conservative opponents "fascists." Again, it would not have made sense to *accuse* Hitler or Mussolini of being fascists. From their point of view, being a fascist was something good, not bad. Thus, even where the descriptive meaning of a word remains more or less fixed, the positive and negative connotations can vary with context. Calling someone a liberal can count as praise, as an attack from the right, or as an attack from the left, depending upon the speaker and the audience.

Finally, positive and negative connotations can be subtle. Consider a word like "clever." Descriptively, it indicates quick mental ability and carries a positive connotation. In contrast, "cunning," which has much the same descriptive content, often carries a negative connotation. It thus makes a difference which one of these words we choose. It also makes a difference where we apply them. You can praise a light opera by calling it clever, but it would surely be taken as a criticism if you called a grand opera clever. This, needless to say, turns upon the rule of Quantity. Grand operas are supposed to be more than clever. When something is supposed to be profound and serious, it is insulting just to call it clever. Prayers, for example, should not be clever.

Sometimes innocuous words can shift connotations. The word "too" is the perfect example of this. This word introduces a negative connotation, sometimes turning a positive quality into a negative one. Compare the following sentences:

John is smart.	John is too smart.
John is honest.	John is too honest.
John is ambitious.	John is too ambitious.
John is nice.	John is too nice.
John is friendly.	John is too friendly.

The word "too" indicates an excess, and thereby contains a criticism. If you look at the items in the second column, you will see that the criticism is sometimes rather brutal—for example, calling someone "too friendly."

Slanting and Persuasive Definitions A particularly subtle form of slanting involves the use of a definition to gain an argumentative advantage. Charles L. Stevenson calls such definitions *persuasive definitions*.[3] Here is an example:

Russian Communism is really state capitalism.

Who would say this? Certainly not a capitalist, who thinks capitalism is a *good* thing and communism is *bad*. Nor would Russian Communists say this, because they think that capitalism is *bad* and have no desire to associate their system with it. On the other hand, this is just the kind of statement that a Chinese Communist might use against the

[3] Charles L. Stevenson, "Persuasive Definitions," *Mind*, XLVII (July, 1938).

Russians. To a Chinese Communist, capitalism is a bad thing; thus calling Russian Communism "state capitalism" applies all the standard attacks against capitalism to the Russians. The pattern looks like this:

| Something to be criticized. | Definitional link | Something considered bad. |

Here is another example that uses the same pattern:

Admissions quotas in favor of minorities are nothing more than reverse discrimination.

Since discrimination is usually thought to be something bad, a person will have a hard time making a case for minority quotas if he is trapped into accepting "reverse discrimination" as a defining characteristic of a system of minority quotas. Sometimes these definitions are crude and heavy handed, for example:

Abortion is fetal murder.

Since murder is, by definition, a wrongful act of killing, this definition assumes the very point at issue. At other times the argumentative move can be quite subtle, for example:

Abortion is the killing of an unborn person.

At first sight, this definition may seem neutral. It does not contain any obviously charged word like "murder." All the same, it is one of the central issues in the debate over abortion whether a human fetus is already a person. This is a matter to be established by argument, not by definition. In general we have a right to be suspicious of anyone who tries to gain an argumentative advantage through an appeal to definitions. Confronted with a definition in the midst of an argument, we should always ask whether the definition clarifies the issues or merely slants them.

What, then, is *slanting*? We shall say that language is slanted when the speaker uses terms with positive and negative connotations *without laying a foundation for doing so*. Here the last clause is important, for we are not proposing a rule that would reject language rich in positive and negative connotations. In the first place, no one would obey such a rule; secondly, if such a rule were followed, our language would be less interesting. The point is this: We have a right to use a term containing, say, an implicit criticism only if we have shown good reasons for this criticism. The word "scoundrel" has a negative connotation. If I simply call someone a scoundrel without giving reasons for doing so, then I am involved in slanting. On the other hand, if I give a detailed account of this person's life showing that he has taken bribes, lied under oath, neglected his duties, harmed innocent people, and been cruel to animals, then calling him a scoundrel is not slanting. It is just the word I want to express a *well-founded* negative attitude. Slanting occurs when we use words carrying a positive or negative connotation without justification. In slanting, we simply help ourselves to such words.

Exercise 8: For each of the following sentences, construct two others—one that reverses the emotive force and one that is more or less neutral. The symbol 0 stands for neutral, + for positive emotive force, and − for negative emotive force.

Example: − Professor Conrad is rude.

  + Professor Conrad is uncompromisingly honest in his criticisms.

  0 Professor Conrad often upsets people with his criticisms.

1. − Martin is a lazy lout.
2. + Brenda is vivacious.
3. + John is a natural leader.
4. + Selby is a methodical worker.
5. − Marsha is a snob.
6. + Clara is imaginative.
7. − Bartlett is a buffoon.
8. − Wayne is a goody-goody.
9. − Sidney talks incessantly.
10. − Dudley is a weenie.
11. ? Floyd is a hotdog. (Decide whether this is + or −.)
12. + Martha is liberated.
13. + Ralph is sensitive.
14. + Betty is a fierce competitor.
15. − Psychology is a trendy department.
16. − This is a Mickey Mouse exercise.

Honors Exercise: Rewrite the following letter to the editor in the style of a neutral analysis of the sources of opposition to former President Nixon's reelection. As far as possible, do not change the factual content.

To the Editor:

  Every long-haired hippie, every left-wing lunatic, every phoney college professor, every socialist school teacher, every bus-crazy judge, every lazy welfare loafer, every yellow-bellied draft-dodger, every blood-stained abortionist, every dope-peddling fiend, every Communist pig, etc. (not to mention innumerable kooks, weirdos, derelicts, and degenerates) is fighting the reelection of President Nixon. Think it over. Which side are you on?

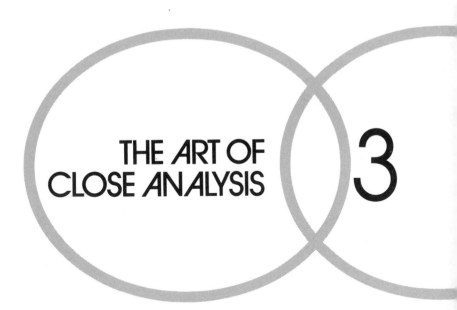

THE ART OF CLOSE ANALYSIS

3

This chapter will be largely dedicated to a single purpose: the close and careful analysis of a speech drawn from the Congressional Record, using the argumentative devices brought together in Chapter 2. The point of this study is to show in detail how these methods of analysis can be applied to an actual argument of some richness and complexity. Though this chapter mainly stresses the importance of analyzing an argument in close detail, it concludes with a discussion of the significance of the standpoint of the argument taken as a whole.

An Extended Example

It is now time to apply all of these notions to a genuine argument. Our example will be a debate that occurred in the House of Representatives on the question whether there should be an increase in the allowance given to members of the House for clerical help—the so-called "clerk hire allowance." The argument against the increase presented by Representative Kyl (Republican, Iowa) will be examined in detail. We will put it under an analytic microscope. The reply made by Representative Mc-Cormack (Democrat, Massachusetts) will be left for analysis as a student exercise.

The choice of this example may seem odd, for the question of clerk hire allowance is not one of the burning issues of our time. This, in fact, is one reason for choosing it. It will be useful to begin with an example where feelings do not run high in order to learn the habit of objective analysis. Later on we shall examine arguments where almost everyone has strong feelings and try to maintain an objective standpoint even there. The example is a good one for two other reasons: (1) it contains most of the argumentative devices we have listed and, (2) relatively speaking, it is quite a strong argument. This last remark may seem ironic after we seemingly tear the argument quite to shreds, but in comparison to other arguments we shall examine, it stands up quite well.

We can begin by reading through the section of the *Congressional Record*[1] without comment:

Clerk Hire Allowance, House of Representatives

Mr. FRIEDEL. Mr. Speaker, by direction of the Committee on House Administration, I call up the resolution (H. Res. 219) to increase the basic clerk hire allowance of each Member of the House, and for other purposes, and ask for its immediate consideration.

The Clerk read the resolution as follows:

Resolved, That effective April 1, 1961, there shall be paid out of the contingent fund of the House, until otherwise provided by law, such sums as may be necessary to increase the basic clerk hire allowance of each Member and the Resident Commissioner from Puerto Rico by an additional $3,000 per annum, and each such Member and Resident Commissioner shall be entitled to one clerk in addition to those to which he is otherwise entitled by law.

Mr. FRIEDEL. Mr. Speaker, this resolution allows an additional $3,000 per annum for clerk hire and an additional clerk for each Member of the House and the Resident Commissioner from Puerto Rico.

---

[1] *Congressional Record,* Vol. 107, Part 3 (March 15, 1961), pp. 4059–60.

Our subcommittee heard the testimony, and we were convinced of the need for this provision to be made. A few Members are paying out of their own pocket for additional clerk hire. This $3,000 is the minimum amount we felt was necessary to help Members pay the expenses of running their offices. Of course, we know that the mail is not as heavy in some of the districts as it is in others, and, of course, if the Member does not use the money, it remains in the contingent fund.

Mr. KYL. Mr. Speaker, will the gentleman yield?

Mr. FRIEDEL. I yield to the gentleman from Iowa |Mr. KYL| for a statement.

Mr. KYL. Mr. Speaker, I oppose this measure. I oppose it first because it is expensive. I further oppose it because it is untimely.

I do not intend to belabor this first contention. We have been presented a budget of about $82 billion. We have had recommended to us a whole series of additional programs or extensions of programs for priming the pump, for depressed areas, for the needy, for unemployed, for river pollution projects, and recreation projects, aid to education, and many more. All are listed as "must" activities. These extensions are not within the budget. Furthermore, if business conditions are as deplorable as the newspapers indicate, the Government's income will not be as high as anticipated. It is not enough to say we are spending so much now, a little more will not hurt. What we spend, we will either have to recover in taxes, or add to the staggering national debt.

The amount of increase does not appear large. I trust, however, there is no one among us who would suggest that the addition of a clerk would not entail allowances for another desk, another typewriter, more materials, and it is not beyond the realm of possibility that the next step would then be request for additional office space, and ultimately new buildings. Some will say, "All the Members will not use their maximum, so the cost will not be great." And this is true. If the exceptions are sufficient in number to constitute a valid argument, then there is no broad general need for this measure. Furthermore, some Members will use these additional funds to raise salaries. Competition will force all salaries upward in all offices and then on committee staffs, and so on. We may even find ourselves in a position of paying more money for fewer clerks and in a tighter bind on per person workload.

This measure proposes to increase the allowance from $17,500 base clerical allowance to $20,500 base salary allowance. No member of this House can tell us what this means in gross salary. That computation is almost impossible. Such a completely absurd system has developed through the years on salary computations for clerical hire that we have under discussion a mathematical monstrosity. We are usually told that the gross allowed is approximately $35,000. This is inaccurate. In one office the total might be less than $35,000 and in another, in complete compliance with the law and without any conscious padding, the amount may be in excess of $42,000. This is possible because of a weird set of formulae which determines that three clerks at $5,000 cost less than five clerks at $3,000. Five times three might total the same as three times five everywhere else in the world—but not in figuring clerk hire in the House.

This is application of an absurdity. It is a violation of bookkeeping principles, accounting principles, business principles and a violation of commonsense. Listen to the formula:

First, 20 percent increase of first $1,200; 10 percent additional from $1,200 to $4,600; 5 percent further additional from $4,600 to $7,000.

Second, after applying the increases provided in paragraph 1, add an additional 14 percent or a flat $250 whichever is the greater, but this increase must not exceed 25 percent.

Third, after applying the increases provided in both paragraphs 1 and 2, add an additional increase of 10 percent in lieu of overtime.

Fourth, after applying the increases provided in paragraphs 1, 2, and 3, add an additional increase of $330.

Fifth, after applying the increases provided in paragraphs 1, 2, 3, and 4, add an additional increase of 5 percent.

Sixth, after applying the increases provided in paragraphs 1, 2, 3, 4, and 5, add an additional increase of 10 percent but not more than $800 nor less than $300 a year.

Seventh, after applying the increases provided in paragraphs 1, 2, 3, 4, 5, and 6, add an additional increase of 7½ percent.

Eighth, after applying the increases provided in paragraphs 1, 2, 3, 4, 5, 6, and 7, add an additional increase of 10 percent.

Ninth, after applying the increases provided in paragraphs 1, 2, 3, 4, 5, 6, 7, and 8, add an additional increase of 7½ percent.

The Disbursing Office has a set of tables to figure house salaries for office staffs and for about 900 other employees. It contains 45 sheets with 40 entries per sheet. In the Senate, at least, they have simplified the process some by figuring their base in multiples of 60, thus eliminating 11 categories. Committee staffers, incidentally, have an $8,880 base in comparison to the House $7,000 base limitation.

Now, Mr. Speaker, I have planned to introduce an amendment or a substitute which would grant additional clerk hire where there is a demonstrable need based on heavier than average population or "election at large" and possible other factors. But after becoming involved in this mathematical maze, I realize the folly of proceeding one step until we have corrected this situation. We can offer all kinds of excuses for avoiding a solution. We cannot offer reasonable arguments that it should not be done or that it cannot be done.

Someone has suggested that the Members of this great body prefer to keep the present program because someone back in the home district might object to the gross figures. I know this is not so. When a Representative is busy on minimum wage, or aid to education, or civil rights, such matters of housekeeping seem too picayune to merit attention. The Member simply checks the table and hires what he can hire under the provisions and then forgets the whole business. But I know the

Members also want the people back home to realize that what we do here is open and frank and accurate, and that we set an example in businesslike procedures. The more we can demonstrate responsibility the greater will be the faith in Congress.

May I summarize. It is obvious that some Members need more clerical help because of large population and large land area. I have been working for some time with the best help we can get, on a measure which would take these items into consideration. Those Members who are really in need of assistance should realize that this temporary, hastily conceived proposition we debate today will probably obviate their getting a satisfactory total solution.

First, we should await redistricting of the Nation.

Second, we should consider appropriate allowance for oversize districts considering both population and total geographic area.

Finally, I hope we can develop a sound and sensible formula for computing salaries of office clerks and other statutory employees in the same category.

Mr. FRIEDEL. Mr. Speaker, I yield 2 minutes to the gentleman from California [Mr. YOUNGER].

Mr. YOUNGER. Mr. Speaker, I take this time simply to state my opposition to this bill, opposition straight across the board. I would favor an increase if it were based on the additional work or the additional population in a district; I think that is justified. It could be worked out at a certain allowance for every additional 250,000 population in the district.

I am opposed to this whole scheme as it is set up. I have had a bill before the committee for 4 or 5 years. This House would not permit any department of the Government to operate the way we operate. It is just as sensible and as profitable for a Congressman to build up a big staff as it is for the head of a bureau to build up a big staff; and in many instances big staffs are being built up right here in our own House. I think this House ought to set a determined example for the departments of Government.

I am opposed to this type of legislation.

Mr. FRIEDEL. Mr. Speaker, I yield 3 minutes to the gentleman from Massachusetts [Mr. McCORMACK].

Mr. McCORMACK. Mr. Speaker I think the RECORD should show that there is definite need for this resolution. I, as a Member of the House as well as majority leader, take my responsibility. I have never apologized to anybody for Members of this House receiving increases in salary throughout the years; as a matter of fact, I think we should further increase our salaries to $25,000. I never apologize for the Members of the House or the Members of the other body having a staff that will enable them to serve the people of their district, of their State, and as Members of Congress the people of the Nation.

Those who object on the grounds some Members raise of the lack of need, do not have to appoint additional help in their offices unless they want to; but certainly those Members should not take the position that because they do not need additional clerk hire that other Members of the House do not either.

This resolution is not for the benefit of any Member of this House; this resolution is for the benefit of the people of America to enable the Members of this House to more effectively and efficiently perform their duties as Members of Congress. So I have no hesitancy in supporting the resolution. I probably will not take advantage of it; I may and I may not. I have not up to date used all of my clerk hire. I may or I may not take advantage of this resolution should it be passed, but I would not want to deny other Members who need additional staff from having it so that they may effectively represent the people of their district here in the Halls of Congress.

Mr. YOUNGER. Mr. Speaker, will the gentleman yield?

Mr. McCORMACK. I am always glad to yield to the gentleman from California.

Mr. YOUNGER. In respect to the gentleman's last statement I may say that never in the 8 years I have been in Congress have I used all my clerk hire allowance, and I have no intention of using this additional allowance.

I think that additional allowance for clerk hire should be on the basis of need. I think in this bill we are hoodwinking the public.

Mr. McCORMACK. I think the weakness of the gentleman's argument is that it does not take into account the volume of work regardless of the number of people in a district. Some Members with a district of 300,000 might have more interested constituents requiring more attention than another Member having a district with 460,000.

In these matters we must treat all alike. As I say, the question of population is not the determining factor as to the prime responsibility of a Member of Congress. A Member from a smaller district may have tremendous mail from all over his State, in fact, from all over the country.

So I do not think a formula based on steps of population increase is a fair one or a good one.

As to the argument of the gentleman from Wisconsin that this resolution is not based on reason, I shall not enter into that at all.

I will say it is commonsense for us to pass this resolution today.

Before going any farther, it will be useful to record your general reaction to this exchange. Perhaps you think that on the whole Kyl gives a more reasoned argument than McCormack. Alternatively, you might think that Kyl is making a big fuss over nothing, trying to confuse people with numbers, and just generally being obnoxious. When you are finished examining this argument in detail, you can look back and ask yourself why you formed this original impression and how, if at all, you have changed your mind.

The first step in the close analysis of an argument is to go through
the text, labelling the various argumentative components we have examined. Here some abbreviations will be useful:

warranting connective	War. Con.
assuring term	As.
hedging term	Hedge
discounting term	Dis.
argumentative performative	Arg. Perf.
parenthetical	Par.
slanting	Slant (+ or −)
persuasive definition	Per. Def. (+ or −)

Even this simple process of labelling brings out features of an argument
that could pass by unnoticed. It also directs us to ask sharp critical questions. To see this, we can look at each part of the argument in detail.

Arg. Perf.

Mr. KYL. Mr. Speaker, I oppose this measure. I
oppose it first because it is expensive. I further oppose it because it is untimely.

War. Con.

This is a model of clarity. By the use of a performative utterance in the
opening sentence, Kyl makes it clear that he opposes the measure. Then
by twice using the warranting connective "because," he gives his two
main reasons for opposing it: *it is expensive* and *it is untimely*. We
must now see if he makes good each of these claims. This paragraph begins the argument for the claim that the measure is expensive:

As.

I do not intend to belabor this first contention.
We have been presented a budget of about $82 bil-
lion. We have had recommended to us a whole series of additional programs or extensions of programs for priming the pump, for depressed areas, for
the needy, for unemployed, for river pollution projects, and recreation projects, aid to education, and **Dis.**
many more. All are listed as "must" activities.
These extensions are not within the budget. Fur-

thermore, if business conditions are as deplorable — **Hedge**
as the newspapers indicate, the Government's income will not be as high as anticipated. It is not — **Dis.**
enough to say we are spending so much now, a little more will not hurt. What we spend, we will
either have to recover in taxes, or add to the stag-
gering national debt.

(a) "I do not intend to belabor this first contention. . . ." This is a pure example of *assuring*. The obvious conversational implication is that the point is so obvious that little has to be said in its support. Yet there is something strange going on here. Having said that he will *not* belabor the claim that the bill is expensive, Kyl actually goes on to say quite a bit on the subject. It is a good idea to look closely when someone says that he or she is not going to do something, for often just the opposite is happening. For example, saying "I am not suggesting that Smith is dishonest" is one way of suggesting that Smith *is* dishonest. If no such suggestion is being made, why raise the issue at all?

(b) Kyl now proceeds in a rather flat way, stating that the proposed budget comes to $82 billion and that it contains many new programs and extensions of former programs. Since these are matters of public record and nobody is liable to deny them, there is no need for guarding or assuring. Kyl also claims, without qualification, that these extensions are not within the budget. This recital of facts does, however, carry an important conversational implication: Since the budget is already out of balance, any further extensions should be viewed with suspicion.

(c) Putting the word "must" in quotation marks, or saying it in a certain tone of voice, is a common device for discounting. The plain suggestion is that some of these measures are *not* must activities at all. We see the same device in a more dramatic fashion when Mark Anthony ironically repeats that "Brutus is an honorable man." Anyway, Kyl here suggests that some of the items already in the budget are not necessary. He does this, of course, without defending this suggestion.

(d) "If business conditions are as deplorable as the newspapers indicate . . . ." This is a clear example of hedging. Kyl is not saying that business conditions are deplorable. For this reason the suggestion that the government's income will be less than anticipated is not given very strong support.

(e) "It is not enough to say we are spending so much now, a little more will not hurt." The opening phrase is, of course, used to discount what follows it. Kyl is plainly rejecting the argument that we are spending so much now, a little more will not hurt. Yet his argument has a peculiar twist, for who would come right out and make such an argument? If you stop to think for a minute, it should be clear that nobody would want to put it that way. A liberal, for example, would use quite different phrasing. He might say something like this: "Considering the large benefits that will flow from this measure, it is more than worth the small costs." What Kyl has done is to attribute a bad argument to his opponents and then discount it in an indignant tone. This is a common device.[2] When we run into the use of a discounting phrase, it is often useful to ask whether anyone would actually argue or speak in the way suggested. When the answer to this question is no, as it often is, it is also useful to ask what the speaker's opponent would have said instead. This leads to a further question: Has the arguer even addressed himself to the *real* arguments of his opponents?

So far, Kyl has not addressed himself to the first main point of his argument, that the measure is *expensive*. This is not a criticism, because he is really making the preliminary point that the matter of expense is significant. Here he has stated some incontestable facts—for example, that the budget is already out of balance. Beyond this he has indicated, with varying degrees of strength, that the financial situation is grave. It is against this background that the detailed argument concerning the cost of the measure is actually presented in the next paragraph.

The amount of increase does not appear large. **— Dis.**

I trust, however, there is no one among us who would suggest that the addition of a clerk would not entail allowances for another desk, another typewriter, more materials, **— As.** and it is not beyond the **— Hedge** realm of possibility that the next step would then be a request for additional office space, and ultimately new buildings. Some will say, "All the Members will not use their maximum, so the cost **Dis. —** will not be great." And this is true. If the exceptions are sufficient in number to constitute a valid argument, then there is no broad general need for **War. Con. —** this measure. Furthermore, some Members will use these additional funds to raise salaries. Competition will force all salaries upward in all offices and then on committee staffs, and so on. We may even **— Hedge** find ourselves in a position of paying more money for fewer clerks and in a tighter bind on per person workload.

---

[2] Another example is that of a professor who spoke to student radicals in the following way: "I can understand that the younger generation wants a free ride—they want to get things without really working for them, but. . . ."

(a) "The amount of increase does not appear large." Words like "appear" and "seem" are sometimes used for hedging, but we must be careful not to apply labels in an unthinking way. The above sentence is the beginning of a *discounting* argument. As soon as you hear this sentence, you can feel that a word like "but" or "however" is about to appear. Sure enough, it does.

(b) "I trust, however, there is no one among us who would suggest that the addition of a clerk would not entail allowances for another desk, another typewriter, more materials . . . ." This is the beginning of Kyl's argument that is intended to rebut the argument that the increase in expenses will not be large. Appearances to the contrary, he is saying, the increase will be large. He then ticks off some additional expenses that are entailed by hiring new clerks. Notice that the whole sentence is covered by the assuring phrase, "I trust . . . that there is no one among us who would suggest . . . ." This implies that anyone who would make such a suggestion is merely stupid. But the trouble with Kyl's argument so far is this: He has pointed out genuine additional expenses, but they are not, after all, very large. It is important for him to get some genuinely large sums of money into his argument. This is the point of his next remark:

(c) "And it is not beyond the realm of possibility, that the next step would then be a request for additional office space, and ultimately new buildings." Here, at last, we have some genuinely large sums of money in the picture, but the difficulty is that the entire claim is totally hedged by the phrase, "it is not beyond the realm of possibility." There are very few things that *are* beyond the realm of possibility. Kyl's problem, then, is this: There are certain additional expenses that he can point to without qualification, but these tend to be small. On the other hand, when he points out genuinely large expenses, he can only do so in a hedged way. So we are still waiting for a proof that the expense will be large. (Parenthetically, it should be pointed out that Kyl's prediction of new buildings actually came true.)

(d) "Some will say, 'All the Members will not use their maximum, so the cost will not be great.' And this is true. If the exceptions are sufficient in number to constitute a valid argument, then there is no broad general need for this measure." This looks like a "tricky" argument, and for this reason alone it demands close attention. The phrase "some will say" is a standard way of beginning a discounting argument. This *is*, in fact, a discounting argument, but its form is rather subtle. Kyl cites what some will say, and then adds, somewhat surprisingly: "And this is true." To understand what is going on here, we must have a good feel for conversational implication. Kyl imagines someone reasoning in the following way:

All the Members will not use their maximum.

So the cost will not be great.

Therefore, since the measure will not be expensive, let's adopt it.

Given the same starting point, Kyl tries to derive just the *opposite* conclusion along the following lines:

All the Members will not use their maximum.

If very few use their maximums, then the cost will not be great.

But if very few use their maximum, then there is no broad general need for this measure.

Therefore, whether it is expensive or not, we should reject this measure.

In order to get clear about this argument, we can put it into schematic form:

Kyl's argument
If (1) expensive, then   → Reject

If (2) inexpensive, then, because that demonstrates no general need,   → Reject

The opposite argument
If (1) inexpensive, then   → Accept

If (2) expensive, then, because that demonstrates a general need,   → Accept

When the arguments are spread out in this fashion, it should be clear that they have equal strength. Both are no good. The question that must be settled is this: Does a genuine need exist that can be met in an economically sound manner? If there is no need for the measure, then it should be rejected however inexpensive. Again, if there is a need, then some expense is worth paying. The real problem is to balance the need against expense and then to decide on this basis whether the measure as a whole is worth adopting. Kyl's argument is a *sophistry* because it has no tendency to answer the real question at hand. By a sophistry we shall mean a clever but fallacious argument intended to establish a point through trickery. Incidentally, it is one of the marks of a sophistical argument that, though it may baffle, it almost never convinces. I think that very few readers will have found this argument persuasive even if they could not say exactly what is wrong with it. The appearance of a sophistical argument (or even a complex and tangled argument) is a sign that the argument is weak. Remember, where a case is strong, people usually argue in a straightforward way. This is illustrated by the second half of Kyl's argument, where he argues directly and strongly that the measure is untimely.

(e) "Furthermore, some Members will use these additional funds to raise salaries. Competition will force all salaries upward in all offices and then on committee staffs, and so on." The word "furthermore" signals that further *reasons* are forthcoming. Here Kyl returns to the argument that the measure is more expensive than it might at first sight appear. Notice that he speaks here in an unqualified way; no hedging appears. Yet the critic is bound to ask whether Kyl has any right to make these projections. Beyond this, Kyl here projects a *parade of horrors*. He pictures this measure leading, by gradual steps, to quite disastrous consequences. Here the little phrase "and so on" carries a great burden in the argument. Once more, we must simply ask ourselves whether these projections seem reasonable.

(f) "We may even find ourselves in a position of paying more money for fewer clerks and in a tighter bind on per person workload." Once more, the use of a strong hedging expression takes back most of the force of the argument. Notice that if Kyl could have said straight out that the measure *will* put us in a position of paying more money for fewer clerks and in a tighter bind on per person workload, that would have counted as a very strong objection. You can hardly do better in criticizing a position than showing that it will have just the opposite result from what is intended. In fact, however, Kyl has not established this, he has only said that this is something that we "may even find."

Before we turn to the second half of Kyl's argument, which we shall see in a moment is much stronger, we should point out that our analysis has not been entirely fair. Speaking before the House of Representatives, Kyl is in an *adversary* situation. He is not trying to prove things for all time; rather, he is responding to a position held by others. Part of what he is doing is *raising objections,* and a sensitive evaluation of the argument demands a detailed understanding of the nuances of the debate. But even granting this, it should be remembered that objections themselves must be made for good reasons. The problem so far in Kyl's argument is that the major reasons behind his objections have constantly been hedged in a very strong way.

Turning now to the second part of Kyl's argument—that the measure is untimely—we see that he moves along in a clear and direct way with really no hedging.

> This measure proposes to increase the allowance from $17,500 base clerical allowance to $20,500 base salary allowance. No member of this House can tell us what this means in gross salary. That computation is almost impossible. Such a completely absurd system has developed through

Hedge

Slant

the years on salary computations for clerical hire
that we have under discussion a (mathematical — *Slant –*
monstrosity.) We are usually told that the gross allowed is approximately $35,000. This is inaccurate.
In one office the total might be less than $35,000
and in another, in complete compliance with the
law and without any conscious padding, the
amount may be in excess of $42,000. This is possi-
Slant – ble because of a (weird set of formulae) which deter-
mines that three clerks at $5,000 cost less than five
clerks at $3,000. Five times three might total the
same as three times five everywhere else in the
world—but not in figuring clerk hire in the House. *Slant–*
    This is application of (an absurdity.) It is a viola-
tion of bookkeeping principles, accounting principles, business principles and a (violation of commonsense.) Listen to the formula:[3]

The main point of the argument is clear enough: Kyl is saying that the
present system of clerk salary allowance is utterly confusing, and this
matter should be straightened out before *any* other measures in this
area are adopted. There is, of course, a great deal of negative slanting in
this passage. Notice the words and phrases that Kyle uses.

completely absurd system

weird set of formulae

a violation of common sense

mathematical monstrosity

an absurdity

There is also a dash of irony in the remark that five times three might
total the same as three times five everywhere else in the world, but not
in figuring clerk hire in the House. Remember, there is nothing wrong
with using slanted language (and irony) if it is deserved. We have a
smear job only when negative slanting is excessive and undeserved.
Looking at the nine-step formula on page 54, you can decide for yourself whether Kyl is on strong grounds in using these negative char-
acterizations.

[3] See page 54 for the formula.

Now, Mr. Speaker, I have planned to introduce an amendment or a substitute which would grant additional clerk hire where there is a demonstrable need based on heavier than average population or "election at large" and possible other factors.

(a) This passage discounts any suggestion that Kyl is unaware that a genuine problem does exist in some districts. It also indicates that he is willing to do something about it.

(b) The phrase "and possible other factors" is not very important, but it seems to be included to anticipate other reasons for clerk hire that should at least be considered.

As. But after becoming involved in this mathematical maze, I realized the folly of proceeding one step until we have corrected this situation. *Slant—*

(a) Here Kyl clearly states his reason for saying that the measure is untimely. Notice that the reason offered has been well documented and is not hedged in by qualifications.

(b) The phrases "mathematical maze" and "folly" are again negatively slanting, but probably justified.

Slant—

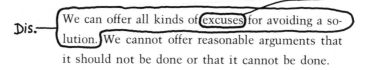

Dis.— We can offer all kinds of excuses for avoiding a solution. We cannot offer reasonable arguments that it should not be done or that it cannot be done.

(a) Notice that the first sentence discounts these "excuses" and that calling them *excuses* is negatively slanting. The second sentence gives assurances that such a solution can be found.

Someone has suggested that the Members of this great body prefer to keep the present program because someone back in the home district might object to the gross figures. I know this is not so. When a Representative is busy on minimum wage, or aid to education, or civil rights, such matters of housekeeping seem too picayune to merit attention. The Member simply checks the table and hires what he can hire under the provisions and then forgets the whole business. But I know the Members also want the people back home to realize

Dis. ———

As.

that what we do here is open and frank and accu- —— Slant +
rate, and that we set an example in businesslike
procedures. The more we can demonstrate responsibility the greater will be the faith in Congress.

(a) Once more the seas of rhetoric run high. Someone (though not
Kyl himself) has suggested that the Members of the House wish to conceal information. He disavows the very thought that he would make
such a suggestion by the sentence "I know this is not so." All the same,
he has gotten this suggestion into the argument.

(b) Kyl then suggests another reason why the Members of the House
will not be concerned with this measure: it is too *picayune*. The last
two sentences discount the suggestion that it is too small to merit close
attention. Even on small matters, the more the House is "open and
frank and accurate," the more it will "set an example in businesslike
procedures" and thus "demonstrate responsibility" that will increase
"the faith in Congress." This is actually an important part of Kyl's argument, for presumably his main problem is to get the other Members of
the House to take the matter seriously.

Arg. Perf. —— May I summarize. It is obvious that some —— As.
Members need more clerical help because of large —— War. Con.
population and large land area. I have been working —— As.
for some time with the best help we can get, on a
measure which would take these items into consid-
As. —— eration. Those Members who are really in need of
assistance should realize that this temporary, hast-
Slant— —— ily conceived proposition we debate today will
Hedge —— probably obviate their getting a satisfactory total
solution.

(a) This is a concise summary. Kyl once more assures the House that
he is aware that a genuine problem exists. He also indicates that he is
working on it.

(b) The phrase "temporary, hastily conceived proposition we debate
today" refers back to his arguments concerning untimeliness.

(c) The claim that "it will probably obviate their getting a satisfactory total solution" refers back to the economic argument. Notice, however, that, as before, the economic claim is hedged by the word "probably."

First, we should await redistricting of the Nation.

> Second, we should consider appropriate allow-
> ance for oversize districts considering both popula-
> tion and total geographic area.
>   Finally, I hope we can develop a (sound and sen- ——— Slant+
> sible) formula for computing salaries of office clerks
> and other statutory employees in the same cate-
> gory.

This is straightforward except that a new factor is introduced: we
should await redistricting of the Nation. This was not mentioned earlier
in the argument, and so seems a bit out of place in a summary. Perhaps
the point is so obvious that it did not need any argument to support it.
On the other hand, it is often useful to keep track of things that are
smuggled into the argument at the very end. If redistricting was about
to occur in the *near* future, this would give a strong reason for delaying
action on the measure. Since the point is potentially so strong, we
might wonder why Kyl has made so little of it. Here, perhaps, we are
getting too subtle.

Exercise 1: Below is reprinted Representative McCormack's reply to
Representative Kyl. Some remarks by Representative Younger are also
included for continuity. Subject this speech to the same close analysis
that we have used in examining Representative Kyl's speech. Who do
you think gets the better of the exchange?

Mr. McCORMACK. Mr. Speaker I think the RECORD should show that there
is definite need for this resolution. I, as a Member of the House as well
as majority leader, take my responsibility. I have never apologized to
anybody for Members of this House receiving increases in salary
throughout the years; as a matter of fact, I think we should further increase our salaries to $25,000. I never apologize for the Members of the
House or the Members of the other body having a staff that will enable
them to serve the people of their district, of their State, and as Members
of Congress the people of the Nation.

Those who object on the grounds some Members raise of the lack
of need, do not have to appoint additional help in their offices unless
they want to; but certainly those Members should not take the position
that because they do not need additional clerk hire that other Members
of the House do not either.

This resolution is not for the benefit of any Member of this House; this
resolution is for the benefit of the people of America to enable the
Members of this House to more effectively and efficiently perform their

duties as Members of Congress. So I have no hesitancy in supporting the resolution. I probably will not take advantage of it; I may and I may not. I have not up to date used all of my clerk hire. I may or I may not take advantage of this resolution should it be passed, but I would not want to deny other Members who need additional staff from having it so that they may effectively represent the people of their district here in the Halls of Congress.

Mr. YOUNGER. Mr. Speaker, will the gentleman yield?

Mr. McCORMACK. I am always glad to yield to the gentleman from California.

Mr. YOUNGER. In respect to the gentleman's last statement I may say that never in the 8 years I have been in Congress have I used all my clerk hire allowance, and I have no intention of using this additional allowance.

I think that additional allowance for clerk hire should be on the basis of need. I think in this bill we are hoodwinking the public.

Mr. McCORMACK. I think the weakness of the gentleman's argument is that it does not take into account the volume of work regardless of the number of people in a district. Some Members with a district of 300,000 might have more interested constituents requiring more attention than another Member having a district with 460,000.

In these matters we must treat all alike. As I say, the question of population is not the determining factor as to the prime responsibility of a Member of Congress. A Member from a smaller district may have tremendous mail from all over his State, in fact, from all over the country.

So I do not think a formula based on steps of population increase is a fair one or a good one.

As to the argument of the gentleman from Wisconsin that this resolution is not based on reason, I shall not enter into that at all.

I will say it is commonsense for us to pass this resolution today.

Exercise 2: Using the Congressional Record, an editorial, a letter to the editor, etc., find an interesting example of an argument and subject it to close analysis. Be sure to label the various argumentative moves and then comment on them. It is also important to get a general sense of context. In particular, you should be alert for the ironic use of an expression which, of course, reverses its normal force.

Exercise 3: Chapter 8, "Issues of Public Concern," offers a series of debates on matters that arouse strong moral and emotional responses. Subject one of these exchanges to close analysis. When you are finished, try to decide how much your own opinions have led you to slant your analysis.

Standpoints

Now that we have looked at Representative Kyl's argument in close detail, we can notice an important feature of the argument as a whole: it is presented from a particular *standpoint*. Kyl puts himself across as a tough-minded, thoroughly honest person who is willing to stand up against majority opinion. This, in fact, may be an accurate representation of his character, but by adopting this standpoint he gains an important argumentative advantage: He suggests that those who disagree with him are a bit soft-minded, not altogether candid, and, anyway, mere tools of the Democratic majority that runs the Congress. By adopting this stance, Kyl casts his opponents in a light that is hardly flattering.

This tactic of adopting a standpoint that puts one's opponent at a disadvantage is a common argumentative device that deserves close attention. A standard ploy is to claim a *middle ground* between two extreme positions. This strategy is used by Paul A. Samuelson in the opening paragraphs of an article published in *Newsweek* under the title "New York Dilemma."

> This is a hard column to write. How easy it would be if one were simpleminded and could baldly assert: "Let New York go down the drain. It couldn't happen to a nicer bunch of fellows anyway. Bankruptcy not only will teach a lesson, punish the guilty and deter those tempted in the future, but it will also be the first step on the road back to fiscal probity."
>
> Likewise, it would be an easy position to hold if one could believe with conviction: "The Federal government should take responsibility for the city's present plight. After all, *the crisis has national not local causes.* Any Puerto Rican or Southerner can freely move into the city. Any well-heeled person can freely move out to the suburbs, thereby avoiding his share of the irreducible fiscal burden of the less fortunate who are left in the city. Only the Federal government has the powers of the purse to take care of the intolerable load now being put on the city and the state . . ."
>
> Neither of these positions is tenable for an intelligent person of goodwill. But where in the wide middle ground between them is the feasible optimum for policy to be found? Here are some tentative economic considerations that may help set bounds on possible policy alternatives.[4]

We thus find Samuelson defining himself as an "intelligent person of goodwill," which is accurate enough, but not very gracious to those who might want to disagree with him in a strong way.

Another device is to seize an extreme position and accuse those who

---

[4] *Newsweek,* November 10, 1975, p. 102.

occupy a middle position of being cowardly, indecisive, or lukewarm. William Lloyd Garrison made brilliant use of this strategy in the first issue of his abolitionist newspaper *The Liberator*. Part of the opening editorial read as follows:

> Assenting to the "self evident truth" maintained in the American Declaration of Independence, "that all men are created equal, and endowed by their Creator with certain inalienable rights—among which are life, liberty and the pursuit of happiness," I shall strenuously contend for the immediate enfranchisement of our slave population. In Park Street Church, on the Fourth of July, 1829, in an address on slavery, I unreflectingly assented to the popular but pernicious doctrine of *gradual* abolition. I seize this opportunity to make a full and unequivocal recantation, and thus publicly to ask pardon of my God, of my country, and of my brethren the poor slaves, for having uttered a sentiment so full of timidity, injustice and absurdity. A similar recantation, from my pen, was published in the *Genius of Universal Emancipation* at Baltimore, in September, 1829. My conscience is now satisfied.
>
> I am aware, that many object to the severity of my language; but is there not cause for severity? I *will be* as harsh as truth, and as uncompromising as justice. On this subject, I do not wish to think, or speak, or write, with moderation. No! no! Tell a man whose house is on fire, to give a moderate alarm; tell him to moderately rescue his wife from the hands of the ravisher; tell the mother to gradually extricate her babe from the fire into which it has fallen;—but urge me not to use moderation in a cause like the present. I am in earnest—I will not equivocate—I will not excuse—I will not retreat a single inch—*AND I WILL BE HEARD*. The apathy of the people is enough to make every statue leap from its pedestal, and to hasten the resurrection of the dead.
>
> It is pretended, that I am retarding the cause of emancipation by the coarseness of my invective and the precipitancy of my measures. *The charge is not true.* On this question my influence,—humble as it is,—is felt at this moment to a considerable extent, and shall be felt in coming years—not perniciously, but beneficially—not as a curse, but as a blessing; and posterity will bear testimony that I was right. I desire to thank God, that he enables me to disregard "the fear of man which bringeth a snare," and to speak his truth in its simplicity and power.[5]

There are a great many devices for establishing an argumentative standpoint that puts the opponent at a disadvantage. Here are just a few:

The disinterested party: Although I have no personal stake in this matter . . .

[5] Richard Heffner, ed., *A Documentary History of the United States* (New York: Mentor Books, 1952), pp. 106–07.

The reasonable man: By now it should be obvious to everyone . . .

The voice in the wilderness: I don't suppose that it will help much to point out that . . .

The world-weary cynic: Are we really going to go through all this again?

Official indignation: It is high time that . . .

The mature person: When I was a child I spoke as a child . . .

The radical: You're either on the bus or off the bus . . .

The plain man: I may not have gone to Harvard but . . .

The expert: Things are not as simple as they might seem.

Sometimes these argumentative moves hit their mark and sometimes they do not. Fair or foul, however, they almost always infuriate those against whom they are directed. If the Expert tells you that things are not as simple as they might seem, this plainly suggests that you are a dope. You have to dig your way out of this hole before you can even get into the argument.

Two additional ploys are worth mentioning: these are used by the *Uplifter* and the *Debaser*. The Uplifter appeals to your better instincts, claiming that in your conscience or in your heart you really *agree.* The Uplifter strikes the pose of bringing you up to his or her level, a particularly obnoxious move when you hold that you *do* disagree, and for perfectly sound and moral reasons. The Debaser is even slimier. The strategy here is to acknowledge all sorts of base motives and low qualities, and then go on to say that everyone else is in the same boat. Where Uplifters lift you up to their preferred heights, Debasers drag you down to their acknowledged depths. Debasers often use the phrase "Let's face it."

"Let's face it, everyone is out to get what he can get for himself."

"Let's face it, you would do the same thing if you thought you could get away with it."

If you disagree, you are accused not only of being naive, but of being dishonest. Debasers pride themselves on admitting to the bad qualities they find in others. It often turns out that Debasers are not so bad as they pretend to be, and Uplifters are almost never as righteous as they assume they are. However this may be, both of these moves often produce strong—even violent—responses.

Exercise 4: Almost any political speech, editorial, or piece of social commentary will be written from a particular standpoint. It is often useful, in analyzing such writing, to identify this standpoint. Using the categories given above—or even better, using some of your own—identify the author's standpoint in a number of arguments of current interest.

FALLACIES OF CLARITY AND RELEVANCE

4

In this chapter we shall examine some of the ways in which arguments can be defective. The defects are considered under two main headings: fallacies of clarity and fallacies of relevance. Fallacies of clarity arise when language is not used precisely enough for the argumentative context. Vagueness and ambiguity, two of the most common results, are defined and discussed in detail. Fallacies of relevance arise when a claim is made which, true or not, has no tendency to establish the point at issue. Though irrelevance comes in endless forms, two kinds are singled out for special attention here: arguments <u>ad hominem</u> and appeals to authority. A central theme of the chapter is that we can speak of fallacies only if we are sensitive to the context of the argument and the conversational implications within it.

Clarity

In a good argument, a person states a conclusion clearly and then, with equal clarity, gives reasons for this conclusion. The arguments of everyday life often fall short of this standard. Usually, unclear language is a sign of unclear thought. There are times, however, when people are intentionally unclear—their goal is to confuse others. This is called *obfuscation.*

Before we look at the various ways in which language can be unclear, a word of caution is needed. There is no such thing as absolute clarity. Whether something is clear or not depends upon the context in which it occurs. A botanist does not use the commonsense vocabulary in describing and classifying plants. At the same time, it would be foolish for a person to use botanical terms in describing the appearance of his backyard. Thus, Aristotle said, it is the mark of an educated person not to expect more rigor than the subject matter will allow. Since clarity and rigor are context-dependent, it takes judgment and good sense to pitch an argument at the right level.

Vagueness Perhaps the most common form of unclarity is *vagueness.* It arises in the following way. Many of our concepts admit of *borderline cases.* The standard example is baldness. A person with a full flowing head of hair is not bald. A person without a hair on his head is bald. In between, however, there is a range of cases where we are not prepared to say definitely whether the person is bald or not. Here we say something less definite, such as this person is "going" bald. Notice that our inability to apply the concept of baldness in this borderline case is not due to ignorance. It will not help, for example, to count the number of hairs on the person's head. Even if we knew the exact number, we would still not be able to say whether the person was bald or not. The same is true of most adjectives that concern properties admitting of degrees—for example, *rich, healthy, tall, wise,* and *ruthless.* We can also encounter borderline cases with common nouns. Consider the common noun *game.* Baseball is a game and so is chess, but how about tossing a frisbee? Is that a game? Is Russian roulette a game? Are prize fighting and bull fighting games? As we try to answer these questions, we feel an inclination to say Yes and an inclination to say No. This uncertainty shows that these concepts admit of borderline cases.

For the most part this feature of our language—that we use terms without sharply defined limits—causes little difficulty. In fact, this is a useful feature of our language, for suppose we *did* have to count the number of hairs on a person's head before we could say whether he was bald or not. Yet difficulties can arise when borderline cases themselves are at issue. Suppose that a state passes a law forbidding all actions that tend to corrupt the public morals. The law is backed up by stiff fines and imprisonment. There will be many cases that clearly fall under this law and many cases that clearly do not fall under it. But in a very wide range of cases, it will just not be clear whether they fall under this law or not. Here we shall say that the law is *vague*; laws are sometimes called unconstitutional for this very reason. In calling the law vague, we are *criticizing* it. We are not simply noticing the existence of borderline cases, for there will usually be borderline cases no matter how careful we are. *We shall say, then, that a concept is vague if, in a given context, it leaves open too wide a range of borderline cases for the successful use of that concept in that context.*

To further illustrate this notion of context dependence, consider the expression "light football player." There are, of course, borderline cases between those football players who are light and those who are not light. But on these grounds alone we would not say that the expression is vague. It is a perfectly serviceable expression, and we can indicate borderline cases by saying that "Jones is a bit light for a football player." Suppose, however, that Ohio State and Cal Tech wish to have a game between their light football players. It is obvious that the previous understanding of what counts as being light is too vague for this new context. At Ohio State, anyone under 210 pounds is considered light. At Cal Tech, anyone over 150 pounds is considered heavy. What is needed then is a ruling—for example, anyone under 175 pounds will be considered a lightweight. This is a common situation. A concept that is perfectly okay in one area becomes vague when applied to some other (usually more specialized) area. This vagueness is removed by adopting more precise rules. Vagueness is resolved by definition.

Exercise 1: Each of the following sentences contains words or expressions that are potentially vague. Resolve this vagueness by replacing the underlined expression with one that is more precise. To do this, you must imagine some context in which the vagueness would make a difference.

For example: Harold has a bad reputation.
　　　　　　　Harold is a known thief.

1. John has a nice personality.
2. Cortisone is a dangerous drug.
3. Marian is a clever girl.
4. Nancy is a terrific tennis player.
5. Mark is a fiend at chess.
6. Sam's loyalty is in question.
7. There's not enough money to go around.
8. We have runaway inflation.
9. Jones won by a landslide.
10. Johnson is no better than he has to be.

Practical problems produced by vagueness may even lead to a lawsuit. The following case turns upon the meaning of the word "chicken":

FRIGALIMENT IMPORTING CO. v. B.N.S. INT'L SALES CORP., S.D. N.Y., 1960, 190 F.Supp. 116. Plaintiff and defendant, a Swiss buyer and a New York seller, respectively, entered into a contract for the sale of "chicken." When the initial shipment arrived in Switzerland, plaintiff found it had received stewing chicken or "fowl," rather than young chicken suitable for broiling or frying, as it had expected. Plaintiff then sued for breach of contract. Judge Friendly of the Second Circuit Court of Appeals, sitting as District Judge, held for defendant.

"The issue is, what is chicken? Plaintiff says 'chicken' means a young chicken, suitable for broiling and frying. Defendant says 'chicken' means any bird of that genus that meets contract specifications on weight and quality, including what it calls 'stewing chicken' and plaintiff pejoratively terms 'fowl'. Dictionaries give both meanings, as well as some others not relevant here. To support its |construction|, plaintiff sends a number of volleys over the net; defendant essays to return them and adds a few serves of its own. . . .

"When all the evidence is reviewed, it is clear that defendant believed it could comply with the contracts by delivering stewing chicken in the 2½–3 lbs. size. Defendant's subjective intent would not be significant if this did not coincide with an objective meaning of 'chicken.' Here it did coincide with one of the dictionary meanings, with the definition in the Department of Agriculture Regulations to which the contract made at least oblique reference, with at least some usage in the trade, with the realities of the market, and with what plaintiff's spokesman had said. Plaintiff asserts it to be equally plain that plaintiff's own subjective intent was to obtain broilers and fryers; the only evidence against this is the material as to market prices and this may not have been sufficiently brought home. In any event it is unnecessary to determine that issue. For plaintiff has the burden of showing that 'chicken' was used in the narrower rather than in the broader sense, and this it has not sustained."

The issue here is whether, in the contract, the word "chicken" was used in a broad or narrow sense. This shows that the word was used in a vague way in the context of this contract. In order to deal with these practical problems of vagueness, every modern society has developed complicated systems for classifying and grading products. Meats are classified as *good, choice, prime,* etc.; eggs as *extra-large, large, medium,* etc.; and in France, where these things matter, wines are classified into categories with various subcategories thrown in. Of course, even these careful and elaborate classifications cannot completely exclude borderline cases, but they limit them and for the most part avoid troublesome vagueness.

Heaps and Slippery Slopes The existence of borderline cases makes possible various styles of fallacious reasoning that have been identified (and used) since ancient times. One such argument was called the argument "from the *heap*," for it was intended to show that there are no heaps. As a variation on this, we will show that there are no rich men. The argument goes as follows:

(1) If someone has one cent, he is not rich.

(2) If someone is not rich, then giving him one cent will not make him rich.

∴ No matter how many times you give a person a cent, he will not pass from being not rich to being rich.

Everyone will agree that there is something wrong with this argument, for if we hand over a billion pennies to someone, that person will be worth ten million dollars. If he or she started out with nothing, that would certainly count as passing from being not rich to being rich.

Although there is some disagreement among philosophers about the correct way to analyze this argument, we can see that it turns upon borderline cases in the following way: If we laid down a ruling (maybe for tax purposes) that anyone with a million dollars or more is rich and anyone with less than this is not rich, then the argument would fail. A person with $999,999.99 would pass from not being rich to being rich when given a single penny. But, of course, we do not use the word "rich" with this precision. We know of some clear cases of people who are rich and some other clear cases of people who are not rich. In between there is a fuzzy area where we are not prepared to say that people either are or are not rich. In this fuzzy area, a penny one way or the other will make no difference. Once we see the form of the argument from the heap, we see how we might "prove" that nobody is tall, fat, or bald and, finally, that there are no heaps. Wherever we find one thing passing over into its opposite through a gradual series of borderline cases, we can pull the following trick: find some increase that will not be large enough to carry us outside the borderline area, and then use the pattern of argument given above.

But what exactly is wrong with the argument from the heap? As a matter of fact, this is not an easy question to answer and remains a subject of debate. Here is one way of viewing this problem. Consider a case where we would all agree that a person would pass from being fat to being thin by losing at least 100 pounds. Now if this person lost an ounce a day for five years, he or she would have lost at least this much. Of course, there would be no particular day on which this person would pass from being fat to being thin. Yet losing an ounce a day for five years is *equivalent to* losing more than 100 pounds. So the argument from the heap seems to depend upon the idea that a series of insignificant changes cannot be equivalent to a significant change. Surely this is a strange assumption. Here we might be met with the reply that, for a change to occur, it must occur at some particular time and place. The answer is that this merely shows a misunderstanding of concepts that admit of borderline cases. We can examine this issue more closely by looking at a near cousin to arguments from the heap—so-called "slippery slope" arguments.

Slippery slope arguments exploit borderline cases in a different way than arguments from the heap. Here, instead of getting trapped in the borderline area, we inch our way through it in order to show that there is no real difference between things at opposite ends of a scale. Whereas the argument from the heap could be used to show that nobody is really bald, a slippery slope argument could be trotted out to show that there is no *real difference* between being bald and not being bald.

Slippery slope arguments are no better than arguments from the heap, but, strangely, they are sometimes taken quite seriously. Consider the difference between living and nonliving things:

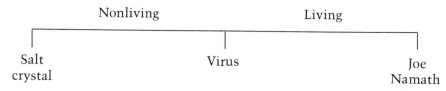

We notice first that a salt crystal is *not* alive. Yet a salt crystal is very similar to other more complex crystals, and these crystals are similar to certain viruses. We might even say that a virus just *is* a highly complex crystalline structure. But a virus is on the borderline between living and nonliving things. A virus does not take nourishment and does not reproduce itself. Instead, a virus invades the reproductive mechanisms of cells and these cells then produce the virus. As viruses become more complex, the differences between them and "higher" life forms become less obvious. Through a whole series of such small transitions, we finally reach a creature who is obviously alive: Joe Namath. So far, we have merely described a series of gradual transitions along a *continuum.* We get a slippery slope argument when we draw the following conclusion from these facts: Therefore there is no genuine difference between living and nonliving things since living processes are nothing more than complex nonliving processes. (By the way, the slippery slope argument can also be run in the opposite way by shifting emphasis: We conclude that everything is really alive, but some things, for example salt crystals, possess a very low level of life.)

Slippery slope arguments have been used to deny the difference between sanity and insanity, health and sickness, and amateur and professional athletics. (We can imagine someone saying that a professional athlete is just an athlete who gets paid more than other athletes who are called "amateurs.") All such arguments depend upon the following principles:

(1) We should not draw a sharp distinction between things that are not significantly different.

(2) If A is not significantly different from B and B is not significantly different from C, then A is not significantly different from C.

This first principle is interesting, complicated, and at least *generally* true. We shall examine it more closely in a moment. The second principle is obviously false. A series of insignificant differences can add up to a significant difference. As Senator Everett Dirksen once said, "A billion dollars here and a billion dollars there can add up to some real money."

Those who use slippery slope arguments often use the phrase "it's just a matter of degree." What is usually wrong with this phrase is the emphasis on the word "just," which suggests that differences of degree don't count. The difference between gluttony and starvation is a matter of degree—how much food you consume—but it is not *only* a matter of degree.

Where do you draw the line? We can now turn to some arguments concerning borderline cases that can be much more important. In the middle of an argument a person can offer a challenge by asking the question, "Where do you draw the line?" This challenge makes sense only when there is a range of intermediate or borderline cases where a line is difficult to draw. But sometimes, even if the line is difficult to draw, this challenge is out of place. If I say that Hank Aaron was a superstar, I am not going to be refuted if I cannot draw a sharp dividing line between athletes who are superstars and those who are not. There are some difficult borderline cases, but Hank Aaron isn't one of them. Nor will we be impressed if someone tells us that the difference between Hank Aaron and the thousands of players who never made it to the major leagues is "just a *matter of degree.*" Of course it is a matter of degree, but the difference in degree is so great that it should be marked by a special word. Arguing that we cannot distinguish things on opposite ends of a scale because we cannot justify any particular dividing point in the middle of the scale is just another variation of the slippery slope argument.

There are, however, occasions when the challenge to draw a line is relevant. For example, most schools and universities have grading systems that draw a fundamental distinction between passing grades and a failing grade. Of course, a person who barely passes a course does not perform very differently from one who barely fails a course, yet they are treated very differently. Students who barely pass a course get credit for it; those who barely fail it do not. This, in turn, can lead to serious consequences in an academic career and even beyond it. It is not unreasonable to ask for a justification of a procedure that treats cases that are so similar in such strikingly different ways. In other words, we are not just being tender-hearted; we are raising an issue of fairness or justice. It seems unfair to treat very similar cases in strikingly different ways, but this occurs any time we draw a sharp line between closely similar cases.

So the question "Where do you draw the line?" sometimes raises a genuine problem. Since drawing a line will make a great deal of difference to those who fall on one side of it or the other, how can it be drawn in a rational and fair way? This is a constant dilemma in making public policy. In considering a poverty program, it will be obvious that certain people are in need of aid and others are not. Yet the program itself must have some specific cut-off point. Those just above this point and those just below it will be treated differently even though the differences between them are negligible.

Sometimes we can find practical ways of dealing with problems of this kind. With a poverty program we can use a graduated scale based on need. Those with a greater need will receive more aid, and the aid will decrease as the cut-off point is approached. In this way, there will be only a small difference between those just below the cut-off point who receive minimal aid and those just above it who receive no aid at all. But sometimes this strategy is not available. Consider the death penalty. Most societies have reserved the death penalty for the most serious crimes. But where should we draw the line between crimes punishable by death and crimes not punishable by death? There is no possibility of introducing a sliding scale, since death does not admit of degrees. It seems to be an unavoidable consequence of the death penalty that similar cases will be treated in radically different ways. A defender of the death penalty can argue that it is fair since once the line is drawn the public will have fair warning about which crimes are subject to the death penalty. It will then be each person's decision whether to cross this line or not. It remains a matter of debate, however, whether the law can be administered in a way that makes this argument plausible. If the laws themselves are administered in an arbitrary way, arguments of this kind lose their force.

The finality and completeness of death raises a profoundly difficult problem in another area too: the legalization of abortion. There are some people who think that abortion is never justified. There are others who think that it doesn't need any justification at all. Between these extremes, there are many people who believe that abortion is justified in certain circumstances but not in others. There are also those who think that abortion should be allowed for a certain number of months of pregnancy, but not thereafter. People in the middle positions face the problem of deciding where to draw a line, and for this reason they are subject to criticism from both extreme positions. This problem admits of no easy solution. Since every line we draw will seem arbitrary to some extent, and since the issues here are profoundly important, the only way a person who holds a middle position can face this problem honestly is to argue that it is better to draw some line—even an arbitrary one—than to draw no line at all.

In an earlier discussion, we saw that, *in general*, we should not draw a sharp distinction between things that are not significantly different. This principle becomes more than a matter of logic when the distinction involves questions of life and death. Yet sometimes we abandon this principle with hardly a thought. There is surely no obvious reason why the voting age should be 18 rather than 17 or 19.[1] The previous voting age of 21 was arbitrary in the same way. But in this area, most people agree that the need to draw a clear line someplace more than outweighs the arbitrariness of drawing it in some particular place. To cite another example, most people agree that it is important to have uniform speed laws for motor vehicles even though it is arbitrary whether the limit is 50, 55, or 60 miles per hour. In other situations, arbitrariness is not so easily accepted. To summarize, the question, "Where do you draw the line?" is sometimes a variation on the slippery slope argument and so is just a quibble, whereas at other times it raises fundamental questions of fairness and justice. We must learn to distinguish the two kinds of cases—dismissing the first and doing the best we can with the second.

Exercise 2: For your own amusement, construct examples of an argument from the heap and a slippery slope argument.

Exercise 3: More seriously, discuss a case where drawing a sharp line can produce important moral, social, or political problems. The arguments on abortion given in Part Two (pages 243–67) may serve this purpose.

Ambiguity The idea of vagueness is based upon a common feature of words in our language. Many of them leave open a range of borderline cases. When these borderline cases cause difficulty, we say that the use of such terms is vague. The notion of ambiguity is also based upon a common feature of our language. Words often have a number of different meanings. For example, *The New Merriam-Webster Pocket Dictionary* has the following entry under the word "cardinal":

Cardinal *adj. 1:* of basic importance: Chief, Main, Primary, *2:* of cardinal red color.

---

[1] An answer to this is that people should be allowed to vote at 18 since they can, in times of war, be drafted at 18. This is not much of an answer, for it is also arbitrary to draft people at the age of 18.

n. 1: an ecclesiastical official of the Roman Catholic Church ranking next below the Pope, *2:* a bright red, *3:* any of several American finches of which the male is bright red.

In the plural, "The Cardinals" is the name of various athletic teams that inhabit St. Louis; "cardinal" is also the name of the numbers used in simple counting.

It is not likely that people could get confused about these very different meanings of the word "cardinal," but we might imagine a priest, a bird watcher, and a baseball fan all hearing the remark: "The cardinals are in town." The priest would prepare for a solemn occasion, the bird watcher would get out his binoculars, and the baseball fan would head for the stadium. If a term is used so that such confusions arise, we say that it is used *ambiguously.*

Examples of ambiguity are perhaps more common in logic texts than in everyday life, for context usually settles which of a variety of meanings is appropriate. Yet sometimes genuine misunderstandings do arise in everyday life. An American and a European discussing "football" may have two different games in mind. The European is talking about what *we* call "soccer"; the American is talking about what *they* call "American football." It is characteristic of the ambiguous use of a term that when it comes to light we are likely to say something like, "Oh, you mean *that* kind of cardinal!" or "Oh, you are talking about *American* football!" In a context where the use of a word is ambiguous, we do not know which of *two* clear meanings to attach to a word. In a context where the use of a word is vague, we cannot attach *any* clear meaning to the use of a word.

So far we have talked about the ambiguity of terms or individual words. But sometimes we do not know what interpretation to give to a phrase or a sentence because its grammar or syntax admits of more than one interpretation. Thus if we talk about *the conquest of the Persians,* we might be referring either to the Persians' conquering someone or to someone's conquering the Persians. Sometimes a sentence admits of a great many possible interpretations. For example, consider the sentence:

Only sons marry only daughters.

One thing that this might mean is that a person who is a male only child will marry a person who is a female only child. Again, it might mean that sons are the only persons who only marry daughters.[2]

The process of rewriting a sentence so that its meaning becomes clear is called *disambiguating.* One way of disambiguating a sentence is to continue it in a way that forces one interpretation. This is a way of filling out a context. Consider the sentence, "Mary had a little lamb."

[2] This example comes from Paul Beneceraph.

Notice how the meaning changes completely under the following continuations:

(1) Mary had a little lamb; he followed her to school.

(2) Mary had a little lamb and then a little broccoli.

Just in passing, it is not altogether obvious how we should describe the ambiguity in the sentence "Mary had a little lamb." The most obvious suggestion is that the word "had" is ambiguous, meaning "owned" on the first reading and "ate" on a second reading. Notice, however, that this also forces alternative readings for the expression "a little lamb." Presumably, it was a small whole live lamb that followed Mary to school, whereas it would have been a small piece of cooked lamb that she ate. So if we try to locate the ambiguity in particular words, we must say that not only the word "had" but also the word "lamb" is being used ambiguously. This is a reasonable approach, but another is available. In everyday speech we often leave things out. Thus, instead of saying "Mary had a little *piece of meat derived from a* lamb *to eat*," we just say "Mary had a little lamb," dropping out the italicized words on the assumption that they will be understood. In most contexts, such deletions cause no misunderstanding. But sometimes deletions are misunderstood, and this can produce ambiguity.

Exercise 4: Show that each of the following sentences admits of at least two interpretations by either rewriting the sentence as a whole in two different ways or expanding the sentence two different ways in order to clarify the context.

Example: Kenneth let us down.
Rewriting: Kenneth lowered us.
             Kenneth disappointed us.
Expanding: Kenneth let us down with a rope.
             Kenneth let us down just when we needed him.

1. The Abbots have to raise all their food.
2. Reggie Jackson was safe at home.
3. Nixon followed Johnson.
4. Marion missed her friends.
5. I don't know what state Meredith is in.
6. Wendy ran the Marathon.
7. Where did you get bitten?
8. There is some explanation for everything.
9. The President sent her congratulations.
10. I cannot recommend him too highly.
11. Visiting professors can be boring.
12. The meaning of the term "altering" is changing.

Equivocation Broadly speaking, to *equivocate* means to use language in a misleading way. More specifically, people equivocate when they shift their position in the course of a discussion or argument. Equivocation is connected with vagueness and ambiguity because they provide the means for making, and masking, such a shift in position. The following series of statements illustrates equivocation:

> All those who claim to be conscientious objectors will be pardoned.

> By a conscientious objector we will mean those persons who actually applied for this status.

> In coming to a decision, a review board will consider the sincerity of this application.

> Evidence of sincerity includes such things as membership in a religious organization that is opposed to all wars, and willingness to accept alternative service.

> Only long-term members of religious organizations opposed to all wars who have volunteered for alternative hazardous duty will be considered genuine conscientious objectors.

Here we move by slow stages from a view that will pardon all conscientious objectors to one that will pardon almost none of them. We can imagine a person sincerely maintaining any one of these positions. But a person who shifts back and forth from one position to another by changing his definition of what counts as a conscientious objection is involved in equivocation.

People often equivocate when they are trying to please a series of audiences with differing views. A study of campaign speeches before different groups shows this at once. People also equivocate when they wish to retreat from an awkward position without actually admitting that they are doing so. A good example of this occurred in the Presidential campaign debates of 1976. In responding to a question concerning foreign affairs, President Gerald Ford remarked that there was

> ... no domination of Eastern Europe and there never will be under a Ford Administration.

When pressed for more details by Max Frankel of the *New York Times*, he went on to say:

> I don't believe, Mr. Frankel, that the Yugoslavians consider themselves dominated by the Soviet Union. I don't believe that the Rumanians

consider themselves dominated by the Soviet Union. I don't believe
that the Poles consider themselves dominated by the Soviet Union.

Each of these countries is independent, autonomous, it has its own
territorial integrity and the United States does not concede that those
countries are under the domination of the Soviet Union. As a matter of
fact, I visited Poland, Yugoslavia and Rumania to make certain that the
people of those countries understood that the President of the United
States and the people of the United States are dedicated to their independence, their autonomy and their freedom.

Ford's remarks were immediately challenged by Jimmy Carter, who
thought it a plain fact that the countries of Eastern Europe are under the
domination of the Soviet Union. After the debate, Brent Snowcroft,
Ford's advisor on national security, answered this criticism by saying:

> I think what the President was trying to say is that we do not recognize
> Soviet domination of Europe.

In succeeding days, the *New York Times* reported these statements
made by the President:

> Last night in the debate I spoke of America's firm support of the aspira-
> tions and the independence of nations of Eastern Europe.

He added that the United States

> . . . has never conceded and never will concede their domination by the
> Soviet Union.

He also said:

> I admire the courage of the Polish people and I always supported the
> hopes of Polish Americans for freedom for their ancestral homeland. It
> is our policy to use every peaceful means to assist countries in Eastern
> Europe in their efforts to become less dependent on the Soviet Union
> and to establish closer and closer ties with the U.S.A.

A day later, the *New York Times* reported the following statement with
President Ford speaking in the third person:

> President Ford does not believe that the Polish people over the long run
> —whether they are in Poland or whether they are Polish-American here
> —will ever condone domination by any foreign force.

Ford said that he recognized that Soviet troops are stationed in Poland and called this "tragic," but said that the Polish

> ... desire for liberty and freedom is just as great as the desire for liberty and freedom of the American people.

Then, after repeating his claim that Yugoslavia and Rumania were not militarily dominated by the Soviet Union, he said:

> I hope and trust that my observations this morning will put an end to a misunderstanding. It was a misunderstanding.

If we go back to the original statement, it makes very little sense to say that President Ford was *misunderstood*. He may have misspoken—he may not have said what he wanted to say—but what he did say had a plain and unmistakable meaning. This series of statements is a particularly fine example of equivocation, because President Ford tried to shift what he meant by the word "domination." At the same time, he never admitted that he was doing this; instead, he attributed his mistake to a misunderstanding by others.

Irrelevance

In a good argument we present statements that are true in order to offer support for some conclusion. One way to mimic arguing without really arguing is to state things that are certainly true, but have no bearing upon the truth of the conclusion. Speaking and arguing in this way violates what Grice calls a rule of Relevance. Now we might wonder why irrelevant remarks can have any influence at all. The answer is that we generally assume that a person's remarks are relevant, for this is one of the conditions for smooth and successful conversation. That it is possible to exploit this natural assumption is shown in the following passage from *The Catcher in the Rye*.

> ... the new elevator boy was sort of on the stupid side. I told him, in this very casual voice, to take me up the Dicksteins' ...
> He had the elevator doors all shut and all, and was all set to take me up, and then he turned around and said, "They ain't in. They're at a party on the fourteenth floor."
> "That's all right," I said. "I'm supposed to wait for them. I'm their nephew."

He gave me this sort of stupid, suspicious look. "You better wait in the lobby, fella," he said.

"I'd like to—I really would," I said. "But I have a bad leg. I have to hold it in a certain position. I think I'd better sit down in the chair outside their door."

He didn't know what the hell I was talking about, so all he said was "oh" and took me up. Not bad, boy. It's funny. All you have to do is say something nobody understands and they'll do practically anything you want them to.[3]

It's clear what is going on here. When someone offers something as a reason, it is conversationally implied that there is some connection between it and the thing you are arguing for. In most cases the connection is obvious, and there is no need to spell it out. In other cases the connection is not obvious, but in the spirit of cooperation others are willing to assume that it exists. In the present case, there seems to be no connection between having a bad leg and sitting in one *particular* chair. Why, then, doesn't the elevator operator challenge this statement? Part of the reason is that it is not easy to challenge what people say; among other things, it is not polite. But politeness doesn't seem to hold the elevator operator back; instead, he does not want to appear stupid. The person who offers a reason conversationally implies a connection and we do not like to admit that we fail to see this connection. This combination of generosity and pride leads us to accept all sorts of irrelevant statements as reasons.

The Presidential campaign debates of 1976 also provided some splendid examples of fallacies of irrelevance. Here is one example involving an exchange with Jimmy Carter:

Question: ... What should the role of the United States in the world be and in that connection, concerning your limited experience in foreign affairs and the fact that you take some pride in being a Washington outsider, don't you think it would be appropriate to tell the American voters, before the election, the people you would like to have in key positions ...

After indicating that it would be inappropriate to announce his appointments at that time, he went on to say:

I've travelled the last twenty-one months among the people of this country. I've talked with them and I've listened. And I've seen it first hand in a very vivid way the deep hurt that's come to this country in

[3] J. D. Salinger, *The Catcher in the Rye* (New York: Bantam Book Co., 1964), pp. 157–58.

the aftermath of Vietnam and Cambodia and Chile and Pakistan and Angola and Watergate, CIA revelations.

Notice that the question itself is not a model of clarity. It falls into three parts. (1) A broad, unfocused question about foreign policy, (2) a reference to Carter's limited experience in foreign affairs, and (3) a direct question about appointments. Carter responds directly to the third item, but he is obviously reacting most strongly to the second aspect of the question because it challenges his qualifications to be President. He speaks of his firsthand knowledge of *the people's concern with* foreign affairs—which is not exactly to the point—and then drifts off into plain irrelevance by referring to Watergate. Hearing this, a visitor from another planet would think that Watergate was a country.

Fallacies of irrelevance are surprisingly common in everyday life. The best strategy for dealing with them is simply to cross out all irrelevant claims and then see what is left. Sometimes nothing is left. On the other hand, we should not be heavy-handed in making charges of irrelevance. Sometimes the occurrence of irrelevance is innocent; good arguments often contain irrelevant asides. More importantly, relevance is often secured by way of a conversational implication, so we really have to know what is going on in a given context in order to decide whether a remark is irrelevant or not.

We can illustrate this last point by examining two classical fallacies of irrelevance: the argument ad hominem and appeals to authority.

Arguments ad Hominem Literally, an *argument ad hominem* is an argument directed against the arguer rather than against his argument or against the conclusion of his argument. On the face of it, this seems to involve irrelevance, for the character of the person should have nothing to do with the truth of what he says or the soundness of what he argues. But consider a case in point:

> A: It is time for the United States to develop more normal relations with Cuba.

> B: Yeah, so you can make a bundle importing cigars from those Commies.

B's reply is certainly an ad hominem attack; it is an attack upon the motives of the speaker and not upon what the speaker has said. Yet the remark is not without some relevance—it is not off the wall. In a conversational exchange, we rely on the integrity of the person who is speaking, and when we have reasons to believe that the person's integrity is questionable, we sometimes say so. This is the significance of B's remark. He points to a fact that gives us some reason not to trust A's integrity in a discussion of U.S. relations with Cuba. We will therefore have to draw a distinction between an ad hominem attack and an ad hominem fallacy. In the context of an argument, we sometimes challenge a person's *right* to perform certain speech acts. Sometimes these attacks are justified, sometimes they are not. They must be judged on their own terms. On the other hand, an attack of this kind is sometimes illicitly turned into an attack upon the *truth* of what a person says or upon the soundness of that person's argument. We then have an instance of an *ad hominem fallacy.* In general, the truth of a statement or the soundness of an argument does not depend upon who produces them.

This difference is illustrated by the Biblical story of Job. Job is described as a person who "was blameless and upright, one who feared God and turned away from evil." Satan challenges God to allow him to subject Job to the worst calamities to see if Job's faith will remain unchanged. After the most extreme misfortune, Job finally cries out and asks why he should be made to suffer so.

> Then the Lord answered Job out of the whirlwind:
>
> Who is this that darkens counsel by words without knowledge?
>
> Gird up your loins like a man.
>
> I will question you, and you shall declare to me.
>
> Where were you when I laid the foundations of the earth?
>
> Tell me, if you have understanding.

God then continues with a long list of matters about which Job is completely ignorant. If we read all this as an answer to Job's complaints, then it must seem an ad hominem fallacy, for how can talk about Job's ignorance justify his apparently unmerited suffering? On the other hand, if we interpret God's statements as an attack upon Job's right to ask such a question, then they will not be read as answers to it, and no fallacy has been committed.

Although there is an important difference between ad hominem attacks and ad hominem fallacies, there is no shortage of the latter. One mark of an ad hominem fallacy is that the personal attack may have nothing to do with the matter at hand. A person's physical appearance, ethnic background, sex, bathing habits, or dress may *sometimes* give us reason to challenge his or her speech acts, but usually they do not. Ad hominem fallacies deal almost exclusively in such matters.

> **Exercise 5**: Ad hominem fallacies are so common that you should have little difficulty finding examples in political speeches, editorials, etc. Collect as many as you can.

Appeals to Authority Often in the midst of an argument we cite an authority to back up what we say. As we saw in Chapter 3, this is a standard way of offering assurances. In citing an authority, instead of giving reasons for what we say, we indicate that someone (the authority cited) could give them. Although logicians sometimes speak of the *fallacy* of appealing to authorities, we should notice in the first place that there is often nothing wrong with citing authorities or experts to support what we say. An authority is a person or institution with a privileged position concerning certain information. Through training, a doctor is an expert on certain diseases. A person who works in the Department of Agriculture can be an expert on America's soybean production. Someone who grew up in the swamps might be an expert on trapping muskrats. Since some people stand in a better position to know things than others, there is nothing wrong with citing them as authorities. In fact, an appeal to experts and authorities is essential if we are to make up our minds on subjects outside our own range of competence.

At the same time, appeals to authority can be abused, and there are some obvious questions we should ask whenever such an appeal is made. Most obviously, we should always ask *whether the authority cited is, in fact, an authority in the area under discussion.* If the answer to this question is *No,* then we are dealing with a fallacy of *relevance.* For example, being a movie star does not qualify a person to speak on the merits of a particular brand of elbow macaroni. Endorsements by athletes of hair cremes, deodorants, beer, and automobiles are in the same boat. Of course, we have to be careful in making this charge. It is possible that Lefty Stone, a famous pitcher, made a thorough investigation of various deodorants before lending his name to one particular product. It is not, however, very likely. But perhaps instead of speaking about the fallacy of the appeal to authority, we might better speak of the fallacy of the appeal to *false* authority.

Not all questions of authority are as trivial as the cases just cited. At one time the Church claimed authority on questions of astronomy, upholding the theory that the sun moves around the earth against the Copernican theory that the earth moves around the sun. There was a period in Russia when the Communist party claimed the authority to reject the Darwinian theory of evolution through natural selection. At a distance it may seem strange that a religious institution should make any claims about a matter in physical science or that a political party should take any stand on an issue of biology. Yet this tendency for institutions to claim authority beyond rational limits has existed throughout human history. Virtually every important intellectual advance has faced the resistance of such institutionalized authorities.

Apart from cases where the opinions of the "authority" cited are obviously irrelevant to the matter at hand, we can still ask *whether the question is of the kind that can be settled by expert opinion.* It is important to raise this issue because experts often disagree. In a criminal trial, one set of expert witnesses may testify that the defendant had been brainwashed and was in no way responsible for his or her actions. A second set of expert witnesses will testify that the defendant was as sane and sober as a judge at the time of the crime. A bewildered jury must decide which (if any) of the experts to trust.

To get a sense of this problem, imagine yourself sitting in the jury trying to decide the following case. In 1920 Mrs. Andree Hahn of Kansas City, Missouri, purchased a painting (entitled *La Belle Ferronnière*) that was supposedly painted by Leonardo da Vinci. On hearing of this sale, Sir Joseph Duveen, an international art dealer, declared that the painting was a fake. He did this publicly, without actually having seen Mrs. Hahn's painting. Such a remark, made by a leading art dealer, naturally lowered the value of the painting and Mrs. Hahn sued. Duveen summoned a gallery of art experts to testify in his behalf that the painting was indeed a fraud. Duveen's leading witness was Bernard Berenson, an art critic of international renown. Part of Berenson's deposition and subsequent cross-examination by Hyacinthe Ringrose, Mrs. Hahn's attorney, has been summarized by Laurie Adams:

> Berenson was Duveen's first Paris witness; his deposition lasted two days and was taken at the offices of the Guaranty Trust Co., 1 rue des Italiens. In view of Berenson's international renown as an art critic, Duveen's attorney opened the deposition with questions on the nature of expertise.

"You have to know the pictures," Berenson explained, "no matter how few or how many, and all the other works of art that practically nobody questions as being by that master. You then get a sense . . . this sort of sixth sense that comes from accumulated experience . . . a sense of the quality of the master, a sense of what that master is up to, what he is likely to do, able to do, and what he is not likely to be able to do. Then you control this by trying to find out what characteristics are recurrent in him and that do not occur in that one picture exclusively. For instance, a certain kind of ear, a certain type of hand, a certain lay of hair, a certain kind of eye, of chin, and so on; certain folds of draperies. When all these things go together in picture after picture, we conclude and are allowed to conclude by all people who allow for evidence, that that is the right kind of evidence; and if that occurs in the picture, then you say that it is a picture by the said master."

Later, under cross-examination, Ringrose launched into an attack on Berenson's description of his own expertise by bringing up the idea of the painter's unconscious. "Do you think it is possible for anybody to identify the unconscious characteristics of a painter?"

"Yes, it is the easiest thing in the world, because he was not trying to disguise them."

"The mystical characteristics?" Ringrose persisted, trying to discredit Berenson's technique by implying that it was vague, unscientific, even ridiculously magical.

"Not at all," asserted Berenson confidently, "It was what he was doing unconsciously; or what he was doing by rote—we all do most of our work by rote. What we do habitually, we always do in the same fashion."

"Didn't you use the word 'mystical' and say that you had ascertained the unconscious characteristics of Leonardo da Vinci by a sort of sixth sense?"

"I did not use it in that sense. I used it in expressing that the moment I see a picture my sixth sense tells me what it is; but not when I describe it. . . . You must distinguish in art criticism between the instantaneous impression, then the attempt to control it by all sorts of other detailed evidence and then the further effort to get the kind of evidence which would appeal to the other man, after you have convinced yourself. . . ."

"Is there any value at all in this so-called 'sixth sense'?"

"To me it is of the highest value, but I keep it to myself. I wouldn't give any value to it unless it was entirely vouched for by detailed counter-examination, counterproof. . . . It is a phrase which is accepted universally and may be called 'accumulated experience.' A man who has been working on a job for forty years gets an accumulated experience which gives him an instantaneous reaction within his field of competence. That is all I mean."[4]

[4] Laurie Adams, *Art on Trial* (New York: Walker and Company, 1976), pp. 80–81.

After listening to this testimony—and to other testimony like it—the majority of the jury (9 - 2) decided that Duveen's experts had not produced credible evidence that Mrs. Hahn's painting was a fraud. The art world was, of course, thunderstruck to see its experts repudiated in this way.

To return to the main point, before we accept expert opinion, we must decide whether expert opinion really exists in a given area. In *Hahn v. Duveen*, the majority of a jury came to the conclusion that for the authenticity of Italian Renaissance painting, the answer is No.

Although this may seem obvious, we often forget to ask *whether the authority has been cited correctly.* When a person cites an authority, he or she is making a factual claim that so and so holds some particular view. Sometimes the claim is false. Here is an example:

> According to medical authorities, poison ivy is contagious when it is oozing.

This is false, for according to medical authorities, poison ivy is never contagious. Yet many people hold that it is contagious, and they think that they have medical opinion on their side. It is hard to deal with people who cite authorities incorrectly, for we do not carry an almanac or encyclopedia around with us. Yet it is a good idea to spot-check appeals to authority, for, short of lying, people often twist authorities to their own opinions.

It is also worth asking *whether the authority cited can be trusted to tell the truth.* To put this more bluntly, we should ask ourselves whether a particular authority has any good reason to lie or misrepresent facts. Presumably, the officials who know most about Russian food production will be the heads of the various agricultural bureaus. But it would be utterly naive to take their reports at face value. Failures in agricultural production have been a standing embarrassment of the Russian economy, and, as a consequence, there is pressure at every level to put a good face on things. Even if the state officials were inclined to tell the truth, which is a charitable assumption, the information they receive is probably not very accurate. But we do not have to consider totalitarian regimes to find instances of deliberate falsification. Oskar Morgenstern remarks that "central banks in many countries, the venerable Bank of England not excepted, have for decades published deliberately misleading statistics, as, for example, when part of the gold in their possession is put under 'other assets' and only part is shown as 'gold.' "[5] Of course, the officials of central banks do not misrepresent their gold holdings out of simple malice; they think that they can gain some advantage through such misrepresentations. So in assessing the trustworthiness of an authority we must really ask two questions: First,

---

[5] Oskar Morgenstern, *On the Accuracy of Economic Observations* (Princeton, N.J.: Princeton University Press, 1963), p. 20.

is the authority really in a position to know, and secondly, do we have good reason to believe that the authority is telling the truth.

One last question we can ask is *why the appeal to authority is being made at all.* To cite an authority is to give assurances and, as we noticed earlier, we usually give assurances to strengthen the weak points in our arguments. It is surprising how often we can see what is wrong with an argument just by noticing where it is backed by appeals to authority. Beyond this, we should be suspicious of arguments that rely on too many authorities. (We might call this the fallacy of excessive footnotes.) Good arguments tend to stand on their own.

To go back to the beginning, in our complicated and specialized world, reliance on experts and authorities is unavoidable. Yet we can still be critical of appeals to authority by asking these questions:

(1) Is the authority cited in fact an authority in the areas under discussion?

(2) Is this the kind of question that can be settled by expert opinion?

(3) Has the authority been cited correctly?

(4) Can the authority cited be trusted to tell the truth?

(5) Why is an appeal to authority being made at all?

Exercise 6: A striking example of disagreements between authorities occurred in a television program produced by Nova entitled "Incident at Brown's Ferry." This script is reproduced in its entirety in Part Two of this book (pp. 191–208). Give your own evaluation of the various authorities. Include the narrator in your assessment.

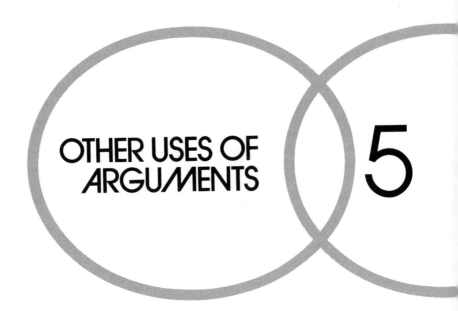

OTHER USES OF ARGUMENTS

5

In earlier chapters we have spoken about arguments as if their only function were to prove something or justify some claim. The purpose of this chapter is to correct this one-sided view by noticing uses of argument other than justification. Sometimes the primary intention of an argument is not to establish some truth, but rather to criticize or refute an argument presented by another. The patterns of <u>refutations</u> mirror the criteria for a sound and significant argument, for the point of a refutory argument is to show that one of these criteria has not been met. Another very important use of arguments is to formulate <u>explanations</u>. In seeking an explanation, we are not trying to prove that something is true; we are trying to understand why it is true. One way of making sense out of a perplexing fact is to show how it can be derived from understood principles. Scientific explanations often have this form.

Refutations

To refute an argument is to show that it is no good. Given the nature of an argument, this can be done in two main ways: (1) we can argue that some of the reasons offered are themselves dubious (or even false) or (2) we can argue that the conclusion does not follow from the reasons presented. It is important to note that a refutory argument does *not* have to prove the opposite of what someone else is arguing. A refutation is sufficient if it raises objections that cannot be answered.

Consider the following example. For centuries many people have believed in astrology. That is, they have believed that their lives are determined by, and therefore can be predicted from, the configuration of the stars at their birth. As evidence for this, astrologers point to successful predictions that they have made. There are two ways in which we might attack the astrologer's claim. First, we might examine the evidence to see just how accurate the predictions were. A second, and often more elegant, form of refutation is to grant the evidence and then argue that it does not establish the conclusion. A beautiful argument of this kind is found in St. Augustine's *Confessions*. St. Augustine was captivated by astrology until his conversion to Christianity. He then abandoned it, he says, for the following simple reason:

> I turned my attention to the case of twins, who are generally born within a short time of each other. Whatever significance in the natural order the astrologers may attribute to this interval of time, it is too short to be appreciated by human observation and no allowance can be made for it in the charts which an astrologer has to consult in order to cast a true horoscope. His predictions, then, will not be true, because he would have consulted the same charts for both Esau and Jacob and would have made the same predictions for each of them, whereas it is a fact that the same things did not happen to them both. Therefore, either he would have been wrong in his predictions or, if his forecast was correct, he would not have predicted the same future for each. And yet he would have consulted the same chart in each case. This proves that if he had foretold the truth, it would have been by luck, not by skill.[1]

It may take a few moments to see the full force of this simple argument, but consider what replies an astrologer might make. He could argue that the small difference in time between the births does make a difference, but since past horoscopes have not been cast on this basis, they must all be incorrect and their success simply luck. On the other

---

[1] St. Augustine, *Confessions*, R. S. Pine-Coffin, trans. (Harmondsworth, England: Penguin Books, 1961), p. 142.

side, if these past horoscopes were correct in ignoring the small time differences, then astrology fails to explain why twins often lead such different lives.

One way for the astrologers to avoid St. Augustine's argument would be to make their claim more modest. Instead of saying that our entire lives are *determined* by the configuration of the heavens at our birth, they could hedge their position by saying that this configuration has an important *influence* on our lives. This move takes some of the excitement out of astrology, for in admitting to *other* influences on our lives, the astrologer can no longer make detailed predictions without having knowledge of the natural and social sciences. But the advantage of this hedging move is that it will allow the astrologer to explain away a great many mistaken predictions. Whenever a particular prediction fails, the astrologer can always say that some other influence interfered with the influence of the stars. If the astrologer is willing to make this move no matter how many predictions come out wrong, then the position is *self-sealing* and so empty of content. (We will examine this notion of a self-sealing position later in this chapter.) So astrologers who wish to maintain that the stars have any influence at all on our lives must produce positive statistical evidence to support their claim. The status of such statistical evidence is examined in a recent textbook on astronomy:

> From time to time astrologers have presented statistical "proofs" of astrology, but without exception when they are checked over by competent mathematicians they are found to be baseless.[2]

That's just like arguing . . . We know that an argument is no good if it starts from true premises and leads to a false conclusion. Often, however, we cannot point this out to refute an argument because the truth or falsity of the conclusion is the very thing at issue. Here a typical device is to point out that by arguing in the same way, we *can* get a result that is unsatisfactory. A wonderfully simple example of this style of argument occurred in the English Parliamentary debate on capital punishment. One member of Parliament was defending the death penalty on the grounds that the alternative, life in prison, was much more cruel. He was met with the following reply: On this principle, those found guilty of first-degree murder ought to be given life in prison and the death penalty should be given to those who commit some lesser offense. Notice that the reply is not decisive as it stands. The first speaker could go on to call for the abolition of life imprisonment and then keep the death penalty as the most severe punishment. Alternatively, he could simply

[2] George O. Abell, *Exploration of the Universe*, 3rd ed. (New York: Holt, Rinehart and Winston, 1975), p. 33.

accept the idea that life imprisonment—not the death penalty—is the most severe penalty and apply it to first-degree murder. In point of fact, however, the first speaker was certainly unwilling to accept either of these alternatives. He simply tried a rhetorical trick and got caught.

Refuting an argument by showing that it is *just like another* argument that is obviously no good is a common device in everyday discussions. Here is another example:

A: If I had a higher salary, I could buy more things, so if everyone had higher salaries, everyone could buy more things.

B: That's just like arguing that if one person stands up at a ball game he will get a better view, so if everyone stands up, everyone will get a better view.

At first sight, it may not be obvious whether A's style of reasoning is valid or not. B's response shows that it is invalid by providing an instance where the same style of reasoning takes us from something true to something false. This, then, is the general method for showing that an argument is invalid: give an example of an argument with the same basic form, where the inference clearly takes us from something true to something false. Admittedly, this procedure is not precise, for we have given no explanation of the notion that two arguments have the *same basic form.* (This topic will be discussed more carefully in Chapters 6 and 7.) Yet it remains a fact that people can often see that two arguments have the same basic form and, through seeing this, decide that an argument presented to them is invalid. This ability is the basis of sound logical judgment. It is also the basis of wit. It's at best mildly funny to say that if God had wanted us to fly, he would have given us wings. You have to be fairly clever to reply at once: "If God had wanted us to stay on the ground, he would have given us roots."

Exercise 1: For each of the following arguments, find another with the same basic form where the premise or premises are true and the conclusion is false.

1. If tea is dangerous, so is coffee.
   Tea isn't dangerous, so coffee isn't either.

2. If a country becomes wealthy, then its people become wealthy as well.

3. You cannot pass a law against dangerous drugs because there is no way of drawing a sharp line between dangerous and nondangerous drugs.

4. If you have never written a novel, then you are in no position to make judgments about novels.

5. If a person has nothing to hide, he or she should not object to being investigated.

6. Women are the natural persons to raise children because they are the ones who give them birth.

7. Radicals should not be granted freedom of speech because they deny this freedom to others.

8. Since everyone acts from his or her own motives, everyone's actions are selfish.

9. Why not smoke? The longer you smoke the longer you live.

Counter-examples So far we have looked at refutations of *arguments*. We have seen that they take two basic forms—they show that the pattern of reasoning is invalid, or they show that the premises themselves are not well-founded. When an argument is refuted, its conclusion has not been shown to be false. As we have seen, we can refute all of the arguments in behalf of astrology but, for all that, the claims of astrologers could still be true. Of course, if we refuted all of these arguments, there would be no *reason* to think that these claims are true.

In contrast, we also speak about refuting a *statement.* This *does* mean showing it to be false. Refutations take various forms, depending upon the form of the statement under attack. For example, if a person claims that all snakes lay eggs, then we need only find one species of snake that does not lay eggs in order to refute the claim. (Here we can cite the black snake, for it bears its young alive.) If the person retreats to the somewhat weaker claim that *most* snakes lay eggs, it becomes much harder to refute his claim. A single example of a snake that bears its young alive is not enough; to refute this claim we would have to show that a majority of snakes do not lay eggs. Here, instead of trying to refute his statement, we may ask him to produce his *argument* in behalf of it. We can then attack this argument. Finally, if the person retreats to the very weak claim that at least some snakes lay eggs, then his statement becomes very difficult to refute. Even if it were false (which it is not), to show this we would have to check every fool snake and establish that it does not lay eggs. So, as a rough-and-ready rule, we can say that the stronger a statement is, the more subject it is to refutation; the weaker it is, the less subject it is to refutation.

Citing the fact that black snakes bear their young alive in order to refute the claim that all snakes lay eggs is called presenting a *counterexample.* The pattern of reasoning is perfectly simple: If someone claims that *everything* of a certain kind has a certain feature, we need only find *one* thing of that kind lacking that feature in order to refute the claim. Although the pattern of argument is simple in form, it is not always easy to think of counter-examples. Some people are much better at it than others. Socrates was a genius in this respect. He wandered through the streets of ancient Athens questioning various people—often important political figures—challenging them to explain what they meant by various terms such as *justice, knowledge, courage, friendship,* and *piety.* As narrated by Plato, these exchanges all fall into a standard pattern: Socrates asks for a definition of some important notion; after some skirmishing, a definition is offered; Socrates immediately finds a counter-example to this definition; the definition is then changed or replaced by another; once more Socrates produces a counter-example; etc. With effortless ease, Socrates seemed able to produce counter-examples to any definition or any principle that others offered. There is no better introduction to the art of giving counter-examples than some specimens of the Socratic method.

In *The Republic,* Socrates is inquiring into the nature of justice. He begins by interrogating Cephalus, an old and distinguished citizen of Athens. Cephalus, in discussing the value of wealth, suggests that justice consists in telling the truth and restoring things we have been entrusted with. The dialogue goes as follows:

> *Cephalus:* Now in this, as I believe, lies the chief value of wealth, not for everyone, perhaps, but for the right-thinking man. It can do much to save us from going to that other world in fear of having cheated or deceived anyone even unintentionally or of being in debt to some god for sacrifice or to some man for money. Wealth has many other uses, of course; but, taking one with another, I should regard this as the best use that can be made of it by a man of sense.

> *Socrates:* You put your case admirably, Cephalus.... But take this matter of doing right: can we say that it really consists in nothing more nor less than telling the truth and paying back anything we may have received? Are not these very actions sometimes right and sometimes wrong? Suppose, for example, a friend who had lent us a weapon were to go mad and then ask for it back, surely anyone would say we ought not to return it. It would not be "right" to do so; nor yet to tell the truth without reserve to a madman.

> *Cephalus:* No, it would not.

> *Socrates:* Right conduct, then, cannot be defined as telling the truth and restoring anything we have been trusted with.[3]

Whereas many of Plato's *Dialogues* show Socrates making fools—and also enemies—of people who claim to know things that they do not

---

[3] *The Republic of Plato,* Francis M. Cornford, trans. (New York: Oxford University Press, 1941), p. 7.

know, other dialogues have a different quality. They show Socrates and his interlocutors involved in a cooperative activity searching after philosophical understanding. The *Theaetetus* is a dialogue of this kind. Theaetetus was a brilliant young man, gifted in mathematics. In the dialogue he and Socrates try (unsuccessfully) to arrive at a correct definition of *knowledge*. They notice an important difference between knowledge and mere belief: It is possible for someone to *believe* something that is false, but it is not possible for someone to *know* something that is false. This leads Theaetetus to suggest a simple definition of knowledge: Knowledge equals true belief. After all, someone cannot have a true belief concerning something that is false. This proposed definition is refuted in the following exchange.

> *Socrates:* [There is] a whole profession to prove that true belief is not knowledge.
>
> *Theaetetus:* How so? What profession?
>
> *Socrates:* The profession of those paragons of intellect known as orators and lawyers. There you have men who use their skill to produce conviction, not by instruction, but by making people believe whatever they want them to believe. You can hardly imagine teachers so clever as to be able, in the short time allowed by the clock, to instruct their hearers thoroughly in the true facts of a case of robbery or other violence which those hearers had not witnessed.
>
> *Theaetetus:* No, I cannot imagine that; but they can convince them.
>
> *Socrates:* And by convincing you mean making them believe something.
>
> *Theaetetus:* Of course.
>
> *Socrates:* And when a jury is rightly convinced of facts which can be known only by an eye-witness, then, judging by hearsay and accept a true belief, they are judging without knowledge, although, if they find the right verdict, their conviction is correct?
>
> *Theaetetus:* Certainly.
>
> *Socrates:* But if true belief and knowledge were the same thing, the best of jurymen could never have a correct belief without knowledge. It now appears that they must be different things.[4]

One thing to notice about both of these counter-examples is that they are *completely decisive.* Cephalus does not stand by his position and argue that it would be right to return the sword to his demented

---

[4] Plato, *Theaetetus*, Francis M. Cornford, trans., in his *Plato's Theory of Knowledge* (New York: Liberal Arts Press, 1957), p. 141.

friend, nor does Theaetetus dig in his heels and insist that the ignorant members of the jury do know that the person is innocent provided only that they believe it and it is true. Faced with the counter-examples, they both retreat at once. Why is this? Why not stay with the definition and reject the counter-examples as false? The answer is that for many concepts there is general agreement about their application to particular cases, even if there is no general agreement about a correct definition. To take an extreme example, everyone agrees that Hitler was a dictator (even Hitler), and no one supposes that Thomas Jefferson was a dictator (even his enemies). So any definition of *a dictator* that would lead us to say that Hitler was not a dictator and Thomas Jefferson was a dictator must be wrong. A less extreme example is the notion of negligence—an idea important in the law. We have some perfectly clear cases of negligence: a person amusing himself by setting off skyrockets in the Sistine Chapel, for example. On the other hand, a person who deliberately drives off a road to avoid striking a child is clearly *not* acting negligently. In between these clear cases there are any number of difficult ones that help give lawyers a living. Because of these borderline cases, no perfectly exact definition of negligence is possible. But any definition of negligence that does not square with the clear cases is just plain wrong, and this can be shown by citing one of these clear cases as a counter-example.

Ethics is an area where arguments often turn upon counter-examples. Although various forms of relativity remain fashionable, in our day-to-day life there is a surprisingly wide range of agreement concerning what actions are right and what actions are wrong. That is, whatever theory we might hold, we usually agree about particular cases. We tend not to notice this agreement because disagreement is interesting and exciting, whereas agreement is not. The task of an ethical theory is to discover those principles which tell us what actions are right and what actions are wrong. One important test of an ethical theory is whether it squares with these clear cases where agreement exists.

Consider the Utilitarian Principle. According to that principle, an action is right if it is the action that will produce the greatest possible total happiness. Admittedly, the idea of happiness is vague and stands in need of explanation. For this discussion, however, we can ignore this complication. At first sight, this principle has much to recommend it. How, we might ask, could it ever be better to act in a way that produces less happiness than would be produced by acting in another way? Furthermore, the world would be a much better place if people uniformly followed this principle. All the same, the Utilitarian Principle is subject to a counter-example that has led most—though not all—philosophers to reject it as the *single* basic principle of ethics. One version of this counter-example goes as follows: It is certainly possible for a society to exist where a small slave population leading a wretched life allows the rest of the population to lead a blissfully happy life. In such a society, any other arrangement would, in fact, lower the total happiness. For example, any attempt to improve the lives of the slaves would be overbalanced by a loss of happiness in the slave-holding class. This may seem like a far-fetched situation, but if it were to occur, the utilitarian would have to approve of this society and argue against any changes in it. To most people this is unacceptable, for it offends our sense of fairness. "Why," we want to ask, "should one segment of society be assigned wretched lives so that others can be happy? How can the society be morally sound when human rights are infringed upon in this way?" Considerations of this kind have led most philosophers to abandon strict utilitarianism as the single principle of morality. Some philosophers have modified the principle to meet objections; some have supplemented it with other principles; some have simply rejected it in favor of some other theory.

Sometimes counter-examples force clarification. Consider the traditional moral precept, "Do unto others as you would have them do unto you." Like utilitarianism, this principle captures an important moral insight, but, if taken quite literally, it is even more subject to counter-examples. Jones, a sado-masochist, enjoys beating other people. When asked whether he would like to be treated in that way, he replies, "Yes." It is obvious that the Golden Rule was not intended to approve of Jones's behavior. The task, then, is to reformulate its principle to avoid this counter-example.

No discussion of counter-examples is complete without a mention of the Morgenbesser Retort. Though the exact story is now shrouded in the mists of time, it has come down to us from the 1950s in the following form. In a lecture, a British philosopher remarked that he knew of many languages where a double negative means an affirmative, but not one language where a double affirmative means a negative. From the back of the room came Morgenbesser's famous retort: "Yeah, Yeah."

Exercise 2: Find a counter-example to each of the following claims.

Examples: Claim: All prime numbers are odd.
Counter-example: 2 is a prime number, but it is not odd.

Claim: "Sugar" is the only word where an s is pronounced sh.
Counter-example: Oh sure.

1. Lightning never strikes twice in the same place.
2. Three points determine a plane.
3. What you don't know can't hurt you.
4. Only the plate umpire can call balls and strikes.
5. You cannot be religious without believing in God.
6. Without poverty there would be no crime.
7. It is always wrong to lie.

Here are two more difficult cases:
1. If it is wrong for one person to do something, then it must be wrong for everyone to do it.
2. There are no rights without corresponding duties.

Self-Sealers and Vacuity It is characteristic of certain positions that no evidence can *possibly* refute them. This may seem like a wonderful feature for a position to have. In fact, however, it usually makes the position useless. We can start with a silly example. A Perfect Sage claims to be able to predict the future in detail. The Perfect Sage's predictions take the following form:

Two weeks from today at 4:37 you are going to be doing . . . *exactly* what you are doing.

This prediction cannot possibly be wrong, but, of course, it doesn't tell us anything in particular about the future. Whatever happens, the prediction is going to be true, and this is just what is wrong with it. The prediction is *empty* or *vacuous.*

People do not, of course, go around making predictions of the kind just noticed, but, strange to say, they sometimes hold positions that are empty or vacuous in just the same way. A clairvoyant claims to be able to predict the future, but every time a prediction fails, he says that this just proves that someone set up bad vibrations that interfered with his visions. If the prediction comes true, that shows his clairvoyance; if it does not come true, that proves interference. No matter what happens, then, the clairvoyant cannot be wrong. So his predictions are as empty and vacuous as those of the Perfect Sage.

Positions that are set up in this way so that nothing can possibly refute them we will call *self-sealers.*[5] A self-sealing position is one that is so constructed that no criticism can possibly be brought against it. This shows its vacuity, and it is precisely for this reason that we reject it.

People do not usually hold self-sealing positions in a blatant way—they tend to back into them. A person who holds that the American economy is controlled by an international Jewish conspiracy will point out people of Jewish extraction (or with Jewish names) who occupy important positions in financial institutions. This at least counts as evidence, though not very strong evidence. There are a great many people in these institutions who are not Jews. To counter this claim, the person now argues that many of these other people are secretly Jews or are tools of the Jewish conspiracy. The Jews have allowed some non-Jews to hold

---

[5] I owe this phrase to Ted Honderich. I do not know whom, if anyone, he owes it to.

important positions in order to conceal their conspiracy. What evidence is there for this? Well, really none, but that only helps to prove how clever the conspiracy is. The position has now become self-sealing, for all evidence cited *against* the existence of the conspiracy will be converted into evidence *for* its cleverness. Unlike our previous examples, which were artificial, reasoning of this kind actually does take place.

Self-sealing arguments are hard to deal with, for people who use them will often shift their ground. A person will begin by holding a significant position that implies that facts are one way rather than another, but under the pressure of criticism he will self-seal it so that no evidence can possibly count against it. That is, he will slide back and forth between two positions—one that is not self-sealed, and so is significant, but subject to criticism, and another that is self-sealed, and so is not subject to criticism, but insignificant. The charge that is leveled against a theory that vacillates in this way is that it is either *trivial* or *false:* trivial if self-sealing, false if not.

One way of challenging a self-sealing position is to ask what possible fact could prove it wrong. This is a good question to ask, but it can be misunderstood and met with the triumphant reply: "Nothing can prove my position wrong, because it is true." A better way to show the insignificance of a self-sealing theory is to put the question in a different form: If your position has any significance, it should tell us that certain things will occur whereas certain other things will not occur. If it cannot do this, it really tells us nothing at all; so please make some specific predictions and we will see how they come out.

Ideologies and world views tend to be self-sealing. The Marxist ideology has this quality. If a revolution occurs, then this was predicted by one part of the theory; if it does not occur, then that too was predicted by another part of the theory. The position also has another quite special twist. If you fail to see the truth of the Marxist ideology, that just shows that your social consciousness has not been raised. The very fact that you reject the Marxist ideology shows that you are not yet capable of understanding it and that you are in need of re-education. This is perfect self-sealing. Sometimes psychoanalytic theory gets involved in this same kind of self-sealing. People who disagree with certain psychoanalytic claims can be accused of repressing these facts. If a boy *denies* that he wants to murder his father and sleep with his mother, this itself is taken as evidence of the strength of these desires and of his unwillingness to acknowledge them. If this kind of reasoning gets out of hand, then psychoanalytic theory also becomes self-sealing and empty. Freud was aware of this danger; this was the basis of his remark that sometimes a cigar is just a cigar.

So far, we have seen two ways in which an argument can be self-sealing: (1) it can invent an *ad hoc* or arbitrary way of dismissing every possible criticism. The clairvoyant and the astrologer can always point to interfering conditions without going to the trouble of saying what they are. The anti-Semite can always cite Jewish cleverness to explain away counter-evidence. (2) A theory can counter criticism by attacking its critics. The critic of Marxism is charged with having a decadent bourgeois consciousness which blinds him to the facts of class conflict. The critic's response to psychoanalytic theory is analyzed (and then dismissed) as repression, a reaction formation, or something or other.

Yet another form of self-sealing is this: Words are used in such a way that a position becomes true *by definition*. For example, a person makes the strong claim that all human actions are selfish. This is an interesting remark, but it seems to be false, for it is easy to think of cases where people have acted in self-sacrificing ways. To counter these obvious objections, the argument takes the following turn: When a person acts in a self-sacrificing way, what he *wants* to do is help another, even at his own expense. This is his desire or his motive, and that is what he acts to fulfill. So the action is selfish after all. It should be obvious that this is a self-sealing move, for it will not help to cite any behavior—even self-destructive behavior—as counter-evidence. If a person desires to harm himself, then he acts to fulfill his desire and the act is again selfish.

It is not hard to see what has happened in this case. The arguer has chosen to use the word "selfish" in a new and peculiar way. A person is said to act selfishly if he acts to do what he desires to do. This is not what we usually mean by this word. We say that a person acts selfishly if he is too much concerned with his own interests at the expense of the interests of others. On this standard use of the word "selfish" there are any number of counter-examples to the claim that all human actions are selfish. But these counter-examples do not apply when the word "selfish" is used in a new way, where "acting selfishly" comes close to meaning just "acting." The point is that under this new meaning of "selfish" it becomes empty (or almost empty) to say that all human actions are selfish. We are thus back to a familiar situation: Under one interpretation (the ordinary interpretation), the claim that all human actions are selfish is interesting, and false. Under another interpretation (an extraordinary interpretation), the claim is true but uninteresting. The position gets all its *apparent* interest and plausibility from a rapid two-step back and forth between these positions.

Self-sealing arguments are not easy to handle, for they change their form under pressure. The best strategy is to begin by charging a person who uses such an argument with saying something trivial, vacuous, or boring. If, to meet this charge, he or she says something quite specific and important, then argument can proceed along normal lines. But it is not always easy to get down to brass tacks in this way. This becomes clear if you examine an argument between a Marxist and a non-Marxist, or between individuals with different religious views. Their positions are sealed against objections from each other, and the arguments are almost always at cross purposes.

Explanations

Explanations answer questions *how* or *why* something happened. We explain how a mongoose got out of his cage by pointing to a hole he dug under the fence. We explain why Smith was acquitted by saying that he got off on a technicality. The purpose of explanations is to make sense out of things. The character of explanations will depend upon the subject matter and the audience. Explanations in science are more technical than those of everyday life, because scientists are addressing their colleagues who are familiar with the subject matter. We explain things in different ways to children and adults. Sometimes simply filling in the details of a story makes an explanation. For example, we can explain how a two-year-old girl foiled a bank robbery by saying that the robber tripped over her while fleeing from the bank. Here we have made sense out of an unusual event by putting it in the context of a plausible *narrative.* It is unusual for a two-year-old girl to foil a bank robbery, but there is nothing unusual about a person tripping over a child when running recklessly at full speed.

Very many of our explanations in everyday life have this narrative form. One standard puzzle specifically calls for this kind of explanation. We are told, for example, of a person who, when alone, always rides an elevator to the eighteenth floor, gets off, and then walks up the remaining five floors to her apartment. We want to know why she behaves in this way. Various lame suggestions are made: she likes to visit people on her way home; she's taking exercise; etc. None of these explanations makes sense because none accounts for the *invariability* of her behavior. Surely she isn't visiting friends when she comes home at five in the morning, nor is this a reasonable time for taking exercise. Her behavior is completely explained, however, when we are told a single fact: that she is quite short and can reach only up to the button for the eighteenth floor. When she is alone, that is as far as she can take the elevator.

Although the narrative is probably the most common form of explanation in everyday life, we also use *arguments* for giving explanations. We can explain a certain event by deriving it from established principles and accepted facts. This derivation has the form of an argument. Although explanations of this kind do occur in daily life, the clearest examples come from science. A scientist can explain the movements of a complex mechanism by deriving them from the laws of mechanics. A psychologist can explain a person's apparently strange behavior by citing laws governing the unconscious mind. Broadly speaking, the pattern of explanation will employ an argument of the following form.

Accepted principles or laws.
A statement of initial conditions.

∴ A statement of the phenomenon to be explained.

By "initial conditions" we mean those facts in the context which, to-

gether with the accepted principles and laws, allow us to derive the result that the event to be explained will occur.

This sounds very abstract, which it is, but one extended example
should clarify these ideas. Suppose we put an ice cube into a glass and
then fill the glass to the very brim. It will look something like this:

What will happen when the ice cube melts? Will the water overflow?
Will it remain at the same level? Will it actually go down? Here we are
asking for a *prediction* and it will, of course, make sense to ask a person
to *justify* whatever prediction he or she makes.

Stumped by this question, we let the ice cube melt to see what happens. In fact, the water level remains unchanged. We are no longer faced
with a problem of prediction, for we can now see what happened: When
ice cubes melt (or, anyway, when *this* ice cube melts), the water level
stays the same (or, at least, it stayed the same in *this* case). After a few
experiments we convince ourselves that this result always occurs. We
now have a new question: *Why* does this occur? In short, we want an
explanation of this phenomenon. The explanation turns upon the law of
buoyancy:

An object is buoyed up by a force equal to the weight of the water it
displaces.

So if we put an object in water, it will continue to sink until it displaces
a volume of water whose weight is equal to its own weight. (An object
heavier than water will continue to sink, but it will feel lighter under
water.) With all this in mind, go back to the original problem. In the following diagram, the shaded area indicates the volume of water displaced
by the ice cube.

We know from the law of buoyancy that the weight of the ice cube will be equal to the weight of the volume of water it displaces. But an ice cube is itself simply water in a solid state. It is a quantity of water equal to the quantity of water it displaces. More simply, when it melts, it will exactly fill in the volume of water it displaced, so the water level will remain unchanged.

We can now see how this explanation conforms to the argumentative pattern mentioned above:

Accepted principles or laws.	(Primarily the law of buoyancy.)
Initial conditions.	(An ice cube floating in a glass of water filled to the brim.)
∴ Phenomenon to be explained.	(The level of the water remaining unchanged after the ice cube melts.)

There are some things to notice about this explanation. First of all, it is a pretty good explanation. People with only a slight understanding of science can follow it and see why the water level remains unchanged. We should also notice that it is not a *complete* explanation, for certain things are simply taken for granted—for example, that things do not change weight when they pass from a solid to a liquid state. To put the explanation into perfect argumentative form, this assumption and many others would have to be stated explicitly. This is never done in everyday life, and is only rarely done in the most exact sciences.

Here is an example of an explanation that is less technical. Houses in Indonesia sometimes have their electrical outlets in the middle of the wall rather than at floor level. Why? A beginning of an explanation is that flooding is a danger in the Netherlands. Citing this fact does not help much, however, unless one remembers that Indonesia was formerly a Dutch colony. Even remembering this leaves gaps in the explanation. We can understand why the Dutch might put their electrical outlets above floor level in the Netherlands. It is safer in a country where flooding is a danger. Is flooding, then, a similar danger in Indonesia? Apparently not. So why did the Dutch continue this practice in Indonesia? To answer this question we must cite another broad principle: Colonial settlers tend to preserve their home customs, practices, and styles. In this particular case, the Dutch continued to build Dutch-looking houses with the electrical outlets where (for them) they are normally placed—that is, in the middle of the wall rather than at floor level.

Even though this is not a scientific explanation, notice that it shares many features of the scientific explanation examined previously. First we have a curious fact: the location of electrical outlets in some houses in Indonesia. By way of explanation, certain important facts are cited:

Indonesia was a Dutch colony.

Flooding is a danger in the Netherlands.

And so on.

These facts are then woven together by certain general principles:

Where flooding is a danger, it is safer to put electrical outlets above floor level.

Colonial settlers tend to preserve their home customs, practices, and styles even when their practical significance is diminished.

And so on.

Taken together, these facts and principles make sense of an anomalous fact, i.e., they explain it.[6]

Explanations are satisfactory for *practical* purposes if they remove bewilderment or surprise. An explanation is satisfactory if it tells us *how* or *why* something happened in a way that is relevant to the concerns of a particular context. But how far can explanations go? In explaining why the water level remains the same when the ice cube melts, we cited the law of buoyancy. Now why should that law be true? What explains it? To explain the law of buoyancy, we would have to derive it from other laws that are more general and, perhaps, more intelligible. In fact, this has been done. Archimedes simultaneously proved and explained the Law of Buoyancy by deriving it from the Laws of the Lever.[7] How about the Laws of the Lever? Can they be proved and explained by deriving them from still higher and more comprehensible laws? Perhaps. Yet reasons give out, and sooner or later explanation and justification come to an end. It is the task of science and all rational inquiry to move that boundary further and further back.

[6] This example comes from my former teacher, Alan Ross Anderson.
[7] This proof, which is a model of elegant scientific reasoning, is given in Part Two of this book (pp. 270–75).

Exercise 3: Experts found the facts reported in the following newspaper article puzzling. Can you think of some explanation for them?

LOCKED DOORS NO BAR TO CRIME, STUDY SAYS

WASHINGTON (UPI) — Rural Americans with locked doors, watchdogs or guns may face as much risk of burglary as neighbors who leave doors unlocked, a federally financed study says.

The study, financed in part by a three-year $170,000 grant from the Law Enforcement Assistance Administration, was based on a survey of nearly 900 families in rural Ohio.

Sixty percent of the rural residents surveyed regularly locked doors, but were burglarized more often than residents who left doors unlocked.

The figures puzzled investigators, too. "A precise explanation of this finding is not possible from these data," they said.

The report also painted a picture of the rural vandal as a youth from a broken home who viewed vandalism as amusement and was involved with a group smoking marijuana or drinking alcohol at the time of the offense.

The survey, released Sunday, was conducted with the help of federal funds by the Ohio State University extension service and the Farm Bureau.

Seventy-eight percent of the residents surveyed kept watchdogs, but the report found they faced as much chance of being victims of burglary, theft or vandalism as neighbors who had no dog.

And while 76 percent of the rural residents surveyed kept guns for protection, they, too, faced the same chance of being a victim of crime as someone without a gun.[8]

Exercise 4: Write a brief explanation of one of the following:

1. Why a lighter-than-air balloon rises.

2. Why there is an infield fly rule in baseball.

3. Why Ronald Reagan did not win the Republican nomination in 1976.

4. Why there are more psychoanalysts in New York City than in any other city or, for that matter, in most countries in the world.

5. Why the cost of food tends to be higher in city slums than in wealthy suburbs.

What facts and what general principles are employed in your explanations? (Don't forget those principles that may seem too obvious to mention.)

Exercise 5: St. Augustine's attempt to explain the existence of evil in a world created by a perfect God is difficult, complex, and subtle. What are the central features of his explanation? How convincing do you find it? (See Part Two, pp. 295–300, in this book.)

---

[8] *Santa Barbara, Calif., News-Press,* Wednesday, February 16, 1977, p. C-11.

Excuses

Sometimes when we have acted in an improper or particularly stupid way, we are asked to explain our actions or explain ourselves. "Why in the world did you do that?" is a request for an explanation of our behavior. Although such explanations lack the rigor of a scientific explanation, they share some of its features. In explaining our behavior we point to certain facts and general principles that together make sense out of what we have done. Take a simple example:

A: Why did you shove Harold into the gulch?

B: He was about to be shot by an assassin.

Here the response makes sense out of a piece of peculiar behavior by citing a single fact: An assassin was about to shoot Harold. But this explanation also depends upon some general principles that are so obvious that we simply take them for granted. For example, we assumed that saving a person's life is, in general, a good thing; that a person in a gulch is less likely to be struck by a bullet than a person standing in plain view; that the amount of harm that might come from falling into a gulch is much less than the harm that would be caused by being struck by a bullet. Against the background of these principles and others, B's remark explains his otherwise inexplicable conduct.

Staying with this same example, we can see that B's remark also justifies his conduct. Not only can we make sense out of what he has done, we are also likely to approve of it. Next, notice what happens when we change the example in the following way:

A: Why did you shove Harold into the gulch?

B: I mistakenly thought that he was about to be shot.

B's remark still explains why he acted as he did. That is, we can still understand his behavior. It no longer justifies, or at least fully justifies, his conduct. Here we would say that B is offering an *excuse* for what he did. Broadly speaking, an excuse is an explanation of human behavior intended to put it in the best possible light. It will often happen that the best possible light will involve the admission of some wrongdoing. In the second dialogue, B admits to having made a mistake. In some contexts this might be a serious admission, but in the present context B does better admitting that he was, perhaps, stupid, rather than acknowledging that he shoved poor Harold into the gulch as a simple act of malice.

We evaluate excuses in much the same way that we evaluate other explanations. An excuse will involve statements of fact and these may be either true or false. We can also challenge the background principles employed in the excuse. We will not be impressed by someone who tells us that he ran seven stoplights so that he would not be late for a kickoff. Getting to a kickoff on time does not warrant such obviously dangerous behavior. Finally, as with other explanations, the facts together with the background principles should make sense out of a piece of behavior.

Presented with an excuse, we can ask the following questions:

(1) Broadly speaking, what are the facts?

(2) With what is the person liable to be charged?

(3) What lesser wrong will the person settle for instead?

(4) How does the explanation accomplish this task?

In our example, (1) B shoved Harold into a gulch. (2) On the face of it, this looks like an attempt to injure Harold. (3) B is willing to admit that he made a mistake of fact. (4) Given this admission, his action can be seen as a laudable, if flawed, attempt to save Harold from death or serious injury.

Exercise 6: Imagine that you have written a letter home asking for money. In the closing paragraph, you feel called upon to offer some excuse for not writing for two months. Write such an excuse (not just an apology) in a perfectly natural way, and then analyze it, using the questions given above.

Exercise 7: In William Shakespeare's Much Ado About Nothing, Benedict, after previously denouncing women and marriage in the strongest terms, is trapped into falling in love with Beatrice. In the following passage he attempts to explain his sudden turnabout. Using the questions given above, analyze this passage.

I may chance have some odd quirks and remnants of wit broken on me because I have railed so long against marriage. But doth not the appetite alter? A man loves the meat in his youth that he cannot endure in his age. Shall quips and sentences and these paper bullets of the brain awe a man from the career of his humor? No, the world must be peopled. When I said I would die a bachelor, I did not think I should live till I were married.[9]

Exercise 8: Find an example of a public official offering an excuse for something he or she has done. Analyze its structure using the four questions above.

---

[9] William Shakespeare, *Much Ado About Nothing*, Act III, Sc. 1.

THE FORMAL
ANALYSIS OF
ARGUMENT:
PART ONE

6

This chapter examines some more technical procedures for analyzing arguments. In particular, we will examine the notion of validity, for this is the central concept of logic. The first part of the chapter shows how the notion of validity first introduced in Chapter 2 can be developed rigorously in one area, the so-called Propositional Logic. This branch of logic deals with those connectives like "and" and "or" that allow us to build up complex propositions from simpler ones. The primary focus of this chapter is theoretical rather than immediately practical. It is intended to provide an insight into the concept of validity by examining it in an ideal setting. The chapter closes with a discussion of the relationship between the ideal language of symbolic logic and the everyday language we actually speak.

Validity and Formal Analysis of Argument

When we carry out an informal analysis of argument, we pay close attention to the key terms used to present the argument and then ask ourselves whether these key terms have been used properly. The procedure is informal because, so far, we have no exact techniques for answering the question: Is such and such a term used correctly? We rely, instead, on logical instincts which, on the whole, are pretty good.

Except in complicated or tricky cases, most people can tell whether one claim follows from another. But if we ask the average intelligent person *why* the one claim follows from the other, he or she will probably have little to say except, perhaps, that it is obvious. That is, it is often easy to see that one claim follows from another, but to explain why turns out to be difficult. This quality of "following from" is called validity, as we saw in Chapter 2. The purpose of this chapter is to get some better idea of this notion—to begin, at least, to understand what we are saying when we assert that one claim follows from another.

The focus of our attention will be the *concept* of validity. We are not, for the time being at least, interested in whether this or that argument is valid—we want to understand validity itself. To this end, the arguments we will examine are so simple that you will not be able to imagine anyone not understanding them at a glance. Who needs logic to deal with arguments of this kind? There is, however, good reason for dealing with simple—*trivially simple*—arguments at the start. The analytic approach to a complex issue is first to break it down into subissues, repeating the process until we reach problems simple enough to be solved. After these simpler problems are solved, we can reverse the process and construct solutions to larger and more complex problems. When done correctly, the *result* of such an analytic process may seem dull and obvious—and it often is. The *discovery* of such a process, in contrast, often demands the insight of genius.

The Propositional Calculus

Conjunction The first system of arguments that we shall examine concerns sentential (or propositional) connections. Sentential connectives are terms that allow us to combine two or more sentences into a single sentence. For example, given the propositions "John is tall" and "Harry is short," we can use the term "and" to *conjoin* them forming a single compound proposition "John is tall and Harry is short." Now let us look carefully at this simple word "and" and ask how it functions. "And," in fact, is a curious word, for it doesn't seem to stand for anything, at least in the way in which a proper name ("Churchill") and a common noun ("dog") seem to stand for things. Instead of asking what this word stands for, we can ask a different question: What *truth conditions* govern this connective? That is, under what conditions are propositions containing this connective true? To answer this question, we imagine every possible way in which the component propositions can be true or false. Then for each combination we decide what truth value to assign to the entire proposition. This may sound complicated, but an example will make it clear:

John is tall.	Harry is short.	John is tall and Harry is short.
T	T	T
T	F	F
F	T	F
F	F	F

Here the first two columns cover every possibility for the component propositions to be either true or false. The third column states the truth value of the whole proposition for each combination. Pretty obviously, the conjunction of two propositions is true if both of the component propositions are true; otherwise it is false.

It should also be obvious that our reflections have not depended upon the particular sentences we have selected. We could have been talking about dinosaurs instead of people, and we still would have come to the conclusion that the conjunction of two propositions is true if both propositions are true, but false otherwise. In order to reflect the generality of our conclusion, we can drop reference to particular sentences altogether and use *variables* instead. Just as the letters x, y, and z can stand for arbitrary numbers in mathematics, we can let the letters p, q, r, s, . . . stand for arbitrary propositions in logic. We will also use the symbol "&" for "and."

Consider the expression "p & q." Is it true or false? There is obviously no answer to this question. This is not because we do not know what "p" and "q" stand for, for in fact "p" and "q" do not stand for anything at all. Thus "p & q" is not a statement, but a pattern for a whole series of statements. To reflect this, we shall say that "p & q" is a *statement form*. It is a pattern, or form, for a whole series of statements, including "John is tall and Harry is short." To repeat the central idea, we can pass from a statement to a statement form by uniformly replacing statements with statement variables.

Statement	*Statement form*
John is tall and Harry is short.	$(p$ & $q)$

When we proceed in the opposite direction by uniformly substituting statements for statement variables, we get what we shall call a *substitution instance* of that statement form.

Statement form	*Substitution instance*
$(p$ & $q)$	Roses are red and violets are blue.

Thus, "John is tall and Harry is short" and "Roses are red and violets are blue" are both substitution instances of the statement form "*p* & *q*." These ideas are perfectly simple, but to get clear about them, it is important to notice that "*p*" can also be a statement form, with "Roses are red and violets are blue" as one of its substitution instances. There is no rule against substituting complex statements for statement variables. Perhaps a bit more surprisingly, our definitions allow "Roses are red and roses are red" to be a substitution instance of "*p* & *q*." We get a substitution instance of a statement form by uniformly replacing the same variable by the same statement throughout. We have not said that different variables must be replaced by different statements throughout. Different variables may be replaced by the same statement, but different statements may not be replaced by the same variable. To summarize this discussion:

"Roses are red and violets are blue" is a substitution instance of "*p* & *q*."

"Roses are red and violets are blue" is a substitution instance of "*p*."

"Roses are red and roses are red" is a substitution instance of "*p* & *q*."

"Roses are red and roses are red" is a substitution instance of "*p* & *p*."

"Roses are red and violets are blue" is not a substitution instance of "*p* & *p*."

"Roses are red" is not a substitution instance of "*p* & *p*."

Exercise 1: The statement "The night is young and you're so beautiful" is a substitution instance of which of the following statement forms?
1. p
2. p & q
3. p & r
4. p & p
5. p or q

Exercise 2: Find three statement forms for which the following statement is a substitution instance:

"The night is young and you're so beautiful and my flight leaves in thirty minutes."

The expression "*p* & *q*" is neither true nor false because it is a *statement form*, not a statement. We get a statement (something that

is either true or false) only when we replace these variables by statements. When such a substitution is made, we get a true statement if both
substituted statements are true; otherwise, we get a false statement.
These reflections are summarized in the following truth-table definition
for conjunction, now using variables where previously we used specific
statements.

p	q	p & q
T	T	T
T	F	F
F	T	F
F	F	F

Next we can look at an argument involving conjunction. Here is one
that is ridiculously simple:

Harry is short and John is tall.
_____
∴ Harry is short.

This argument is obviously valid. But why is the argument valid? Why
does the conclusion follow from the premise? The answer in this case
seems obvious, but we will spell it out in detail as a guide for more difficult cases. Suppose we replace these particular statements by statement
forms, using a different variable for each distinct statement throughout
the argument. This yields what we shall call the following *argument
form:*

p & q
_____
∴ p

This is a pattern for endlessly many arguments, each of which is called
a substitution instance of this argument form. Every argument that has
this general form will also be valid. It really doesn't matter which propositions we put back into this schema; the resulting argument will be
valid—so long as we are careful to substitute the same statement for the
same variable throughout.

Let us pursue this matter further. If an argument has true premises
and a false conclusion, then we know at once that it is invalid. But in
saying that an argument is *valid,* we are not only saying that it does not
have true premises and a false conclusion; we are saying that the argument *cannot* have a false conclusion when the premises are true. By
that we mean that the argument has a structure that rules out the very
possibility of true premises and a false conclusion. We can appeal to the
notion of an argument form to make sense out of this idea. A somewhat
more complicated truth table will make this clear:

		Premise	*Conclusion*
p	q	p & q	p
T	T	T	T
T	F	F	T
F	T	F	F
F	F	F	F

The first two columns give all the combinations for the truth values of the statements that we might substitute for *p* and *q*. The third column gives the truth value of the premise for each of these combinations and, finally, the fourth column gives the truth value for the conclusion for each combination. (Here, of course, this merely involves repeating the first column. Later on, things will become more complicated and interesting.) If we look at this truth table, we see that no matter how we make substitutions for the variables, we never get a case where the premise is true and the conclusion is false. Here it is important to remember that a valid argument can have false premises, for one proposition can follow from another that is false. Of course, an argument that is sound cannot have a false premise, since a sound argument is defined as a valid argument with true premises.[1]

Let us summarize this discussion. In the case we have examined, validity depends upon the form of an argument and not upon its particular content. A first principle, then, is this:

> An argument is valid if it is an instance of a valid argument form.

So the argument "Harry is short and John is tall, therefore Harry is short" is valid because it is an instance of the valid argument form "*p* & *q* ∴ *p*." Next we must ask what makes an argument form valid. The answer to this is given in this principle:

> An argument form is valid if it has no substitution instances where the premises are true and the conclusion is false.

We have just seen that the argument form "*p* & *q* ∴ *p*" meets this test. The truth-table analysis showed that. Incidentally, we can use the same truth table to show that the following argument is valid:

John is tall.	p
Harry is short.	q
∴ John is tall and Harry is short.	∴ (p & q)

---

[1] The difference between validity and soundness is explained in Chapter 2.

The argument on the left is a substitution instance of the argument form on the right, and a glance at the truth table will show that there is never a case where all the premises (i.e., p and q) are true and the conclusion (i.e., p & q) is false. This pretty well tells the story of the logical properties of the connective we call conjunction.

Notice that we have not said that *every* argument that is valid is so by virtue of its form. There may be arguments where the conclusion plainly does follow from the premises but where we cannot show that the argument's validity is a matter of its logical form. Explaining validity by means of logical form has been an ideal of logical theory, but there are arguments, many of them quite commonplace, where this ideal has not been fulfilled. At present, however, we shall only consider cases where the strategy we used for analyzing conjunction continues to work.

Disjunction Just as we can form a conjunction of two propositions by using the connective "and," we can form a *disjunction* of two propositions by using "or," as in the following compound sentence:

John will win or Harry will win.

Again, it is easy to see that the truth of this whole statement depends upon the truth of the component statements. If they are both false, then the statement as a whole is false. If just one of them is true, then the statement as a whole is true. But suppose they are both true, what shall we say then? Sometimes when we say "either–or" we seem to rule out the possibility of both. "You may have chicken or steak" probably means that you cannot have both. Sometimes, however, both is not ruled out—for example, when we say to someone, "If you want to see tall mountains, go to California or Colorado." So one way (in fact, the standard way) to deal with this problem is to say that "or" has two meanings: one *exclusive*, which rules out both, and one *inclusive*, which does not rule out both. We could thus give two truth-table definitions, one for each of these senses of the word "or":

	Exclusive			*Inclusive*	
p	q	p or q	p	q	p or q
T	T	F	T	T	T
T	F	T	T	F	T
F	T	T	F	T	T
F	F	F	F	F	F

For reasons that will become clear in a moment, we will adopt the inclusive sense of the word "or." Where necessary, we will define the exclusive sense using the inclusive sense as a starting point. Logicians symbolize *disjunctions* using the connective "v." The truth table for this connective has the following form:

p	q	p v q
T	T	T
T	F	T
F	T	T
F	F	F

We shall look at some arguments involving this connective in a moment.

Negation With conjunction and disjunction, we begin with two propositions and construct a new proposition from them. There is another way in which we can construct a new proposition from another—through *denying* it. Given the proposition "John is clever," we can get a new proposition "John is not clever" simply by inserting the word "not" in the correct place in the sentence. What, exactly, does the word "not" mean? This can be a difficult question to answer, especially if we begin with the assumption that all words stand for things. Does it stand for nothing or, maybe, nothingness? Although some respectable philosophers have sometimes spoken in this way, it is important to see that the word "not" does not stand for anything at all. It has an altogether different function in the language. To see this, think how conjunction and disjunction work. Given two propositions, the word "and" allows us to construct another proposition that is true only when both original propositions are true, and is false otherwise. Turning to disjunction, given two propositions, the word "or" allows us to construct another proposition that is false only when both the original propositions are false, and true otherwise. (Our truth-table definitions reflect these facts.) Using these definitions as a model, how should we define *negation*? A parallel answer is that the negation of a proposition is true just in case the original proposition is false and it is false just in case the original proposition is true. Using the symbol ~ to stand for negation, this gives us the following truth-table definition:

p	~p
T	F
F	T

How Truth Functional Connectives Work We have now defined *conjunction, disjunction,* and *negation.* That, all by itself, is sufficient to complete the branch of modern logic called Propositional Logic. The definitions themselves may seem peculiar. They do not look like the definitions we find in a dictionary. But the form of these definitions is important, for it tells us something interesting about the character of

such words as "and," "or," and "not." Two things are worth noting:
(1) These expressions are used to construct new propositions from old.
(2) The newly constructed proposition is always a *truth function* of
the original propositions—that is, the truth value of the new proposition
is always determined by the truth value of the original propositions.
For this reason they are called *truth functional connectives*. (Of course,
with negation, we start with a *single* proposition.) For example, suppose
that A and B are two true propositions and G and H are two false propositions. We can then determine the truth values of more complex
propositions built from them using conjunction, disjunction, and negation. Sometimes the correct assignment is obvious at a glance:

A & B	True
A & G	False
~G	True
A v H	True
~A · G	False

As in mathematics, parentheses can be used to distinguish groupings.
Parentheses bring out an important difference between the following
two expressions:

~A & G   ~(A & G)

Notice that in one expression the negation symbol applies only to the
proposition *A*, whereas in the other expression it applies to the entire
proposition (A & G). The first expression above is false, then, and the
second expression is true.

As expressions become more complex, we reach a point where it is
no longer obvious how the truth values of the component propositions
determine the truth value of the entire proposition. Here a regular
procedure is helpful. The easiest method is to fill in the truth values of
the basic propositions and then, step by step, make assignments progres-
sively wider, going from the inside out. For example:

$$
\begin{array}{c}
\sim((A \ v \ G) \ \& \ \sim(\sim H \ \& \ B)) \\
(T \ v \ F) \ \& \ \sim(\sim F \ \& \ T) \\
(T \ v \ F) \ \& \ \sim(T \ \& \ T) \\
T \ \& \ \sim(T) \\
\sim(T \ \& \ F) \\
\sim \ (F) \\
T
\end{array}
$$

With very little practice, you can master this technique in dealing with
even highly complex examples.

Exercise 3: Given that A, B, and C are true propositions and X, Y, and Z are false propositions, determine the truth values of the following complex propositions.

1. (A v Z) & B
2. ~(Z v Z)
3. ~~(A v B)
4. (A v X) & (B v Z)
5. (A & X) v (B & Z)
6. ~(A v (Z v X))
7. ~(A v ~(Z v X))
8. ~Z v (Z & A)
9. A v ((~B & C) v ~(~B v ~(Z v B)))
10. A & ((~B & C) v ~(~B v ~(Z v B)))

But what is the point of all this? In everyday life we rarely run into an expression as complicated as the one given in our example. Our purpose here is to sharpen our sensitivity concerning the way in which truth functional connectives work, and then to express our insights in clear ways. This is important because the validity of many arguments depends upon the logical features of these truth functional connectives. We can now turn directly to this subject.

Earlier we saw that every argument of the form "p & q ∴ p" will be valid. This is obvious in itself, but we saw that this claim could be justified by an appeal to truth tables. A truth-table analysis shows us that an argument of this form can never have an instance where the premise is true and the conclusion is false. We can now apply this same technique to arguments that are more complex. In the beginning we will take arguments that are still easy to follow without the use of technical help. At the end, we will consider some arguments that most people cannot follow without guidance.

Consider the following argument:

Harry is spending his summer in Florida or California. Harry is not spending his summer in California or New York. Therefore, Harry is spending his summer in Florida.

We can use the following abbreviations:

A = Harry is spending his summer in Florida.
B = Harry is spending his summer in California.
C = Harry is spending his summer in New York.

Using these abbreviations, and then substituting the variables p, q, and r, the argument looks like this:

A v B	p v q
~(B v C)	~(q v r)
∴ A	∴ p

The expression on the right gives the argument *form* of the argument presented on the left. To see whether the argument is valid, we ask if the argument form is valid. The procedure is cumbersome, but perfectly mechanical:

			Pr.		*Pr.*	*Cn.*
p	q	r	(p v q)	(q v r)	~(q v r)	p
T	T	T	T	T	F	T
T	T	F	T	T	F	T
T	F	T	T	T	F	T
T	F	F	T	F	T	T
F	T	T	T	T	F	F
F	T	F	T	T	F	F
F	F	T	F	T	F	F
F	F	F	F	F	T	F

Notice that there is only one combination of truth values where both premises are true, and in that case the conclusion is true as well. So the original argument is valid since it is an instance of a valid argument form, i.e., an argument form with no instances of true premises combined with a false conclusion.

This last truth table may need some explaining. First, why do we get eight rows in this truth table where before we got only four? The answer to this is that we need to test the argument form for *every possible combination of truth values* for the component propositions. With two variables, there are four combinations: (TT), (TF), (FT), and (FF). With three variables, there are eight combinations: (TTT), (TTF), (TFT), (TFF), (FTT), (FTF), (FFT), and (FFF). The general rule is this: If an argument form has n variables, the truth table used in its analysis must have 2^n rows. For four variables there will be sixteen rows; for five variables, thirty-two rows; for six variables, sixty-four rows; etc. You can be sure that you capture all possible combinations of truth values by using the following pattern in constructing the columns of your truth table:

First column	*Second column*	*Third column*	*Etc.*
First half T's, second half F's	First quarter T's, second quarter F's	First eighth T's, second eighth F's	

A glance at the earlier examples in this chapter will show that we have been using this pattern. Of course, as soon as an argument becomes very complex, these truth tables become very large indeed. But there is no need to worry about this, since we will not consider complex arguments. (Those who do turn to a computer for help.)

The style of the truth table above is also significant. The premises (Pr.) are plainly labeled and so is the conclusion (Cn.). A line is drawn under every row where the premises are all true. (In this case, there is only one such row.) If the conclusion on this line is also true, it is marked "O.K." If every line where the premises are all true is okay, the argument form is valid. Marking all this out may seem rather childish, but it is worth doing. First, it helps guard against mistakes; more importantly, it draws one's attention to the purpose of the procedure being used. Cranking out truth tables without understanding what they are about does not enlighten the mind or elevate the spirit.

For the sake of contrast, we can next consider an invalid argument:

Harry is spending his summer in Florida or California.
Harry is not spending his summer both in California and New York.

∴ Harry is spending his summer in Florida.

Using the same abbreviations as earlier for Harry's vacation plans, this becomes:

Argument	*Argument form*
A v B	p v q
~(B & C)	~(q & r)
∴ A	∴ p

Truth-table analysis:

p	q	r	(p v q)	(q & r)	~(q & r)	p	
			Pr.		*Pr.*	*Cn.*	
T	T	T	T	T	F	T	
T	T	F	T	F	T	T	O.K.
T	F	T	T	F	T	T	O.K.
T	F	F	T	F	T	T	O.K.
F	T	T	T	T	F	F	
F	T	F	T	F	T	F	NO *Invalid*
F	F	T	F	F	T	F	
F	F	F	F	F	T	F	

This time, we find four rows where all the premises are true. In three cases the conclusion is true as well, but in one case the conclusion is false. The argument form is thus invalid, since it is possible for it to have a substitution instance where all the premises are true and the conclusion is false. In the present case, this possibility arises in the sixth row of the truth table, where A would be false, B true, and C false.

Exercise 4: Using the truth-table technique outlined above, test the following argument forms for validity:

1. p v q
   p
   ———
   ∴ ~q

2. ~(p v q)
   ———
   ∴ ~q

3. ~(p & q)
   ~q
   ———
   ∴ ~p

4. p
   ~(p v q)
   ———
   ∴ ~q

5. p
   ~(p v q)
   ———
   ∴ r

6. (p & q) v (p & r)
   ———
   ∴ p & (q v r)

7. (p v q) & (p v r)
   ———
   ∴ p & (q v r)

8. p & q
   ———
   ∴ (p v r) & q

Some Further Connectives

We have developed the logic of propositions using only three basic notions corresponding (perhaps roughly) to the English words "and," "or,"

and "not." Now let us go back to the question of the two possible senses
—exclusive and inclusive—of the word "or." Sometimes "or" seems to
rule out the possibility that both options are open; at other times "or"
seems to allow this possibility. This is the difference between exclusive
and inclusive disjunction, respectively.

Suppose we use the symbol ᵥᵥ to stand for exclusive disjunction. (After this discussion, we will not use it again.) We could then define this
new connective in the following way:

(p ᵥᵥ q) = (by definition) ((p v q) & ~(p & q))

It is not hard to see that the expression on the right side of this definition
captures the force of exclusive disjunction. Since we can always define
exclusive disjunction when we want it, there is no need to introduce it
into our system of basic notions.

> **Exercise 5**: Construct a truth-table analysis of the expression on the right
> side of the above definition and compare it with the truth-table definition
> of exclusive disjunction given on page 121.

Actually, in analyzing arguments we have been defining new logical
connectives without much thinking about it. For example, *not both p
and q* was symbolized as "~(p & q)." *Neither p nor q* was symbolized as
"~(p v q)." Let us look more closely at the example "~(p v q)." Perhaps
we should have symbolized it as "~p & ~q." As a matter of fact, we could
have used this symbolization, for the two expressions amount to the
same thing. Again, this may be obvious, but we can prove it by using a
truth table in yet another way. Compare the truth-table analysis of these
two expressions:

p	q	~p	~q	(~p & ~q)	(p v q)	~(p v q)
				*	*	
T	T	F	F	F	T	F
T	F	F	T	F	T	F
F	T	T	F	F	T	F
F	F	T	T	T	F	T

Under "~p & ~q" we find the column (FFFT), and we find the same sequence under "~(p v q)." This shows that for every possible substitution
we make, these two expressions will yield statements of the same truth

value. We shall say that these statement forms are *truth-functionally equivalent.*

Given the notion of truth-functional equivalence, the possibility of more than one translation can often be solved. If two translations are truth-functionally equivalent, then it does not matter which one we use in testing for validity. Of course, some translations will seem more natural than others. For example, "p v q" is truth-functionally equivalent to:

$$\sim((\sim p \ \& \ \sim p) \ \& \ (\sim q \ v \ \sim q))$$

The first expression is obviously more natural than the second, even though they are truth-functionally equivalent.

So far in this chapter we have seen that by using conjunction, disjunction, and negation, it is possible to construct complex statements out of simple statements. A distinctive feature of compound statements constructed in these three ways is that the truth of the compound statement is always a function of the truth of its component propositions. Thus, these three notions allow us to construct truth-functionally compound statements. Some arguments depend for their validity simply upon these truth-functional connectives. When this is so, it is possible to test for validity in a purely mechanical way. This can be done through the use of truth tables. Thus, in this area at least, we are able to give a clear account of validity and to specify exact procedures for testing for validity. Now we shall go on to examine an area where the application of this approach is more problematic. It concerns *conditionals.*

Conditionals

Conditionals often occur in arguments. They have the form, "If _____, then _____." Sometimes conditionals appear in the indicative mood:

If it rains, the crop will be saved.

Sometimes they occur in the subjunctive mood:

If it had rained, the crop would have been saved.

There are also conditional imperatives:

If a fire breaks out, call the fire department first!

There are conditional promises:

If you get into trouble, give me a call and I promise to help you.

Indeed, conditionals get a great deal of use in our language, and they very often appear in arguments. It is important, therefore, to understand them.

Unfortunately, there is no general agreement among experts about the correct way to analyze conditionals. We shall simplify matters by considering only *indicative* conditionals, but even here there is no settled opinion about the correct position to adopt. It may seem surprising that disagreement should exist concerning such a simple and fundamental notion as the if-then construction. Nonetheless, be prepared that this discussion will have none of the settled character of the previous one. First we shall describe the most standard treatment of conditionals; second, we shall consider a number of alternatives to it.

For conjunction, disjunction, and negation, the truth-table methods provided an approach that was at once plausible and effective. An indicative conditional is also compounded out of two simpler propositions, and this suggests that we might be able to offer a truth-table definition for conditionals as well. What should the truth table look like? When we try to answer this question, we get stuck almost at once, for it is unclear how we should fill in the table in three out of four cases.

p	q	If p, then q.
T	T	?
T	F	F
F	T	?
F	F	?

Let us call "*p*" the *antecedent* of this conditional and "*q*" its *consequent*. It seems obvious that a conditional cannot be true if the antecedent is true and the consequent false. We record this by putting an F in the second row. But suppose *p* and *q* are replaced by two arbitrary true propositions, say, "two plus two equals four" and "Chile is in South America." What shall we say about the conditional:

If two plus two equals four, then Chile is in South America.

The first thing to say is that this is a very strange statement, because the arithmetic remark in the antecedent doesn't seem to have anything to do with the geographical remark in the consequent. So this conditional is odd—indeed, extremely odd—but is it true or false? At this point a reasonable response is bafflement.

Now consider the following argument, which is intended to solve all these problems by giving good reasons for assigning truth values in each row of the truth table. One thing that seems obvious is that if "If p, then q" is true, then it is not the case that "p" is true and "q" is false. That in turn means that "$\sim(p \ \& \sim q)$" must be true. Now let's reason in the opposite direction. Suppose that we know that "$\sim(p \ \& \sim q)$" is true. For this to be true, "$p \ \& \sim q$" must be false. We know that from the truth-table definition of negation. Next let us suppose that "p" is true. Then "$\sim q$" must be false. We know that from the truth-table definition of conjunction. Finally, if "$\sim q$" is false, then "q" itself must be true. This line of reasoning is supposed to show that we can derive "If p, then q" from "Not both p and not q." The first step in the argument was intended to show that we can derive "Not both p and not q" from "If p, then q." But if each of these expressions is derivable from the other, this suggests that they are equivalent. We use this background argument as a justification of the following definition:

If p, then q = (by definition) Not both p and not q.

We can put this into symbols using a horseshoe to symbolize conditionals:

p ⊃ q = (by definition) ~(p & ~q)

Given this definition, we can now construct the truth table for indicative conditionals. It is simply the truth table for "$\sim(p \ \& \sim q)$":

p	q	~(p & ~q)	(p ⊃ q)	(~p v q)
T	T	T	T	T
T	F	F	F	F
F	T	T	T	T
F	F	T	T	T

Notice that "$(\sim p \text{ v } q)$" is also truth-functionally equivalent to the other expressions. We have included "$(\sim p \text{ v } q)$" because traditionally it has been used to define "$p \supset q$." For reasons that are now obscure, when a conditional is defined in this truth-functional way, it is called a *material conditional*.

Now let us suppose, for the moment, that the notion of a material conditional corresponds exactly with our idea of an indicative conditional. What would follow from this? The answer is that we could treat conditionals in the same way in which we have treated conjunction, disjunction, and negation. A conditional would be just one more kind of truth-functionally compound statement capable of definition by truth tables. Furthermore, arguments that depend upon this notion (together with conjunction, disjunction, and negation) could be settled by appeal to truth-table techniques. Let us pause for a moment to examine this.

One of the most common patterns of reasoning is called *modus ponens*. It looks like this:

If p, then q.   p ⊃ q
p   p
_____   _____
∴ q   ∴ q

The truth-table definition of material implication shows at once that this pattern of argument is valid.

Pr.		Pr.	Cn.	
p	q	p ⊃ q	q	
T	T	T	T	O.K. *Valid*
T	F	F	F	
F	T	T	T	
F	F	T	F	

Exercise 6: Show that the argument form called modus tollens is valid. It looks like this:

p ⊃ q
~q
_____
∴ ~p

These same techniques allow us to show that one of the traditional fallacies is, indeed, a fallacy. It is called the fallacy of denying the antecedent, and it looks like this:

p ⊃ q
~p
_____
∴ ~q

The truth-table analysis showing the invalidity of this argument has the following form:

		Pr.	Pr.	Cn.	
p	q	p ⊃ q	−p	−q	
T	T	T	F	F	
T	F	F	F	T	
F	T	T	T	F	NO *Invalid*
F	F	T	T	T	OK.

Exercise 7: A second standard fallacy is called affirming the consequent. It looks like this:

$$p \supset q$$
$$q$$
$$\therefore p$$

Using truth-table techniques, show that this argument form is invalid.

We can examine one last argument that has been historically significant. It is called the *hypothetical syllogism* and has the following form:

$$p \supset q$$
$$q \supset r$$
$$\therefore p \supset r$$

Since we are dealing with an argument form containing three variables, we must perform the boring task of constructing a truth table with eight rows:

			Pr.	Pr.	Cn.	
p	q	r	p ⊃ q	q ⊃ r	p ⊃ r	
T	T	T	T	T	T	O.K.
T	T	F	T	F	F	
T	F	T	F	T	T	*Valid*
T	F	F	F	T	F	
F	T	T	T	T	T	O.K.
F	T	F	T	F	T	
F	F	T	T	T	T	O.K.
F	F	F	T	T	T	O.K.

This is fit work for a computer, not for a human being, but it is important to see that it actually works.

Why is it important to see that these techniques work? Most people, after all, could see that hypothetical syllogisms are correct without going through all this tedious business. We seem only to be piling boredom on top of triviality. This protest deserves an answer. Suppose we ask someone *why* he or she thinks that the conclusion follows from the premises in a hypothetical syllogism. The person might answer that anyone can see that—something, by the way, that is false. Beyond this he or she might say that it all depends upon the meanings of the words, or that it is all a matter of definition. But if we go on to ask *which words* and *what definitions,* most people will fall silent. What we have done is to discover that the validity of some arguments depends upon the meanings of such words as "and," "or," "not," and "if–then." We have then gone on to give explicit definitions of these terms—definitions, by the way, that help us to see how these terms function in an argument. Finally, by getting all these *simple* things right, we have produced what is called a *decision procedure* for determining the validity of every argument involving conjunction, disjunction, negation, and conditionals. Our truth-table techniques give us an automatic procedure for settling questions of validity in this area. In fact, truth-table techniques have practical applications, for example, in computer programming. But the important point here is that through understanding how these techniques work, we can gain a deeper insight into the notion of validity.

> **Exercise 8**: Using the truth-table techniques employed above, test the following argument forms for validity. (For your own entertainment, guess about the validity of the argument form before working it out.)
>
> 1. p ⊃ q
>   _____
>   ∴ q ⊃ p
>
> 2. p ⊃ q
>   _____
>   ∴ ~q ⊃ ~p
>
> 3. (p v q) ⊃ r
>   _____
>   ∴ p ⊃ r
>
> 4. (p & q) ⊃ r
>   _____
>   ∴ p ⊃ r
>
> 5. p ⊃ q
>   q ⊃ r
>   _____
>   ∴ p ⊃ (q & r)
>
> 6. (p v q) & (p v r)
>   ~r
>   _____
>   ∴ ~q ⊃ p
>
> 7. (p ⊃ q) & (p ⊃ ~r)
>   r & ~q
>   _____
>   ∴ ~p
>
> 8. p ⊃ q
>   q ⊃ r
>   _____
>   ∴ ~r ⊃ ~p

9. $p \supset (q \supset r)$

$\therefore (p \& q) \supset r$

10. $p \supset (q \supset r)$

$p \supset q$

$\therefore r$

Logical Language and Everyday Language

Early in this chapter we started out by talking about such common words as "and" and "or," and then slipped over to talking about *conjunction* and *disjunction*. The transition was a bit sneaky, but intentional. To understand what is going on here, we can ask how closely these logical notions we have defined match their everyday counterparts. We will start with conjunction, and then come back to the more difficult question of conditionals. At first sight, the match seems to be very bad indeed.

In everyday discourse, we do not go about conjoining random bits of information. We do not say, for example, that two plus two equals four and Chile is in South America. We already know why we do not say such things, for unless the context is quite extraordinary, this is bound to violate the rule of Relevance. But if we are interested in validity, the rule of Relevance—together with all other pragmatic rules—is simply beside the point.

The formal notion of conjunction is also insensitive to another important feature of our everyday discourse: context. It reduces all conjunctions to their bare truth-functional content. We have already seen that the following remarks have a very different force in the context of an argument:

The ring is beautiful, but expensive.
The ring is expensive, but beautiful.

These two remarks will mean opposite things in the context of an actual argument, but from a purely formal point of view they are equivalent. We can translate the first sentence as "*B & E*" and the second as "*E & B.*" Their truth-functional equivalence is too obvious to need proof.

It might seem that if formal analysis cannot distinguish an "and" from a "but," then it can hardly be of any use at all. This is not true. A formal analysis of an argument will tell us just one thing: whether the argument is valid or not. If we expect the analysis to tell us more than this, we will be disappointed. It is important to remember two things:

(1) we expect arguments to be valid; (2) usually we expect much more than this from an argument. To elaborate upon the second point, we usually expect an argument to be sound as well as valid—we expect the premises to be true. Beyond this, we expect the argument to be informative, intelligible, convincing, and so forth. Validity, then, is an important aspect of an argument and formal analysis helps us to evaluate it. But validity is not the only aspect of an argument that concerns us; in many contexts it is not even our chief concern.

We can now look at our analysis of conditionals, for here we find some striking departures between the logician's analysis and everyday use. The following arguments are all valid:

(1) p
∴ q ⊃ p

(2) ~p
∴ p ⊃ q

(3) p & ~p
∴ q

(4) q
∴ p v ~p

We can see that these arguments are all valid by checking them with the following truth table:

p	q	~p	~q	q ⊃ p	~p ⊃ q	p & ~p	p v ~p
T	T	F	F	T	T	F	T
T	F	F	T	T	T	F	T
F	T	T	F	F	T	F	T
F	F	T	T	T	F	F	T

Yet, though valid, all these argument forms seem odd—so odd that they have actually been called *paradoxical*. The first argument form seems to say this: if a proposition is true, then it is implied by any proposition whatsoever. Here is an example of an argument that satisfies this argument form and is therefore valid:

Lincoln was President.

If water is hard, Lincoln was President.

This is a *very* peculiar argument to call valid. First we want to know what water has to do with Lincoln's having been President. Beyond this, how can his having been President depend upon the falsehood that water is hard? We can give these questions even more force by noticing that even the following argument is valid:

Lincoln was President.

If Lincoln was not President, then Lincoln was President.

This is an instance of the valid argument form: "p $\therefore$ $\sim p \supset p$."

The other three argument forms are also paradoxical. They seem to say the following things: (2) A false proposition implies anything whatsoever. (3) Anything whatsoever follows from a contradiction. ("p & $\sim p$" is the statement form for a *contradiction*, or what people sometimes call a self-contradiction. Look at the truth table and you will see that it is false for all possible truth value combinations.) (4) A tautology may be validly inferred from any proposition whatsoever. (Logicians call "p v $\sim p$" the statement form for *tautologies*. Just the reverse of a contradiction, a tautology is true no matter what truth values are assigned to its constituent parts.)

At this point, nonphilosophers become impatient, whereas philosophers become worried. We started out with principles that seemed to be both obvious and simple. Now, quite suddenly, we are being overwhelmed with a whole series of peculiar results. What in the world has happened, and what should be done about it? Philosophers remain divided in the answers they give to these questions. The responses fall into two main categories: (1) Simply give up the idea that conditionals can be defined truth-functionally and search for a different and better analysis of conditionals that avoids the difficulties involved in truth-functional analysis. (2) Take the difficult line and argue that there is nothing wrong with calling the above argument forms valid.

The first approach is highly technical and cannot be pursued in detail in this book. The general idea is this: Instead of identifying "If p, then q" with "Not both p and not q," identify it with "Not *possibly* both p and not q." This provides a stronger notion of a conditional and avoids some—though not all—of the suspicious arguments noticed above. This theory is given a systematic development by offering a logical analysis of the notion of *possibility*. This branch of logic is called *modal logic*, and has shown remarkable development in recent years.

Paul Grice, whose theories played a prominent part in Chapter 1, has taken the second line. He acknowledges—as anyone must—that the four argument forms above are decidedly odd. He denies, however, that this oddness has anything to do with *validity*. Validity concerns one thing and one thing only: An argument is valid if it is an instance of an argument form that never takes us from true premises to a false conclusion. The above arguments are valid by this definition of validity. Of course, arguments can be defective in all sorts of other ways. Look at the third and fourth arguments. Since "q" can be replaced by any proposition (true or false), the rule of Relevance will often be violated. It is worth pointing out violations of the rule of Relevance, but, according to Grice, this has nothing to do with validity. Now if we look at the first two arguments we see that they can also lead to arguments that contain a violation of the rule of Relevance. They also invite violations of the rule of Quantity. A conditional will be true just in case the consequent is true. Given this, it doesn't matter whether the antecedent is true or false. Again, a conditional is true just in case the antecedent is false—and it doesn't matter, given this, whether the consequent is true or false. Yet it can be very misleading to *use* a conditional on the basis of these logical features. For example, it would be very misleading for a museum guard to say, "If you give me five dollars, then I will let you into the exhibition," when, in fact, he will let you in in any case. For Grice, this is misleading since it violates the rule of Quantity. Yet, strictly speaking, it is not false. Strictly speaking, it is true.

The Grice line is attractive, for, among other things, it allows us to accept the truth-functional account of conditionals with all its simplicity. Yet sometimes it is difficult to swallow. Consider the following remark:

If God exists, then there is evil in the world.

If Grice's analysis is correct, even the most pious will have to admit that this conditional is true provided only that he is willing to admit that there is evil in the world. Yet this conditional plainly suggests that God's existence has something to do with the evil in the world, and the pious will wish to deny this suggestion. Grice would agree: The conditional plainly suggests that there is some connection between God's existence and the evil in the world—presumably, that is the point of connecting them in a conditional. All the same, this is something that is suggested, not asserted, and once more we come to the conclusion that this conditional is misleading—and therefore in need of criticism and correction—but still, strictly speaking, true.

Philosophers and logicians have had various responses to Grice's position. No consensus has emerged on this issue. The author of this book finds it on the whole convincing and we shall adopt it in this book. This will have two advantages: (1) This appeal to pragmatics fits in well with our previous discussions and (2) it provides a way of keeping the logic simple and within the range of a beginning student. Other philosophers and logicians continue to work toward a definition superior to the truth-table definition for indicative conditionals.

Other Conditionals in Ordinary Language So far we have considered only one form in which conditionals appear in everyday language: the indicative conditional "If p, then q." But, as we have noted, conditionals come in a variety of forms and some of them demand subtle treatment.

We can first consider the contrast between constructions using "if" and those using "only if":

(1) I'll clean the barn *if* Hazel will help me.

(2) I'll clean the barn *only if* Hazel will help me.

Adopting the following abbreviations:

B = I'll clean the barn
H = Hazel will help me

the first sentence is translated as follows:

(1) H ⊃ B

Notice that in the prose version of (1), the antecedent and consequent appear in reverse order. "*q* if *p*" means the same thing as "If *p*, then *q*."

How shall we translate the second sentence? Here we should move slowly and first notice what seems incontestable: If Hazel does not help me, then I will not clean the barn. This is translated in the following way:

(2) ~H ⊃ ~B

And that is equivalent to:

(2) B ⊃ H²

A more difficult question arises when we ask whether an implication runs the other way. When I say that I will clean the barn only if Hazel will help me, am I committing myself to cleaning the barn if she does help me? There is a strong temptation to answer this question "yes" and then give a fuller translation of (2) in the following way:

(2) (B ⊃ H) & (H ⊃ B)

Logicians call such two-way implications *biconditionals,* and we shall discuss them in a moment. But adding this second conjunct is almost surely a mistake, for we can think of parallel cases where we would not be tempted to include it. A government regulation might read as follows:

A person is eligible for retirement only if he or she is past 65.

From this it does not follow that anyone past 65 is eligible for retirement, for there may be other requirements as well.

Why were we tempted to use a biconditional in translating sentences containing the connective "only if"? Why, that is, are we tempted to think that the statement "I'll clean the barn only if Hazel will help me" implies "If Hazel helps me, then I will clean the barn"?

---

² If this equivalence is not obvious, it can be quickly established by using a truth table.

The answer turns upon the notion of conversational implication first met in Chapter 1. If I am *not* going to clean the barn, whether Hazel helps me or not, then it will be misleading—a violation of the rule of Quantity—to say that I will clean the barn only if Hazel helps me. For this reason, in many contexts, the use of a sentence of the form "*p* only if *q*" will conversationally imply a commitment "*p* if and only if *q*."

We can next look at sentences of the form "*p* if and only if *q*"—so-called biconditionals. If I say that I will clean the barn if and only if Hazel will help me, then I am saying that I will clean it if she helps and I will not clean it if she does not help. Translated, this becomes:

$$(H \supset B) \mathrel{\&} (\sim H \supset \sim B)$$

This is equivalent to:

$$(H \supset B) \mathrel{\&} (B \supset H)$$

We thus have an implication going both ways—the characteristic form of a biconditional. In fact, constructions containing the expression "if and only if" do not often appear in everyday speech. They appear almost exclusively in technical or legal writing. In ordinary conversation, we capture the force of a biconditional by saying something like this:

I will clean the barn, but only if Hazel helps me.

The decision whether to translate a remark of everyday conversation into a conditional or a biconditional is often subtle and difficult. We have already noticed that the use of sentences of the form "*p* only if *q*" will often conversationally imply a commitment to the biconditional "*p* if and only if *q*." In the same way, the *use* of the conditional "*p* if *q*" will also often carry this same implication. If I plan to clean the barn whether Hazel helps me or not, it will certainly be misleading—again, a violation of the rule of Quantity—to say that I will clean the barn *if* Hazel helps me.

So far, then, we have the following results:

(1) "*q* if *p*" translates "$(p \supset q)$." However, the use of "*q* if *p*" often has the conversational force of a biconditional.

(2) "*q* only if *p*" translates "$(q \supset p)$." However, the use of "*q* only if *p*" often has the conversational force of a biconditional.

(3) "*q* if and only if *p*" translates "$(p \supset q) \mathrel{\&} (q \supset p)$." The biconditional, "*q* if and only if *p*," is more often conversationally implied than explicitly stated in everyday discourse.

We can close this discussion by considering one further, rather difficult, case. What is the force of saying "*p unless q*"? Is this a biconditional, or just a conditional? If it is just a conditional, which way does the implication go? There is a strong temptation to treat this as a biconditional, but the following example shows this to be wrong:

Carter will not win re-election unless he carries the Northeast.

This sentence clearly indicates that Carter will not win re-election if he does not carry the Northeast. Using abbreviations:

N = Carter will carry the Northeast.
W = Carter will win reelection.
~N ⊃ ~W

The original statement does not imply—even conversationally—that he will win re-election if he does carry the Northeast. The expression "~*p* unless *q*" means the same thing as the expression "*p* only if *q*," and they both translate:

(p ⊃ q)

Summary In this chapter we have tried to get a clear conception of the notion of validity in one particular area. We have studied the logic of truth-functionally compound statements. These are arguments that depend for their validity on the logical properties of *conjunction, disjunction, negation,* and *material implication.* We have offered truth-table definitions of these notions and laid down a truth-table method for testing the validity of arguments that turn upon these connectives. Although we have not shown this, we have, in fact, developed a method for testing the validity of *all* arguments whose validity depends upon the character of these truth-functional connectives.

Exercise 9: Translate each of the following sentences into symbolic notation, using the suggested symbols as abbreviations.

(1) The Reds will win only if the Dodgers collapse. (R,D)
(2) The Steelers will win if their defense holds up. (S,D)
(3) If it rains or snows, the game will be called off. (R,S,O)
(4) Unless there is a panic, stock prices will continue to rise. (P,R)
(5) If the house comes up for sale and if I have money in hand, I will bid on it. (S,M,B)
(6) You can be a success if only you try. (S,T)

(7) You will get a good bargain provided you get there early. (B,E)

(8) You cannot lead a happy life without friends. (Let H = "You can lead a happy life," and let F = "You have friends.")

Exercise 10: Translate each of the following arguments into symbolic notation. Then (1) test the argument for validity using truth-table techniques and (2) comment upon any violations of conversational rules.

Example: Harold is clever, so if Harold isn't clever, then Anna isn't clever either. (H, A)

$$\frac{H}{\sim H \supset \sim A} \qquad \frac{p}{\sim p \supset \sim q}$$

(1)

Pr.				Cn.	
p	q	~p	~q	~p⊃~q	
T	T	F	F	T	O.K.
T	F	F	T	T	O.K.
F	T	T	F	F	
F	F	T	T	T	

(2) The argument violates the rule of Relevance.

(1) Jones is brave, so Jones is brave or Jones is brave. (J)

(2) The Democrats will run either Jones or Smith. If Smith runs they will lose the South and if Jones runs they will lose the North. So the Democrats will lose either the North or South. (J, S, D, N)

(3) Although Brown will pitch, the Rams will lose. If the Rams lose, their manager will get fired, so their manager will get fired. (B, L, F).

(4) America will win the Olympics unless Russia does and Russia will win the Olympics unless East Germany does, so America will win the Olympics unless East Germany does. (A, R, E).

(5) If you dial 0, you will get the operator, so if you dial 0 and do not get the operator, then there is something wrong with the telephone. (D, O, W)

(6) The Republicans will carry either New Mexico or Arizona, but since they will carry Arizona they will not carry New Mexico. (A, N).

(7) John will play only if the situation is hopeless, but the situation will be hopeless, so John will play. (P, H)

(8) a. Carter will win the election whether he wins Idaho or not, therefore Carter will win the election. (C, I).

b. Carter will win the election, therefore Carter will win the election whether he wins Idaho or not. (C, I).

c. Carter will win the election, therefore Carter will win the election whether he wins a majority or not. (C, M).

(9) If you flip the switch then the light will go on, but if the light goes on, then the generator is working; so if you flip the switch, then the generator is working. (F, L, G)
(This example is due to Charles L. Stevenson.)

THE FORMAL ANALYSIS OF ARGUMENT: PART TWO

7

In Chapter 6 we saw how validity can depend upon the external connections between propositions. By examining in detail the theory of immediate inference and the theory of the categorical syllogism, this chapter will demonstrate how validity can depend on the internal structure of propositions. Our interest in these two branches of logic is mostly theoretical. Understanding the theory of the syllogism deepens our understanding of validity even if this theory is, in most cases, difficult to apply directly to complex arguments of daily life.

Armed with the techniques developed in Chapter 6, we can look at the following argument:

> All squares are rectangles.
> All rectangles have parallel sides.
> _____
> ∴ All squares have parallel sides.

At a glance it is obvious that the conclusion follows from the premises —it is a valid argument. Furthermore, if it is valid, it must be valid in virtue of its *form*. In order to show the form of this argument, we might try something of the following kind:

$$p \supset q$$
$$\underline{q \supset r}$$
$$p \supset r$$

BUT THIS IS A MISTAKE, and a bad mistake. We have used the letters "p," "q," and "r" as *propositional variables*—they stand for arbitrary propositions. But the proposition "All squares are rectangles" is not itself composed of two propositions.

In fact, if we attempt to translate the above argument into the language of the propositional calculus, we get the following result:

$$p$$
$$\underline{q}$$
$$\therefore r$$

This, of course, is not a valid argument form. But if we look back at the original argument we see that it is obviously valid. This shows that the Propositional Logic—however adequate it is in its own areas—is not capable of explaining the validity of *all* valid arguments. To broaden our understanding of the notion of validity, we will examine a branch of logic developed in ancient times, *the theory of the syllogism*.

Categorical Propositions

In the argument above, the first premise asserts some kind of relationship between squares and rectangles; the second premise asserts some kind of relationship between rectangles and things with parallel sides; finally, *in virtue of this*, the conclusion asserts a relationship between squares and things having parallel sides. Our task, now, is to understand these relationships as clearly as possible so that we can discover the *basis* for the validity of this argument. Again we shall adopt the strategy of starting from very simple cases and using the insights gained there for dealing with more complicated cases.

A natural way to represent the relationships expressed by the propositions in an argument is through diagrams. Suppose we draw one circle standing for all things that are squares and another circle standing for all things that are rectangles. The claim that all squares are rectangles may be represented by placing the circle representing squares completely inside the circle representing rectangles.

Another way of representing this relationship is to begin with overlapping circles.

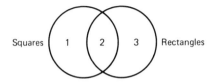

We then shade out the portions of the circles that represent nothing. Since all squares are rectangles, there is nothing that is a square that is not a rectangle—that is, there is nothing in region 1. So our diagram looks like this:

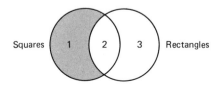

Either method of representation seems plausible. We shall, however, use the system of overlapping circles because in the long run they actually work better. They are called Venn diagrams.

Having examined *one* relationship that can exist between two classes, it is natural to wonder what other relationships might exist. Going to the opposite extreme from our first example, two classes may have *nothing* in common. The proposition "No triangles are squares" expresses such a relationship. We diagram this by indicating that there is nothing in common between squares and triangles.

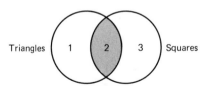

In these first two extreme cases we have indicated that one class is either completely included in another ("All squares are rectangles") or completely excluded from another ("No triangles are squares"). Sometimes, however, we make the weaker remark that two classes have at least *some* things in common. We say, for example, that "some aliens are spies." How shall we indicate this on the following diagram?

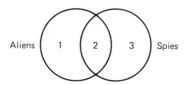

In this case, we do not want to cross out any whole region. We do not want to cross out region 1 because we are not saying that *all* aliens are spies. Plainly, we do not want to cross out region 2, for we are actually saying that some persons are both aliens and spies. Finally, we do not want to cross out region 3, for we are not saying that all spies are aliens. Saying that some aliens are spies does not rule out the possibility that some spies are homegrown.

It is plain, then, that we need some new device to represent claims that two classes have at least *some* members in common. We shall do this in the following way:

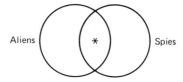

Here the asterisk indicates that there is at least one person who is both an alien and a spy. Notice, by the way, that we are departing a bit from an everyday way of speaking. "Some" is usually taken to mean *more than one*; here we let it mean *at least one*. In fact, this makes things simpler and will really cause no trouble.

Given this new method of diagramming class relationships, we can immediately think of other possibilities. The following diagram indicates that there is someone who is an alien but not a spy. In more natural language, it represents the claim that *some aliens are not spies.*

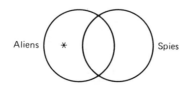

Next we can indicate that there is someone who is a spy but not an alien. More simply, we are representing the claim that *some spies are not aliens*.

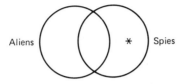

Finally, we can indicate that there is someone who is neither a spy nor an alien:

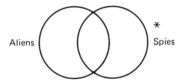

Domain of Discourse

The last example raises a special problem. When we try to think of something that is neither a spy nor an alien, we naturally think of a *person*—say, Dorothy Hamill. But how about Mt. Whitney and the number seven? Neither of these things is either a spy or an alien. Yet it seems odd to say that Mt. Whitney is neither a spy nor an alien. How could it be either of these things? Talk about spies and aliens typically concerns people. We can put it this way: Talking about spies and aliens normally *presupposes* that we are considering only persons. To reflect the notion of limiting our discussion to a certain kind of thing, we will make our diagrams a bit more elaborate. We will enclose the intersecting circles with a box that indicates the *domain of discourse* (DD). Some examples will make this clear:

1. All squares are rectangles (domain of discourse: plane figures):

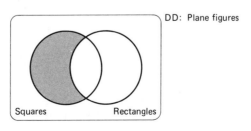

2. Some aliens are not spies (domain of discourse: people):

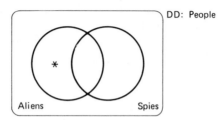

Deciding upon a domain of discourse is somewhat arbitrary. It depends upon good sense and present interests. In the first example, we might have taken *four-sided figures* as the domain of discourse, and perhaps in the second example *people in the United States* might have done perfectly well. Actually, we will be quite casual about specifying a domain of discourse, and will only do so when it serves some useful purpose.

The Four Basic Propositions

It is easy to see that two classes can be related in a great many different ways. Nonetheless, it is possible to examine all these relationships in terms of four basic propositions:

A: All *A* is *B*.   I: Some *A* is *B*.
E: No *A* is *B*.   O: Some *A* is not *B*.

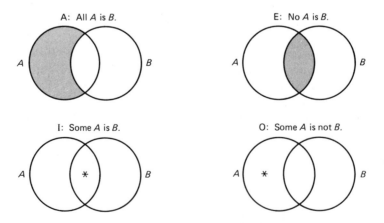

These basic propositions, together with their labels and diagrams, should be memorized because they will be used constantly.

Exercise 1: Using just the four basic propositions, indicate what information is given in each of the following diagrams:

Example:

No A is B.
Some A is not B.
Some B is not A.
No B is A.

1.

2.

3.

4.

5.

6.

Existential Import

We must now turn to a difficult problem that logicians have not fully settled. Usually when we make a statement it is obvious that we are *talking about* certain things. If someone claims that all whales are mammals, he is then talking about whales and saying that they are mammals. That is, in making this statement about whales, he *seems to be taking for granted the existence of whales.* He is not exactly saying that there are whales, yet his remark commits him to the existence of whales. To mark this commitment, we can put an asterisk (*) into our diagram for the A proposition:

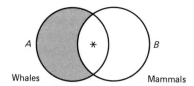

Whales   Mammals

We now see at once that if *all whales are mammals*, then *at least some whales are mammals*. This is not a very exciting inference, but one that strikes us as valid. We can now see why this inference is valid by noticing that the diagram for the A proposition given above already contains the information contained in the I proposition given below:

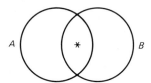

In the same way, we can see why the proposition "No aliens are spies" implies the proposition "Some aliens are not spies." In saying that no aliens are spies, we seem to be committing ourselves to the existence of aliens and saying of them that none of them are spies. If we reflect this commitment in the diagram for the E proposition, as follows,

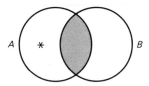

we see at once that it implies the O proposition which, as we know, is represented in the following way:

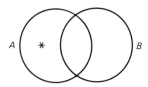

So far, then, everything seems simple enough. We can understand the relationships between the A and I as well as the E and O propositions simply by marking the commitment to existence in the A and E propositions. The difficulty is that we sometimes seem to use both the A and E propositions without any such existential commitment. If I say that all dwarfs are small, I am not committing myself to the existence of dwarfs; I am speaking about fictitious or mythical creatures. There are problems concerned with fictitious things, but they will not concern us here. A more difficult problem arises with a remark of the following kind: "All trespassers will be fined." In saying this, I am not committing myself to the existence of trespassers; I am only saying, *"If* there are trespassers, *then* they will be fined." Given this one example of an A proposition that carries no commitment concerning things referred to in the subject term, it is easy to think of many others.

Once more, then, we must make a decision. (Remember that we had to make decisions concerning the truth-table definitions of both disjunction and implication.) Classical logic was developed on the assumption that both the A and E propositions carry existential import. Modern logic makes the opposite decision, treating the claim that all men are mortal as equivalent to the claim that if someone is a man, then he is mortal. This way of speaking carries no commitment to the existence of men. If we want to indicate the existence of men, then we must say so explicitly. The difference is shown in the following diagrams:

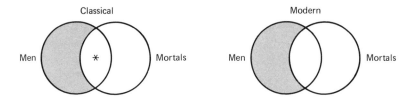

An important consequence of this difference is that in the classical approach the A proposition implies the I proposition, whereas in the modern approach it does not.

Which approach shall we adopt? In the long run, the modern approach has proved a more powerful method. All the same, there is something beautiful about the classical approach and it is worth exploring in its own right. Our decision, then, is this: We will adopt the modern approach and not assign existential import to the A and E propositions. At the same time, we can develop the classical approach simply by adding an indication of existential commitment where it is needed. In this way we can examine both the modern and the classical approach to this area of logic.

The Classification of the Basic Propositions

Traditionally, these basic propositions have been classified under the following distinctions:

    Quality: Affirmative/Negative
    Quantity: Universal/Particular

Quality The A and I propositions are affirmative propositions, and the E and O propositions are negative propositions. The intuitive difference between an affirmative proposition and a negative proposition seems obvious: In an affirmative proposition we *affirm* something; in a negative proposition we *deny* or *negate* something. Yet it is not always easy to apply this distinction to particular cases. Is the following proposition affirmative or negative?

John is absent.

If you decide that it is negative because absent just means "not here," then how do you classify this proposition?

John is not absent.

It seems odd to call a proposition affirmative when it has the transparent form of a denial.

Fortunately, in the present context, we do not have to worry about such questions. We shall classify propositions in terms of their form and not in terms of the meaning of the subject and predicate words. Thus the same thought can be expressed in propositions of different forms. For example:

All clergy are noncombatants.
No clergy are combatants.

Although these propositions express the same thought, the first is an A proposition, the second is an E proposition. For evident reasons, then, we call the E and the O propositions negative, and the A and the I propositions affirmative.

Quantity The A and E propositions are *universal* propositions, and the I and O propositions are *particular* propositions. The distinction between universal and particular propositions turns upon the character of the subject term in the proposition. In a universal proposition we speak about *all* of the members of the subject class; in a *particular* proposition we speak about *some* of them. So the A proposition is said to be universal and the I and O propositions are said to be particular. It does not take much thought to see that the E proposition is universal. If I say that no *A* is *B*, I am plainly speaking of *all* the things that are *A* and saying that none of them is *B*. We can summarize this nomenclature in the following table:

		Quality	
		Affirmative	Negative
Quantity	Universal	A	E
	Particular	I	O

The Square of Opposition

We can now examine some logical relationships that obtain between these four basic propositions. The first system of relationships form what has been called the *square of opposition*. The approach here is classical, with existential commitment indicated for the A and E propositions.

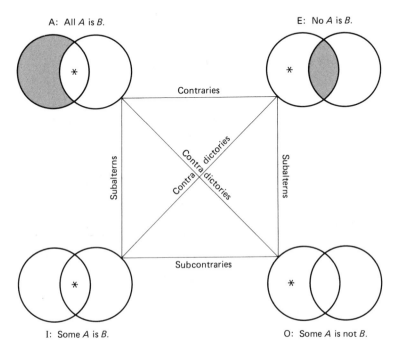

A: All *A* is *B*.

E: No *A* is *B*.

Contraries

Contradictories

Contradictories

Subalterns

Subalterns

Subcontraries

I: Some *A* is *B*.

O: Some *A* is not *B*.

This diagram shows the relationship that each proposition has to the other three. All of these relationships have specific names which are explained below.

Contraries The A and E propositions are *contraries* of one another. That is, they are so related that:

(1) They cannot both be true.

(2) They can, however, both be false.

In common life, the idea of contraries is captured by the notion that one thing is the *complete opposite* of another. The complete opposite of "Everyone is here" is "No one is here." Clearly, such complete opposites cannot both be true at once. If we look at the diagrams for the A and E propositions, we see this at once. The middle region of the A proposition diagram shows the existence of something that is both *A* and *B*, whereas the middle region of the E proposition diagram is shaded out, showing that nothing is both *A* and *B*. It should also be clear that both the A and E propositions may be false. Suppose that there is some *A* that is *B* and also some *A* that is not *B*:

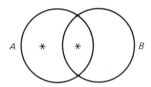

Going from left to right, the first asterisk shows that "All *A* is *B*" is false; the second asterisk shows that "No *A* is *B*" is false.

Contradictories The A and O propositions are contradictories of one another, and so are the E and I propositions. The most obvious example of a contradictory pair of propositions is a proposition and its explicit denial, i.e., pairs of the form: "*p*" and "*~p*." If we look at the square of opposition, we see that the O proposition is the denial of the A proposition. These contradictory pairs are so related that:

(1) They cannot both be true.

(2) They cannot both be false.

More simply, contradictory pairs of propositions always have *opposite* truth values.

Once more these relationships are reflected in the diagrams we have drawn for these propositions. Here we will only examine the A and O propositions.

A: All *A* is *B*.

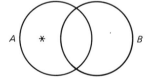

O: Some *A* is not *B*.

It is easy to see that these two propositions cannot both be true, for the second diagram has an asterisk in a region that is shaded out in the first diagram. But why must at least one of these propositions be true? Actually, it is rather easy to explain this in the *modern* approach, where there is no existential commitment for the A and E propositions. The explanation in the classical approach is more complicated.

In the modern approach we can represent the denial of a proposition by a simple procedure. The only information given in our diagram is represented either by *shading out* some region, thereby indicating that

nothing exists in it, or by *putting an asterisk* in a region, thereby indicating that something does exist in it. We are given no indication about
unmarked regions. To represent the denial of a proposition, we simply
reverse the information in the diagram. That is, where there is an asterisk, we put in shading; where there is shading, we put in an asterisk.
Everything else is left unchanged. Thus in the modern approach, we can
see at once that the A and O propositions are denials of one another so
that they must always take opposite truth values.

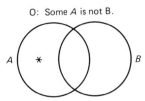

The situation in the classical interpretation is much less tidy. The basic
idea in the classical approach is that in asserting that all *A* is *B*, we are
committing ourselves to the existence of things that are *A*. We reflect
this commitment by putting an asterisk in the middle region of the diagram for the A proposition. But now the interpretation of the denial of
this proposition is no longer a straightforward business of reversing information. The following is *not* what we want:

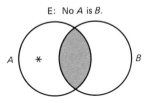

Here we have wound up with the wrong result, for we want the O proposition to be the contradiction of the A proposition and not the E proposition. The result we do want is this:

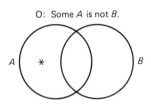

To get the right result, we shall make the following ruling: Even in the
classical approach we shall ignore existential import, except in those
cases where a particular inference depends upon it. In those cases, *we*

shall plug in the existential import only after all other logical maneuvers have been made. So we are back to our simple modern diagram:

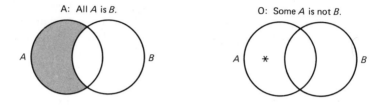

A: All *A* is *B*.

O: Some *A* is not *B*.

There is no need here to further decorate this diagram with indications of existential import, since nothing turns upon it.

Subcontraries The I and O propositions are *subcontraries* of one another. Here the pattern is just the reverse of the pattern of contraries:

(1) Both can be true.

(2) Both cannot be false.

As with contraries, this relationship holds on the classical approach because of the commitment to the existence of items in the classes we speak about. (The relationship of subcontraries does not hold on the modern approach.) To see how this works out, compare the diagrams for the I and O propositions:

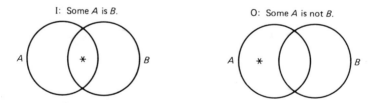

I: Some *A* is *B*.

O: Some *A* is not *B*.

Consider just the left-hand side of this diagram:

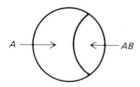

We know that in the classical approach, a presuppositional asterisk must go into this diagram somewhere. But if the asterisk goes into the overlapping region *AB*, then the I proposition is true; if the asterisk goes into the nonoverlapping region of A, then the O proposition is true. So at least one of them is true. Finally, nothing rules out the possibility that there might be an asterisk in each region. In that case both the I and the O propositions would be true, and the situation would look like this:

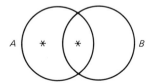

Subalternation *Subalternation* is the relationship that holds down the sides of the square of opposition. Quite simply, the A proposition implies the I proposition and the E proposition implies the O proposition. Again, this relationship depends upon the existential commitment found in the classical approach, and does not hold in the modern approach. We can use our diagrams for testing these implications in the following way: First diagram the premise, and then diagram the conclusion. If the inference from premise to conclusion is valid, then the information contained in the diagram for the conclusion must already be contained in the information given in the diagram for the premise. The validity for subalternation is illustrated by the following diagrams:

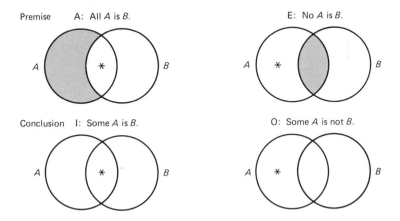

Another way of describing this test is as follows: Draw both the diagram for the premise and the conclusion, and then try to add the information contained in the diagram for the conclusion to the diagram for the premise. If the argument is valid, that information is already present in the diagram for the premise and no addition to it is needed.

We can summarize the information given by the classical square of opposition using two charts. We shall ask two questions. First, for each proposition, what consequences follow from the assumption that it is true?

		A	E	I	O
	A	T	F	T	F
Assumed true	E	F	T	F	T
	I	?	F	T	?
	O	F	?	?	T

Secondly, for each proposition, what consequences follow from the assumption that it is false?

		A	E	I	O
	A	F	?	?	T
Assumed false	E	?	F	T	?
	I	F	T	F	T
	O	T	F	T	F

Pragmatics and the Square of Opposition

As we have examined the classical treatment of the square of opposition, we have seen that at almost every turn the argument depended upon the notion of existential commitment. The one exception was the relationship of contradictories, but in all other cases we have to make this commitment explicit in order to show that the relationships hold. We might say that the classical approach depends upon making *explicit* what is *implicit* in the use of these basic propositions.

We can now look at a different approach that is familiar to us from earlier discussions. Instead of saying that the A proposition *implies* the existence of things that are *A*, we can say that the *use* of an A proposition *normally conversationally implies that the person believes that there are things that are A.* We have to speak in this qualified way because there are times when the use of an A proposition has no such conversational implication. Remember the example of someone saying, "All trespassers will be fined." This does not conversationally imply that the person who says it believes that there will be trespassers. (Having announced this, he may now believe just the opposite.) Reflections of this kind lead to a different way of treating the square of opposition. We can take the logically simple approach of dropping the assumption that the A and E propositions carry existential import. We then get the result that *only* the relationships of contradictories continue to hold. All the other relationships now fail.

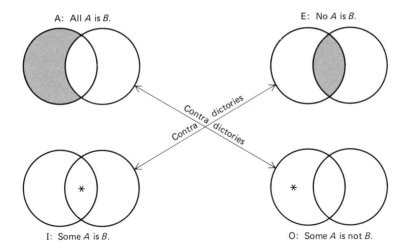

This is all that is left of the traditional square of opposition in the modern approach.

We can, however, reflect more of the traditional relationships by adding to this square the conversational implications that arise in standard contexts:

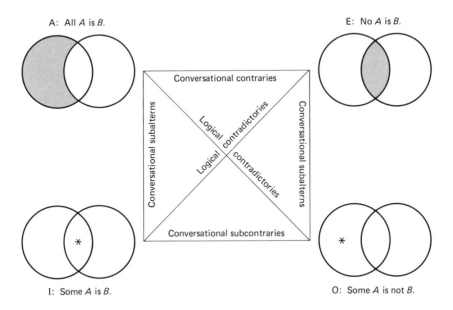

Here only the relationship of contradictories is a logical one; all the other relationships depend upon conversational implication and thus are labeled as conversational relationships.

Will it make much difference whether we adopt the classical or the modern approach to the propositions that form the square of opposition?

For some purposes it will hardly make any difference at all. In the practical affairs of life it usually does not make any difference whether something is logically implied *by what is said* or conversationally implied *by the saying of it.* In fact, it is only relatively recently that philosophers have become aware of this difference in something like a clearheaded way. Yet from the point of view of logical theory, the distinction is crucial. When we mix up logical implications and conversational implications, our logic first of all becomes very complicated. This comes out, for example, in trying to explain contradictories on the classical square of opposition.

Beyond leading to complications, mixing up logical and conversational implication can actually lead to inconsistency. This can be illustrated by noticing another way that conversational rules apply to the use of the propositions on the square of opposition. The use of these propositions is governed by Grice's rule of Quantity—that is, where justified, we are expected to use the stronger A or E propositions rather than the weaker I or O propositions. Thus when we use either the I or O propositions, we conversationally imply that we are not in a position to use the stronger A or E propositions. A simple example will show how this works: Filled with greed, a person takes every last piece of candy from a box. When asked if he has taken the candy, he replies, "I took some of the candy." Now, strictly speaking, this is true. The person did take some of the candy. Yet his remark plainly suggests that he took *only* some of it. Here the violation of the conversational rule is so extreme that it is tempting to call the person's reply an outright lie. In general, then, the use of an I proposition by a speaker contextually implies that the speaker does not believe the A proposition to be true; sometimes it implies, even more strongly, that he knows the A proposition to be false. We get this stronger implication when the speaker is in a position to know whether the A proposition is true or not. For example, the person who takes all the candy is obviously in a position to know what he has done. It is for this reason that his remark conversationally implies the *denial* of the assertion that he took all of the candy.

Now the very same relationship holds between the weak O proposition and the strong E proposition. The use of an O proposition by a speaker conversationally implies that the speaker does not believe the E proposition, and sometimes, even more strongly, that he knows it not to be true. This leads to a result that squares with our commonsense understanding of language: When someone says, "Some are ..." this conversationally implies "Some are not ..."; conversely, when someone says, "Some are not ..." this conversationally implies "Some are...." In general, then, the use of one subaltern conversationally implies that the use of the other subaltern is also okay.[1]

[1] Remember that conversational rules, unlike logical rules, hold only in general, for one conversational rule can be affected and overridden by another.

We are now in a position to see how mixing up conversational rules with logical rules can lead to lunacy. Consider the following line of reasoning.

(1) All aliens are spies.
∴ (2) Some aliens are spies.
∴ (3) Some aliens are not spies.

∴ (4) If all aliens are spies, some aliens are not spies.

In this strange argument, we wind up with a proposition implying its own denial, a result we expect to get *only* when we start out from a self-contradictory proposition. It is not hard to see what has gone wrong here. The step from (1) to (2) is a logical implication in the classical approach, and a conversational implication in the modern approach. On the other hand, the step from (2) to (3) must be a conversational implication in either approach. In the conclusion both steps are treated as logical implications, and disaster results.

Exercise 2: Give a similar explanation of the fallacies in the following lines of reasoning:

(1) If you have an obligation to do something, then you are permitted to do it.
If you are permitted to do something, then you are permitted not to do it.

∴ If you have an obligation to do something, then you are permitted not to do it.

Less seriously:

(2) If something is good, then it is not bad.
If something is not bad, then it is not so good.

∴ If something is good, then it is not so good.

This last example shows that mixing up logical implications with conversational implications can lead to unwanted results. This, however, does not settle the issue between the classical and the modern approach to the existential import of these basic propositions. A logician is free to argue that existential import is logically implied—not merely conversationally implied—by the A and E propositions. He can then develop his theory accordingly. There is nothing incoherent about such an approach. This text adopts the modern approach for three reasons:

(1) It yields a simpler logical system.

(2) It is part of a much wider system that has proved extraordinarily successful.

(3) It fits in well with the general approach of distinguishing logical implications from conversational implications.

The Theory of Immediate Inference

The theory of immediate inference concerns arguments with the following features:

(1) They have a single premise. (That is why the inference is called immediate.)

(2) They involve only the four basic propositions.

Of course, there are all sorts of other arguments involving just one premise, but those involving the four basic propositions have been singled out for special attention. These inferences deserve special attention because they occur quite often in everyday reasoning.

We already know about one immediate inference: subalternation. In the classical theory, but not in the modern theory, we can always derive an I proposition from an A proposition, and we can always derive an O proposition from an E proposition. Here we shall consider three standard patterns of immediate inference: conversion, obversion, and contraposition. We will adopt the modern approach, but we will notice where the classical approach differs from it.

Conversion *Conversion* is the simplest immediate inference we shall consider. We convert a proposition simply by reversing the subject term and the predicate term. By the subject term, we simply mean the term that occurs in the grammatical subject; by the predicate term, we mean the term that occurs in the grammatical predicate. In the proposition "All spies are aliens," "spies" is the subject term and "aliens" is the predicate term. In this case identifying the predicate term is straightforward, since the grammatical predicate is a noun—a predicate nominative. Often, however, we have to change the grammatical predicate from an adjective to a noun phrase in order to get a noun that refers to a class of things. Though it is a bit artificial, we can always use this device. "All spies are dangerous" becomes "All spies are dangerous things." Here "spies" is the subject term and "dangerous things" is the predicate term. The reason we must make this change is that when we convert a proposition, we need a noun phrase to go into the place of the grammatical subject. In English we cannot say "All dangerous are spies," but we can say "All dangerous things are spies."

We want to know when this operation of conversion is legitimate. That is, we want to know when conversion yields a *valid* immediate inference. To answer this question we can examine the four basic propositions to see what happens when conversion is attempted. Two cases are obvious at first sight. Both the I and the E propositions validly convert. From the I proposition, "Some *S* is *P*," we may validly infer "Some *P* is *S*."

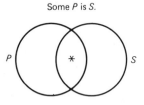

From the E proposition, "No *S* is *P*," we may validly infer "No *P* is *S*."

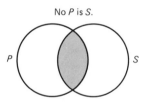

Notice that in these cases the converse of the proposition has exactly the same diagram as the original proposition. This shows that the I proposition not only *implies* its converse, but is *logically equivalent* to it; the implication runs both ways. It should also be obvious that the O proposition cannot, in general, be converted validly. From "Some *S* is not *P*," we may not, in general, infer "Some *P* is not *S*."[2]

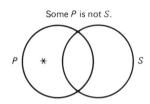

---

[2] There are some strange cases—logicians call them degenerate cases—where inferences of this pattern are valid. For example, from *Some men are not men,* we may validly infer that *Some men are not men.* Here, by making the subject term and the predicate term the same, we trivialize conversion. Keeping cases of this kind in mind, we must say that in general, but not always, the conversion of an O proposition does not yield a valid inference. In contrast, the set of valid inferences holds in all cases, including degenerate cases.

Finally, we can see that the A proposition does not validly convert, either. From "All *S* is *P*," we may not, in general, infer "All *P* is *S*."

Everything that we have said so far is true in both the modern and the classical approach. To see this, we need only add the symbols indicating existential commitment to the above diagrams and then notice that the reasoning remains unchanged. But there is one important difference between the classical and the modern approach. Given the existential commitment in the classical approach, we may infer from *All S is P* that *Some P is S*. That inference does not hold in the modern approach:

Classical: All *S* is *P*.   *Some P* is *S*.

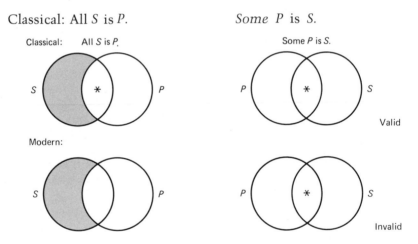

The classical conversion of an A proposition into an I proposition is called *conversion by limitation* since the original universal claim is limited to a particular claim. The following table summarizes these relationships:

Proposition	Conversion	Status
A: All *S* is *P*.	Some *P* is *S*.	Implication by limitation—classical theory only
E: No *S* is *P*.	No *P* is *S*.	Logically equivalent
I: Some *S* is *P*.	Some *P* is *S*.	Logically equivalent
O: Some *S* is not *P*.	Some *P* is not *S*.	Does not hold

Obversion Before we can deal with *obversion,* we must define the notion of a *complementary class.* The idea is simple enough: given any class C, its complementary class is just all of those things that are not in C. One standard way of referring to a complementary class is to use the prefix "non." Here are some examples:

Class	Complementary class
Republicans	Non-Republicans
Voters	Nonvoters
Combatants	Noncombatants

If we look at the class of non-Republicans, we see that it is a mixed bag, for as we have defined the notion it includes everything that is not a Republican. This includes coyotes, subatomic particles, prime numbers, the top ten record hits, and the British royal family. Of course, in everyday life we certainly do not wish to include all these things in our notion of a non-Republican. When we speak about non-Republicans, the context will usually make it clear that we are referring to politicians, voters, or party members. We can capture this idea by using a notion introduced earlier: that of a *domain of discourse.* We might say that the domain of discourse here includes all those who are members of American political parties. A non-Republican is someone in this domain of discourse who is not a Republican. We can represent this using the following diagram:

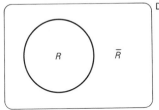

DD: Members of American political parties

A bar over a letter indicates a complementary class. In this case $\bar{R}$ means the class of non-Republicans. As indicated earlier, sometimes it is useful to specify the domain of discourse, sometimes it is not. In this book we will worry about the domain of discourse only when it serves some useful purpose.

We can now define the immediate inference called *obversion.* To pass from a basic proposition to its obverse:

(1) We reverse the *quality* of the proposition, from affirmative to negative or negative to affirmative as the case may be.

(2) We replace the predicate term by its complementary term.

Starting with "All men are mortal," this two-step process works as follows:

All men are mortal.

(1) Reversing the quality yields: No men are mortal.

(2) Replacing the predicate term by its converse yields: No men are nonmortal.

This final proposition is the obverse of "All men are mortal."

We now want to know when this operation of obversion is legitimate—that is, we want to know when obversion yields a valid immediate inference. The answer to this is that a proposition is always *logically equivalent* to its obverse in both the classical and the modern interpretation. To show this, we can run through the four propositions. Since all these equivalences hold between a proposition and its *obverse*, there is no need to draw a diagram twice. The reader should, however, check to see whether the diagram is accurate for both propositions.

A: "All *S* is *P*" is logically equivalent to "No *S* is non-*P*."

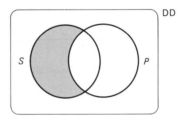

In this diagram, the class of things that are non-*P* includes all those things in the domain of discourse that are not in *P*. We can see that there is nothing in the class of things that are *S* that is also in the complimentary class of *P*, because all the things in *S* are in the class *P*. This may sound a bit complicated, but with a very little thought the validity of inferences through obversion becomes quite obvious.

E: "No *S* is *P*" is logically equivalent to "All *S* is non-*P*."

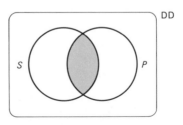

I: "Some S is P" is logically equivalent to "Some S is not non-P."

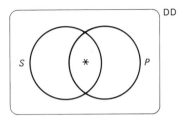

O: From "Some S is not P," we may validly infer that "Some S is non-P."

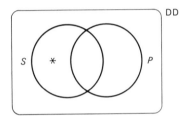

It is important to see that the final inference is a genuine inference and not a mere repetition. "Some S is not P" is an O proposition, whereas "Some S is non-P" is an I proposition. That is, the first proposition formulates a negative proposition—it indicates that there is at least one thing that is not in a certain class. The second proposition is an affirmative proposition, for it indicates that something is in a given class—in this case, a complementary class.

Contraposition *Contraposition* is the final relationship we shall examine. We get the contrapositive of a proposition by the following two-step process:

    (1) We convert the proposition.

    (2) We replace *both* terms by their complementary terms.

For example, starting with "All men are mortal," this two-step process works as follows:

    All men are mortal.

    (1) Converted, this proposition becomes:
    All mortal (things) are men.

    (2) Replacing each term by its complementary term we get:
    All nonmortal (things) are non-men.

This final proposition is the contrapositive of "All men are mortal."

Following our previous pattern, we must now ask when the contrapositive can be validly inferred from a given proposition. Here the situation is pretty much the reverse of what we discovered for conversion:

A: "All S is P" is logically equivalent to "All non-P is non-S."

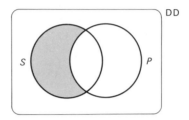

E: From "No S is P" we may not, in general, infer "No non-P is non-S."

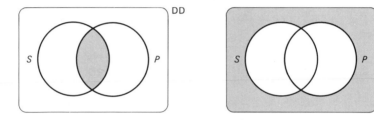

But in the classical approach, though not in the modern approach, *contraposition by limitation* does hold, i.e., from "No S is P" we may infer "Some non-P is not non-S."[3]

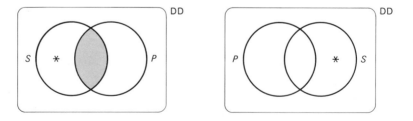

I: From "Some S is P," we may not, in general, infer "Some non-P is non-S."

---

[3] At first sight this proposition may seem hard to understand, but with a little thought it actually makes sense.

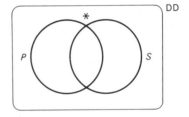

O: "Some *S* is not *P*" is logically equivalent to "Some non-*P* is not non-*S*."

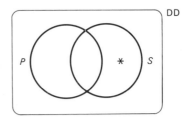

The following table summarizes all these equivalence relationships. The two items in parentheses are not equivalent but are only implied, and they hold only in the classical interpretation.

Proposition	Obversion	Conversion	Contraposition
All *S* is *P*.	No *S* is non-*P*.	(Some *S* is *P*.)	All non-*P* is non-*S*.
No *S* is *P*.	All *S* is non-*P*.	No *P* is *S*.	(Some non-*P* is not non-*S*.)
Some *S* is *P*.	Some *S* is not non-*P*.	Some *P* is *S*.	XXXXXXXXXX
Some *S* is not *P*.	Some *S* is non-*P*	XXXXXXXXXX	Some non-*P* is not non-*S*.

If we compare some of the propositions we have been studying with remarks that we make in everyday life, some of them, at least, will seem very artificial. It is hard to imagine a case where we would actually say "Some nonspies are not nonaliens." It would certainly be easier to say "Some nonspies are aliens," which is its equivalent through *obversion*. We can then *convert* this: "Some aliens are nonspies." This is still somewhat unnatural, so by using obversion again we get the natural remark, "Some aliens are not spies." Actually, we could have gotten this result immediately through applying *contraposition* to the original remark. (This shows that the contrapositive of a proposition is the obverse of the converse of the obverse of that proposition—something you need not commit to memory!)

In fact, we do *sometimes* find ourselves in contexts where we use some of these complicated sentences. Discussing the voting patterns of nonresidents, we might find ourselves saying that some nonresidents are not nonvoters. Given the context, this remark loses much of its oddness. Usually, however, we choose simple clear formulations; the ability to do this depends upon an implicit understanding of the logical relationships within this system of propositions. Here we are trying to bring this implicit understanding to the surface so that we can understand it better. That is, we are trying to give clear rules for inferences that we make routinely in everyday life.

Exercise 3: For each of the following propositions, decide by using appropriate diagrams which of the above immediate inferences hold. For example:

All ministers are noncombatants.

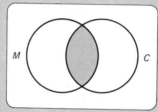

DD: People

Obverse: No ministers are combatants.

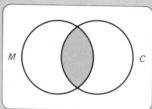

DD: People

VALID

Converse: All noncombatants are ministers.

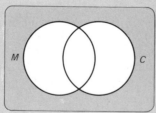

DD: People

INVALID

Contrapositive: All non-noncombatants are nonministers. Or more simply: All combatants are nonministers.

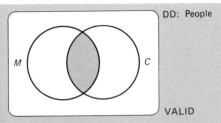

DD: People

VALID

(1) Some dudes are not cowards.
(2) All nonresidents are taxpayers.
(3) Some nonaligned nations are wealthy (nations).
(4) No daughters are sons.
(5) No nonnegotiable stocks are safe (stocks).
(6) All that glitters is not gold.
(7) Some people cannot be bought.
(8) There is no such thing as a bad boy.

Exercise 4: Put the following sentences into plain, respectable English. Indicate the immediate inference or immediate inferences you have used to do so. (Be careful!)
(1) No noncombatant is a minister.
(2) Some nonresident is not a non-nonvoter.
(3) Not all snakes are not dangerous (things).
(4) No all-the-time losers are non-nonpersons.

The Theory of the Syllogism

In an immediate inference, we draw a conclusion directly from a single proposition. The traditional theory of immediate inference explores such inferences as they arise for the basic A E I O propositions. The square of opposition answers the following question: Given the truth or falsity of one of these basic propositions, what, if anything, may we infer concerning the truth or falsity of the remaining basic propositions? We have now extended the theory of immediate inference to include the *conversion* of terms and the construction of *complementary* classes.

The next step in developing the traditional theory concerning these basic propositions is to consider arguments containing two premises rather than just one. An important group of such arguments is called *categorical syllogisms*. The basic idea behind these arguments is commonsensical. Suppose I wish to prove that "All S is P"—whatever S or P might be. A proof should present some *link* or *connection* between S and P. This link can be some other term we shall label M. In a syllogism we establish a relationship between the terms S and P through some middle term M.

We can now define a categorical syllogism more carefully.

(1) A categorical syllogism is constructed from the basic A, E, I, and O propositions.

(2) Given that the conclusion will contain two terms S and P, we can place the following restrictions on the premises.
   (i) There are only two premises.
   (ii) One premise contains the term S. (This is called the minor premise.)
   (iii) One premise contains the term P. (This is called the major premise.)
   (iv) Each premise contains the middle term M.

Traditionally, the major premise is stated first, the minor premise second. Here are some examples of syllogisms.

All rectangles have four sides.   (Major premise)
All squares are rectangles.   (Minor premise)
$\therefore$ All squares have four sides.   (Conclusion)

Subject term   = Squares
Predicate term = Being four-sided
Middle term   = Rectangles

Schematically, the argument looks like this:

All M is P
All S is M
$\therefore$ All S is P.

Here is a syllogism containing a negative premise.

No ellipses have sides.
All circles are ellipses.
$\therefore$ No circles have sides.

Schematically:

No M is P.
All S is M.
$\therefore$ No S is P.

Finally, here is an example of a syllogism containing a particular proposition.

All squares have equal sides.
Some squares are rectangles.

∴ Some rectangles have equal sides.

Schematically:

All *M* is *P*.
Some *M* is *S*.

∴ Some *S* is *P*.

Valid and Invalid Syllogisms

The examples given so far have all been of valid syllogisms—it should be obvious in each case that the conclusion does follow from the premise. It is possible to construct an argument that meets the definition of a categorical syllogism but is still invalid. A glaringly invalid argument will make this clear.

Some figures are circles.
Some figures are squares.

∴ All squares are circles.

This is a dreadful argument, but still it is a categorical syllogism. It is an *invalid* categorical syllogism.

Since some categorical syllogisms are valid whereas others are invalid, it will be important to have some systematic method for evaluating them. This subject has been explored for more than two thousand years, and a variety of analytical techniques has been developed. We shall use Venn diagrams.

Venn Diagrams for Syllogisms

In the previous section we used Venn diagrams to test the validity of immediate inferences. In a categorical syllogism, three terms appear; thus we are dealing with three classes. To reflect this, we will use diagrams of the following kind:

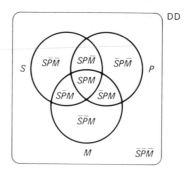

The diagram has eight different compartments:

$$
\begin{array}{ccc}
S & P & M \\
S & P & \overline{M} \\
S & \overline{P} & M \\
S & \overline{P} & \overline{M} \\
\overline{S} & P & M \\
\overline{S} & P & \overline{M} \\
\overline{S} & \overline{P} & M \\
\overline{S} & \overline{P} & \overline{M}
\end{array}
$$

Notice that if something is not an S nor a P nor an M, it falls completely outside the system of overlapping circles. In every other case, a thing is assigned to some compartment within the system of overlapping circles.

To test the validity of a syllogism using Venn diagrams, we first fill in the diagram to reflect the content of the premises. If the argument is valid, then the conclusion will already be contained in the diagram. To see this, consider the diagrams for examples already considered:

> All rectangles are four-sided.
> All squares are rectangles.
> ───────────────────────────
> ∴ All squares are four-sided.

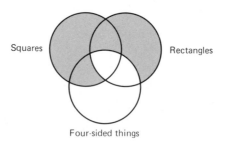

Notice that all the things that are squares are corralled into the region of things that are four-sided. So the argument is valid.

No ellipses have sides.
All circles are ellipses.
_____
∴ No circles have sides.

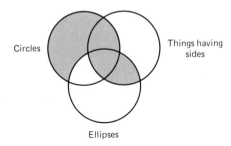

We diagram the conclusion "No circles have sides" as follows:

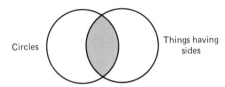

That information is already contained in the Venn diagram for the premises.

All squares have equal sides.
Some squares are rectangles.
_____
∴ Some rectangles have equal sides.

It is a good strategy to diagram a universal proposition before we diagram a particular proposition. The diagram for the above argument looks like this:

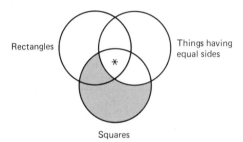

The conclusion—that there is something that is a rectangle that is equal-sided—appears in the diagram for the premises.

Existential Import

In the discussion of immediate inferences, we raised the question whether the universal propositions—the A and the E propositions—carried existential import. That is, when we assert that "All *S* is *P*" or that "No *S* is *P*," are we committing ourselves to the existence of *S*s and *P*s? The ruling for traditional logic was that these propositions *do* carry existential import. The same ruling holds for the traditional theory of the syllogism. So far we have continued to employ the modern approach that does not assign existential import to the A and E propositions.

We can begin our study of this matter with an example that has had a curious history:

> All rectangles are four-sided.
> All squares are rectangles.
>
> ∴ *Some* squares are four-sided.

The argument is peculiar because the conclusion is weaker than it needs to be. We could, after all, conclude that *all* squares are four-sided. The argument thus violates the conversational rule of Quantity; perhaps for this reason, this syllogism was often not included in traditional lists of valid syllogisms. Yet the argument is valid on the traditional interpretation of existential import and our diagram should show this.

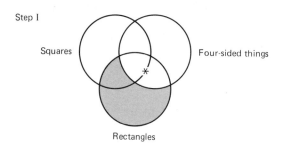

Step I

Squares — Four-sided things

Rectangles

Notice that the asterisk is placed on the line dividing regions *SPM* and $\overline{S}PM$ since we are not in a position to put it into one region rather than the other. We now draw in the second premise:

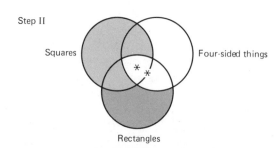

Step II

Squares — Four-sided things

Rectangles

As expected, the conclusion that some squares are four-sided is already diagrammed, so the argument is valid—provided that we commit ourselves to the existential import of A propositions.

Since classical logicians tended to ignore the previous argument, their writings did not bring out the importance of existential import in evaluating it. There is, however, an argument that did appear on the classical lists that makes clear the demand for existential commitment. These are syllogisms of the following kind:

> All *M* is *P*.
> All *M* is *S*.
> —————
> ∴ Some *S* is *P*.

This is diagrammed as follows:

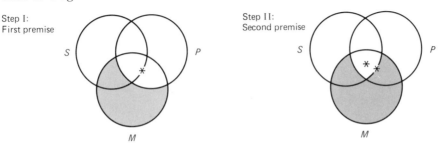

Step I:
First premise

Step II:
Second premise

Again we see that the conclusion follows, but only if we diagram the universal propositions to indicate existential import. This, then, is an argument that was declared valid in the traditional approach, but invalid in the modern approach.

So far we have looked only at valid arguments. Here are some patterns for invalid arguments. The conclusion is diagrammed at the right. It is evident that this diagram is not already contained in the diagram for the premises. The arrows show differences in informational content.

> All *M* is *P*.
> All *M* is *S*.
> —————
> ∴ All *S* is *P*.

All *S* is *P*.

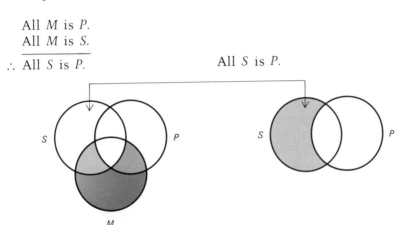

Some *M* is *P*.
Some *S* is *M*.
——————
∴ Some *S* is *P*.   Some *S* is *P*.

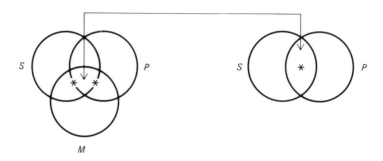

Examine this diagram closely. Notice that in saying "Some *M* is *P*," we had to put the asterisk *on* the line dividing *S* and *P*, since we were not given information saying whether anything falls into *S* or not. For the same reason we had to put the asterisk *on* the line dividing *S* and *P* when diagramming "Some *M* is *S*." The upshot was that we did not indicate that anything exists in the region of overlap between *S* and *P*. But this is what the conclusion demands, so the argument is invalid.

No *M* is *P*.
No *S* is *M*.
——————
∴ No *S* is *P*.   No *S* is *P*.

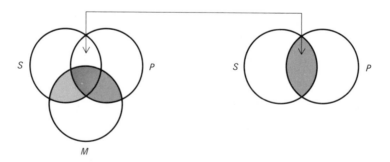

Again we see that this argument is invalid.

The method of Venn diagrams is adequate for deciding the validity or invalidity of all possible syllogisms. Furthermore, it is easy to distinguish between syllogisms that are classically valid and those that are valid in the modern interpretation of existential import. To get the classical theory, we simply include the presuppositions of existential import in our diagrams; in the modern approach we do not do this.

Exercise 5: Adopting the modern approach, test the following syllogisms for validity by using Venn diagrams.

1. All M is P.
    All M is S.
    _____
    ∴ All S is P.

2. No M is P.
    Some S is M.
    _____
    ∴ Some S is not P.

3. No P is M.
    Some S is not M.
    _____
    ∴ Some S is not P.

4. All M is P.
    Some S is not M.
    _____
    ∴ Some S is not P.

5. Some P is M.
    Some S is not M.
    _____
    ∴ Some S is not P.

6. All M is P.
    No S is M.
    _____
    ∴ No S is P.

7. All P is M.
    No S is M.
    _____
    ∴ No S is P.

8. All P is M.
    All S is M.
    _____
    ∴ All S is P.

9. No S is M.
    Some M is P.
    _____
    ∴ Some S is P.

10. No P is M.
    Some S is M.
    _____
    ∴ Some S is not P.

Problems in Applying the Theory of the Syllogism

After students have mastered the techniques for evaluating syllogisms, they naturally turn to arguments that arise in daily life and attempt to use these newly acquired skills. They are usually disappointed with the results. The formal theory of the syllogism seems to bear little relationship to everyday arguments, and there doesn't seem to be any easy way to bridge the gap.

This gap between formal theory and its application occurs for a number of reasons. First, as we saw in Chapter 1, our everyday discourse leaves much unstated. Many things are conversationally implied rather than explicitly asserted. Moreover, we do not feel called upon to say many things that are matters of common agreement. Before we can apply the theory of the syllogism to everyday arguments, these things that are simply understood must be *made explicit.* This is often illuminating and sometimes boring, but it usually involves a great deal of work. Second, the theory of the syllogism applies to statements only in a highly stylized form. Before we apply the theory of the syllogism to an argument, we must cast its premises and conclusion into the basic A, E, I, and O forms. This is not always easy either. Finally, there are arguments that the theory of the syllogism is not adequate to evaluate. We saw earlier in this chapter that propositional logic is not adequate to evaluate arguments whose validity depends upon the *internal* structure of propositions. For this reason, we went beyond propositional logic to study the theory of immediate inference and the theory of the syllogism, which do explore this internal structure of propositions. Although this is still a matter of some dispute, most logicians agree that developments beyond the theory of immediate inference and the theory of the syllogism are needed for the analysis of many, quite ordinary, arguments. Here is one example:

> George is taller than Harry by a head.
> _____
> ∴ George is taller than Harry.

It is hard to imagine an argument that is more obviously valid, yet its validity cannot be shown by the classical theory of immediate inference or syllogism. (In fact, the correct analysis of this argument is still a matter of debate.)

Why study the theory of the syllogism at all, if it is hard to apply in some circumstances and perhaps impossible to apply in others? The answer to this question was given at the beginning of Chapter 6: The study of formal logic is important because it deepens our insight into the central notion of logic, *validity.* Furthermore, the argument forms we have studied do underlie much of our everyday reasoning, but so much else is going on in a normal conversational setting that this dimension is hardly evident. By examining arguments in idealized forms, we can study their validity in isolation from all the other factors at work in a rich conversational setting.

There is a difference, then, between the techniques developed in Chapters 1 to 5 and the techniques developed in these last two chapters. The first five chapters presented methods of *informal* analysis that may be applied directly to the rich and complex arguments that arise in everyday life. These methods of analysis are not wholly rigorous, but they do provide practical guides for the analysis and evaluation of actual arguments. These two chapters concerning *formal* logic have the opposite tendency. In comparison with the first five chapters, the level of rigor is very high, but the range of application is correspondingly smaller. In general, it is accurate to say that the more rigor and precision you want, the less you can talk about.

A System of Rules for Evaluating Syllogisms

The method of Venn diagrams that we have used in this chapter is probably the most natural technique for analyzing syllogisms, since the relationship between overlapping figures is a clear analogy for the relationship between classes. Another method for evaluating syllogisms employs a system of rules. While this system has less intuitive appeal than Venn diagrams, it is easier to apply. The procedure is to lay down a set of rules such that any syllogism that satisfies all of the rules is valid and any syllogism that fails to satisfy any one of them is invalid. A concise summary of one such system is presented here.

Distribution The central idea for one system of rules is that of the *distribution* or *extension* of a term. The basic idea is that a term is used distributively in a proposition if it is used to refer to the whole of a class or to all of the members in it. We shall first simply state the distributional properties for each of the basic A, E, I, and O propositions and then try to make sense out of this notion.

Proposition	Subject	Predicate
A	Distributed	Undistributed
E	Distributed	Distributed
I	Undistributed	Undistributed
O	Undistributed	Distributed

The two universal propositions A and E have distributed subject terms. In the I and the O propositions we speak about *some S*, therefore the subject term is undistributed for these propositions.

The reasoning runs smoothly for the subject term, but the predicate

term is not so easy to deal with. Notice that there is no word like
"some" or "all" governing the predicate term.

The reasoning concerning the predicate term usually proceeds along
the following lines: Suppose we assert that no squares are circles.

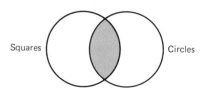

For this to be true, there can be no square that is identical with *any* circle. The appearance of the word "any" shows that the predicate term is
distributed in the E proposition. Consider next the O proposition. Some
S is not *P*. For this to be true, there must be some *S* that is not identical
with *any* *S*. Again, the appearance of the word "any" shows that the
predicate term is distributed. Our test for the distribution of terms is
then to compare the basic A E I O proposition with a counterpart identity statement as follows:

A: All *S* is *P*.   For *any* *S* there is *some* *P* that is identical with
                it.
E: No *S* is *P*.   For *any* *S* there is not *any* *P* that is identical
                with it.
I: Some *S* is   For *some* *S* there is *some* *P* that is identical with
     P.   it.
O: Some *S* is   For *some* *S* there is not *any* *P* that is identical
     not *P*.   with it.

This comparison gives the pattern for the distribution of terms noticed
earlier.

Quality Along with the notion of distribution, the system of rules we
are discussing here also uses the idea of the *quality* of a proposition—
whether it is affirmative or negative. The following rules are adequate
for testing the validity of categorical syllogisms.

Quality:
(1) Nothing follows from two negative premises.

(2) If one premise is negative, then the conclusion must be negative as well.

Distribution:
(3) The middle term must be distributed at least once.

(4) The subject term may not be distributed in the conclusion if it is not distributed in the premises.

(5) The predicate term may not be distributed in the conclusion if it is not distributed in the premises.

The fallacies that result from violating these rules are called by the following names:

Quality:

(1) The Fallacy of Two Negative Premises

(2) The Fallacy of Drawing an Affirmative Conclusion from an Argument with a Negative Premise

Distribution:

(3) The Fallacy of the Undistributed Middle

(4) The Fallacy of the Illicitly Distributed Subject

(5) The Fallacy of the Illicitly Distributed Predicate

Quantity The rules on distribution and quality are adequate for the analysis of syllogisms in the classical interpretation. The modern interpretation requires a further rule of *quantity.*

Quantity:

(6) A particular conclusion cannot be derived from two universal premises.

Corresponding to this there is, in the modern approach, a fallacy:

(6) The Fallacy of Deriving a Particular Conclusion from Universal Premises

The following devices facilitate the application of these rules. Mark the propositions in the syllogism "+" or "−" to indicate quality. Circle all terms that are distributed, leaving all undistributed terms uncircled. This makes it easy to see if the first five rules of the syllogism have been satisfied, and so whether the syllogism is valid or invalid in the classical approach. No special devices are needed to check the additional sixth rule needed in the modern approach.

The following examples illustrate these methods:

(1) + All Ⓜis P
+ All Ⓢis M Valid
∴ + All Ⓢis P

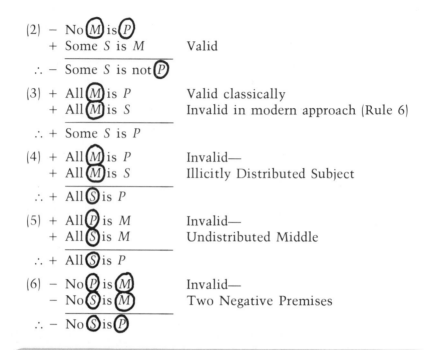

(2)   –   No $\textcircled{M}$ is $\textcircled{P}$
     +   Some S is M Valid
$\therefore$ –   Some S is not $\textcircled{P}$

(3)   +   All $\textcircled{M}$ is P Valid classically
     +   All $\textcircled{M}$ is S Invalid in modern approach (Rule 6)
$\therefore$ +   Some S is P

(4)   +   All $\textcircled{M}$ is P Invalid—
     +   All $\textcircled{M}$ is S Illicitly Distributed Subject
$\therefore$ +   All $\textcircled{S}$ is P

(5)   +   All $\textcircled{P}$ is M Invalid—
     +   All $\textcircled{S}$ is M Undistributed Middle
$\therefore$ +   All $\textcircled{S}$ is P

(6)   –   No $\textcircled{P}$ is $\textcircled{M}$ Invalid—
     –   No $\textcircled{S}$ is $\textcircled{M}$ Two Negative Premises
$\therefore$ –   No $\textcircled{S}$ is $\textcircled{P}$

Exercise 6: Using the system of rules we have developed, test the syllogisms given on page 181 for validity. Where a fallacy occurs, give the name of that fallacy.

Honors Exercise: To a person familiar with computer programming, this system of rules immediately suggests that a program can be written for the evaluation of syllogisms. In fact, such a program can be written and is only moderately difficult. The first problem is to find some method for encoding all possible syllogisms. After this, the notions of distribution and quality must be given mathematical analogues. In writing such a program, there is a good chance that the programmer will discover on his own large portions of Medieval logic.

PART TWO

SPECIMENS OF ARGUMENTS

PART TWO
SPECIMENS OF ARGUMENTS

The arguments collected in Part Two serve two purposes. The first is to supply case material for exercising the art of close analysis. This is the primary intention of the material presented in Chapter 8, "Issues of Public Concern." Chapter 3 carefully examined a speech made by Representative Kyl on the issue of clerk hire allowances—not a matter to arouse strong emotions or rabid interest. The blandness of the issue, together with the high quality of the argument, made this speech a good model for analysis, for a disinterested attitude toward the content of an argument makes it easier to concentrate upon its structure. But it is artificial to consider only safe topics, for in daily life we often have strong feelings concerning the arguments we encounter. Chapter 8 therefore considers arguments on topics that are both controversial and of current interest. They are also issues on which individual citizens may be called upon to express their opinions at the ballot box. The first debate concerns the safety of atomic power plants; the second concerns issues of affirmative action and so-called reverse discrimination.

The second purpose of Part Two is to examine the distinctive character of arguments as they arise in different fields or areas. The procedures developed in Part I are general enough to be applied to arguments in any field, but Chapters 9-13 illustrate that arguments arising in law, morals, science, theology, and philosophy each have distinctive features. This is obvious in the case of legal arguments, where specific rules are laid down to control an argument as it moves within a system of laws, precedents, and constitutional guarantees. Legal arguments have a character or personality that reflects the distinctive role they play. The same can be said about scientific, theological, and philosophical arguments. Of course, as matters become more technical, it becomes harder for the general reader to follow the nuances of an argument. But with patience and close attention, it is possible for the nonprofessional to develop an appreciation for the brilliance and subtlety of a legal opinion or the elegance of a scientific explanation. It may come as a surprise how similar arguments in these areas are, in both their strengths and their weaknesses, to arguments of everyday life.

ISSUES OF PUBLIC CONCERN

8

As citizens of a democracy, we are often called upon to make decisions on complex public issues. Sometimes we express our decisions indirectly by voting for leaders who represent or support certain policies. Sometimes, though less frequently, we express our opinions directly by participating in a public referendum. Often a reasonable and intelligent person will find these public issues profoundly perplexing. The available facts may be scattered and fragmentary. Our informants may be biased and interested parties. We may find ourselves drawn in opposite directions by competing moral and social principles. We may have prejudices of our own to overcome. The problem in a situation of this kind is to find ways of bringing intelligence to bear upon the question. Methods of close analysis will not do this automatically or infallibly, but they do help to guide our reflections and make them more self-consciously critical.

Safety in Nuclear Power Plants

Our first specimen of a public debate shows how bewildering a public issue can be. The debate concerns the safety of atomic power plants. First of all, the problem is urgent. During a time of energy shortage, we must either build atomic power plants or immediately develop alternative sources of energy. Furthermore, the stakes are high. If atomic power plants are unsafe, then the potential danger could be catastrophic. On top of this, there are sharp disagreements among experts on a whole range of topics beyond the safety of atomic power plants. This includes their effects on the environment, their immunity to terrorist attack, and so on. As responsible citizens we cannot simply consult experts on such questions; we must choose between them. Finally, and not insignificantly, the fear of an atomic holocaust is deeply engrained in our psyches. Whether fears concerning atomic power plants are reasonable fears is itself a question of importance.

We derive our information concerning public issues from a number of sources, including news reports, editorials, paid advertisements, and, likely as not, television specials. The material given below is the "unofficial public service transcript" of a television program entitled "Incident at Brown's Ferry," produced by WGBH in Boston for *Nova*. The incident in question was a fire that occurred at the nuclear power plant in Brown's Ferry, Alabama, causing 150 million dollars in damages and losses. *Nova* used this event as the starting point for a program examining the growing issue of the safety of nuclear power plants.

A close analysis of this transcript will involve virtually all of the techniques discussed in Part I of this book. One of the main problems is deciding upon the credibility of various experts in an area where few citizens have technical knowledge of their own. It is also important to pay close attention to the role of the narrator in this transcript. He does not pretend to be a neutral observer, but quite plainly advocates one side of the issue. There is nothing improper about this. It is simply important to remember that the narrator is one of the parties to the dispute, not the judge.

The transcript raises a whole series of questions for close analysis. Is the program reasonably fair in presenting all sides of the issue? Are the critics of atomic energy clear-headed and precise in their objections? Are the defenders of atomic energy responsive to these criticisms? Beyond such broad questions, the transcript contains many subtle details that are worth examining. Notice the two closing graphics. One states that "the Nuclear Regulatory Commission declined repeated invitations to appear in this film"; the other cites Albert Einstein's statement that it is important for the people of America to participate in the formulation of national policies concerning atomic energy. Why does the program end in just this way?

Incident at Brown's Ferry

NOVA

NARRATOR: On March 22, 1975 a workman in the world's largest nuclear power plant was checking for air leaks by using a candle flame. A fire started.... It went out of control ... burned for 7 hours ... resulted in 150 million dollars in damage and loss to this plant. The chief government investigator of this incident at Brown's Ferry, Alabama concluded it raised embarrassing questions about the safety of reactors throughout the United States. If the Brown's Ferry incident had been the worst possible nuclear accident, a recent government study called the Rasmussen Report predicts it could have immediately killed over 3,000 people, 45,000 more would have been severely injured from radiation, 300,000 more would suffer long-term health problems, including cancer and genetic defects. An area the size of the state of Pennsylvania would have been contaminated, and there would have been 15 billion dollars in property damage. But on the other hand, the Rasmussen Report predicts that the odds of any single individual getting killed in a nuclear plant accident in any given year are only 1 in 5 billion. Despite this predicted low risk, nuclear power as a safe energy source has become an emotional public issue that won't go away. Protests like this one [shown] at Seabrook, New Hampshire in 1976, ballot measures, lawsuits, grassroots action in America and European cities ... the cutting edge of the environmental movement.

In this film NOVA examines the growing nuclear safety issue. How the issue is resolved could have consequences affecting everyone on this planet. The 57 nuclear plants now operating in the United States supply 9 percent of the nation's electricity. About 150 plants operate in other countries around the world. Another 260 are under construction, and as many as one thousand are planned for completion by the year two thousand. If the nuclear industry has its way, they will be supplying half of the world's energy as the 21st century begins. The nuclear safety debate emerged in the early 1970's as a public issue after decades of private scientific dispute. In early 1975 pioneer nuclear physicist Ralph Lapp organized a petition in which eminent scientists declared themselves in favor of nuclear power as a safe energy source.

LAPP: In my opinion nuclear power is the very real answer to generating adequate amounts of electricity in the future for a dynamic American economy.

NARRATOR: A few months after Lapp's petition, another group of eminent scientists released a counter statement urging caution and stressing development of alternate energy sources. A leader in this drive was Henry Kendall, MIT physics professor and founder of the Union of Concerned Scientists.

KENDALL: Almost any source of energy in our society has less inherent risk than nuclear power, in my opinion. Nuclear power, with its enormous accumulations of radioactivity, can cause prompt death, can cause death by cancer, birth defects, and many other kinds of damage. It is potentially the most hazardous thing that we can incorporate in our society.

NARRATOR: Willard Libby, Nobel chemist, former member of the Atomic Energy Commission, a signer of the Lapp petition.

LIBBY: I think atomic power is an absolute necessity, and we have every reason to believe in its safety. We have a marvelous record. No major industry has ever been started that has a better record than the atomic power industry.

NARRATOR: Linus Pauling, another Nobel chemist and Nobel Peace Prize winner for alerting the world to radiation dangers from nuclear bomb testing. He supported Henry Kendall's declaration.

PAULING: I believe that nuclear power plants are unsafe, that they damage human beings, and are a real hazard.

NARRATOR: With scientists lining up on opposing sides, it was almost inevitable that the issue developed into a ballot measure question. In 1976, voters in seven different states struggled with the issue as they tried to decide how to vote.

MAN: Are we going to have enough electricity to continue living the style of life that we have been ... that I at least, I've been living?

WOMAN: The only thing I hear is money and comfort. Does it mean anything safe for our kids, or is it all the time material? I hear material, that's all I hear. This is a housewife talking baby talk.

SECOND WOMAN: I'm really very worried about the genetic problem that can be caused by radioactivity. I don't like the thought of my children having children that are mutants. That really upsets me a great deal.

SECOND MAN: You're making damn sure that they're not gonna have these plants unless they're so safe that you could put all the babies in Oregon in them and they'd be in terrific shape.

THIRD MAN: But the fact is, when you're dealing with nuclear power and radioactive materials, there's a higher standard of care. And there has to be, and you know there is a dispute, you know, on it, how safe should it be? And we're saying that it should be safer than it is.

NARRATOR: Anthony Roisman, a Washington attorney representing nuclear power opponents.

ROISMAN: I don't think that anybody is able to say at this time that nuclear power is safe, but I'm not sure that anybody can say conclusively that it's not safe. I think it's a question which has not yet been resolved. The issue is what do you do if you don't know the answer.

NARRATOR: If the answer can be figured out, it begins with knowing how a nuclear plant works. In the simplest terms, you start with uranium pellets . . . the pellets are fitted into 30 to 40 thousand fuel rods . . . long thin tubes made of a special metal alloy . . . the core—or heat source—of a large modern nuclear reactor. Control rods are interspersed with the fuel rods. All the rods are enclosed in a reactor vessel, in turn enclosed by larger and larger protective structures, often ending with the familiar dome. The fission process—the splitting of uranium atoms—begins when the control rods are separated from the fuel rods. Water surrounding the rods is heated under pressure to 600 degrees by the fission process and turns into steam. The steam circulates under pressure of one thousand pounds per square inch. Three hundred and fifty thousand gallons of water travel through the reactor core every minute. Then, in the form of pressurized steam, it travels through pipes—at high speed—and turns huge turbine generators that produce electricity. The process is similar to a coal or oil plant, except for the fuel and its special problems. If a large cooling pipe breaks this would stop the normal flow of water that keeps the fuel rods safely covered. Radioactive 600 degree water would spurt out of the pipe under great pressure as radioactive steam. As the water level dropped, the core would get hotter, a dangerous uncontrollable melting of the fuel rods would begin, leading to massive release of radiation—resulting in death, disease, contamination and long-term genetic defects. Plant designers recognize that pipe ruptures could occur. So all modern reactors have emergency systems to maintain the supply of coolant to the reactor core. But this emergency water must reach the core within a few minutes to prevent a melting and the release of radiation. All emergency systems are monitored and can be operated, if necessary, in the control room. Here, personnel are alerted to the need to use emergency systems by a vast array of lights and gauges. These devices are connected to a large number of cables, which are collected in long trays in a cable-spreading room, beneath the control room. The thousands of cables—a kind of central nervous system for the plant—are sorted out and routed to the valves, pumps and instruments that make the emergency systems work. It is extremely complex and crucial to the safety of the plant and to the ultimate safety of the public. Nuclear plants contain enormous amounts of radioactive materials. So extraordinary measures are normally taken inside the plants to protect workers from excessive irradiation. Workers routinely wear protective clothing and masks. They check themselves daily with radiation monitors to make sure they are not contaminated. In some plants workers are checked periodically from head to toe, in a Whole Body Counter. This is to make sure that radiation accumulated in their bodies has not exceeded government established permitted limits. These are fixed at two levels: one for workers, a lower one for the public. But some scientists contend both levels increase the chances of illness, especially cancer. The only really safe radiation level, they believe, is no radiation, inside or outside the plants. Ralph Lapp sees it another way.

LAPP: People who travel in airplanes get more radiation dose than the whole nuclear industry put together. That's on the basis of high altitude air travel where because of the fact that you're closer to space—more radiation comes through from outer space—you get a radiation dose. What I would urge is that the American people understand that radiation is all around you. You live in a sea of it.

PAULING: This natural background causes about 10 percent, an estimated 10 percent of the defective children who are born; the gene mutations producing these defective children. And about 10 percent of cases of cancer. This doesn't mean that it's all right to add another one percent as might be done by the high energy radiation from nuclear power plants, if there were a lot of them. This additional one percent means thousands of additional defective children born into the world, and thousands of additional cases of cancer. So this argument is a false and misleading one.

NARRATOR: Beyond this permitted radiation hazard to workers and the public, there is the larger fear of an accidental and catastrophic radiation release.
      How close was the Brown's Ferry incident to such a catastrophe? March 22, 1975. 12:20 P.M. Unit One of the plant. Polyurethane—a spongy foam—was being used to fill a 2″ by 4″ hole in the wall, where cables lead from the cable room to the reactor building. This was done to prevent any potential escape of radiation from the reactor building into the main part of the plant, and perhaps out into the surrounding area. To make sure the foam had in fact sealed the hole, a candle was lit and workers watched the flame to see if it was moved by escaping air. The foam caught on fire. Then the cable insulation. The air draft sucked the fire into the hole, then began to burn cable insulation inside the cable room. After fifteen minutes spent trying to snuff the fire out with rags, a decision was made to sound the fire alarm inside the plant. And so the incident at Brown's Ferry was underway. Superintendent Jim Green.

GREEN: I think there's a lot of misunderstanding on just what the fire was. Now, it was confined to one room, and the room was a concrete room and it was confined entirely to wiring. It was not a nuclear accident and we demonstrated that even under these most adverse conditions the plant could be shut down safely.

KENDALL: The Brown's Ferry accident was a very close call. I've studied it, my colleagues have studied it. We've talked to nuclear engineers at the Brown's Ferry plant who wish to remain anonymous and they've told us, and we agree, that that accident was in fact a close call.

NARRATOR: What exactly happened at Brown's Ferry? The record shows that it was the third fire caused by candle flames and foam. The first two were minor,

but no change in airleak-testing procedure was made. After this fire began, like
in so many accidents, a series of incredible unpredicted human and mechanical
failures had started. Wrong numbers were posted and called to sound the fire
alarms. There was insufficient breathing apparatus for fire-fighters and the system to refill the air supply was broken. After the fire was over, insurance inspectors said that it was "inexcusable" that the trays holding the cables were so
crowded together that ordinary fire extinguishers would not reach in. As the fire
spread, the chemical fire extinguisher in the cable room which was supposed to
trigger automatically didn't. A metal plate covered the hand switch so it
couldn't even be turned on manually. The spray nozzle of a hose would not let
the water reach the flames. Twenty minutes after the fire started, operators in
the control room noticed smoke leaking in, lights randomly blinking on and off,
a drop in the power output of the reactor. They noticed that all the emergency
cooling systems pumps had unexpectedly started. At 12:51, a half-hour after the
fire began, the problem had become so severe it was decided to "scram" the
reactor, which means reinserting the control rods between the fuel rods to shut
the operation down. The heat in the core cannot turn off instantly; it continues
to be produced for months after a "scram." So cooling water must constantly
cover the fuel, even after the control rods are in, to prevent a meltdown and release of radiation. Despite earlier specific warnings by government inspectors,
some of the cables for the main emergency system as well as its backup systems
were all in the same or nearby cable trays. This was in direct violation of federal
safety regulations. As the insulation around the cables continued to burn, the
emergency cooling systems were shorted out. At 12:55 the entire electrical supply to control and power these systems was lost. By then crucial monitoring instruments had failed. Engineers could no longer measure temperature or radiation in the core. Athens, Alabama is the nearest town with a fire department,
ten miles away. Chief Artie Bumpus takes up the story:

BUMPUS: Well, they called us a little after one o'clock and when we arrived
there was some wires afire, a lot of wires, several hundred. And they was using
their chemicals on it, dry chemicals and CO_2. We surveyed the situation and we
also tried the chemicals they was using and some of ours, but it failed to put
the fire out. And we saw right off that we was going to have to use something
else and of course water, being the best extinguishing agent, we recommended
that.

NARRATOR: With the fire still burning, and the emergency systems out of action, the water level dropped from its normal 200" down to an alarming 48". After several hours it was discovered that depressurizing the water would allow a
low pressure pump—not part of the emergency systems—to supply enough water to keep the core covered. This makeshift arrangement is what saved the core
from a catastrophic meltdown. Around 7 o'clock Chief Bumpus' suggestion to
use water was finally listened to and the cable fire was put out in 15 minutes.
Why didn't they use water 5 hours earlier?

BUMPUS: We didn't, could not get permission to use it. We was under their supervision down there and they wouldn't let us use water.

NARRATOR: Problems were not confined to the interior of the plant. The cable fire inside made it impossible to use automatic monitors to check for possible radiation release around the outside of the plant. Air samples were taken in two towns close to Brown's Ferry. But in Decatur, directly downwind, the man who was sent to check the radiation monitor had a surprise.

SAYWELL: This monitor was not operable at all on the day of the fire.

NARRATOR: If radioactive material from Brown's Ferry had been carried downwind to Decatur, instant knowledge was essential to protect the public. Because the first monitor was not working, it was necessary to drive to another. But that air sampler was not designed to give instant information. The filter had to be sent to a laboratory hundreds of miles away for analysis, which took two days. And local civil defense officials—in charge of evacuation plans—did not hear about the fire until two days after it was over.

GREEN: The core was never in danger of melting down throughout the fire event.

KENDALL: The circumstances of that accident would only had to have been casually different and there could well have been—almost certainly could have been—a catastrophic release of radioactivity. That's no cause for complacency. That's a severe and sharp warning.

NARRATOR: Both superintendent Green and Kendall's views appear to be justified: radiation did not leak out of the plant, but it seems to have been a close call. How could a major safety problem develop at a facility like Brown's Ferry? There had been two major safety reviews of the plant by the federal government, 207 on-site safety inspections between 1966—when they began construction—and the 1975 fire. Brown's Ferry was presumably licensed to operate under the strictest of federal regulations.

KENDALL: The worst accident we've had in the nuclear program, the fire at Brown's Ferry, was almost entirely the result of regulatory failure to correct problems that had been identified, to reduce the sensitivity of emergency systems to total failure.

LAPP: I find that the regulation of nuclear power plants is extremely tough, tougher than it was in the past; and I think that the regulation is perhaps going overboard. I think we're getting too much regulation.

ROISMAN: They've always regulated them to the possible, not to what is required. And I think that that is probably the single biggest flaw in the theory that the agency is vigorously regulating nuclear power. If it were regulating nuclear power, at least one utility sometime would have found the regulations so onerous that they would have sued them or sought relief. That's never happened. And I think that suggests that the agency has always been careful to be just as tough as the industry could take, but never any tougher. And I don't think that that is sufficiently tough.

NARRATOR: The Atomic Energy Act, signed by President Eisenhower in 1954, set up an agency that both promoted and regulated commercial use of the new peaceful atom. Under the Atomic Energy Commission—the A.E.C.—small experimental plants were begun. But private firms resisted getting into the atomic business without insurance protection, and insurance firms were unwilling to provide adequate coverage for this new hazard. Congress urged the A.E.C. to study power plant safety, hoping the findings would encourage insurance firms to provide coverage. The report came out in 1957, but was not generally publicized. It concluded that the outside limits of damage from a nuclear plant accident would result in 3,400 people killed within 15 miles of the plant; 43,000 would suffer severe radiation sickness in an area 44 miles from the plant; 182,000 people in a 200-mile circle would double their chances of getting cancer from radiation exposure. And there would be 7 billion dollars in property damage. With these gloomy figures in mind, A.E.C. Chairman Lewis Strauss led efforts to get the Price-Anderson Act passed. This meant federal tax money provided most of the 560 million dollars in insurance coverage since private insurance was reluctant. Commercial utilities then began to move into atomic energy on a larger scale. Larger, presumably safer, nuclear plants began operation. So with this experience record and the Price-Anderson Act up for possible renewal, it was expected that a new 1965 A.E.C. safety study would present a more favorable insurance picture. By this time—even with evacuation taken into account —27,000 deaths were estimated from a major accident; 73,000 would suffer severe radiation sickness; 300,000 would have greater risk of cancer. Property damage would total 17 billion dollars. The Price-Anderson Act was renewed, still at the 560 million dollar level. How enough people could get out of a major metropolitan center in enough time was not clarified. Significantly, the study concluded there was no rational way of working out the chances of such a disaster ever occurring, because there had not been a long enough history of nuclear plant operations on which to base a responsible prediction. They went on to say that it was "difficult to prove that nuclear power plants were safe enough to build." At first the A.E.C. claimed the new, ominous figures did not exist. Instead, leaving out the numbers, they reported that a major nuclear plant accident would "not be less, and under some circumstances would be substantially more, than the consequences reported" in 1957. The actual figures were kept secret for eight years, until Henry Kendall and the Union of Concerned Scientists used the Freedom of Information Act to open A.E.C. files. They found the safety regulators of the agency had been consistently overruled by the more powerful reactor-development branch. As a result in 1974 the agency was abolished. The Energy Research and Development Administration took over nuclear power promotion; N.R.C.—the Nuclear Regulatory Commission—now licenses plants and regulates safety. Ralph Lapp welcomed the change.

LAPP: The Atomic Energy Commission hadn't always behaved in the best way in the public sense. But now we have an open agency. You can get in. I can get in and do get into the Energy Research and Development Administration and the Nuclear Regulatory Commission. And to my mind, the openness of the industry is a real requirement, and I think it's satisfied today.

NARRATOR: The secret 1965 study decided it was impossible to determine the odds of an accident occurring in a nuclear plant. Nevertheless, with increased pressure by concerned scientists the A.E.C. began a new study in 1972. This was led by Norman Rasmussen, M.I.T. professor of nuclear engineering. The four million dollar study was released by the new Nuclear Regulatory Commission in October, 1975. For the first time, the government tried to estimate both chances and consequences of nuclear plant accidents.

RASMUSSEN: What we did was examine the plant and find out what kind of failures could release significant amounts of radioactivity. As engineers that's not so hard to do. And then we examined how likely it was to have failures of this type in the plant. Let's presume one of these failures is the rupture of a large pipe. How do we know how likely that is? Well, we examine how often pipes have failed in nuclear power plant accidents, in oil refineries, in fossil fuel plants, in chemical plants. We took the accumulated experience of the last few decades to get an idea of how likely that event was to occur. The same kind of investigation was made to find out how likely a valve is to fail, or a motor is to fail to operate, or any one of a number of the components in the plant that might contribute to the release of radioactivity.

NARRATOR: The Rasmussen Report rekindled the safety debate because it claimed to have examined, identified and established—with computer analysis —the risk of every possible radiation-releasing accident that could occur in a nuclear plant. Keith Miller of the University of California, computer consultant to the N.R.C., has his own outspoken private views.

MILLER: The entire basis of the Rasmussen Report is that somehow we trust them to have been able to think of every possible thing which could go wrong in a nuclear reactor, and analyze it. Here we've got a relatively new product, we've got thousand megawatt reactors and there's only a few units in operation for only a few years. Nevertheless, they seem to claim to have the analytical ability by testing this component, testing that component, guessing this probability, and that probability, to totally analyze the system, everything that might humanly go wrong with this manufacturer's operation, and end up telling us that here's a new product and it's going to be reliable for twenty thousand years. As an applied mathematician, I'm just amazed. I just can't believe it. What you can do with a large scale computer and a little of mathematical analysis.

RASMUSSEN: We as engineers can think of only the failures that we as engineers have come to recognize or imagine can happen in these kinds of systems. There may be a kind of failure that we've never thought of and never seen. However, for that to be true, it would also have to be a very unlikely failure because we've been looking and working with systems of this kind for nearly a century. That is, systems that pump water, pipe it around, turn turbine valves and so on. So for there to be a whole new mechanism that we've never thought of or contemplated it would have to be very unlikely. If it's very unlikely then it isn't going to contribute very much to the probability of failure of the plant.

KENDALL: In order to prove that a reactor is safe—and this has never been done —one has to identify all the important accidents, each one in this complex structure. Rasmussen claims he's done that. I don't believe it. And we have too many examples in our society of unexpected events and this is even more true in the complex and intricate structure of a nuclear reactor.

NARRATOR: We live in a dangerous world. The Rasmussen study compared the chances of a nuclear plant accident with a variety of natural and man-created accidents. The average chance of any individual dying in a fire in a given year is one in 25,000. This tragedy is in Sao Paulo, Brazil. The odds of any person dying from an airplane crash in any given year are one in 100,000 . . . of dying from an auto accident, one in 4,000. The odds of someone drowning, perhaps from a flood like the Teton Dam disaster in Idaho, are one in 30,000. The odds diminish when it comes to natural disasters like hurricanes or tornadoes . . . one in 2-and-a-half million. Without taking into account long-term radiation effects, Rasmussen's study contends that the odds are one in 5 billion that any individual will die in any given year from a nuclear plant accident—about as remote as you can get. George Kistiakowsky, Harvard chemistry professor, Science Advisor to President Eisenhower at the time the Atomic Energy Act was passed.

KISTIAKOWSKY: It is very difficult for me to accept assertions of the Rasmussen Report. And I should say that that's partly, this is because of my long experience with Atomic Energy Commission bureaucracy. In all my many years dealing with Washington, I would say that that bureaucracy is the most arrogant bureaucracy in the federal government. It's one whose motto seems to be the public be damned. And yet it is not the most intelligent, most competent bureaucracy. And it's the same bureaucracy which prepared, under Rasmussen's management, that report. So why should I believe it?

NARRATOR: The critics reject Rasmussen's odds. What do they think are the correct odds of a major nuclear plant disaster?

KENDALL: I believe and many colleagues agree with this, that if the program continues as it is now that within the next ten years, twenty years, perhaps twenty-five years, that there will be an accident of important size, one that would cause a crippling of the nuclear reactor program in the United States.

NARRATOR: Carl Hocevar, who resigned from the nuclear industry in 1974, has a more fundamental reservation about the Rasmussen Report.

HOCEVAR: Rasmussen does not take into the, take into account at all the possibility that the safety system itself may be improperly designed. He assumes that it is properly designed, and that occasionally a pump or something might fail. Okay? That is one of the reasons why he gets so, gets such relatively low probabilities for an accident. We don't know that that safety system will work 99 times out of a hundred. He's just assuming it will work that many times, and there's test data to prove, or to indicate that that may very well not be the case.

NARRATOR: For many years the government has been running tests trying to prove that the emergency systems in already operating nuclear plants will work, if a major cooling pipe breaks. These tests are done using computer analysis and scale models of nuclear plants. Until 1976 all tests failed. The heated pressurized water in the scale models did not allow the emergency cooling water to get to the core. And the computers couldn't accurately predict what was going to happen. So if a cooling pipe in a full-size plant actually does break, no one can yet say with certainty that the emergency systems will really work. Most of the tests are being done at the National Engineering Laboratory in Idaho. In this test, a miniature heating system is being subjected to a "blowdown"—the term describing what happens when a large cooling pipe breaks.

MAN: Three ... two ... one ... zero. We've got a blowdown.

NARRATOR: Temperature changes, water flows, pressures and other measurements from the small-scale system are combined into a computer code. Results from tests on full-scale reactor components are also included. This computer code is then used to predict how a full-scale reactor will behave during a real pipe break accident. It is not entirely theoretical, but it is not exactly the real thing either. Carl Hocevar, who worked on the project, had doubts about it.

HOCEVAR: We're taking a computer code which has been partially verified, with a system that is only one two-thousandth as large as the big machine, and we're saying that, on the basis of what we know on a small scale, we can predict what's going to happen on a big scale. And physics doesn't work that way.

NARRATOR: One partial answer to this problem may be the LOFT reactor— standing for Loss Of Fluid Test. Using nuclear fuel, LOFT will be subjected to a real pipe break accident, and the emergency core cooling system tested. But LOFT is still a scale model, one sixtieth the volume of a full-scale nuclear plant. Are scale model tests of nuclear plants adequate? Manager of the LOFT test program, Dr. Larry Ybarrando.

YBARRANDO: Scale models that we are using are indeed somewhat similar also to scale models which are used in other industries, for instance in the modeling of dams and flood situations, where people predict when the river is going to crest and how much land it is going to flood and for how long. The Army Corps of Engineers uses scale models for those types of things. For years we have tested aircraft in wind tunnels, rockets in wind tunnels.

MILLER: We have here with reactors a situation which is much, much more highly complex, much more difficult to do than aerodynamics. Yet in aerodynamics only recently have we been able to use computer programs with great success for the design of aircraft. And there, of course, we build the aircraft, and there we have constant interconnections between the computer programs, and we can check them out against wind tunnel tests. We build the aircraft, we fly it. We put a pilot in it, a test pilot. We don't go loading the public on this based completely on computer predictions.

LAPP: Large-scale, or full-scale testing of safety systems is not common to engineering. One does not test the San Francisco Golden Gate Bridge full-scale because it's too expensive. Nor does one test the Empire State Building full-scale by starting a fire in the basement and seeing if you can put it out. I mean, you just don't do it that way. What you do is you take the best engineering judgement that you can of the systems and where it is necessary to scale up a system, you do, but you do it on the basis of reasonable extrapolation or extension of your knowledge. Thus it is probably never going to be possible to test a nuclear reactor full-scale unless there is a true accident.

NARRATOR: With full-scale testing out of the question, all that seems to be left is a legacy of test failures using disputed computer codes. These same computer models are the basis for the licensing of nuclear plants by the federal government.

MILLER: Licensing computer models on which we test whether the present pressurized water reactors have adequate core coolant systems, depends upon the same codes which for 5 years have even been able to, unable to predict what happens in these small-scale experiments. Now when we go to the full size, there's room for a vast margin of error. We may be fooling the American government and public, and, what's more disturbing to me, we have indications that we're actually fooling the Nuclear Regulatory Commission and the licensing people within that commission. And there's just not enough leeway with the present system for error in our computerized analysis. If we make too many mistakes in our computerized analysis, this system will not be effective. It won't work.

NARRATOR: The Idaho facility primarily deals with pressurized water reactors. General Electric, which designs and manufactures boiling water reactors, the other major type, does its own safety testing in San Jose, California. G.E. does a variety of safety tests—this one tests the ability of separate parts of nuclear plants to withstand severe earthquakes. The fundamental behavior of steam injected into cold water is investigated. This test relates to what may happen if the emergency system is called into play. Sections of metal pipe are broken to study the behavior of cracks. Ultrasonic scanners verify that the pipes and welding used in the plants have no flaws. In early 1976 three nuclear engineers who worked at the San Jose facility quit because in spite of the testing programs, they felt nuclear power can never be made safe. One was Richard Hubbard.

HUBBARD: I resigned from my management position with General Electric because of my concerns about reactor safety. Design deficiencies that we were finding in the field and in our new, larger scaled-up products, in the regulatory deficiencies, and the quality deficiencies that I had experienced.

NARRATOR: Salomon Levy is General Electric's chief nuclear engineer in San Jose.

LEVY: I want to assure you that safety comes first in any of our work. Profits or economics clearly are secondary. You know that I could tell you personally that I would quit this corporation if at any time I felt that I had to do one thing for profit when I felt that I had to do the opposite for safety.

NARRATOR: Hubbard and his colleagues testified before Congress and the California legislature on what they thought had been going wrong.

HUBBARD: We pointed out that the G.E. containment on 19 of the operating plants in the United States—nearly a third of them—could not contain an accident. That over 20 forces had not been considered. Well, in this case the regulatory process worked because soon thereafter those plants were ordered to update their containment. We brought up that there are vibrations inside the cores of the reactors that weren't understood. Pipes were cracking and instruments were vibrating against fuel channels. Well, G.E.'s response to that was—we're building an 18 million dollar test facility. And I read in our San Jose newspaper last week that they may have it built by 1978. Maybe we'll have some tests by 1980.

LEVY: I think in reality the issues they've raised were on the way to being solved. I think certain cases I think there was some acceleration of the programs because they have focused attention on some of these problems and, clearly, as I have indicated before, we believe we have to be responsive to these criticisms.

NARRATOR: As chief nuclear engineer Levy indicates, resignations from the industry has led to acceleration in some safety testing. But that still leaves the public waiting until 1980 when vital tests are scheduled for completion. And what if these tests in San Jose or Idaho show that emergency systems in currently operating nuclear plants are faulty? Should the plants then be refitted to include better systems?

LAPP: Well, I think that you're limited there by the practicality of engineering a system that's been in operation and it would seem to me that the real issue is what is the safety margin that is built into the system, what is the probability that you would have an accident? That has been, I think, carefully examined by the Rasmussen study, and you see that whole emergency core cooling system is called into play only in the event of emergency. So you must ask yourself how likely is the emergency, and then back it up by saying, then, how probable is it that the emergency system will not work.

NARRATOR: If, as Ralph Lapp suggests, existing emergency systems cannot be changed even if tests show they are inadequate, then why bother to do the tests? James Zane of the Idaho testing program.

ZANE: The work we're doing today is trying to get an in-depth understanding or to get precision in our analytical models so we can make a case for perhaps removing some of those conservatisms in the licensing process. Perhaps give them a little more latitude in the power densities they run at.

NARRATOR: In other words, it appears that the computer and scale model Idaho tests are not designed to make plants safer, but to verify the safety of existing plants and possibly relax licensing standards for new plants. Keith Miller sees potential safety problems with this strategy.

MILLER: It's bad enough that they're telling the American leaders in public that these things are so grossly safe, but perhaps even worse is that there's indications that people within the Nuclear Regulatory Commission, the commissioners themselves—I have a letter from the chairman of the Nuclear Regulatory Commission—these people themselves are believing these grossly optimistic predictions. And that can be extremely dangerous. We can just wipe away certain problems in nuclear safety research and, such as trying to design a more adequate emergency core coolant system because we say, ah, that's totally improbable. And that can lead to a great relaxation in standards. It can lead to a great inadequacy in our safety systems for our nuclear industry.

NARRATOR: How do the critics propose that the problems of possibly inadequate safety systems can be solved? Attorney Anthony Roisman.

ROISMAN: I think a good starting point for knowing that plants are safe is to have the Advisory Committee on Reactor Safeguards, which reports to the Nuclear Regulatory Commission, issue a report that says there are no more unresolved safety problems in our judgment. Their last report had about 30 and they have had that number for quite a few years.

LAPP: Yes, the Nuclear Regulatory Commission has an Advisory Committee on Reactor Safeguards, which lists a number of unresolved technical issues. But that does not mean they are without solution. What that means is that the experts are requiring additional verification, additional research to give us an added margin of safety for those issues. I think that the whole question of technical issues of safety has been blown into the open now, the sunshine has come in because of these three G.E. engineers who resigned and who essentially cleaned the files out; they purged the system.

NARRATOR: In September, 1976 Unit One of Brown's Ferry—a plant designed by General Electric with safety systems tested in San Jose—went back into operation: the world's largest nuclear plant, supplying 1,000 megawatts of power to the Tennessee Valley in northern Alabama. Superintendent Jim Green.

GREEN: As a result of the fire we've certainly had a number of safety reviews and incorporated a number of modifications so that the plant is now safer than it was before.

BUMPUS: Since the fire they have put in sprinkler systems down there to protect these wires and they also put in more stand-pipe fire hose and things. The old saying is, "Wait 'til the mule gets out and then close the barn door."

NARRATOR: The cables where the fire had started have been realigned so that emergency systems are separated. And the cables are now covered with a fireproof material. G.E.'s chief nuclear engineer agrees that the incident at Brown's Ferry led to design changes in other plants.

LEVY: Subsequent to that plant, I think we have made some design changes in some of these plants. Learning from that experience we have assured ourselves that if a fire would take place it would be terminated quite a bit more rapidly and have arranged our electrical cables in a way that if a fire occurs in one area, we could still get the signals to all of our instruments by having the cable come from a completely separated area.

NARRATOR: Meanwhile, the new policy for checking air leak at Brown's Ferry, according to the Alabama press, is to use feathers. What are the odds of another incident like the one that happened at Brown's Ferry? Norman Rasmussen.

RASMUSSEN: Sure it could happen again. The crudest kind of statistics would say, we've now had about 250 to 300 plant years of operation. We've had one such event. So the first rough estimate statistically is that the occurrence of such an event is one in 200 per plant per year.

NARRATOR: The fact is that, worldwide, the nuclear industry has never produced the ultimate catastrophe. However, there have been many nuclear plants where unanticipated problems have occurred. At Windscale, England there was a fire and partial core meltdown in 1957. Radioactive materials escaped to nearby pastureland; traces were found hundreds of miles away. Radioactive Iodine 131, passed on to humans through contaminated cows' milk, can cause leukemia and thyroid cancer. Thousands of gallons of milk were dumped. In 1966 at Unit One of the Fermi plant near Detroit there was another partial core meltdown. The plant has closed permanently. In 1970 the huge Commonwealth

Edison plant near Chicago was shut down after 50,000 gallons of radioactive water and steam escaped from the reactor vessel. There were 17 major shutdowns in the first 19 months of operation of the Vermont Yankee plant because of safety violations, fuel rods buckling, and other equipment failures. At Millstone in Connecticut pipe cracks and leaks of sea water into the cooling system led to a six-month shutdown in 1972. Turkey Point near Miami, Florida—five failures of cooling pumps, leakage of radioactive water. Indian Point, near New York City—the government safety inspector quit in 1976, urging the plant be shut down immediately because "it's almost an accident waiting to happen." Indian Point is still operating. In another plant whose name still remains secret, radioactive water was mixed up with water for the plant's drinking fountains. In 1974 reporting on the many nuclear plant incidents, an A.E.C. report said that none threatened public health, but added "The absence of more serious effects is largely the result of good luck." Strict licensing and regulation should provide greater assurance than "good luck"—but will it ever be possible that the licensing process can guarantee that a Brown's Ferry-type accident—or worse—won't occur in another nuclear plant? Carl Hocevar.

HOCEVAR: The licensing process is basically only as good as man is. If we're infallible and we can think of all the things that can occur, maybe we can develop a failsafe licensing process. Since we didn't anticipate what happened at Brown's Ferry, and I suspect we can't anticipate a lot of other things that are going to happen in the future—I'm basing that on past experience—we do not have an infallible licensing process.

NARRATOR: Infallible or not, billions of dollars have been invested in hundreds of new plants that are planned or under construction, no matter what the critics say. Do the critics want to close this huge industry down?

MILLER: I'm not suggesting that we do away with nuclear power. We have some serious technical difficulties with nuclear power right now though, and these need to be solved.

KENDALL: If the problems can be resolved, nuclear power can make a useful contribution to the nation's energies. If these safety problems cannot be resolved, then nuclear power is an unacceptable energy source and ultimately will simply have to be phased out.

ROISMAN: Put it on the back shelf, use the technologies in other areas—energy conservation and other kinds of energy that we know are safe—until such time as nuclear power is either proven to be safe, or proven to be not safe. And in the meantime, phase out those construction permits and operating licenses that are in existence and halt the issuance of new ones.

KENDALL: The nuclear program in this country has developed for 25 years. There are immense investments in it now. There's professional pride associated with it, and there's been the hope for many years that nuclear power would supply cheap, inexpensive safe electricity. As someone said, too cheap to meter. This promise is a bit tarnished now. In order to turn this around one needs citizen action because of the immense size of the industry. Its immense political clout. But this can be done. It's being done now in the area of nuclear reactor safety by citizens groups and it needs the support of the American people.

NARRATOR: Citizen groups have indeed organized successful drives to put nuclear plant safety on state ballots. Volunteers and voters at large focused on the growing controversy.

LINORE: I don't consider myself on any level an expert, but I just understand that I want to take care of the environment. And if I can do it this way, by just saying, "Hey, let's be reasonable. Let's just be careful," and I think that's all the proposition is. It's just a plea to be careful.

DOCTOR: Not having tested the safety systems and not having any solution for the waste storage, to me is incredible. Because the amount of radioactivity that's there now is exceedingly toxic and there are a great number of people in the medical community that are very much worried and very concerned with the consequences of a massive accident.

DARLENE: My children and myself, we're the ones who are going to pay the price if nuclear power is not safe enough. And, therefore, I think we need to be very actively involved in the decision.

NARRATOR: The nuclear industry—with federal help—fought back. They stressed their safety records, and introduced economic fears, as this campaign ad demonstrates.

KATHY HIGLEY: Hello, I'm Kathy Higley. I'm majoring in physical chemistry at Reed College, and I operate our research nuclear reactor. A lot of students like myself will soon be out of school and looking for jobs. Our energy supply is very important to us. No energy—no jobs. Please join me and vote "no" on measure 9. It would ban further development of nuclear power, a clean and safe energy source. Vote "no" on 9, and beat the ban.

NARRATOR: As nuclear power becomes a public issue, the technical complications are reduced to bumper stickers and 30-second TV spots, as in this advertisement.

ANNOUNCER FROM AD: The utilities say nuclear power is safe, but ask about radioactive waste leaks and that series of so-far small accidents, and they admit there are a few bugs. Still they say, it's worth the danger. But is it? Shouldn't we prove that nuclear emergency systems are safe before we build more plants? Measure 9 simply says, yes. But then you're taking the risk. You have to decide.

NARRATOR: All 1976 ballot measures lost, but the debate is not over. The California legislature did pass three laws that achieved the goals of the ballot proponents in that state. President Carter endorsed the Oregon ballot measure in his election campaign. Congress is taking a new look. New state ballot drives are underway, so citizens will continue to be asked to decide these issues. But should this be a voting matter, or should it simply be left to the experts?

PAULING: Everyone should decide these important questions. I do think that scientists have a special role to play. They may understand the technical aspects of these problems better than other people. I think that they have the duty of explaining them. Not only explaining, presenting the facts, but also expressing their own opinions. That's why I say that I am opposed to nuclear power plants and I say why I am.

LAPP: I happen to believe that the citizen has a very real interest in nuclear safety because, after all, he is the person who is at risk. On the other hand, there's a great gap separating the public from the expert. The expert presumably knows what the technology is, what its risks are; but the expert is also a specialist who has a limited frame of reference and sometimes a limited vocabulary. And the public is not apt to understand him very well. Therefore, it seems to me that this is a question of great delicacy for democracy, because sooner or later you have to trust somebody, and if you don't trust government, who do you trust?

DARLENE CARLSON: On the one hand, the industry says everything is fine. On the other hand, we hear people in positions of importance saying everything is not fine. And so I'm caught in the middle then. Whom am I supposed to believe?

NARRATOR: Leading international scientists disagree, so how can the ordinary citizen ever make a sound voting decision?

RASMUSSEN: Leading international scientists disagree on most everything is, ah, certainly true, especially when they're talking about things outside their field of expertise. And so one has to judge how well a man has studied and understood the issue he's talking about. Does he fully know the details of it, because scientists are no better than anybody else at making a decision in a technical area, unless it's one that they've studied.

KENDALL: Citizens are able to understand these issues. They are able to resolve the conflicting claims, and the whole history of the nuclear program with its difficulties, its poor reliability, its poor accident record speaks for itself, and is one of the reasons why the nuclear program is in so much trouble presently.

NARRATOR: Pressure by citizen groups, scientists and the growing number of people who quit the industry and the government agencies, all have helped focus attention on the whole question of whether or not nuclear power has yet been proven to be a safe energy source. For any improvements or changes, it seems likely the same kind of pressure will have to intensify. Those opposed to our growing dependence on nuclear power will have to press for major commitments to energy conservation, and intensive development of alternate energy sources. Those in favor will have to hope that the ultimate accident will never happen. Meanwhile, nuclear power plant risks continue—how high or low we probably will never really know. Should we continue to live with a technology with such potential hazards? A technology that—like the incident at Brown's Ferry—can be disrupted by a candle flame?

GRAPHIC: "The Nuclear Regulatory Commission declined repeated invitations to appear in this film."

GRAPHIC: "... to the village square we must carry the facts of atomic energy ... from there must come America's voice."   Albert Einstein

Affirmative Action and Reverse Discrimination

The basic issue concerning affirmative action quotas and the "reverse discrimination" that they may cause is easily stated. If a quota is established guaranteeing that a certain percentage of positions will go to members of minority groups, then it is possible for the following situation to arise: A is a member of a minority included in the quota whereas B is not. B is in every other way more qualified for the position than A. A receives one of these positions, and B does not. (The position might be a job supported by a government contract, a place in an entering law school class, etc.)

Those who oppose affirmative action quotas claim that this result amounts to discrimination in reverse, since B's race is a factor, perhaps even the determining factor, in his or her failure to receive a position that A receives. Those who favor affirmative action goals or quotas usually argue that they are the only effective means for overcoming centuries of past discrimination.

Two strong and articulate statements of the opposing views on this subject are presented below. The first is a speech made by Senator James L. Buckley on presenting a bill entitled the "Antidiscrimination Act of 1976." Buckley's central argument is that the system of affirmative action quotas developed by the United States Department of Health, Education and Welfare (HEW) derives no legitimacy from the Civil Rights Act of 1964 or from President Lyndon B. Johnson's Executive Order No. 11246. Since these are the only possible sources of legal legitimacy, Buckley argues, the system of quotas has no *legal* justification at all. In a sub-argument, rather reminiscent of Kyl's speech, Buckley produces a parade of horrors showing, to his satisfaction, that HEW often acts in arbitrary, capricious, and even silly ways. Of course, the underlying argument, or perhaps assumption, of Buckley's position is that discrimination on the basis of race, color, religion, sex, or national origin is always wrong and should not be part of a national policy, no matter how laudable its goals might be.

An opposing position is stated by Jack Greenberg, director-counsel of the National Association for the Advancement of Colored People (NAACP) Legal Defense Fund, Inc. Greenberg's statement opposes Buckley's position in a fundamental way. He first argues that we commonly use other criteria than "best qualified" in assigning jobs or admitting people into schools. Considerations of merit are sometimes overriden in order to give preference to veterans, those with seniority, and the handicapped, for example, and such practices are justified in terms of their general social benefits. Greenberg then argues that the long tradition of discriminating against minorities can be overcome only by strong measures, and that in this case, as in others, the claims of merit must be modified to achieve an important social goal.

Affirmative Action: Congressional Statement
JAMES L. BUCKLEY

Mr. BUCKLEY. Mr. President, 12 years ago, the United States made it illegal to discriminate in employment on grounds of race, color, religion, sex, and national origin. That was accomplished when the Civil Rights Act of 1964 became law, and it was properly heralded as the end of one era and the beginning of another. What had been a readily accepted element of the American tradition, equality of opportunity, was made a matter of legal right for all Americans.

There is no question but that some Americans, most notably for reasons of race, were being denied equality of opportunity. This legislation, not only defined legal rights and duties, but it also proved to have a profound and largely beneficial social impact on the United States. Whatever enforcement problems have subsequently developed, the case for the passage of the law has, it seems to me, been fully vindicated. But, unfortunately, there is more to the story of the Civil Rights Act of 1964 and the national commitment to end discrimination.

To understand the present problem one must go through the details of the legislation in question. First, title VI of the Civil Rights Act of 1964 requires that any program or activity, including State and local government, which receives Federal financial assistance must, as a matter of law, treat all participants equally without regard to race, religion, color, sex, or national origin. The act, in title VII, further prohibits any Federal contractors, private employers, or labor organizations from discriminating against applicants for employment on any of the above grounds. In effect, the Congress in passing the legislation was ab-

* *Congressional Record,* Vol. 122, No. 28 (March 2, 1976).

stracting the social policy articulated in Brown against Board of Education, the landmark school segregation case handed down in 1954 by the U.S. Supreme Court, and extending it to Federal programs and private employment. The policy was one in which discrimination on grounds of race, religion, color, sex, or national origin was prohibited as constituting the antithesis of the principles of individual equality, individual dignity, and individual justice on which the American Nation was founded; principles which the civil rights movement was designed to translate into full practice.

The second step in the process was taken on September 24, 1965, when then President Lyndon Johnson issued Executive Order No. 11246 requiring Federal contractors to take affirmative action "to insure that applicants are employed, and that employees are treated during employment, without regard to their race, creed, color, or national origin." Later a sex discrimination prohibition was added to the affirmative action requirements.

The point was clear: The policy of the U.S. Government was not only to prohibit discrimination on the grounds of race, religion, color, sex, or national origin, but to force action to end inherently discriminatory practices. There would be no substantial issue today if, in the intervening years, the Federal Government had not changed its policy. While the civil rights law has not been amended with respect to any of the anti-discrimination provisions and while the Executive orders have not been revised in any substantial way, the policies of the Federal Government have changed substantially. It is to this change that the legislation I am today introducing is addressed.

Lest there be any doubt about congressional intent behind the Civil Rights Act, and specifically on the question of the nature of discrimination, the Senator from Minnesota (Mr. HUMPHREY), a leading supporter of the act, stated that there "must be an intention to discriminate" before one could be held to have violated the law. He also stated that the act "does not require an employer to achieve any kind of racial balance in his work force by giving any kind of preferential treatment to any individual or group—the express requirement of intent" would prevent de facto circumstances from being manipulated into a finding of discrimination. Senators CASE of New Jersey and CLARK of Pennsylvania joined Senator HUMPHREY in that analysis.

The first notable change came in February 1970, when the Department of Labor adopted regulations which included the language:

> An affirmative action program is a set of specific result-oriented procedures to which a contractor commits himself to apply every good faith. The objective of these procedures plus such efforts is equal employment opportunity.

It is important to make note of the point that within this rather obscure rhetoric is the redefinition of "opportunity" to mean "result." The transposition of Federal policy occurred when opportunity was defined in terms of result, or in the later language of composition.

A more explicit change in Federal policy came about in late 1971 with the adoption of revised order No. 4 by the U.S. Department of Labor, which was adopted pursuant to both the Civil Rights Act and the Executive order. In revised order No. 4, there is no attempt to define "discrimination," as such. A reading of the order requires the conclusion that for purposes of affirmative action requirements, discrimination is equated with "underutilization," which is defined "as having fewer minorities or women in a particular job classification than would reasonably be expected under their availability." The order then details a long series of factors which are to be relied upon in determining whether there is "underutilization."

But the unreasonableness or lack thereof of the criteria begs any serious questions of public policy. Wherever in the law did the doctrine of "underutilization" become the controlling factor in determining whether a party subject to the Civil Rights Act was in violation of the act?

The change came about subtly, through the use of the relatively anonymous mechanism of rulemaking whereby an enforcing agency, such as the Department of Health, Education, and Welfare—HEW—can expand and even redefine the essence of the law it is supposed to enforce. The legal requirement which was initially intended to guarantee equality of opportunity was now being defined as specifically requiring the manipulation of results. It is at that point that the prohibition against discrimination was turned into a positive duty to discriminate. There is no way to insure a certain result other than by discriminating.

There are a number of examples which illustrate the point. One of the most striking is to be found in the case of the University of California, at Berkeley, of all places, where the Federal Government relied solely upon the racial and sex composition of the work force to prove a violation of the Civil Rights Act. In June 1971, HEW descended upon the campus to conduct a compliance review. The study lasted for 1½ years.

Berkeley personnel did their best to supply all of the data HEW requested. The review culminated in a demand that the university adopt an affirmative action hiring program, although the university was never specifically charged with having discriminatory hiring practices. Nor was the university told what it had to do. The frustration of the university was best expressed by Robert Kerley, the vice chancellor for administration, who said:

> It was a bit like being in a ballgame against a team that was making
> up the rules as it went along.

The university never really had the benefit of a clearcut Government position. There was never any explicit charge or specific demand.

The responsibility for developing an "acceptable"—to HEW—affirmative action program was on the university. What the university was required to overcome was not a charge of discrimination, but of "underutilization" of minorities, a determination that was in part based upon the population composition of the bay area. What that had to do with Berkeley's hiring practices is unclear, but it was part of the utilization formula against which the university was judged by bureaucrats having the discretionary power to withhold substantial Federal funding.

In order to come into compliance with the Civil Rights Act, as imple-
mented by HEW and its guidelines, and to retain the $2.8 million in Federal con-
tracts which the university held, the campus administration commenced to
gather the necessary data in order to develop "goals"—quotas—which would
bring the school up to full "utilization." The project was costly, consuming the
time of 10 staff members and countless hours of many others connected with
the university. But the first Berkeley plan did not satisfy the HEW officials and
the threat to cut off the Federal contracts was carried out, resulting in the delay
of $2.8 million in contracts and no doubt creating severe administration prob-
lems with staff payroll and other budgetary obligations. Still HEW did not take
an overt position on what would constitute "compliance."

Faced with such an intolerable situation, the university had its own statistics department develop plans for hiring minority personnel, with specific goals
and timetables. The plan was acceptable to HEW. The utilization formula which
was agreed to called for, among other things, certain goals which implied that
the university was "under-quota" or "under-utilizing" minority personnel. Included in the plan was the university's commitment to hire 1.38 black professors in the social welfare department and 1.39 Spanish surnamed and Native
Americans—Indians—as professors in the civil engineering department. Monitoring the affirmative action program continues to cost the university at least
$400,000 per year. We must remember all this comes against a background
wherein the university was not charged with discrimination. But in order to
come into "compliance," the university would most certainly have to discriminate and expend substantial resources.

In a less complex situation, but one which is just as outrageous, Congress-
woman Edith Greene, in November 1972, testified in a House of Representatives
hearing regarding her own city of Portland, Oreg., which was found to be in non-
compliance by HEW. Portland, with a black population of 5 percent of the total,
had minority representation in the school system of 15 percent of the whole. But
because Portland did not have 15 percent representation in each and every job
classification within the school system, the city was found to be guilty of discrimination as defined by HEW.

As recently as August 1975, HEW made a computer run to determine what
school systems, if any, assigned faculty to schools in majority/minority patterns
that did not mathematically reflect the ratios within the school system in which
they were employed. Ninety school systems, including Buffalo, N.Y., were in-
dicted by computer for no reason other than the fact that the school administra-
tions had not kept the ratios relatively uniform in schools throughout the system. Here there was not even a charge of underutilization. It was asserted that
random assignment was per se discrimination. In Buffalo, and perhaps elsewhere, HEW withheld Federal funds under the authority of the Civil Rights Act.

In another recent case, the Department of Justice, using the goals and guidelines theory of discrimination developed by the Departments of Labor and HEW,
filed a civil rights suit against the Sheet Metal Workers Union, Local 28, of
New York City. The suit charged the union with discrimination. The allegation
of discrimination relied upon the composition of the union membership for

proof of discrimination. A court-ordered quota has been set requiring the union to hire minorities until the membership in the union has been brought up to 29 percent minority. But again, as in the cases brought under agency guidelines, there was no charge of discrimination as such. Underutilization was held to be discrimination, pure and simple.

A second element, in the case of the Sheet Metal Workers Union, was a test administered by the union as part of the application process for apprenticeships. In the landmark Griggs against Duke Power Co. case, the Supreme Court held that when a test eliminates more minorities than nonminorities, it becomes the duty of those administering the test to prove its relevance to the job. But since that decision, EEOC and others have moved Federal Government policy to the point where validation of the test is a practical impossibility. Prof. Nathan Glazer's research in "Affirmative Discrimination"—New York Basic Books, 1975—forced him to conclude that the only test which could be safely administered was a typing test, and the Equal Employment Opportunity Commission is not entirely sure about that. But because minorities in New York City did not do as well as nonminorities in the test scores, the Court upheld that the minorities had been "victimized" and ordered the union to eliminate the test and to pay back pay to those allegedly victimized. But all of this happened in spite of section 703(h) of the Civil Rights Act, where the clear meaning of the language restricts the review of tests to the question of whether they are "designed, intended, or used to discriminate because of race, color, religion, sex, or national origin."

To comply with the Federal district court order, the Sheet Metal Workers Union has been ordered to discriminate, even against those longstanding members presently unemployed and standing by until construction work again becomes available. Nothing in the court's decision addressed the rights of those who would now be discriminated against and the justice due them. Again, this is all against a background where there is no charge of discrimination.

There is also the problem of costs. The Congressional Research Service has, at my request, been collecting what data there is on the question of the financial costs of the affirmative action programs now being imposed. CRS found that the costs of affirmative action for the Federal Government alone in fiscal year 1976 are estimated at, unbelievably, $329,296,367. The estimated costs to higher education for the academic year 1974–75 was more than $75 million. The study is not complete, but the initial indication is that the costs are literally astronomical.

After having complained to the executive agencies over the past years over these distributors of the concept of civil rights, I am now convinced that the only solution rests with the Congress of the United States. While it seems to me that the 1964 act makes the congressional intent crystal clear, others in the Federal Government, courts and agencies alike, have succeeded in perverting the law to the point of rendering it unrecognizable.

Discriminatory hiring practices have no place in our country. America should pride itself upon guaranteeing each of its citizens an equal opportunity to earn a decent living. To benefit one man at the expense of another, for reasons no more relevant than sex, or race, or national origin, is a perversion of civil rights. Reverse discrimination is discrimination, and it was discrimination the Congress prohibited 12 years ago.

Consequently, today I am introducing the Antidiscrimination Act of 1976. The legislation is designed to reinforce the 1964 law and to clarify any ambiguities which may have been created through agency rulemaking and overly broad court decision.

The bill contains three major provisions:

First. It would reaffirm the Federal Government's role in requiring as a condition of receipt of any grant or contract that the recipient submit an affirmative action program which assures nondiscrimination on the basis of race, religion, color, national origin, or sex, along the lines of Executive Order No. 11246. Such programs would not be allowed to impose the establishment of employment goals, timetables, or quotas based on race, religion, color, national origin, or sex.

Any affirmative action program undertaken by contractors, grantees, private employers, or labor organizations, whether fashioned by a Federal agency or a Federal court, would be limited to attempts to expand the pool of applicants or participants. Plans could include an expansion of recruiting practices, including, but not necessarily limited to the expansion of normal advertising and promotion methods, consistent with the financial ability of the concerned parties to undertake such a program. Such programs could—in fact should—preclude any qualifications that are unrelated to job requirements, and hence a potential vehicle for discrimination.

The goal would be to insure that no particular group would encounter any unusual difficulty in seeking out information regarding the opportunity which is advertised, or in being judged on the basis of qualifications alone.

Second. In all cases arising under the law of the United States, or any Federal regulation or Executive order, where the Federal Government seeks a finding of discrimination, no finding would be allowed solely on the basis of the composition of the workforce or membership in the business, union, or program. Such statistical data would be admissible as evidence, however, in any hearing before an appropriate agency or court.

Third. The Antidiscrimination Act of 1976 would prohibit the Federal Government from requiring that data be collected regarding race, color, religion, sex, or national origin. The acceptance by the Government of such information would be limited to discovery proceedings under the direction of a Court.

There is a certain difficulty in offering this legislation. The plain meaning of the original legislative language does not need changing. Moreover, this legislation would not be offered but for the actions taken and interpretations made by the various departments and agencies charged with enforcing the law.

The challenge before the Congress is to do away with quotas, goals, and timetables which necessarily result in discrimination against some for the benefit of others. There is no suggestion made by me that we as a nation withdraw one iota from our commitment to end discrimination on the grounds of race, religion, color, sex, or national origin. To the contrary, the legislation I am offering today will, if enacted into law, reinforce the principles of nondiscrimination and equality of opportunity that are essential to a just and free society.

Affirmative Action, Quotas and Merit

JACK GREENBERG

The moral legitimacy of affirmative action and quotas favoring racial minorities must be assessed in a social and historical context, in the light of the many conflicting values that our society holds.

Traditionally, we profess reliance upon grades, scores and experience as bases upon which to assign jobs or admit to schools those who by these prevailing measures of competence are said to be most qualified.

Recently, as a result of litigation, we have found that these criteria often fail to select the best candidates or are not job-related. But when it works, the merit standard often picks those who do in fact perform better, and by offering incentive probably makes society more productive.

However, many dissimilar, widely accepted or barely tolerated criteria that serve other values often are designed to select persons other than those best qualified.

A tenured professor will hold his position in spite of competition from younger, better, more vigorous scholars. Tenure is thought, however, to serve the important societal interest in academic freedom by enabling teachers to take controversial positions without fear and by shielding them against petty politics.

Seniority rights advance individual security, worker satisfaction and job loyalty by promoting older workers although younger persons may be objectively more qualified, while, paradoxically, compulsory retirement favors younger persons over older, experienced, and perhaps more competent workers.

The union shop favors a union member against a superior outside competitor in the belief that a strong labor movement is more important than the employers' right to hire and fire on the basis of whim, or merit.

Hiring and promotional preferences granted to veterans express national gratitude for military sacrifice and expressly subordinate claims of superior persons without military experience.

Even the most prestigious schools consider more than marks as criteria for admission—to obtain a geographically and otherwise diverse student body and thereby enhance the educational experience of all. Some admissions officers contend that if "all other things are equal" they will favor a great industrial or financial family by admitting one of its children. Perhaps this helps raise funds.

There are not many in positions of influence who have not been asked to help a relative or friend get a job or be admitted to a school. This is called word-of-mouth recruitment, "old boy network," or "pull." It is natural to assist friends and useful to have additional information about candidates. But persons not plugged into the network do not have the same access.

One would imagine, to pick only names from the past, that Carnegies and Morgans did not travel a rough road in getting an education and obtaining employment. Inheritability of wealth is an economic incentive, and strengthens the

* *The New York Times*, February 7, 1976, p. 21.

family, although some see unfairness in benefiting those who played no part in creating the wealth.

The general, sometimes grudging, sometimes comfortable acceptance of antimerit preferences requires close scrutiny of arguments that affirmative action for blacks violates America's merit ethic.

Even the most conservative must agree that the historic injustices that America has heaped upon its black citizens are beyond calculation.

After the abolition of the inhumane institution of slavery, racial segregation and discrimination persisted in virtually the same form, almost unchecked for generations.

In our lifetime, Washington, D.C., as well as other portions of our nation, compared with Capetown, South Africa, in the entrenchment of apartheid, and lynchings were frequent.

Black unemployment remains about double white unemployment, and health, housing and other inequities persist.

America's historic public and private racial discrimination has left a legacy of inequality and inopportunity, and infuses virtually every major social problem: unemployment, poverty, crime, welfare, slum housing.

The mere assertion of new policy with respect to black citizens has not adequately changed the social situation. To select someone for employment or school on the basis of race, as a means of breaking the cycle of inferior education, poverty, unemployment, and damaged families, has at least as great moral justification as the many criteria we use other than so-called merit.

LEGAL REASONING

9

At first sight, it might seem that the pattern of legal reasoning should be simple and straightforward. A legal issue, it might seem, looks like this: A criminal law exists prohibiting a certain kind of behavior and assigning a punishment to those who violate it. A person is accused of violating this law, so a trial is held to decide whether *in fact* he has done so. If the jury decides the facts show that he has, they find him guilty. The judge then hands down the punishment stated in the statute. Or, in a civil suit, one party sues another for breach of contract. Since states have laws governing the formation of contracts, once more a trial is held to decide whether *in fact* a breach of contract (as defined by these statutes) has occurred. If a breach of contract is found, then the judge awards damages as the law prescribes.

Actually, some cases do fall into this simple pattern, but the most interesting ones do not. In order for a case to be settled in this mechanical way, both the law and the facts must be clear. Often they are not. Starting from the side of the law, statutes and regulations are often vague. For example, a law may insist that people show "reasonable care" not to harm the person or property of another. Needless to say, there is no sharp line between conduct that shows reasonable care and conduct that does not. To cite another example, antitrust laws prohibit "combinations in restraint of trade"—a notion that may be widely interpreted. The situation becomes more complicated when we take into account the *common law* tradition of English and American law. A particular decision must be made in the context of past decisions and, as far as possible, be consistent with them. The most obvious difficulty with

this is that the past decisions may not be consistent with each other.
There can also be conflicts between statutes and the common law, between interpretations of statutes, between different statutes, between
jurisdictions. We can add to this the complication that a given case may
"fall between the cracks." Human beings have a remarkable ability to
produce weird cases that would tax even the wisdom of Solomon.

Turning now to facts, they must be established through testimony,
and this testimony can also contain conflicts. In a criminal procedure,
the prosecution must establish its case beyond a "reasonable doubt" (another inherently vague expression). In a civil case the situation is different. Although the procedural rules can be very complicated, the general
idea is this. The case is won by the party who shows that the *preponderance* of evidence favors his or her side of the case. Although this is a bit
too simple, it is sometimes said that if the scales tip ever so slightly in
favor of A rather than B, then A wins the case. The complicated rules
that govern civil procedures are intended to guarantee that each party
has a fair chance to show that the preponderance of evidence falls on his
or her side of the case.

Together, the vagueness and conflicts within the *law* and the indeterminacy of *facts* often make it impossible to settle legal disputes in
a mechanical way. Of course, vagueness and conflict are not special to
the law, and it often happens that available facts are not conclusive. But
outside the law, we can often just let matters ride—we can postpone a
decision until further facts are established, or even declare that the issues are too vague to admit of any decision. This is rarely an option in
a legal case. If A sues B, then either A or B must win. Throwing the case
out of court amounts to ruling in favor of the defendant. A decision
must be made, and usually in a relatively short period of time. Many legal decisions must be made in a context of vague and perhaps conflicting laws, mixed precedents, and incomplete information—all under the
pressure of time.

With all this in mind, we can see why, as Edward Levy has remarked, legal reasoning is *analogical*.[1] By this he does not mean that
every argument that takes place in a court of law is analogical, for many
of the arguments—perhaps most—are guided by common-sense standards. But given the indeterminacies we have noticed, a legal situation
may look like this:

Laws and precedents   Laws and precedents
favorable to A.   favorable to B.

Fact
situation

---

[1] Edward Levi, *An Introduction to Legal Reasoning* (Chicago: University of Chicago
Press, 1963). There is no better introduction to the study of legal reasoning than this fine
little book.

The attorney for A will try to establish and then stress those facts that bring the case under laws and precedents favorable to his client's side of the case. B's attorney will, of course, proceed in the opposite direction. It is important to see that this debate can take place even when there is *no* disagreement concerning facts. By stressing certain similarities and playing down others, each attorney will try to move the case under those laws and precedents that favor his client's side of the case. Exchanges will often have the following form:

A: Your honor, may I remind the court that in cases of this kind
   it has always held . . .

B: Your honor, the case before us is of an entirely different sort
   from those just cited . . .

The pattern of argument here is analogical because the whole point is to get the court to agree that the particular case is *more like* one line of cases than another.

Analogy in Legal Reasoning

The analogical aspect of legal reasoning is illustrated by the following classic case from the law of contracts: *Hawkins v. McGee.* McGee performed an operation on Hawkins that proved unsuccessful, and Hawkins sued for damages. He did not sue on the basis of malpractice, however, but on the basis of breach of contract. His attorney argued that the doctor initiated a contractual relationship by saying "I will guarantee to make the hand a hundred percent perfect hand." The attorney for the surgeon replied that these words, even if uttered, would not be an offer of a contract, but merely an *expression of strong belief.* The issue before the court, then, was to decide which is the more plausible way of interpreting this *speech act.* More precisely, the court was asked to rule on a *question of law* as opposed to a *question of fact.* The question of fact took the following form:

Did the defendant make the statement attributed to him?

This is a question appropriately settled by a jury.

If the doctor did make the statement attributed to him, would
it amount to an offer of a contract?

This is not a question for a jury, but for a judge, to decide, and if it is answered No, then the case should have been thrown out of court rather than sent to the jury. This was the basis for an appeal. The court decided that the remarks attributed to the doctor could more reasonably be

viewed as an offer of a contract than as an expression of strong belief.
It thus rejected the appeal on this question of law and ruled that the
lower court was correct in submitting the case to the jury for a determination of the question of fact.[2]

Hawkins v. McGee

BRANCH, J. 1. The operation in question consisted in the removal of a considerable quantity of scar tissue from the palm of the plaintiff's right hand and the
grafting of skin taken from the plaintiff's chest in place thereof. The scar tissue
was the result of a severe burn caused by contact with an electric wire, which
the plaintiff received about nine years before the time of the transactions here
involved. There was evidence to the effect that before the operation was performed the plaintiff and his father went to the defendant's office, and that the
defendant in answer to the question, ''How long will the boy be in the hospital?'' replied, ''Three or four days, . . . not over four; then the boy can go home
and it will be just a few days when he will go back to work with a perfect hand.''
Clearly this and other testimony to the same effect would not justify a finding
that the doctor contracted to complete the hospital treatment in three or four
days or that the plaintiff would be able to go back to work within a few days
thereafter. The above statements could only be construed as expressions of opinion or predictions as to the probable duration of the treatment and plaintiff's resulting disability, and the fact that these estimates were exceeded would impose
no contractual liability upon the defendant. The only substantial basis for the
plaintiff's claim is the testimony that the defendant also said before the operation was decided upon, ''I will guarantee to make the hand a hundred per cent
perfect hand'' or ''a hundred per cent good hand.'' The plaintiff was present
when these words were alleged to have been spoken, and, if they are to be
taken at their face value, it seems obvious that proof of their utterance would
establish the giving of a warranty in accordance with his contention.

The defendant argues, however, that even if these words were uttered by
him, no reasonable man would understand that they were used with the intention of entering into any ''contractual relation whatever,'' and that they could
reasonably be understood only ''as his expression in strong language that he believed and expected that as a result of the operation he would give the plaintiff
a very good hand.'' It may be conceded, as the defendant contends, that, before
the question of the making of a contract should be submitted to a jury, there is
a preliminary question of law for the trial court to pass upon, i.e. ''whether the

---

* Supreme Court of New Hampshire, 1929, 84 N.H. 114, 146 A. 641.
[2] It does not matter that nothing was put in writing. In general, verbal contracts are binding if it can be shown that the verbal agreement did take place. More technically, a signed
document is not a contract but evidence of one. A verbal agreement, though sometimes
harder to prove, can also be evidence of a contract.

words could possibly have the meaning imputed to them by the party who founds his case upon a certain interpretation," but it cannot be held that the trial court decided this question erroneously in the present case. It is unnecessary to determine at this time whether the argument of the defendant, based upon "common knowledge of the uncertainty which attends all surgical operations," and the improbability that a surgeon would ever contract to make a damaged part of the human body "one hundred per cent perfect," would, in the absence of countervailing considerations, be regarded as conclusive, for there were other factors in the present case which tended to support the contention of the plaintiff. There was evidence that the defendant repeatedly solicited from the plaintiff's father the opportunity to perform this operation, and the theory was advanced by plaintiff's counsel in cross-examination of defendant that he sought an opportunity to "experiment on skin grafting," in which he had had little previous experience. If the jury accepted this part of plaintiff's contention, there would be a reasonable basis for the further conclusion that, if defendant spoke the words attributed to him, he did so with the intention that they should be accepted at their face value, as an inducement for the granting of consent to the operation by the plaintiff and his father, and there was ample evidence that they were so accepted by them. The question of the making of the alleged contract was properly submitted to the jury.

The Law of Torts

Some of the most complicated legal cases have arisen in the law of torts. A *tort* is defined as a wrongful act (with the exception of those acts involving a breach of contract) for which an injured party can recover damages in a civil action. In an ideally simple situation, A acts in a negligent way that leads directly to an injury to an innocent party, B. B sues and recovers for the injuries resulting from A's action. For example, A throws a bottle out of his car window that strikes and shatters a ceramic deer on B's lawn. B sues A and recovers the cost of replacing his ceramic deer. Here the law squares with our rough-and-ready sense of justice. But cases rarely appear in this ideal form. Consider the following possible changes in this case:

(1) Actually, B threw the bottle at A, who was peacefully and legally sitting in his car, then A threw it back, accidentally shattering B's ceramic deer.

(2) The bottle was, in fact, a Molotov cocktail thrown into the car by a third party, C. A *instinctively* threw it out, shattering B's ceramic deer.

(3) Same as (2), except that it was B who threw the Molotov cocktail into A's car.

(4) Same as (3), but A quite *deliberately* threw the Molotov cocktail at B's ceramic deer as an act of retaliation.

(5) A negligently threw the bottle out of his car window, and it was then carried a half mile by a tornado before landing on and shattering B's ceramic deer.

(6) A negligently threw the bottle out of his car window, but it ricocheted off an illegally driven motorcycle before hitting and shattering B's ceramic deer.

(7) The ceramic deer was a priceless Etruscan sculpture that no reasonable person would leave in his or her yard.

(8) There was an ordinance in the town prohibiting lawn ornaments in yards facing public thoroughfares.

In law schools, a set of examples of this kind is called a *series of hypotheticals.* These hypotheticals introduce variations on the original simple case. The first four form a progression, whereas each of the last four goes off on a tangent of its own. As these hypotheticals become more complex and remote from the original paradigm, our common-sense views of justice no longer yield simple answers and the legal issues themselves become difficult. The examination of such a series of hypotheticals is ideal for studying the law governing a particular area. It also brings out the character of legal reasoning: it is not always a mechanical procedure of applying a set of laws to a set of facts.

These hypothetical cases may seem artificial. In a way they are, and in a way they are not. They are artificial because each hypothetical is intended to isolate a single aspect of the legal situation for special investigation. Genuine cases are rarely this tidy. On the other hand, if it is thought that these hypotheticals are artificial because the facts imagined are bizarre or strange, this is simply a mistake. Cases exist corresponding to each of the hypotheticals listed above, and many genuine cases are even more exotic. Consider the famous case of *Palsgraf v. Long Island Railroad Co.*[3] Helen Palsgraf sued the Long Island Railroad for injuries she received while standing on a platform of one of its stations. The extraordinary set of facts surrounding this case is given at the opening of Chief Justice Cardozo's opinion:

---

[3] Although not the stuff of a Perry Mason television show, the case was one of high legal significance—even drama. Justices Cardozo and Andrews, who wrote the opposing opinions, were distinguished legal figures, and both—quite self-consciously—thought of themselves as making legal history. A fascinating account of the actual development of the case is given in James Noonan, *Justice and the Masks of the Law* (New York: Farrar, Straus and Giroux, 1976).

Palsgraf v. Long Island Railroad Co.

CARDOZO, C.J. Plaintiff was standing on a platform of defendant's railroad after buying a ticket to go to Rockaway Beach. A train stopped at the station, bound for another place. Two men ran forward to catch it. One of the men reached the platform of the car without mishap, though the train was already moving. The other man, carrying a package, jumped aboard the car, but seemed unsteady as if about to fall. A guard on the car, who had held the door open, reached forward to help him in, and another guard on the platform pushed him from behind. In this act, the package was dislodged, and fell upon the rails. It was a package of small size, about fifteen inches long, and was covered by a newspaper. In fact it contained fireworks, but there was nothing in its appearance to give notice of its contents. The fireworks when they fell exploded. The shock of the explosion threw down some scales at the other end of the platform, many feet away. The scales struck the plaintiff, causing injuries for which she sues.

Helen Palsgraf won her suit in the lower courts, and the Long Island Railroad carried its appeal to the highest court in the State of New York. This court ruled in favor of the Long Island Railroad, reversing the decision of the lower courts by a margin of four to three.

The leading idea of Justice Cardozo's majority opinion is that the conductors in the employ of the Long Island Railroad were in no way negligent *relative to Mrs. Palsgraf.* Presumably their conduct was negligent relative to the person who attempted to board the train. (Among other things, the door should have been closed when the train was in motion; the conductors should have warned the passenger not to board the train; they should not have helped him to do so; etc.) Yet Mrs. Palsgraf was not in the class of the foreseeable victims of this negligence. So as a *matter of law* Cardozo held that Mrs. Palsgraf had no right to recover for her injuries and, speaking for the majority of the court, reversed the decisions of the lower courts, assigning court costs to Mrs. Palsgraf.

The remainder of Cardozo's opinion, with some technical material deleted, follows:

The conduct of the defendant's guard, if a wrong in its relation to the holder of the package, was not a wrong in its relation to the plaintiff, standing far away. Relatively to her it was not negligence at all. Nothing in the situation gave notice that the falling package had in it the potency of peril to persons thus removed. Negligence is not actionable unless it involves the invasion of a legally protected interest, the violation of a right. "Proof of negligence in the air, so to speak, will not do" (Pollock, *Torts* [11th ed.], p. 455; *Martin* v. *Herzog,* 228 N.Y.

* Court of Appeals of New York. 1928, 248 N.Y. 339; 162 N.E. 99.

164, 170; *cf.* Salmond, *Torts* [6th ed.]. p. 24). "Negligence is the absence of care, according to the circumstances" (WILLES, J., in *Vaughan* v. *Taff Vale Ry. Co.*, 5 H. & N. 679; 1 Beven, *Negligence* [4th ed.], 7). The plaintiff as she stood upon the platform of the station might claim to be protected against intentional invasion of her bodily security. Such invasion is not charged. She might claim to be protected against unintentional invasion by conduct involving in the thought of reasonable men an unreasonable hazard that such invasion would ensue. These, from the point of view of the law, were the bounds of her immunity, with perhaps some rare exceptions, survivals for the most part of ancient forms of liability, where conduct is held to be at the peril of the actor. If no hazard was apparent to the eye of ordinary vigilance, an act innocent and harmless, at least to outward seeming, with reference to her, did not take to itself the quality of a tort because it happened to be wrong, though apparently not one involving the risk of bodily insecurity, with reference to some one else. "In every instance before negligence can be predicated of a given act, back of the act must be sought and found a duty to the individual complaining, the observance of which would have averted or avoided the injury." . . . "The ideas of negligence and duty are strictly correlative" (BOWEN, L.J., in *Thomas* v. *Quartermaine*, 18 Q.B.D. 685, 694). The plaintiff sues in her own right for a wrong personal to her, and not as the vicarious beneficiary of a breach of duty to another.

A different conclusion will involve us, and swiftly too, in a maze of contradictions. A guard stumbles over a package which has been left upon a platform. It seems to be a bundle of newspapers. It turns out to be a can of dynamite. To the eye of ordinary vigilance, the bundle is abandoned waste, which may be kicked or trod on with impunity. Is a passenger at the other end of the platform protected by the law against the unsuspected hazard concealed beneath the waste? If not, is the result to be any different, so far as the distant passenger is concerned, when the guard stumbles over a valise which a truckman or a porter has left upon the walk? The passenger far away, if the victim of a wrong at all, has a cause of action, not derivative, but original and primary. His claim to be protected against invasion of his bodily security is neither greater nor less because the act resulting in the invasion is a wrong to another far removed. In this case, the rights that are said to have been invaded, are not even of the same order. The man was not injured in his person nor even put in danger. The purpose of the act, as well as its effect, was to make his person safe. If there was a wrong to him at all, which may very well be doubted, it was a wrong to a property interest only, the safety of his package. Out of this wrong to property, which threatened injury to nothing else, there has passed, we are told, to the plaintiff by derivation or succession a right of action for the invasion of an interest of another order, the right to bodily security. The diversity of interests emphasizes the futility of the effort to build the plaintiff's right upon the basis of a wrong to some one else. The gain is one of emphasis, for a like result would follow if the interests were the same. Even then, the orbit of the danger as disclosed to the eye of reasonable vigilance would be the orbit of the duty. One who jostles one's neighbour in a crowd does not invade the rights of others standing at the outer fringe when the unintended contact casts a bomb upon the ground. The wrongdoer as to them is the man who carries the bomb, not the one who explodes it without suspicion of the danger. Life will have to be made over, and human nature transformed, before prevision so extravagant can be accepted as the form of conduct, the customary standard to which behaviour must conform.

The argument for the plaintiff is built upon the shifting meanings of such words as "wrong" and "wrongful", and shares their instability. What the plaintiff must show is "a wrong" to herself, *i.e.*, a violation of her own right, and not merely a wrong to some one else, nor conduct "wrongful" because unsocial, but not a "wrong" to any one. We are told that one who drives at reckless speed through a crowded city street is guilty of a negligent act and, therefore, of a wrongful one irrespective of the consequences. Negligent the act is, and wrongful in the sense that it is unsocial, but wrongful and unsocial in relation to other travellers, only because the eye of vigilance perceives the risk of damage. If the same act were to be committed on a speedway or a race course, it would lose its wrongful quality. The risk reasonably to be perceived defines the duty to be obeyed and risk imports relation; it is risk to another or to others within the range of apprehension. . . . This does not mean, of course, that one who launches a destructive force is always relieved of liability if the force, though known to be destructive, pursues an unexpected path. "It was not necessary that the defendant should have had notice of the particular method in which an accident would occur, if the possibility of an accident was clear to the ordinary prudent eye". . . . Some acts, such as shooting, are so imminently dangerous to any one who may come within reach of the missile, however unexpectedly, as to impose a duty of prevision not far from that of an insurer. Even today, and much oftener in earlier stages of the law, one acts sometimes at one's peril. . . . Under this head, it may be, fall certain cases of what is known as transferred intent, an act wilfully dangerous to A resulting in misadventure in injury to B. . . . These cases aside, wrong is defined in terms of the natural or probable, at least when unintentional. . . . The range of reasonable apprehension is at times a question for the court, and at times, if varying inferences are possible, a question for the jury. Here, by concession, there was nothing in the situation to suggest to the most cautious mind that the parcel wrapped in newspaper would spread wreckage through the station. If the guard had thrown it down knowingly and wilfully, he would not have threatened the plaintiff's safety, so far as appearances could warn him. His conduct would not have involved, even then, an unreasonable probability of invasion of her bodily security. Liability can be no greater when the act is inadvertent.

Negligence, like risk, is thus a term of relation. Negligence in the abstract, apart from things related, is surely not a tort, if indeed it is understandable at all. . . . Negligence is not a tort unless it results in the commission of a wrong, and the commission of a wrong imports the violation of a right, in this case, we are told, the right to be protected against interference with one's bodily security. But bodily security is protected, not against all forms of interference or aggression, but only against some. One who seeks redress at law does not make out a cause of action by showing without more that there has been damage to his person. If the harm was not wilful, he must show that the act as to him had possiblities of danger so many and apparent as to entitle him to be protected against the doing of it though the harm was unintended. Affront to personality is still the keynote of the wrong. . . .

The law of causation, remote or proximate, is thus foreign to the case before us. The question of liability is always anterior to the question of the measure of the consequences that go with liability. If there is no tort to be redressed, there is no occasion to consider what damage might be recovered if there were a finding of a tort. We may assume, without deciding, that negligence, not at large or in the abstract, but in relation to the plaintiff, would entail liability for any and all consequences, however novel or extraordinary. . . .

The judgment of the Appellate Division and that of the Trial Term should be reversed, and the complaint dismissed, with costs in all courts.

Starting from the same set of facts, Justice Andrews reasons along different lines and comes to the opposite conclusion. He begins by rejecting Cardozo's innovation that recovery be limited (primarily, at least) to people in the class of foreseeable victims of a negligent act. (This portion of Andrews' opinion is not given below.) He then treats the case along the more traditional lines of *proximate cause*. For Andrews, the basic question is whether the connection between the negligent actions and Mrs. Palsgraf's injuries were sufficiently close for the actions to constitute the proximate cause of the injuries. In contrast, Cardozo says that "the law of causation, remote or proximate, is . . . foreign to the case before us." Andrews attempts to explain, through a series of analogies and metaphors, what he understands by a proximate cause.

Although it is clear that Cardozo and Andrews view this case in entirely different ways, it is still not clear why they should arrive at opposing conclusions. (Indeed, as you read Andrews' opinion, you can get the feeling that he is going to come out against Mrs. Palsgraf rather than for her.) His reasoning runs as follows: the problem at hand is one of *drawing a line* between a proximate and a remote cause. This, he argues, cannot be settled as a *matter of law*, so, without either agreeing or disagreeing with the verdict, Andrews concludes that the matter was properly submitted to a jury for determination, and there is no legal basis for overturning its decision.

What is a cause in a legal sense, still more what is a proximate cause, depends in each case upon many considerations, as does the existence of negligence itself. Any philosophical doctrine of causation does not help us. A boy throws a stone into a pond. The ripples spread. The water level rises. The history of that pond is altered to all eternity. It will be altered by other causes also. Yet it will be forever the resultant of all causes combined. Each one will have an influence. How great only omniscience can say. You may speak of a chain, or, if you please, a net. An analogy is of little aid. Each cause brings about future events. Without each the future would not be the same. Each is proximate in the sense it is essential. But that is not what we mean by the word. Nor on the other hand do we mean sole cause. There is no such thing.

Should analogy be thought helpful, however, I prefer that of a stream. The spring, starting on its journey, is joined by tributary after tributary. The river, reaching the ocean, comes from a hundred sources. No man may say whence any drop of water is derived. Yet for a time distinction may be possible. Into the clear creek, brown swamp water flows from the left. Later, from the right comes water stained by its clay bed. The three may remain for a space, sharply divided. But at last inevitably no trace of separation remains. They are so commingled that all distinction is lost.

As we have said, we cannot trace the effect of an act to the end, if end there is. Again, however, we may trace it part of the way. A murder at Serajevo may be the necessary antecedent to an assassination in London twenty years hence. An overturned lantern may burn all Chicago. We may follow the fire from the shed to the last building. We rightly say the fire started by the lantern caused its destruction.

A cause, but not the proximate cause. What we do mean by the word "proximate" is that, because of convenience, of public policy, of a rough sense of justice, the law arbitrarily declines to trace a series of events beyond a certain point. This is not logic. It is practical politics. Take our rule as to fires. Sparks from my burning haystack set on fire my house and my neighbour's. I may recover from a negligent railroad. He may not. Yet the wrongful act as directly harmed the one as the other. We may regret that the line was drawn just where it was, but drawn somewhere it had to be. We said the act of the railroad was not the proximate cause of the neighbour's fire. Cause it surely was. The words we used were simply indicative of our notions of public policy. Other courts think differently. But somewhere they reach the point where they cannot say the stream comes from any one source.

Take the illustration given in an unpublished manuscript by a distinguished and helpful writer on the law of torts. A chauffeur negligently collides with another car which is filled with dynamite, although he could not know it. An explosion follows. A, walking on the sidewalk nearby, is killed. B, sitting in a window of a building opposite is cut by flying glass. C, likewise sitting in a window a block away, is similarly injured. And a further illustration: A nursemaid ten blocks away, startled by the noise, involuntarily drops a baby from her arms to the walk. We are told that C may not recover but A may. As to B it is not a question for court or jury. We will all agree that the baby might not. Because, we are again told, the chauffeur had no reason to believe his conduct involved any risk of injuring either C or the baby. As to them he was not negligent.

But the chauffeur, being negligent in risking the collision, his belief that the scope of the harm he might do would be limited is immaterial. His act unreasonably jeopardized the safety of any one who might be affected by it. C's injury and that of the baby were directly traceable to the collision. Without that, the injury would not have happened. C had the right to sit in his office, secure from such dangers. The baby was entitled to use the sidewalk with reasonable safety.

The true theory is, it seems to me, that the injury to C, if in truth he is to be denied recovery, and the injury to the baby, is that their several injuries were not the proximate result of the negligence. And here not what the chauffeur had reason to believe would be the result of his conduct, but what the prudent would foresee, may have a bearing—may have some bearing, for the problem of proximate cause is not to be solved by any one consideration. It is all a question of expediency. There are no fixed rules to govern our judgment. There are simply matters of which we may take account. We have in a somewhat different connection spoken of "the stream of events". We have asked whether that stream was deflected—whether it was forced into new and unexpected channels: . . . This is rather rhetoric than law. There is in truth little to guide us other than common sense.

There are some hints that may help us. The proximate cause, involved as it may be with many other causes, must be, at the least, something without which the event would not happen. The court must ask itself whether there was a natural and continuous sequence between cause and effect. Was the one a substantial factor in producing the other? Was there a direct connection between them, without too many intervening causes? Is the effect of cause on result not too attenuated? Is the cause likely, in the usual judgment of mankind, to produce the result? Or, by the exercise of prudent foresight, could the result be foreseen? Is the result too remote from the cause, and here we consider remoteness in time and space. . . . Clearly we must so consider, for the greater the distance either in time or space, the more surely do other causes intervene to affect the result. When a lantern is overturned, the firing of a shed is a fairly direct consequence. Many things contribute to the spread of the conflagration—the force of the wind, the direction and width of streets, the character of intervening structures, other factors. We draw an uncertain and wavering line, but draw it we must as best we can.

Once again, it is all a question of fair judgment, always keeping in mind the fact that we endeavour to make a rule in each case that will be practical and in keeping with the general understanding of mankind.

Here another question must be answered. In the case supposed, it is said, and said correctly, that the chauffeur is liable for the direct effect of the explosion although he had no reason to suppose it would follow a collision. "The fact that the injury occurred in a different manner than that which might have been expected does not prevent the chauffeur's negligence from being in law the cause of the injury." But the natural results of a negligent act—the results which a prudent man would or should foresee—do have a bearing upon the decision as to proximate cause. We have said so repeatedly. What should be foreseen? No human foresight would suggest that a collision itself might injure one a block away. On the contrary, given an explosion, such a possibility might be reasonably expected. I think the direct connection, the foresight of which the courts speak, assumes prevision of the explosion, for the immediate results of which, at least, the chauffeur is responsible.

It may be said this is unjust. Why? In fairness he should make good every injury flowing from his negligence. Not because of tenderness toward him we say he need not answer for all that follows his wrong. We look back to the catastrophe, the fire kindled by the spark, or the explosion. We trace the consequences, not indefinitely, but to a certain point. And to aid us in fixing that point we ask what might ordinarily be expected to follow the fire or the explosion.

This last suggestion is the factor which must determine the case before us. The act upon which defendant's liability rests is knocking an apparently harmless package onto the platform. The act was negligent. For its proximate consequences the defendant is liable. If its contents were broken, to the owner; if it fell upon and crushed a passenger's foot, then to him; if it exploded and injured one in the immediate vicinity, to him also as to A in the illustration. Mrs. Palsgraf was standing some distance away. How far cannot be told from the record—apparently 25 to 30 feet, perhaps less. Except for the explosion, she would not have been injured. We are told by the appellant in his brief, "It cannot be denied that the explosion was the direct cause of the plaintiff's injuries." So it was a substantial factor in producing the result—there was here a natural and continuous sequence—direct connection. The only intervening cause was that, instead of blowing her to the ground, the concussion smashed the weighing machine which in turn fell upon her. There was no remoteness in time, little in space. And surely, given such an explosion as here, it needed no great foresight to predict that the natural result would be to injure one on the platform at no greater distance from its scene than was the plaintiff. Just how no one might be able to predict. Whether by flying fragments, by broken glass, by wreckage of machines or structures no one could say. But injury in some form was most probable.

Under these circumstances I cannot say as a matter of law that the plaintiff's injuries were not the proximate result of the negligence. That is all we have before us. The court refused to so charge. No request was made to submit the matter to the jury as a question of fact, even would that have been proper upon the record before us.

The Question of Constitutionality

The most fundamental questions in our legal system concern *constitutionality*. No law may conflict with rights guaranteed by the Constitution. This is an area where disagreement is possible, and the Supreme Court of the United States is the final arbiter of such disagreements. The cases that follow concern the so-called "separate but equal" doctrine that was used to justify racial segregation laws in various states. This doctrine first made its appearance in the Supreme Court in the case of *Plessy v. Ferguson* (1896). Here the Court ruled that a Louisiana statute enforcing the segregation of races in certain forms of public transportation was not unconstitutional. In particular, the Court ruled that this statute did not violate Thirteenth or Fourteenth Amendment guarantees. Justice Brown delivered the opinion of the Court, and Justice Harlan wrote the dissenting opinion. In 1954, in *Brown v. Board of Education*, the Supreme Court considered the doctrine of "separate but equal" as it applied in a different area: *public education*. It concluded that "in the field of public education the doctrine of 'separate but equal' has no place." The Court was unanimous in its decision and Chief Justice Earl Warren wrote the opinion of the Court.

These three opinions differ strikingly in style. Justice Brown's is scholarly and is carefully argued on fairly narrow legal grounds. Justice Harlan's opinion is written from a much broader historical perspective and is infused with moral concern. At first glance, the Warren opinion may seem too casual for a decision of such fundamental historical importance.

Parts of the long opinions of Justices Brown and Harlan have been omitted. The shorter Warren opinion is given almost in its entirety; only the closing instructions concerning implementation are omitted.

Plessy v. Ferguson

Mr. Justice Brown delivered the opinion of the Court.

This case turns upon the constitutionality of an act of the general assembly of the state of Louisiana, passed in 1890, providing for separate railway carriages for the white and colored races.

The 1st section of the statute enacts "that all railway companies carrying passengers in their coaches in this state shall provide equal but separate accommodations for the white and colored races, by providing two or more passenger coaches for each passenger train, or by dividing the passenger coaches by a partition so as to secure separate accommodations: *Provided,* That this section shall not be construed to apply to street railroads. No person or persons shall be permitted to occupy seats in coaches other than the ones assigned to them, on account of the race they belong to."

By the 2d section it was enacted "that the officers of such passenger trains shall have power and are hereby required to assign each passenger to the coach or compartment used for the race to which such passenger belongs; any passenger insisting on going into a coach or compartment to which by race he does not belong, shall be liable to a fine of $25 or in lieu thereof to imprisonment for a period of not more than twenty days in the parish prison, and any officer of any railroad insisting on assigning a passenger to a coach or compartment other than the one set aside for the race to which said passenger belongs, shall be liable to a fine of $25, or in lieu thereof to imprisonment for a period of not more than twenty days in the parish prison; and should any passenger refuse to occupy the coach or compartment to which he or she is assigned by the officer of such railway, said officer shall have power to refuse to carry such passenger on his train, and for such refusal neither he nor the railway company which he represents shall be liable for damages in any of the courts of this state." . . .

The information filed in the criminal district court charged in substance that Plessy, being a passenger between two stations within the state of Louisiana, was assigned by officers of the company to the coach used for the race to which he belonged, but he insisted upon going into a coach used by the race to

* 163 U.S. 537 1896.

which he did not belong. Neither in the information nor plea was his particular race or color averred.

The petition for the writ of prohibition averred that petitioner was seven eighths Caucasian and one eighth African blood; that the mixture of colored blood was not discernible in him, and that he was entitled to every right, privilege, and immunity secured to citizens of the United States of the white race; and that, upon such theory, he took possession of a vacant seat in a coach where passengers of the white race were accommodated, and was ordered by the conductor to vacate said coach and take a seat in another assigned to persons of the colored race, and having refused to comply with such demand he was forcibly ejected with the aid of a police officer, and imprisoned in the parish jail to answer a charge of having violated the above act.

The constitutionality of this act is attacked upon the ground that it conflicts both with the 13th Amendment of the Constitution, abolishing slavery, and the 14th Amendment, which prohibits certain restrictive legislation on the part of the states.

1. That it does not conflict with the 13th Amendment, which abolished slavery and involuntary servitude, except as a punishment for crime, is too clear for argument. . . .

. . . Indeed, we do not understand that the 13th Amendment is strenuously relied upon by the plaintiff in error in this connection.

2. By the 14th Amendment, all persons born or naturalized in the United States, and subject to the jurisdiction thereof, are made citizens of the United States and of the state wherein they reside; and the states are forbidden from making or enforcing any law which shall abridge the privileges or immunities of citizens of the United States, or shall deprive any person of life, liberty, or property without due process of law, or deny to any person within their jurisdiction the equal protection of the laws. . . .

The object of the amendment was undoubtedly to enforce the absolute equality of the two races before the law, but in the nature of things it could not have been intended to abolish distinctions based upon color, or to enforce social, as distinguished from political, equality, or a commingling of the two races upon terms unsatisfactory to either. Laws permitting, and even requiring their separation in places where they are liable to be brought into contact do not necessarily imply the inferiority of either race to the other, and have been generally, if not universally, recognized as within the competency of the state legislatures in the exercise of their police power. The most common instance of this is connected with the establishment of separate schools for white and colored children, which have been held to be a valid exercise of the legislative power even by courts of states where the political rights of the colored race have been longest and most earnestly enforced. . . .

[Justice Brown next reviews a whole series of cases where statutes similar to the one in question have been upheld as constitutional.]

It is . . . suggested by the learned counsel for the plaintiff in error that the same argument that will justify the state legislature in requiring railways to provide separate accommodations for the two races will also authorize them to require separate cars to be provided for people whose hair is of a certain color, or who are aliens, or who belong to certain nationalities, or to enact laws requiring colored people to walk upon one side of the street, and white people upon the other, or requiring white men's houses to be painted white, and colored men's black, or their vehicles or business signs to be of different colors, upon the theory that one side of the street is as good as the other, or that a house or vehicle of one color is as good as one of another color. The reply to all this is that every exercise of the police power must be reasonable, and extend only to such laws as are enacted in good faith for the promotion of the public good, and not for the annoyance or oppression of a particular class. Thus in *Yick Wo* v. *Hopkins* it was held by this court that a municipal ordinance of the city of San Francisco to regulate the carrying on of public laundries within the limits of the municipality violated the provisions of the Constitution of the United States if it conferred upon the municipal authorities arbitrary power, at their own will, and without regard to discretion, in the legal sense of the term, to give or withhold consent as to persons or places, without regard to the competency of the persons applying, or the propriety of the places selected for the carrying on of the business. It was held to be a covert attempt on the part of the municipality to make an arbitrary and unjust discrimination against the Chinese race. While this was the case of a municipal ordinance a like principle has been held to apply to acts of a state legislature passed in the exercise of the police power.

So far, then, as a conflict with the 14th Amendment is concerned, the case reduces itself to the question whether the statute of Louisiana is a reasonable regulation, and with respect to this there must necessarily be a large discretion on the part of the legislature. In determining the question of reasonableness it is at liberty to act with reference to the established usages, customs, and traditions of the people, and with a view to the promotion of their comfort, and the preservation of the public peace and good order. Gauged by this standard, we cannot say that a law which authorizes or even requires the separation of the two races in public conveyances is unreasonable or more obnoxious to the 14th Amendment than the acts of Congress requiring separate schools for colored children in the District of Columbia, the constitutionality of which does not seem to have been questioned, or the corresponding acts of state legislatures.

We consider the underlying fallacy of the plaintiff's argument to consist in the assumption that the enforced separation of the two races stamps the colored race with a badge of inferiority. If this be so, it is not by reason of anything found in the act, but solely because the colored race chooses to put that construction upon it. The argument necessarily assumes that if, as has been more than once the case, and is not unlikely to be so again, the colored race should become the dominant power in the state legislature, and should enact a law in precisely similar terms, it would thereby relegate the white race to an inferior position. We imagine that the white race, at least, would not acquiesce in this assumption. The argument also assumes that social prejudices may be overcome by legislation, and that equal rights cannot be secured to the negro except by an enforced commingling of the two races. We cannot accept this proposition. If the two races are to meet on terms of social equality, it must be the result of natural affinity, a mutual appreciation of each other's merits and a voluntary consent of individuals. As was said by the court of appeals of New York in *People* v. *Gallagher*, "this end can neither be accomplished nor promoted by laws which conflict with the general sentiment of the community upon whom they are designed to operate. When the government, therefore, has secured to each of its citizens equal rights before the law and equal opportunities for improvement and progress, it has accomplished the end for which it is organized and performed all of the functions respecting social advantages with which it is endowed." Legislation is powerless to eradicate racial instincts or to abolish distinctions based upon physical differences, and the attempt to do so can only result in accentuating the difficulties of the present situation. If the civil and political rights of both races be equal, one cannot be inferior to the other civilly or politically. If one race be inferior to the other socially, the Constitution of the United States cannot put them upon the same plane. . . .

The judgment of the Court below is therefore affirmed.

Mr. Justice Harlan dissenting. . . .

In respect of civil rights, common to all citizens, the Constitution of the United States does not, I think, permit any public authority to know the race of those entitled to be protected in the enjoyment of such rights. Every true man has pride of race, and under appropriate circumstances, when the rights of others, his equals before the law, are not to be affected, it is his privilege to express such pride and to take such action based upon it as to him seems proper. But I deny that any legislative body or judicial tribunal may have regard to the race of citizens when the civil rights of those citizens are involved. Indeed such legislation as that here in question is inconsistent, not only with that equality of rights which pertains to citizenship, national and state, but with the personal liberty enjoyed by every one within the United States.

The 13th Amendment does not permit the withholding or the deprivation of any right necessarily inhering in freedom. It not only struck down the institution of slavery as previously existing in the United States, but it prevents the imposition of any burdens or disabilities that constitute badges of slavery or servitude. It decreed universal civil freedom in this country. This court has so adjudged. But that amendment having been found inadequate to the protection of the rights of those who had been in slavery, it was followed by the 14th Amendment, which added greatly to the dignity and glory of American citizenship, and to the security of personal liberty, by declaring that "all persons born or naturalized in the United States, and subject to the jurisdiction thereof, are citizens of the United States and of the state wherein they reside," and that "no state shall make or enforce any law which shall abridge the privileges or immunities of citizens of the United States; nor shall any state deprive any person of life, liberty, or property without due process of law, nor deny to any person within its jurisdiction the equal protection of the laws." These two amendments, if enforced according to their true intent and meaning, will protect all the civil rights that pertain to freedom and citizenship. . . .

These notable additions to the fundamental law were welcomed by the friends of liberty throughout the world. They removed the race line from our governmental systems. They had, as this court has said, a common purpose, namely, to secure "to a race recently emancipated, a race that through many generations have been held in slavery, all the civil rights that the superior race enjoy." They declared, in legal effect, this court has further said, "that the law in the states shall be the same for the black as for the white; that all persons, whether colored or white, shall stand equal before the laws of the states, and, in regard to the colored race, for whose protection the amendment was primarily designed, that no discrimination shall be made against them by law because of their color." We also said: "The words of the amendment, it is true, are prohibitory, but they contain a necessary implication of a positive immunity, or right, most valuable to the colored race—the right to exemption from unfriendly legislation against them distinctively as colored—exemption from legal discriminations, implying inferiority in civil society, lessening the security of their enjoyment of the rights which others enjoy, and discriminations which are steps toward reducing them to the condition of a subject race." It was consequently adjudged that a state law that excluded citizens of the colored race from juries because of their race and however well qualified in other respects to discharge the duties of jurymen was repugnant to the 14th Amendment. At the present term, referring to the previous adjudications, this court declared that "underlying all of those decisions is the principle that the Constitution of the United States, in its present form, forbids, so far as civil and political rights are concerned, discrimination by the general government or the states against any citizen because of his race. All citizens are equal before the law."

The decisions referred to show the scope of the recent amendments of the Constitution. They also show that it is not within the power of a state to prohibit colored citizens, because of their race, from participating as jurors in the administration of justice.

It was said in argument that the statute of Louisiana does not discriminate against either race, but prescribes a rule applicable alike to white and colored citizens. But this argument does not meet the difficulty. Everyone knows that the statute in question had its origin in the purpose, not so much to exclude white persons from railroad cars occupied by blacks, as to exclude colored people from coaches occupied by or assigned to white persons. Railroad corporations of Louisiana did not make discrimination among whites in the matter of accommodation for travelers. The thing to accomplish was, under the guise of giving equal accommodation for whites and blacks to compel the latter to keep to themselves while traveling in railroad passenger coaches. No one would be so wanting in candor as to assert the contrary. The fundamental objection, therefore, to the statute, is that it interferes with the personal freedom of citizens. "Personal liberty," it has been well said, "consists in the power of locomotion, of changing situation, or removing one's person to whatsoever places one's own inclination may direct, without imprisonment or restraint, unless by due course of law." If a white man and a black man choose to occupy the same public conveyance on a public highway, it is their right to do so, and no government, proceeding alone on grounds of race, can prevent it without infringing the personal liberty of each.

It is one thing for railroad carriers to furnish, or to be required by law to furnish, equal accommodations for all whom they are under a legal duty to carry. It is quite another thing for government to forbid citizens of the white and black races from traveling in the same public conveyance, and to punish officers of railroad companies for permitting persons of the two races to occupy the same passenger coach. If a state can prescribe as a rule of civil conduct, that whites and blacks shall not travel as passengers in the same railroad coach, why may it not so regulate the use of the streets of its cities and towns as to compel white citizens to keep on one side of the street and black citizens to keep on the other? Why may it not, upon like grounds, punish whites and blacks who ride together in street cars or in open vehicles on a public road or street? Why may it not require sheriffs to assign whites to one side of a court-room and blacks to the other? And why may it not also prohibit the commingling of the two races in the galleries of legislative halls or in public assemblages convened for the political questions of the day? Further, if this statute of Louisiana is consistent with the personal liberty of citizens, why may not the state require the separation in railroad coaches of native and naturalized citizens of the United States, or of Protestants and Roman Catholics?

The answer given at the argument to these questions was that regulations of the kind they suggest would be unreasonable, and could not, therefore, stand before the law. Is it meant that the determination of questions of legislative power depends upon the inquiry whether the statute whose validity is questioned is, in the judgment of the courts, a reasonable one, taking all the circumstances into consideration? A statute may be unreasonable merely because a sound public policy forbade its enactment. But I do not understand that the courts have anything to do with the policy or expediency of legislation. A statute may be valid, and yet upon grounds of public policy may well be characterized as unreasonable. Mr. Sedgwick correctly states the rule when he says that the legislative intention being clearly ascertained, "the courts have no other duty to perform than to execute the legislative will, without any regard to their views as to the wisdom or justice of the particular enactment." There is a dangerous tendency in these latter days to enlarge the functions of the courts, by means of judicial interference with the will of the people as expressed by the legislature. Our institutions have the distinguishing characteristic that the three departments of government are co-ordinate and separate. Each must keep within the limits defined by the Constitution. And the courts best discharge their duty by executing the will of the lawmaking power, constitutionally expressed, leaving the results of legislation to be dealt with by the people through their representatives. Statutes must always have a reasonable construction. Sometimes they are to be construed strictly; sometimes literally, in order to carry out the legislative will. But however construed, the intent of the legislature is to be respected, if the particular statute in question is valid, although the courts, looking at the public interests, may conceive the statute to be both unreasonable and impolitic. If the power exists to enact a statute, that ends the matter so far as the courts are concerned. The adjudged cases in which statutes have been held to be void, because unreasonable, are those in which the means employed by the legislature were not at all germane to the end to which the legislature was competent.

The white race deems itself to be the dominant race in this country. And so it is, in prestige, in achievements, in education, in wealth, and in power. So, I doubt not that it will continue to be for all time, if it remains true to its great heritage and holds fast to the principles of constitutional liberty. But in view of the Constitution, in the eye of the law, there is in this country no superior, dominant, ruling class of citizens. There is no caste here. Our Constitution is color-blind, and neither knows nor tolerates classes among citizens. In respect of civil rights, all citizens are equal before the law. The humblest is the peer of the most powerful. The law regards man as man, and takes no account of his surroundings or of his color when his civil rights as guaranteed by the supreme law of the land are involved. It is therefore to be regretted that this high tribunal, the final expositor of the fundamental law of the land, has reached the conclusion that it is competent for a state to regulate the enjoyment by citizens of their civil rights solely upon the basis of race.

In my opinion, the judgment this day rendered will, in time, prove to be quite as pernicious as the decision made by this tribunal in the *Dred Scott Case*. It was adjudged in that case that the descendants of Africans who were imported into this country and sold as slaves were not included nor intended to be included under the word "citizens" in the Constitution, and could not claim any of the rights and privileges which that instrument provided for and secured to citizens of the United States; that at the time of the adoption of the Constitution they were "considered as a subordinate and inferior class of beings, who had been subjugated by the dominant race, and, whether emancipated or not, yet remained subject to their authority, and had no rights or privileges but such as those who held the power and the government might choose to grant them." The recent amendments of the Constitution, it was supposed, had eradicated these principles from our institutions. But it seems that we have yet, in some of the states, a dominant race, a superior class of citizens, which assumes to regulate the enjoyment of civil rights, common to all citizens, upon the basis of race. The present decision, it may well be apprehended, will not stimulate aggressions, more or less brutal and irritating, upon the admitted rights of colored citizens, but will encourage the belief that it is possible, by means of state enactments, to defeat the beneficent purposes which the people of the United States had in view when they adopted the recent amendments of the Constitution, by one of which the blacks of this country were made citizens of the United States and of the states in which they respectively reside and whose privileges and immunities, as citizens, the states are forbidden to abridge. Sixty millions of whites are in no danger from the presence here of eight millions of blacks. The destinies of the two races in this country are indissolubly linked together, and the interests of both require that the common government of all shall not permit the seeds of race hate to be planted under the sanction of law. What can more certainly arouse race hate, what more certainly create and perpetuate a feeling of distrust between these races, than state enactments which in fact proceed on the ground that colored citizens are so inferior and degraded that they cannot be allowed to sit in public coaches occupied by white citizens? That, as all will admit, is the real meaning of such legislation as was enacted in Louisiana. . . .

The arbitrary separation of citizens, on the basis of race, while they are on a public highway, is a badge of servitude wholly inconsistent with the civil freedom and the equality before the law established by the Constitution. It cannot be justified upon any legal grounds.

If evils will result from the commingling of the two races upon public highways established for the benefit of all, they will be infinitely less than those that will surely come from state legislation regulating the enjoyment of civil rights upon the basis of race. We boast of the freedom enjoyed by our people above all other peoples. But it is difficult to reconcile that boast with a state of the law which, practically, puts the brand of servitude and degradation upon a large class of our fellow citizens, our equals before the law. The thin disguise of "equal" accommodations for passengers in railroad coaches will not mislead anyone, or atone for the wrong this day done. . . .

I am of opinion that the statute of Louisiana is inconsistent with the personal liberty of citizens, white and black, in that state, and hostile to both the spirit and letter of the Constitution of the United States. If laws of like character should be enacted in the several states of the Union, the effect would be in the highest degree mischievous. Slavery as an institution tolerated by law would, it is true, have disappeared from our country, but there would remain a power in the states, by sinister legislation, to interfere with the full enjoyment of the blessings of freedom; to regulate civil rights, common to all citizens, upon the basis of race; and to place in a condition of legal inferiority a large body of American citizens, now constituting a part of the political community, called the people of the United States, for whom and by whom, through representatives, our government is administered. Such a system is inconsistent with the guarantee given by the Constitution to each state of a republican form of government, and may be stricken down by congressional action, or by the courts in the discharge of their solemn duty to maintain the supreme law of the land, anything in the Constitution or laws of any state to the contrary notwithstanding.

For the reasons stated, I am constrained to withhold my assent from the opinion and judgment of the majority.

Brown v. Board of Education

Mr. Chief Justice Warren delivered the opinion of the Court.

These cases come to us from the States of Kansas, South Carolina, Virginia, and Delaware. They are premised on different facts and different local condi-

• 347 U.S. 483 1954.

tions, but a common legal question justifies their consideration together in this consolidated opinion.

In each of the cases, minors of the Negro race, through their legal represen-tatives, seek the aid of the courts in obtaining admission to the public schools of their community on a nonsegregated basis. In each instance, they had been denied admission to schools attended by white children under laws requiring or permitting segregation according to race. This segregation was alleged to deprive the plaintiffs of the equal protection of the laws under the Fourteenth Amend-ment. In each of the cases other than the Delaware case, a three-judge federal district court denied relief to the plaintiffs on the so-called "separate but equal" doctrine announced by this Court in *Plessy* v. *Ferguson*. Under that doctrine, equality of treatment is accorded when the races are provided substantially equal facilities, even though these facilities be separate. In the Delaware case, the Supreme Court of Delaware adhered to that doctrine, but ordered that the plaintiffs be admitted to the white schools because of their superiority to the Ne-gro schools.

The plaintiffs contend that segregated public schools are not "equal" and cannot be made "equal," and that hence they are deprived of the equal protec-tion of the laws. Because of the obvious importance of the question presented, the Court took jurisdiction. Argument was heard in the 1952 Term, and reargu-ment was heard this Term on certain questions propounded by the Court.

Reargument was largely devoted to the circumstances surrounding the adoption of the Fourteenth Amendment in 1868. It covered exhaustively consid-eration of the Amendment in Congress, ratification by the states, then existing practices in racial segregation, and the views of proponents and opponents of the Amendment. This discussion and our own investigation convince us that, al-though these sources cast some light, it is not enough to resolve the problem with which we are faced. At best, they are inconclusive. The most avid propo-nents of the post-War Amendments undoubtedly intended them to remove all legal distinctions among "all persons born or naturalized in the United States." Their opponents, just as certainly, were antagonistic to both the letter and the spirit of the Amendments and wished them to have the most limited effect. What others in Congress and the state legislatures had in mind cannot be deter-mined with any degree of certainty.

An additional reason for the inconclusive nature of the Amendment's his-tory, with respect to segregated schools, is the status of public education at that time. In the South, the movement toward free common schools, supported by general taxation, had not yet taken hold. Education of white children was largely in the hands of private groups. Education of Negroes was almost non-existent, and practically all of the race were illiterate. In fact, any education of Negroes was forbidden by law in some states. Today, in contrast, many Negroes have achieved outstanding success in the arts and sciences as well as in the business and professional world. It is true that public school education at the time of the Amendment had advanced further in the North, but the effect of the Amend-ment on Northern States was generally ignored in the congressional debates. Even in the North, the conditions of public education did not approximate those existing today. The curriculum was usually rudimentary; ungraded schools were common in rural areas; the school term was but three months a year in many states; and compulsory school attendance was virtually unknown. As a consequence, it is not surprising that there should be so little in the history of the Fourteenth Amendment relating to its intended effect on public education.

In the first cases in this Court construing the Fourteenth Amendment, decided shortly after its adoption, the Court interpreted it as proscribing all state-imposed discriminations against the Negro race. The doctrine of "separate but equal" did not make its appearance in this Court until 1896 in the case of *Plessy* v. *Ferguson* involving not education but transportation. American courts have since labored with the doctrine for over half a century. In this Court, there have been six cases involving the "separate but equal" doctrine in the field of public education. In *Cumming* v. *County Board of Education* and *Gong Lum* v. *Rice* the validity of the doctrine itself was not challenged. In more recent cases, all on the graduate school level, inequality was found in that specific benefits enjoyed by white students were denied to Negro students of the same educational qualifications. In none of these cases was it necessary to re-examine the doctrine to grant relief to the Negro plaintiff. And in *Sweatt* v. *Painter* the Court expressly reserved decision on the question whether *Plessy* v. *Ferguson* should be held inapplicable to public education.

In the instant cases, that question is directly presented. Here, unlike *Sweatt* v. *Painter*, there are findings below that the Negro and white schools involved have been equalized, or are being equalized, with respect to buildings, curricula, qualifications and salaries of teachers, and other "tangible" factors. Our decision, therefore, cannot turn on merely a comparison of these tangible factors in the Negro and white schools involved in each of the cases. We must look instead to the effect of segregation itself on public education.

In approaching this problem, we cannot turn the clock back to 1868 when the Amendment was adopted, or even to 1896 when *Plessy* v. *Ferguson* was written. We must consider public education in the light of its full development and its present place in American life throughout the Nation. Only in this way can it be determined if segregation in public schools deprives these plaintiffs of the equal protection of the laws.

Today, education is perhaps the most important function of state and local governments. Compulsory school attendance laws and the great expenditures for education both demonstrate our recognition of the importance of education to our democratic society. It is required in the performance of our most basic public responsibilities, even service in the armed forces. It is the very foundation of good citizenship. Today it is a principal instrument in awakening the child to cultural values, in preparing him for later professional training, and in helping him to adjust normally to his environment. In these days, it is doubtful that any child may reasonably be expected to succeed in life if he is denied the opportunity of an education. Such an opportunity, where the state has undertaken to provide it, is a right which must be made available to all on equal terms.

We come then to the question presented: Does segregation of children in public schools solely on the basis of race, even though the physical facilities and other "tangible" factors may be equal, deprive the children of the minority group of equal educational opportunities? We believe that it does.

In *Sweatt* v. *Painter* in finding that a segregated law school for Negroes could not provide them equal educational opportunities, this Court relied in large part on "those qualities which are incapable of objective measurement but which make for greatness in a law school." In *McLaurin* v. *Oklahoma State Regents* the Court, in requiring that a Negro admitted to a white graduate school be treated like all other students, again resorted to intangible considerations: ". . . his ability to study, to engage in discussions and exchange views with other students, and, in general, to learn his profession." Such considerations apply with added force to children in grade and high schools. To separate them from others of similar age and qualifications solely because of their race generates a feeling of inferiority as to their status in the community that may affect their hearts and minds in a way unlikely ever to be undone. The effect of this separation on their educational opportunities was well stated by a finding in the Kansas case by a court which nevertheless felt compelled to rule against the Negro plaintiffs:

> "Segregation of white and colored children in public schools has a detrimental effect upon the colored children. The impact is greater when it has the sanction of the law; for the policy of separating the races is usually interpreted as denoting the inferiority of the negro group. A sense of inferiority affects the motivation of a child to learn. Segregation with the sanction of law, therefore, has a tendency to [retard] the educational and mental development of negro children and to deprive them of some of the benefits they would receive in a racial[ly] integrated school system."

Whatever may have been the extent of psychological knowledge at the time of *Plessy* v. *Ferguson,* this finding is amply supported by modern authority. Any language in *Plessy* v. *Ferguson* contrary to this finding is rejected.

We conclude that in the field of public education the doctrine of "separate but equal" has no place. Separate educational facilities are inherently unequal. Therefore, we hold that the plaintiffs and others similarly situated for whom the actions have been brought are, by reason of the segregation complained of, deprived of the equal protection of the laws guaranteed by the Fourteenth Amendment. . . .

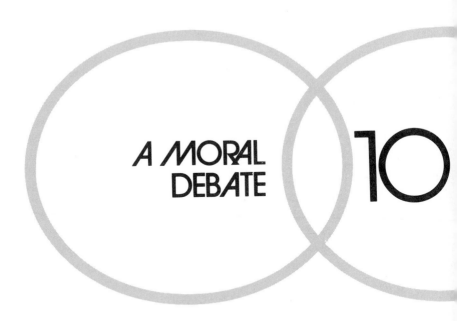

A MORAL DEBATE 10

Legal reasoning is possible because there is a shared framework of laws, precedents, procedures, etc.; it is interesting and complex because conflicts (and, hence, disagreements) can arise within this framework. A parallel situation exists for moral reasoning except that the potential for disagreement seems even greater. People in our society accept a great many moral principles as a matter of course. If a policy has no other consequence but to produce widespread misery, it is rejected out of hand. We share a conception of justice that includes, among other things, equality of opportunity and equality before the law. Most people have a conception of human dignity: a human being is not merely a thing to be used and disposed of for personal advantage. To the extent that views of this kind are widely shared and generally acknowledged, a moral community exists and moral discussion, including moral *disagreement*, is possible.

The idea that moral disagreement presupposes a system of shared moral principles may seem paradoxical, but it is not. Our moral disagreements typically arise when there is a *conflict* between moral principles, and people are inclined to resolve this conflict in different ways. If a person cannot see the moral difference between eating a carrot and eating his brother-in-law, we will not be able to get on a sufficient footing with him even to disagree. (This does not mean, of course, that cannibalism is always wrong, but even cannibals recognize that human beings are not just a different food.) The most serious and perplexing disagreements take place when people agree on principles such as welfare, justice, and human dignity, and yet, by weighing these principles differently or seeing the situation in a different light, arrive at opposing conclusions. It is a disagreement of this kind that we shall examine in this chapter.

It is important to see that we are not here concerned with *ethical theory*. An ethical theory is an attempt to establish the fundamental principle (or principles) by which actions are judged morally right or wrong. A great many such theories have been developed in the history of philosophy. Each has shed some light into the character of our moral thought, but none has received general acceptance. One such theory, ethical skepticism, holds, in effect, that there are no rational procedures for settling ethical disputes. Perhaps ethical skepticism is true, but until it is shown to be true, it would be foolish to abandon our serious concern with ethical issues. In any case, there is no reason to postpone discussion of special moral problems until agreement arises concerning the correct ethical theory. No one thinks that our courts should go into recess until the basic problems in jurisprudence have been resolved.

The Question of Abortion

The two selections given below concern the moral and, to a lesser extent, the legal issues raised by abortion. This is an area where people often gravitate toward extreme positions and express themselves in extreme language. But between the extremes of abortion on demand and the absolute prohibition of abortion there is a range of positions that generate serious and complex moral argumentation. In her essay, "A Defense of Abortion," Judith Jarvis Thomson defends an extensive (though not absolute) right to abortion. Her argument depends upon stressing the similarities between this disputed right and other human rights that are generally acknowledged. Baruch A. Brody adopts a different standpoint in his essay, "Abortion and the Sanctity of Human Life." He begins with the assumption (which Thomson acknowledges, at least for the sake of argument), that the fetus is a human being with a right to life. He then asks under what circumstances the rights of the pregnant woman should take precedence over the rights of the fetus. His answer is that a woman's right to abortion is extremely limited.

Both arguments bring out the analogical character of moral reasoning in a clear-cut way. They also show that the way in which an issue is raised will have an important influence on an argument. Starting out with the rights of a pregnant woman, Thomson asks when these should be set aside in favor of the acknowledged rights of the fetus. Reasoning from this perspective, she is able to find analogical arguments that support an extensive right to abortion. In contrast, Brody takes the rights of the fetus as his starting point and then challenges those analogical arguments that would deprive the fetus of its right to life. The outcome of this reasoning is that the fetus has an extensive right to life and, therefore, the right to abortion must be very limited.

A Defense of Abortion[1]

JUDITH JARVIS THOMSON

Most opposition to abortion relies on the premise that the fetus is a human being, a person, from the moment of conception. The premise is argued for, but, as I think, not well. Take, for example, the most common argument. We are asked to notice that the development of a human being from conception through birth into childhood is continuous; then it is said that to draw a line, to choose a point in this development and say "before this point the thing is not a person, after this point it is a person" is to make an arbitrary choice, a choice for which in the nature of things no good reason can be given. It is concluded that the fetus is, or anyway that we had better say it is, a person from the moment of conception. But this conclusion does not follow. Similar things might be said about the development of an acorn into an oak tree, and it does not follow that acorns are oak trees, or that we had better say they are. Arguments of this form are sometimes called "slippery slope arguments"—the phrase is perhaps self-explanatory —and it is dismaying that opponents of abortion rely on them so heavily and uncritically.

I am inclined to agree, however, that the prospects for "drawing a line" in the development of the fetus look dim. I am inclined to think also that we shall probably have to agree that the fetus has already become a human person well before birth. Indeed, it comes as a surprise when one first learns how early in its life it begins to acquire human characteristics. By the tenth week, for example, it already has a face, arms and legs, fingers and toes; it has internal organs, and brain activity is detectable.[2] On the other hand, I think that the premise is false, that the fetus is not a person from the moment of conception. A newly fertilized ovum, a newly implanted clump of cells, is no more a person than an acorn is an oak tree. But I shall not discuss any of this. For it seems to me to be of great interest to ask what happens if, for the sake of argument, we allow the premise. How, precisely, are we supposed to get from there to the conclusion that abortion is morally impermissible? Opponents of abortion commonly spend most of their time establishing that the fetus is a person, and hardly any time explaining the step from there to the impermissibility of abortion. Perhaps they think the step too simple and obvious to require much comment. Or perhaps instead they are simply being economical in argument. Many of those who defend abortion rely on the premise that the fetus is not a person, but only a bit of tissue that will become a person at birth; and why pay out more arguments than you have to? Whatever the explanation, I suggest that the step they take is

* *Philosophy and Public Affairs*, Vol. 1, No. 1 (Fall 1971), pp. 47-66.
[1] I am very much indebted to James Thomson for discussion, criticism, and many helpful suggestions.
[2] Daniel Callahan, *Abortion: Law, Choice and Morality* (New York, 1970), p. 373. This book gives a fascinating survey of the available information on abortion. The Jewish tradition is surveyed in David M. Feldman, *Birth Control in Jewish Law* (New York, 1968), Part 5, the Catholic tradition in John T. Noonan, Jr., "An Almost Absolute Value in History," in *The Morality of Abortion*, ed. John T. Noonan, Jr. (Cambridge, Mass., 1970).

neither easy nor obvious, that it calls for closer examination than it is commonly given, and that when we do give it this closer examination we shall feel inclined to reject it.

I propose, then, that we grant that the fetus is a person from the moment of conception. How does the argument go from here? Something like this, I take it. Every person has a right to life. So the fetus has a right to life. No doubt the mother has a right to decide what shall happen in and to her body; everyone would grant that. But surely a person's right to life is stronger and more stringent than the mother's right to decide what happens in and to her body, and so outweighs it. So the fetus may not be killed; an abortion may not be performed.

It sounds plausible. But now let me ask you to imagine this. You wake up in the morning and find yourself back to back in bed with an unconscious violinist. A famous unconscious violinist. He has been found to have a fatal kidney ailment, and the Society of Music Lovers has canvassed all the available medical records and found that you alone have the right blood type to help. They have therefore kidnapped you, and last night the violinist's circulatory system was plugged into yours, so that your kidneys can be used to extract poisons from his blood as well as your own. The director of the hospital now tells you, "Look, we're sorry the Society of Music Lovers did this to you—we would never have permitted it if we had known. But still, they did it, and the violinist now is plugged into you. To unplug you would be to kill him. But never mind, it's only for nine months. By then he will have recovered from his ailment, and can safely be unplugged from you." Is it morally incumbent on you to accede to this situation? No doubt it would be very nice of you if you did, a great kindness. But do you *have* to accede to it? What if it were not nine months, but nine years? Or longer still? What if the director of the hospital says, "Tough luck, I agree, but you've now got to stay in bed, with the violinist plugged into you, for the rest of your life. Because remember this. All persons have a right to life, and violinists are persons. Granted you have a right to decide what happens in and to your body, but a person's right to life outweighs your right to decide what happens in and to your body. So you cannot ever be unplugged from him." I imagine you would regard this as outrageous, which suggests that something really is wrong with that plausible-sounding argument I mentioned a moment ago.

In this case, of course, you were kidnapped; you didn't volunteer for the operation that plugged the violinist into your kidneys. Can those who oppose abortion on the ground I mentioned make an exception for a pregnancy due to rape? Certainly. They can say that persons have a right to life only if they didn't come into existence because of rape; or they can say that all persons have a right to life, but that some have less of a right to life than others, in particular, that those who came into existence because of rape have less. But these statements have a rather unpleasant sound. Surely the question of whether you have a right to life at all, or how much of it you have, shouldn't turn on the question of whether or not you are the product of a rape. And in fact the people who oppose abortion on the ground I mentioned do not make this distinction, and hence do not make an exception in the case of rape.

Nor do they make an exception for a case in which the mother had to spend the nine months of her pregnancy in bed. They would agree that would be a great pity, and hard on the mother; but all the same all persons have a right to life, the fetus is a person, and so on. I suspect, in fact, that they would not make an exception for a case in which, miraculously enough, the pregnancy went on for nine years or even the rest of the mother's life.

Some won't even make an exception for a case in which continuation of the pregnancy is likely to shorten the mother's life; they regard abortion as impermissible even to save the mother's life. Such cases are nowadays very rare, and many opponents of abortion do not accept this extreme view. All the same, it is a good place to begin: a number of points of interest come out in respect to it.

1. Let us call the view that abortion is impermissible even to save the mother's life "the extreme view." I want to suggest first that it does not issue from the argument I mentioned earlier without the addition of some fairly powerful premises. Suppose a woman has become pregnant, and now learns that she has a cardiac condition such that she will die if she carries the baby to term. What may be done for her? The fetus, being a person, has a right to life, but as the mother is a person too, so has she a right to life. Presumably they have an equal right to life. How is it supposed to come out that an abortion may not be performed? If mother and child have an equal right to life, shouldn't we perhaps flip a coin? Or should we add to the mother's right to life her right to decide what happens in and to her body which everybody seems to be ready to grant—the sum of her rights now outweighing the fetus' right to life?

The most familiar argument here is the following. We are told that performing the abortion would be directly killing[3] the child, whereas doing nothing would not be killing the mother, but only letting her die. Moreover, in killing the child, one would be killing an innocent person, for the child has committed no crime, and is not aiming at his mother's death. And then there are a variety of ways in which this might be continued. (1) But as directly killing an innocent person is always and absolutely impermissible, an abortion may not be performed. Or, (2) as directly killing an innocent person is murder, and murder is always and absolutely impermissible, an abortion may not be performed.[4] Or, (3) as one's duty to refrain from directly killing an innocent person is more stringent than one's duty to keep a person from dying, an abortion may not be performed. Or, (4) if one's only options are directly killing an innocent person or

---

[3] The term "direct" in the arguments I refer to is a technical one. Roughly what is meant by "direct killing" is either killing as an end by itself, or killing as a means to some end, for example, the end of saving someone else's life. See note 6, below, for an example of its use.

[4] Cf. *Encyclical Letter of Pope Pius XI on Christian Marriage*, St. Paul Editions (Boston, n.d.), p. 32: "however much we may pity the mother whose health and even life is gravely imperiled in the performance of the duty allotted to her by nature, nevertheless what could ever be a sufficient reason for excusing in any way the direct murder of the innocent? This is precisely what we are dealing with here." Noonan (*The Morality of Abortion*, p. 43) reads this as follows: "What cause can ever avail to excuse in any way the direct killing of the innocent? For it is a question of that."

letting a person die, one must prefer letting the person die, and thus an abortion may not be performed.[5]

Some people seem to have thought that these are not further premises which must be added if the conclusion is to be reached; but that they follow from the very fact that an innocent person has a right to life.[6] But this seems to me to be a mistake, and perhaps the simplest way to show this is to bring out that while we must certainly grant that innocent persons have a right to life, the theses in (1) through (4) are all false. Take (2), for example. If directly killing an innocent person is murder, and thus is impermissible, then the mother's directly killing the innocent person inside her is murder, and thus is impermissible. But it cannot seriously be thought to be murder if the mother performs an abortion on herself to save her life. It cannot seriously be said that she *must* refrain, that she *must* sit passively by and wait for her death. Let us look again at the case of you and the violinist. There you are, in bed with the violinist, and the director of the hospital says to you, "It's all most distressing, and I deeply sympathize, but you see this is putting an additional strain on your kidneys, and you'll be dead within the month. But you *have* to stay where you are all the same. Because unplugging you would be directly killing an innocent violinist, and that's murder, and that's impermissible." If anything in the world is true, it is that you do not commit murder, you do not do what is impermissible, if you reach around to your back and unplug yourself from that violinist to save your life.

The main focus of attention in writings on abortion has been on what a third party may or may not do in answer to a request from a woman for an abortion. This is in a way understandable. Things being as they are, there isn't much a woman can safely do to abort herself. So the question asked is what a third party may do, and what the mother may do, if it is mentioned at all, is deduced, almost as an afterthought, from what it is concluded that third parties may do. But it seems to me that to treat the matter in this way is to refuse to grant to the mother that very status of person which is so firmly insisted on for the fetus. For we cannot simply read off what a person may do from what a third party may do. Suppose you find yourself trapped in a tiny house with a growing child. I mean a very tiny house, and a rapidly growing child—you are already up against the wall of the house and in a few minutes you'll be crushed to death. The child on the other hand won't be crushed to death; if nothing is done to stop him from growing he'll be hurt, but in the end he'll simply burst open the house

---

[5] The thesis in (4) is in an interesting way weaker than those in (1), (2), and (3): they rule out abortion even in cases in which both mother *and* child will die if the abortion is not performed. By contrast, one who held the view expressed in (4) could consistently say that one needn't prefer letting two persons die to killing one.

[6] Cf. the following passage from Pius XII, *Address to the Italian Catholic Society of Midwives:* "The baby in the maternal breast has the right to life immediately from God.— Hence there is no man, no human authority, no science, no medical, eugenic, social, economic or moral 'indication' which can establish or grant a valid juridical ground for a direct deliberate disposition of an innocent human life, that is a disposition which looks to its destruction either as an end or as a means in another end perhaps in itself not illicit. The baby, still not born, is a man in the same degree and for the same reason as the mother" (quoted in Noonan, *The Morality of Abortion,* p. 45).

and walk out a free man. Now I could well understand it if a bystander were to say, "There's nothing we can do for you. We cannot choose between your life and his, we cannot be the ones to decide who is to live, we cannot intervene." But it cannot be concluded that you too can do nothing, that you cannot attack it to save your life. However innocent the child may be, you do not have to wait passively while it crushes you to death. Perhaps a pregnant woman is vaguely felt to have the status of house, to which we don't allow the right of self-defense. But if the woman houses the child, it should be remembered that she is a person who houses it.

I should perhaps stop to say explicitly that I am not claiming that people have a right to do anything whatever to save their lives. I think, rather, that there are drastic limits to the right of self-defense. If someone threatens you with death unless you torture someone else to death, I think you have not the right, even to save your life, to do so. But the case under consideration here is very different. In our case there are only two people involved, one whose life is threatened, and one who threatens it. Both are innocent: the one who is threatened is not threatened because of any fault, the one who threatens does not threaten because of any fault. For this reason we may feel that we bystanders cannot intervene. But the person threatened can.

In sum, a woman surely can defend her life against the threat to it posed by the unborn child, even if doing so involves its death. And this shows not merely that the theses in (1) through (4) are false; it shows also that the extreme view of abortion is false, and so we need not canvass any other possible ways of arriving at it from the argument I mentioned at the outset.

2. The extreme view could of course be weakened to say that while abortion is permissible to save the mother's life, it may not be performed by a third party, but only by the mother herself. But this cannot be right either. For what we have to keep in mind is that the mother and the unborn child are not like two tenants in a small house which has, by an unfortunate mistake, been rented to both: the mother *owns* the house. The fact that she does adds to the offensiveness of deducing that the mother can do nothing from the supposition that third parties can do nothing. But it does more than this: it casts a bright light on the supposition that third parties can do nothing. Certainly it lets us see that a third party who says "I cannot choose between you" is fooling himself if he thinks this is impartiality. If Jones has found and fastened on a certain coat, which he needs to keep him from freezing, but which Smith also needs to keep him from freezing, then it is not impartiality that says "I cannot choose between you" when Smith owns the coat. Women have said again and again "This body is *my* body!" and they have reason to feel angry, reason to feel that it has been like shouting into the wind. Smith, after all, is hardly likely to bless us if we say to him, "Of course it's your coat; anybody would grant that it is. But no one may choose between you and Jones who is to have it."

We should really ask what it is that says "no one may choose" in the face of the fact that the body that houses the child is the mother's body. It may be simply a failure to appreciate this fact. But it may be something more interesting, namely the sense that one has a right to refuse to lay hands on people, even where it would be just and fair to do so, even where justice seems to require that somebody do so. Thus justice might call for somebody to get Smith's coat back from Jones, and yet you have a right to refuse to be the one to lay hands on Jones, a right to refuse to do physical violence to him. This, I think, must be granted. But then what should be said is not "no one may choose," but only "*I* cannot choose," and indeed not even this, but "*I* will not *act*," leaving it open that somebody else can or should, and in particular that anyone in a position of authority, with the job of securing people's rights, both can and should. So this is no difficulty. I have not been arguing that any given third party must accede to the mother's request that he perform an abortion to save her life, but only that he may.

I suppose that in some views of human life the mother's body is only on loan to her, the loan not being one which gives her any prior claim to it. One who held this view might well think it impartiality to say "I cannot choose." But I shall simply ignore this possibility. My own view is that if a human being has any just, prior claim to anything at all, he has a just, prior claim to his own body. And perhaps this needn't be argued for here anyway, since, as I mentioned, the arguments against abortion we are looking at do grant that the woman has a right to decide what happens in and to her body.

But although they do grant it, I have tried to show that they do not take seriously what is done in granting it. I suggest the same thing will reappear even more clearly when we turn away from cases in which the mother's life is at stake, and attend, as I propose we now do, to the vastly more common cases in which a woman wants an abortion for some less weighty reason than preserving her own life.

3. Where the mother's life is not at stake, the argument I mentioned at the outset seems to have a much stronger pull. "Everyone has a right to life, so the unborn person has a right to life." And isn't the child's right to life weightier than anything other than the mother's own right to life, which she might put forward as ground for an abortion?

This argument treats the right to life as if it were unproblematic. It is not, and this seems to me to be precisely the source of the mistake.

For we should now, at long last, ask what it comes to, to have a right to life. In some views having a right to life includes having a right to be given at least the bare minimum one needs for continued life. But suppose that what in fact *is* the bare minimum a man needs for continued life is something he has no right at all to be given? If I am sick unto death, and the only thing that will save my life is the touch of Henry Fonda's cool hand on my fevered brow, then all the same, I have no right to be given the touch of Henry Fonda's cool hand on my fevered brow. It would be frightfully nice of him to fly in from the West Coast to provide it. It would be less nice, though no doubt well meant, if my friends flew out to the West Coast and carried Henry Fonda back with them. But I have no right at all against anybody that he should do this for me. Or again, to return to the story I told earlier, the fact that for continued life that violinist needs the continued use of your kidneys does not establish that he has a right to be given the continued use of your kidneys. He certainly has no right against you that *you* should give him continued use of your kidneys. For nobody has any right to use your kidneys unless you give him such a right; and nobody has the right against you that you shall give him this right—if you do allow him to go on using your kidneys, this is a kindness on your part, and not something he can claim from you as his due. Nor has he any right against anybody else that *they* should give him continued use of your kidneys. Certainly he had no right against the Society of Music Lovers that they should plug him into you in the first place. And if you now start to unplug yourself, having learned that you will otherwise have to spend nine years in bed with him, there is nobody in the world who must try to prevent you, in order to see to it that he is given something he has a right to be given.

Some people are rather stricter about the right to life. In their view, it does not include the right to be given anything, but amounts to, and only to, the right not to be killed by anybody. But here a related difficulty arises. If everybody is to refrain from killing that violinist then everybody must refrain from doing a great many different sorts of things. Everybody must refrain from slitting his throat, everybody must refrain from shooting him—and everybody must refrain from unplugging you from him. But does he have a right against everybody that they shall refrain from unplugging you from him? To refrain from doing this is to allow him to continue to use your kidneys. It could be argued that he has a right against us that *we* should allow him to continue to use your kidneys. That is, while he had no right against us that we should give him the use of your kidneys, it might be argued that he anyway has a right against us that we shall not now intervene and deprive him of the use of your kidneys. I shall come back to third-party interventions later. But certainly the violinist has no right against you that *you* shall allow him to continue to use your kidneys. As I said, if you do allow him to use them, it is a kindness on your part, and not something you owe him.

The difficulty I point to here is not peculiar to the right to life. It reappears in connection with all the other natural rights; and it is something which an adequate account of rights must deal with. For present purposes it is enough just to draw attention to it. But I would stress that I am not arguing that people do not have a right to life—quite to the contrary, it seems to me that the primary control we must place on the acceptability of an account of rights is that it should turn out in that account to be a truth that all persons have a right to life. I am arguing only that having a right to life does not guarantee having either a right to be given the use of or a right to be allowed continued use of another person's body—even if one needs it for life itself. So the right to life will not serve the opponents of abortion in the very simple and clear way in which they seem to have thought it would.

4. There is another way to bring out the difficulty. In the most ordinary sort of case, to deprive someone of what he has a right to is to treat him unjustly. Suppose a boy and his small brother are jointly given a box of chocolates for Christmas. If the older boy takes the box and refuses to give his brother any of the chocolates, he is unjust to him, for the brother has been given a right to half of them. But suppose that, having learned that otherwise it means nine years in

bed with that violinist, you unplug yourself from him. You surely are not being unjust to him, for you gave him no right to use your kidneys, and no one else can have given him any such right. But we have to notice that in unplugging yourself, you are killing him; and violinists, like everybody else, have a right to life, and thus in the view we were considering just now, the right not to be killed. So here you do what he supposedly has a right you shall not do, but you do not act unjustly to him in doing it.

The emendation which may be made at this point is this: the right to life consists not in the right not to be killed, but rather in the right not to be killed unjustly. This runs a risk of circularity, but never mind: it would enable us to square the fact that the violinist has a right to life with the fact that you do not act unjustly toward him in unplugging yourself, thereby killing him. For if you do not kill him unjustly, you do not violate his right to life, and so it is no wonder you do him no injustice.

But if this emendation is accepted, the gap in the argument against abortion stares us plainly in the face: it is by no means enough to show that the fetus is a person, and to remind us that all persons have a right to life—we need to be shown also that killing the fetus violates its right to life, i.e., that abortion is unjust killing. And is it?

I suppose we may take it as a datum that in a case of pregnancy due to rape the mother has not given the unborn person a right to the use of her body for food and shelter. Indeed, in what pregnancy could it be supposed that the mother has given the unborn person such a right? It is not as if there were unborn persons drifting about the world, to whom a woman who wants a child says "I invite you in."

But it might be argued that there are other ways one can have acquired a right to the use of another person's body than by having been invited to use it by that person. Suppose a woman voluntarily indulges in intercourse, knowing of the chance it will issue in pregnancy, and then she does become pregnant; is she not in part responsible for the presence, in fact the very existence, of the unborn person inside her? No doubt she did not invite it in. But doesn't her partial responsibility for its being there itself give it a right to the use of her body?[7] If so, then her aborting it would be more like the boy's taking away the chocolates, and less like your unplugging yourself from the violinist—doing so would be depriving it of what it does have a right to, and thus would be doing it an injustice.

And then, too, it might be asked whether or not she can kill it even to save her own life: If she voluntarily called it into existence, how can she now kill it, even in self-defense?

The first thing to be said about this is that it is something new. Opponents of abortion have been so concerned to make out the independence of the fetus, in order to establish that it has a right to life, just as its mother does, that they have tended to overlook the possible support they might gain from making out that the fetus is *dependent* on the mother, in order to establish that she has a

---

[7] The need for a discussion of this argument was brought home to me by members of the Society for Ethical and Legal Philosophy, to whom this paper was originally presented.

special kind of responsibility for it, a responsibility that gives it rights against her which are not possessed by any independent person—such as an ailing violinist who is a stranger to her.

On the other hand, this argument would give the unborn person a right to its mother's body only if her pregnancy resulted from a voluntary act, undertaken in full knowledge of the chance a pregnancy might result from it. It would leave out entirely the unborn person whose existence is due to rape. Pending the availability of some further argument, then, we would be left with the conclusion that unborn persons whose existence is due to rape have no right to the use of their mothers' bodies, and thus that aborting them is not depriving them of anything they have a right to and hence is not unjust killing.

And we should also notice that it is not at all plain that this argument really does go even as far as it purports to. For there are cases and cases, and the details make a difference. If the room is stuffy, and I therefore open a window to air it, and a burglar climbs in, it would be absurd to say, "Ah, now he can stay, she's given him a right to the use of her house—for she is partially responsible for his presence there, having voluntarily done what enabled him to get in, in full knowledge that there are such things as burglars, and that burglars burgle." It would be still more absurd to say this if I had had bars installed outside my windows, precisely to prevent burglars from getting in, and a burglar got in only because of a defect in the bars. It remains equally absurd if we imagine it is not a burglar who climbs in, but an innocent person who blunders or falls in. Again, suppose it were like this: people-seeds drift about in the air like pollen, and if you open your windows, one may drift in and take root in your carpets or upholstery. You don't want children, so you fix up your windows with fine mesh screens, the very best you can buy. As can happen, however, and on very, very rare occasions does happen, one of the screens is defective; and a seed drifts in and takes root. Does the person-plant who now develops have a right to the use of your house? Surely not—despite the fact that you voluntarily opened your windows, you knowingly kept carpets and upholstered furniture, and you knew that screens were sometimes defective. Someone may argue that you are responsible for its rooting, that it does have a right to your house, because after all you *could* have lived out your life with bare floors and furniture, or with sealed windows and doors. But this won't do—for by the same token anyone can avoid a pregnancy due to rape by having a hysterectomy, or anyway by never leaving home without a (reliable!) army.

It seems to me that the argument we are looking at can establish at most that there are *some* cases in which the unborn person has a right to the use of its mother's body, and therefore *some* cases in which abortion is unjust killing. There is room for much discussion and argument as to precisely which, if any. But I think we should side-step this issue and leave it open, for at any rate the argument certainly does not establish that all abortion is unjust killing.

5. There is room for yet another argument here, however. We surely must all grant that there may be cases in which it would be morally indecent to detach a person from your body at the cost of his life. Suppose you learn that what the violinist needs is not nine years of your life, but only one hour: all you need

do to save his life is to spend one hour in that bed with him. Suppose also that letting him use your kidneys for that one hour would not affect your health in the slightest. Admittedly you were kidnapped. Admittedly you did not give anyone permission to plug him into you. Nevertheless it seems to me plain you *ought* to allow him to use your kidneys for that hour—it would be indecent to refuse.

Again, suppose pregnancy lasted only an hour, and constituted no threat to life or health. And suppose that a woman becomes pregnant as a result of rape. Admittedly she did not voluntarily do anything to bring about the existence of a child. Admittedly she did nothing at all which would give the unborn person a right to the use of her body. All the same it might well be said, as in the newly emended violinist story, that she *ought* to allow it to remain for that hour—that it would be indecent in her to refuse.

Now some people are inclined to use the term "right" in such a way that it follows from the fact that you ought to allow a person to use your body for the hour he needs, that he has a right to use your body for the hour he needs, even though he has not been given that right by any person or act. They may say that it follows also that if you refuse, you act unjustly toward him. This use of the term is perhaps so common that it cannot be called wrong; nevertheless it seems to me to be an unfortunate loosening of what we would do better to keep a tight rein on. Suppose that box of chocolates I mentioned earlier had not been given to both boys jointly, but was given only to the older boy. There he sits, stolidly eating his way through the box, his small brother watching enviously. Here we are likely to say "You ought not to be so mean. You ought to give your brother some of those chocolates." My own view is that it just does not follow from the truth of this that the brother has any right to any of the chocolates. If the boy refuses to give his brother any, he is greedy, stingy, callous— but not unjust. I suppose that the people I have in mind will say it does follow that the brother has a right to some of the chocolates, and thus that the boy does act unjustly if he refuses to give his brother any. But the effect of saying this is to obscure what we should keep distinct, namely the difference between the boy's refusal in this case and the boy's refusal in the earlier case, in which the box was given to both boys jointly, and in which the small brother thus had what was from any point of view clear title to half.

A further objection to so using the term "right" that from the fact that A ought to do a thing for B, it follows that B has a right against A that A do it for him, is that it is going to make the question of whether or not a man has a right to a thing turn on how easy it is to provide him with it; and this seems not merely unfortunate, but morally unacceptable. Take the case of Henry Fonda again. I said earlier that I had no right to the touch of his cool hand on my fevered brow, even though I needed it to save my life. I said it would be frightfully nice of him to fly in from the West Coast to provide me with it, but that I had no right against him that he should do so. But suppose he isn't on the West Coast. Suppose he has only to walk across the room, place a hand briefly on my brow—and lo, my life is saved. Then surely he ought to do it, it would be indecent to refuse. Is it to be said "Ah, well, it follows that in this case she has a right to the touch of his hand on her brow, and so it would be an injustice in him to refuse"? So that I have a right to it when it is easy for him to provide it, though no right when it's hard? It's rather a shocking idea that anyone's rights should fade away and disappear as it gets harder and harder to accord them to him.

So my own view is that even though you ought to let the violinist use your kidneys for the one hour he needs, we should not conclude that he has a right to do so—we should say that if you refuse, you are, like the boy who owns all the chocolates and will give none away, self-centered and callous, indecent in fact, but not unjust. And similarly, that even supposing a case in which a woman pregnant due to rape ought to allow the unborn person to use her body for the hour he needs, we should not conclude that he has a right to do so; we should conclude that she is self-centered, callous, indecent, but not unjust, if she refuses. The complaints are no less grave; they are just different. However, there is no need to insist on this point. If anyone does wish to deduce "he has a right" from "you ought," then all the same he must surely grant that there are cases in which it is not morally required of you that you allow that violinist to use your kidneys, and in which he does not have a right to use them, and in which you do not do him an injustice if you refuse. And so also for mother and unborn child. Except in such cases as the unborn person has a right to demand it—and we were leaving open the possibility that there may be such cases—nobody is morally *required* to make large sacrifices, of health, of all other interests and concerns, of all other duties and commitments, for nine years, or even for nine months, in order to keep another person alive.

6. We have in fact to distinguish between two kinds of Samaritan: the Good Samaritan and what we might call the Minimally Decent Samaritan. The story of the Good Samaritan, you will remember, goes like this:

A certain man went down from Jerusalem to Jericho, and fell among thieves, which stripped him of his raiment, and wounded him, and departed, leaving him half dead.

And by chance there came down a certain priest that way; and when he saw him, he passed by on the other side.

And likewise a Levite, when he was at the place, came and looked on him, and passed by on the other side.

But a certain Samaritan, as he journeyed, came where he was and when he saw him he had compassion on him.

And went to him, and bound up his wounds, pouring in oil and wine, and set him on his own beast, and brought him to an inn, and took care of him.

And on the morrow, when he departed, he took out two pence, and gave them to the host, and said unto him, ''Take care of him: and whatsoever thou spendest more, when I come again, I will repay thee.''

(Luke 10:30-35)

The Good Samaritan went out of his way, at some cost to himself, to help one in need of it. We are not told what the options were, that is, whether or not the priest and the Levite could have helped by doing less than the Good Samaritan did, but assuming they could have, then the fact they did nothing at all shows they were not even Minimally Decent Samaritans, not because they were not Samaritans, but because they were not even minimally decent.

These things are a matter of degree, of course, but there is a difference, and it comes out perhaps most clearly in the story of Kitty Genovese, who, as you will remember, was murdered while thirty-eight people watched or listened, and did nothing at all to help her. A Good Samaritan would have rushed out to give direct assistance against the murderer. Or perhaps we had better allow that it would have been a Splendid Samaritan who did this, on the ground that it would have involved a risk of death for himself. But the thirty-eight not only did not do this, they did not even trouble to pick up a phone to call the police. Minimally Decent Samaritanism would call for doing at least that, and their not having done it was monstrous.

After telling the story of the Good Samaritan, Jesus said "Go, and do thou likewise." Perhaps he meant that we are morally required to act as the Good Samaritan did. Perhaps he was urging people to do more than is morally required of them. At all events it seems plain that it was not morally required of any of the thirty-eight that he rush out to give direct assistance at the risk of his own life, and that it is not morally required of anyone that he give long stretches of his life—nine years or nine months—to sustaining the life of a person who has no special right (we were leaving open the possibility of this) to demand it.

Indeed, with one rather striking class of exceptions, no one in any country in the world is *legally* required to do anywhere near as much as this for anyone else. The class of exceptions is obvious. My main concern here is not the state of the law in respect to abortion, but it is worth drawing attention to the fact that in no state in this country is any man compelled by law to be even a Minimally Decent Samaritan to any person; there is no law under which charges could be brought against the thirty-eight who stood by while Kitty Genovese died. By contrast, in most states in this country women are compelled by law to be not merely Minimally Decent Samaritans, but Good Samaritans to unborn persons inside them. This doesn't by itself settle anything one way or the other, because it may well be argued that there should be laws in this country—as there are in many European countries—compelling at least Minimally Decent Samaritanism.[8] But it does show that there is a gross injustice in the existing state of the law. And it shows also that the groups currently working against liberalization of abortion laws, in fact working toward having it declared unconstitutional for a state to permit abortion, had better start working for the adoption of Good Samaritan laws generally, or earn the charge that they are acting in bad faith.

I should think, myself, that Minimally Decent Samaritan laws would be one thing, Good Samaritan laws quite another, and in fact highly improper. But we

[8] For a discussion of the difficulties involved, and a survey of the European experience with such laws, see *The Good Samaritan and the Law*, ed. James M. Ratcliffe (New York, 1966).

are not here concerned with the law. What we should ask is not whether anybody should be compelled by law to be a Good Samaritan, but whether we must
accede to a situation in which somebody is being compelled—by nature, perhaps
—to be a Good Samaritan. We have, in other words, to look now at third-party
interventions. I have been arguing that no person is morally required to make
large sacrifices to sustain the life of another who has no right to demand them,
and this even where the sacrifices do not include life itself; we are not morally
required to be Good Samaritans or anyway Very Good Samaritans to one another. But what if a man cannot extricate himself from such a situation? What
if he appeals to us to extricate him? It seems to me plain that there are cases
in which we can, cases in which a Good Samaritan would extricate him. There
you are, you were kidnapped, and nine years in bed with that violinist lie ahead
of you. You have your own life to lead. You are sorry, but you simply cannot
see giving up so much of your life to the sustaining of his. You cannot extricate
yourself, and ask us to do so. I should have thought that—in light of his having
no right to the use of your body—it was obvious that we do not have to accede
to your being forced to give up so much. We can do what you ask. There is no
injustice to the violinist in our doing so.

7. Following the lead of the opponents of abortion, I have throughout been
speaking of the fetus merely as a person, and what I have been asking is whether
or not the argument we began with, which proceeds only from the fetus' being
a person, really does establish its conclusion. I have argued that it does not.

But of course there are arguments and arguments, and it may be said that
I have simply fastened on the wrong one. It may be said that what is important
is not merely the fact that the fetus is a person, but that it is a person for whom
the woman has a special kind of responsibility issuing from the fact that she is
its mother. And it might be argued that all my analogies are therefore irrelevant
—for you do not have that special kind of responsibility for that violinist, Henry
Fonda does not have that special kind of responsibility for me. And our attention
might be drawn to the fact that men and women both *are* compelled by law to
provide support for their children.

I have in effect dealt (briefly) with this argument in section 4 above; but a
(still briefer) recapitulation now may be in order. Surely we do not have any
such "special responsibility" for a person unless we have assumed it, explicitly
or implicitly. If a set of parents do not try to prevent pregnancy, do not obtain
an abortion, and then at the time of birth of the child do not put it out for adoption, but rather take it home with them, then they have assumed responsibility
for it, they have given it rights, and they cannot *now* withdraw support from it
at the cost of its life because they now find it difficult to go on providing for it.
But if they have taken all reasonable precautions against having a child, they do
not simply by virtue of their biological relationship to the child who comes into
existence have a special responsibility for it. They may wish to assume responsibility for it, or they may not wish to. And I am suggesting that if assuming responsibility for it would require large sacrifices, then they may refuse. A Good
Samaritan would not refuse—or anyway, a Splendid Samaritan, if the sacrifices

that had to be made were enormous. But then so would a Good Samaritan assume responsibility for that violinist; so would Henry Fonda, if he is a Good Samaritan, fly in from the West Coast and assume responsibility for me.

8. My argument will be found unsatisfactory on two counts by many of those who want to regard abortion as morally permissible. First, while I do argue that abortion is not impermissible, I do not argue that it is always permissible. There may well be cases in which carrying the child to term requires only Minimally Decent Samaritanism of the mother, and this is a standard we must not fall below. I am inclined to think it a merit of my account precisely that it does *not* give a general yes or a general no. It allows for and supports our sense that, for example, a sick and desperately frightened fourteen-year-old schoolgirl, pregnant due to rape, may *of course* choose abortion, and that any law which rules this out is an insane law. And it also allows for and supports our sense that in other cases resort to abortion is even positively indecent. It would be indecent in the woman to request an abortion, and indecent in a doctor to perform it, if she is in her seventh month, and wants the abortion just to avoid the nuisance of postponing a trip abroad. The very fact that the arguments I have been drawing attention to treat all cases of abortion, or even all cases of abortion in which the mother's life is not at stake, as morally on a par ought to have made them suspect at the outset.

Secondly, while I am arguing for the permissibility of abortion in some cases, I am not arguing for the right to secure the death of the unborn child. It is easy to confuse these two things in that up to a certain point in the life of the fetus it is not able to survive outside the mother's body; hence removing it from her body guarantees its death. But they are importantly different. I have argued that you are not morally required to spend nine months in bed, sustaining the life of that violinist; but to say this is by no means to say that if, when you unplug yourself, there is a miracle and he survives, you then have a right to turn round and slit his throat. You may detach yourself even if this costs him his life; you have no right to be guaranteed his death by some other means, if unplugging yourself does not kill him. There are some people who will feel dissatisfied by this feature of my argument. A woman may be utterly devastated by the thought of a child, a bit of herself, put out for adoption and never seen or heard of again. She may therefore want not merely that the child be detached from her, but more, that it die. Some opponents of abortion are inclined to regard this as beneath contempt—thereby showing insensitivity to what is surely a powerful source of despair. All the same, I agree that the desire for the child's death is not one which anybody may gratify, should it turn out to be possible to detach the child alive.

At this place, however, it should be remembered that we have only been pretending throughout that the fetus is a human being from the moment of conception. A very early abortion is surely not the killing of a person, and so is not dealt with by anything I have said here.

Abortion and the Sanctity of Human Life
BARUCH A. BRODY

One of our most fundamental moral intuitions is that, except in the most extreme circumstances, it is wrong to take a human life. This intuition is, however, not very precise, partially because of the vagueness of "extreme circumstances" and partially because of the unclarity about what is a human life. The problem about abortion is a difficult one just because of this latter unclarity. There are those who, with good reason, claim that a foetus is a human being the taking of whose life is, except in the most extreme circumstances, wrong; destroying a foetus, according to this position, is just as wrong as the taking of any other human life. There are, however, others who claim, with equally good reason, that a foetus is not a human being and that, therefore, its destruction is permissible in many cases in which it would be wrong to take a human life. Because it is so difficult, given the vagueness of "human life," to decide which of these claims about the foetus is correct, it is very difficult to decide when, if ever, an abortion is morally[1] permissible.

I should like, in this paper, to consider the following issue: if a foetus is a human being the destruction of which is as wrong as the taking of any human life, are there any extreme circumstances in which an abortion would still be morally permissible? In particular, would it be permissible in order to save the life of the mother?

There are three reasons for being concerned with this question: (a) it just may be the case that a foetus is a human being. If so, then an answer to our question will be the answer to the question as to whether it actually is permissible to perform an abortion in order to save the life of the mother; (b) given that we do not know whether the foetus is a human being, it would be helpful to have an answer to our question for if (as seems possible) it is that it would still be permissible to perform the abortion, then we will at least know that an abortion is permissible in some of the cases in which the need for it is greatest; (c) a consideration of this issue may shed some light upon what are the extreme circumstances in which it is permissible to take a human life.

I

The most obvious reason for supposing that it is permissible to perform an abortion in order to save the life of the mother, even though the foetus is a human being, is that such an abortion would be a permissible act of defending oneself. After all, the foetus's continued existence poses a threat to the life of the

* *American Philosophical Quarterly*, Vol. 10, No. 2 (April 1973), pp. 133—40.
[1] This is a question about morals, not about the legal question of whether there should be laws prohibiting abortion. On that issue, see my "Abortion and the Law," *Journal of Philosophy*, 1971.

mother which she can meet, if necessary, by the taking of the life of the foetus.[2]

This simple argument from the right to kill the pursuer will not do for there is an important difference between the case of an abortion and the normal case of killing the pursuer. In the normal case of killing the pursuer, B is attempting to take A's life and is responsible for that attempt. It is this guilt which, together with the fact that A will die unless B is stopped, seems to justify the taking of B's life. In the case of an abortion, however, the situation is quite different. Leaving aside for now—we shall return to it later on—the question as to whether the foetus is attempting to take the mother's life, we can certainly agree that the foetus is not responsible for such an attempt (if it is occurring), that the foetus is therefore totally innocent, and that the taking of his life cannot therefore be compared to the ordinary case of killing the pursuer.[3]

Let us put this point another way. Consider the following case: there is just enough medicine to keep either A or B alive; B legitimately owns it, and will not give it to A. In this case, the continued existence of B certainly poses a threat to the life of A; A can survive only if B does not survive. Still, one would not say that it is permissible for A to kill B in order to save A's life. Why not? How does this case differ from the ordinary case of killing the pursuer? The simplest answer is that in this case, while B's continued existence poses a threat to the life of A, B is not guilty of attempting to take A's life; he is not even attempting to do so. On the other hand, in the ordinary case of a pursuer, B is guilty of attempting to kill A. Now if we consider the case of a foetus whose continued existence poses a threat to the life of the mother, we see that it is like the medicine-case and not like the ordinary case of killing the pursuer. The foetus does pose a threat to the life of its mother, but it is not guilty of attempting to take its mother's life. Consequently, analogously to the medicine-case, the mother (or her agent) could not justify destroying the foetus on the ground that it is a permissible act of killing the pursuer.

This objection, while persuasive, is not entirely convincing, and something more must be said about the whole matter of pursuers before we can definitely decide whether an abortion to save the life of the mother could be viewed as a permissible act of killing the pursuer. If we look again at a normal pursuer case, we see that there are three factors involved:

(1) the continued existence of B poses a threat to the life of A, a threat that can be met only by the taking of B's life,

---

[2] To be sure, it is the abortionist, and not the mother, who will destroy the fetus, but that is irrelevant. To begin with, in such cases, it is permissible for him whose life is threatened (A) to, if necessary, either take the life of him (B) who threatens him or call upon someone else to do so. And more importantly, it seems permissible (and perhaps even obligatory in some cases) for a third person to take B's life in order to save A's life even if A has not called upon him to do so (we leave aside the question as to whether it is permissible if A objects). For this reason, it seems better to say that it is permissible to take the life of the pursuer, when necessary to save the life of the pursued, rather than to say that it is permissible to take lives, when necessary for self-defense. On this point, see *Talmud Sanhedrin* 72b–75a.

[3] This is, essentially, the argument of Pius XI (in *Casti Connubii*, Section 64).

(2) B is justly attempting to take A's life,

(3) B is responsible for his attempt to take A's life.

In the medicine-case, only condition (1) was satisfied, and our intuitions that it would be wrong for A to take B's life in that case are justified by the fact that the mere satisfaction of (1) does not guarantee that killing B will be a justifiable act of killing a pursuer. But it would be rash to conclude, as we did, that all of conditions (1)-(3) must be satisfied before one has a case in which the killing of B will be a justifiable act of killing a pursuer. What would happen, for example, if conditions (1) and (2), but not (3), were satisfied?

There are good reasons for supposing that the satisfaction of (1) and (2) is sufficient for someone's being justified in taking B's life as an act of killing the pursuer. Consider, for example, a normal case of pursuit (e.g., where B is about to shoot A and the only way in which A can stop him is by killing him first) with the modification that B is a minor who is not responsible for his attempt to take A's life.[4] In this case, conditions (1) and (2) but not (3) are satisfied. Still, despite the fact that (3) is not satisfied, it seems that A may justifiably take B's life because doing so is a permissible act of killing a pursuer. So guilt of the pursuer is not a requirement for legitimate cases of killing the pursuer.[5]

Are there any cases in which the satisfaction of (1) and something weaker than (2) is sufficient for A's justifiably killing B as an act of killing a pursuer? It seems that there are. Consider, for example, the following case: B is about to press a button that apparently turns on a light and there is no reason for him to suspect what is the case, viz., that his doing so will blow up a bomb that will destroy A. Moreover, the only way in which we can stop B and save A's life is by taking B's life (there is no opportunity to warn him, etc.). In such a case, neither conditions (2) nor (3) are satisfied. B is not attempting to take A's life and, *a fortiori*, he is not responsible for, or guilty of, any such attempt. Nevertheless, one is inclined to say that this is still a case in which one would be justified in taking B's life in order to save A's life, that this is a legitimate case of killing a pursuer.

How does this case differ from the medicine-case? Or, to put our question another way, what condition (other than (2)) in addition to (1) is satisfied in this case, but not in the medicine-case, and is such that its satisfaction (together with the satisfaction of (1)) is sufficient to justify our killing B as an act of killing a pursuer? As we think about the two cases, the following idea seems to suggest itself: there is, in this case, some action that B is doing (pressing the button) that results in A's death and which is such that if B knew about this result and still did the action voluntarily he would be to blame for the loss of A's life. In this

---

[4] This point, and its significance, was first pointed out by R. Huna when he said (*Talmud Sanhedrin*, 72b) that a pursuer who is a minor can be stopped even by killing him.

[5] It should be noted that this point wreaks havoc with a very plausible analysis of why we are justified in taking the life of the pursuer. According to this analysis, B's guilt for his attempt to take A's life together with the threat that his continued existence poses for A's life justifies the taking of B's life. Or, to put this analysis another way, B's guilt makes A's life take precedence over B's. We now see that this intuitively plausible analysis cannot be right. After all, in cases where conditions (1) and (2) but not (3) are satisfied, B has incurred no guilt for his attempt to take A's life and his guilt cannot therefore be used to explain why we are justified in taking B's life in order to save A's life.

case, if B knew that A would die if he pressed the button and still pressed it voluntarily, he would be to blame[6] for the loss of A's life. In the medicine-case, on the other hand, there is no such action. It is true that B's refusing to give A the medicine does result in A's death. But even if he knows that and still voluntarily refuses to give A the medicine, he is not to blame for the loss of A's life. A man is not obligated to give up his life to save the life of another person and he is not to blame for the loss of that other person's life when he does refuse to sacrifice himself. It would seem then that it is sufficient, for A to be justified in taking B's life as an act of killing a pursuer, that, in addition to the satisfaction of condition (1), the following condition be satisfied:

> (2') B is doing some action that will lead to A's death and is such that if B is a responsible person who did it voluntarily knowing that this result would come about, B will be to blame for the loss of A's life.

To summarize, then, our general discussion of killing the pursuer, we can say that if conditions (1) and (2) or (2') are satisfied, one would be justified in taking B's life in order to save A's life.[7] The satisfaction of (3) is not required.

Let us return now to the problem of abortion and, working with the assumption that the foetus is human, apply these results to the case of the foetus whose continued existence poses a threat to the life of his mother and see whether, in that case, it would be permissible, as an act of killing a pursuer, to abort the foetus in order to save the mother. The first thing that we should note is that our initial objection to the claim that the foetus could be aborted because its abortion is a permissible act of killing a pursuer is mistaken. Our objection was that the foetus is not responsible for any attempt to take the life of the mother, that the foetus is innocent. But that only means that condition (3) is not satisfied and we have seen that the satisfaction of (3) is not necessary.

Is, then, the aborting of a foetus when necessary to save the life of the mother a permissible act of killing a pursuer? Well, in such cases, condition (1) is satisfied, so the only question that we have to consider is whether (2) or (2') is also satisfied. It is clear that (2) is not satisfied. The foetus, after all, has neither the beliefs nor the intentions that would be necessary for any of his actions (if he does act) to be an attempt, on his part, to take the life of his mother. Nor is (2') satisfied. Even if we endow the foetus with the beliefs and intentions of an adult, none of his actions are such that his doing them would result in his being to blame for the loss of his mother's life. The most that he would then be trying to do is to grow to maturity and be born mortally, and even a super-endowed foetus would not, because he tried to do that, be to blame for the resulting loss of his mother's life.[8]

---

[6] He need not be the only one to blame. The person who placed the bomb might also be responsible. All that is required is that he be to blame.

[7] We leave open the question as to whether the satisfaction of either (2) or (2') is necessary.

[8] This is presumably what the Talmud means when (op. cit.) it rejects the justification of its being a killing of a pursuer because "only heaven is pursuing her." The talmudic justification (in Ohalot, 7:2) for abortions in the cases we have been considering is that the foetus does not have the same right to life as an ordinary human being. An examination of that claim, however, lies beyond the scope of this paper.

We conclude, therefore, that the mother cannot justify aborting her foetus, even when its continued existence threatens her life, on the grounds that it is a permissible taking of the life of a pursuer. What we must now consider is the possibility that there could be some other justification for aborting the foetus in that case even if the foetus is human.

II

Are there any cases in which it would be permissible to take one life to save another although they are not cases of killing a pursuer? The following seem to be such cases (even if a bit overdramatic—overdramatic cases are still cases):

(a) By a series of accidents for which no one is to blame, it has come about that the five people in room r_2 and the one person in room r_1 will be blown up by a bomb in the next sixty seconds. The only way to prevent this is to defuse the bomb by blowing up its triggering mechanism which is in room r_1. Unfortunately, this necessarily means that the person in r_1 will also be blown up. He is, however, the only one who will die; if you do nothing, all of the six people in question will die. It does seem that one ought to blow up that triggering mechanism and save those lives even if it does mean taking the life of the person in r_1.

(b) A small village is surrounded by a hostile group of brigands who demand that the villagers kill Joe, an innocent villager whom the brigands dislike. If the villagers do not do this, the brigands threaten to (and the villagers have every reason to believe that they will) destroy the village and everyone in it (including Joe). The village is cut off from outside help and giving in to their demands is the only way to save the village. Again, it does seem that one ought to save the life of the villagers even if it does mean taking Joe's life.

How are we to account for these cases? Why, in these cases, is it permissible (and perhaps even obligatory) to take the life of one person in order to save the life of others? Remember, these are not cases of killing a pursuer; only condition (1) is met in any of them. At least three answers suggest themselves:

(I) In these cases, the person whose life you will be taking is going to die anyway. If you take his life, however, you can save those other lives. Taking his life is an optimal act since no lives are sacrificed and some are gained, and that is why it is okay to take his life. In general, it is permissible to take B's life to save A's life if B is going to die anyway and taking B's life is the only way of saving A's life.

(II) In these cases, it is a question of sacrificing one life to save many other lives. While the life to be sacrificed is tremendously valuable, so are all the lives that can be saved, and when we weigh them, we find that the many lives outweigh the one. This may, of course, seem like a harsh attitude, but it would be even harsher to forget about the many lives you can save by sentimentally refusing to take one life.

In general, it is okay to take B's life to save the lives of A and C (where A ≠ C) if taking B's life is the only way of saving their lives.

(III) In these cases, one does not intend to take the life of anyone; what one is trying to do is to save some lives. The loss of life is an unintended, although certainly foreseen, consequence of a perfectly permissible (and perhaps even obligatory) action. In general, it is okay to do an action that will result in the taking of A's life if you do not intend that result, although it may be foreseen, and the intended results outweigh this unfortunate unintended result.

Of these three accounts, it seems that the third is the least satisfactory. To begin with, it rests upon the dubious distinction between the intended results of an action and the foreseen inevitable consequences of it. Secondly, and perhaps even more seriously, it supposes that the distinction is relevant to the moral evaluation of the action (and not merely the agent). This seems highly questionable. Finally, it does not really handle the second of our cases. When, in that case, the villagers take Joe's life, the taking of Joe's life is precisely what they intend to bring about by, and is not a mere inevitable consequence of, their action. To be sure, it is not the ultimate purpose of their action, but that is irrelevant. So the third account doesn't even explain why it is permissible for them to take Joe's life.

We turn then to the more plausible accounts, (I) and (II). What is the difference between them? The first says that, in our cases, it is permissible to take someone's life just because he will die anyway. The second says that, in our cases, it is permissible to take someone's life because doing that will result in the saving of the most possible lives. These two accounts will, then, disagree in cases where a person would survive if you did not take his life but the taking of his life would result in the saving of many other lives. According to our first account, it would be wrong for you, in such a case, to take that person's life; one cannot sacrifice someone's life to save the life of some other people. According to our second account, however, it would be permissible, in such cases, to kill that person in order to save the other people. After all, one would still be maximizing the number of lives saved.

Once one sees that this is the fundamental difference between the two accounts, one also sees what is wrong with (II). It, in a way, is very much like standard utilitarian theories. Analogously to the utilitarian maximization of happiness, it claims that, in cases like ours, the right action is the one that maximizes the number of human lives saved. And like standard utilitarian theories, it does not do justice to considerations of fairness. We object, on grounds of lack of fairness, to actions that maximize human happiness by making some few people suffer in order that many will be happy. We should similarly object, on the same grounds of lack of fairness, to actions that maximize the number of lives saved by sacrificing some few lives (that would not otherwise be lost) to save a larger number of lives. (I), in contrast, is not open to such objections. It only allows one to take B's life when not taking it won't make a difference, when he will die anyway. In such cases, B is not being treated unfairly, and given that taking his life will save these other lives, it is permissible (and perhaps even obligatory) to do so.

This point emerges even more clearly if we imagine the following two modifications of cases (a) and (b):

(a') By a series of accidents for which no one is to blame, it has come about that the five people in room r_2 (and only they) will be blown up by a bomb in the next sixty seconds. The only way to prevent this is to defuse the bomb by blowing up its triggering mechanism in room r_1, but this means that the single person in room r_1 will die.

(b') A small village is surrounded by a hostile group of brigands who, interested (for their own diabolic reasons) in seeing that the villagers kill an innocent man, demand that the villagers kill Joe. If the villagers do not do this, the brigands threaten to (and the villagers have every reason to believe that they will) kill all of the village leaders (this does *not* include Joe). The village is cut off from outside help and giving in to their demands is the only way to save the village leaders.

The important thing to note here is that, according to (II), we should still blow up the triggering mechanism and the villagers should still kill Joe. After all, it is still a question of taking one life to save others. But this just seems mistaken; the acts in question would be wrong because they would be unfair to the man in r_1 and to Joe. Only account (I) takes this into consideration and says, correctly, that it would be wrong for us, in cases (a') and (b'), to kill the man in r_1, or to kill Joe, although it would be permissible for us to do that in cases (a) and (b). It would seem, therefore, that (I) is to be preferred to (II).

It might be objected that we are introducing, in our objection to (II), an asymmetry between taking lives and saving lives that is not justified. After all, while we have been concerned with the unfairness to the man whose life might be taken by us, we have not, it could be argued, been properly concerned with the unfairness to the men whose lives will be lost if we don't act. Why should their lives be sacrificed in order to spare the life of the other man? Isn't that unfair to them?

In a way, I agree with this objection. I have supposed that there is asymmetry between the two; however, this supposition seems justified. Consider, once more, case (a'). If I destroy the triggering mechanism, then I will not have met an obligation that I have toward the man in room r_1, viz., the obligation not to take his life. And when I try to justify not meeting that obligation by saying that I did so in order to save the lives of some other people, it seems open for someone to object that I am acting unfairly to this man by neglecting this vital obligation I have toward him so that others will benefit. The situation is very different if I don't destroy the triggering mechanism. Then, there is no obligation that I have towards the people in r_2 that I have, unfairly, not met. After all, even if one agrees that a man has an obligation to save the lives of his fellow human beings,[9] that obligation is certainly not present when I can only save their lives by taking other lives. The same point can, of course, be made about (b').

This reply depends, of course, upon the assumption that, in cases like (a') and (b'), the obligation to a man not to take his life remains while the obligation

[9] Even this is unclear. It may only be a good thing that one do it; the claim that there is an obligation is, of course, much stronger than that, and it may be too strong.

towards a man to save his life does not. But this is quite plausible; the former obligation is clearly more important than the latter and is present in a great many cases in which the latter is not. After all, while I am normally under an obligation to another man not to take his life even though this means my losing my own life (and even more so if it only means a worsening in the quality of my life or a loss of all I possess), I certainly am not normally under an obligation[10] to another man to save his life at the cost of my own life (or even at the cost of a significant lowering in the quality of my life or of the loss of all that I possess).

If, then, we agree[11] to accept (I) rather than (II) as our account of why, in the cases that we are considering, it is permissible to take some lives to save others, how, working upon our assumption that the foetus is human, does that affect what we think about the problem of abortion? It seems that its major effect is the following: we have to distinguish two types of cases in which we might want to abort the foetus to save the mother. In one case, if we do nothing, the foetus will survive and the mother will die. Such cases are, of course, only possible at the very end of pregnancy. In such a case, we ought not to abort the foetus, for taking its life to save the life of the mother would be unfair. On the other hand, we may have a case in which, if we do nothing, neither the mother nor the foetus will survive. In such a case, aborting the foetus is not unfair to it, and given the truth of (I), it follows that it is permissible for us to abort it to save the mother if this is the only way to save her.[12]

We seem to have found one case in which, even if we assume that the foetus is a human being entitled to all of the rights to life had by any other human being, it would be permissible to abort the foetus to save the life of its mother. But our argument for this claim depends upon the truth of (I), and since this principle is not unproblematic, we must turn to a further consideration of it.

III

There is a standard objection against (I) that must be considered first. The rationale behind (I) is that, in such cases, everything is gained and nothing is lost by taking the life of the individual in question. From the point of view of lives saved, this seems correct; no additional lives will be lost, and some will be saved, by taking the life of that individual. But aren't there other respects in which something will be lost, in which something bad will have occurred? Won't a murder be committed by you, one that would not otherwise be committed? Therefore, it is simply not true that nothing is lost by taking that person's life.

Proponents of this objection often embellish it with references to the mortal sin that one would commit by this act of murder and to the punishment which

---

[10] One may suppose, however, that this would be a saintly act. But, especially if one is opposed to suicidal acts or to martyrdom, one may not even suppose this. See, on this point, Zevin's Le'or HaHalacha (Tel Aviv: 1957), pp. 14–16.

[11] (1) is, essentially, the opinion of R. Yochanan in (Jerusalem Talmud, Trumah, chapter 8) his discussion of the biblical case of Sheva ben Bichri. For a full account of the talmudic debate on that case, see Maimonides, Laws of the Foundations of the Tora, 5, 5 and the commentaries on his discussion.

[12] This point was well made in Responsa Panim Me'irot (Sulzbach: 1738), vol. III, no. 8.

will be forthcoming as a consequence of this. Such embellishments, like the original objection, rest upon the presupposition that some evil act, viz., an act of murder, has been committed. I turn therefore to a consideration of this presupposition.

One obviously has to distinguish four possible descriptions of A's taking the life of B: (1) A has taken B's life, (2) A has taken the life of an innocent man B, (3) A has taken the life of an innocent man B who is not pursuing A, and (4) A has murdered B. There clearly are cases in which (1) and, as we saw in Section I, (2) are correct descriptions of an action but (4) is not. In a way, the question that we considered in the last section was whether there could be cases in which (3) would be a correct description of an act but (4) would not. The defenders of (1) say that there are such cases; these are the cases in which B would die anyway. The proponents of our objection would deny this. But they cannot assume that their denial is correct in the course of their arguments without being circular. This is, however, precisely what they do. In trying to show that it would be wrong, in such cases, for A to take B's life, they assume that doing that would be murder, that doing that would be an unjustified taking of a human life, and by assuming that, they beg the question.

There are, however, more serious objections to (I), ones that can be met only by modifying that principle, and we turn therefore to a consideration of them. To begin with, whenever one takes B's life to save A's life, B is going to die anyway. It's just a matter of time for all of us. So, as (I) now stands, one can always take someone's life if it is the only way of saving the life of someone else, and this is clearly mistaken. Obviously, we need some condition that is stronger than "B is going to die anyway."

Two suggested modifications of (I) seem plausible. They are:

(I') It is permissible to take B's life to save A's life if B is going to die anyway in a relatively short time and taking B's life is the only way of saving A's life.

(I'') It is permissible to take B's life to save A's life if taking B's life is the only way of saving A's life and, if nothing is done, the same event will cause the death of A and B.

Looking at our examples (a) and (b), we see how these modified principles work. (I') allows for the killing of the man in r_1 because he will die anyway in the next sixty seconds and it allows for the killing of Joe because he will die anyway when (in the near future) the brigands destroy the village. (I'') allows for the killing of the man in r_1, because, if nothing is done, he and the people in r_2 will both be killed by the bomb's explosion and it allows for the killing of Joe because, if nothing is done, he and all of the villagers will be killed in the brigands' destruction of the village. On the other hand, neither (I') nor (I'') will allow us to take the life of any B to save the life of any A when that is the only way to do so. After all, in the normal case, B is not going to die anyway in a relatively short period of time, and, if nothing is done, the event that causes B to die (when he does eventually die) will not be the same event as the one that caused A's death.

In trying to decide between (I') and (I''), it will be helpful if we see more clearly the differences in their implications. A consideration of the following two modifications of our original bombing case helps bring out these differences:

(a'') By a series of accidents for which no one is to blame, it has come about that the five people in room r_2 (and only they) will be blown up by a bomb in the next sixty seconds. The only way to prevent this is to defuse the bomb by blowing up its triggering mechanism in room r_1, but this means that the single person in room r_1 will die; however, he will die anyway from cancer within the next few hours.

(a''') By a series of accidents for which no one is to blame, it has come about that the five people in room r_2 (and only they) will be blown up by a bomb in the next sixty seconds. The only way to prevent this is to defuse the bomb by blowing up its triggering mechanism in room r_1, but this means that the single person in room r_1 will die. If nothing is done, he will be wounded by the explosion of the bomb and will even eventually die from these wounds; however, he will live for a few years leading a restricted life.

(I') allows for the killing of the man in r_1 in case (a'') because he will die anyway in a relatively short time, but it does not allow for the killing of the man in r_1 in case (a''') since he will live on for some years. (I''), on the other hand, allows for the killing of the man in r_1 in case (a''') since, if nothing is done, his death will be caused by the same explosion that kills the people in r_2, but it does not allow for the killing of the man in r_1 in case (a'') since, if nothing is done, his death will be caused by his cancer and not by the explosion that will kill the people in r_2.

Which, if either, of these principles is correct? One thing seems pretty clear. The whole rationale, in cases like the ones we are considering, for taking some life to save others is that he whose life will be taken loses nothing of significance and is not therefore being treated unfairly. But if, as in cases like (a'''), he will live if we do nothing for a considerable amount of time, our taking his life now means that we will have unfairly subjected him to a significant loss. Consequently, the whole rationale for the taking of lives in such cases collapses, and, in cases like (a'''), it would be unfair and wrong to take that person's life. Since, however, (I') allows for the killing of the man in r_1 in case (a'''), it is mistaken.

We see, then, that the question of how long B is going to live is central to the question as to whether we can kill him to save A. What we must now consider is whether anything else plays a role, and, in particular, whether the nature of the cause of B's death if we do nothing is at all relevant. To put the question another way, is (I') true or must we add to it the additional condition that, if nothing is done, the same event will cause the death of A and B?

It is extremely difficult to answer this question. On the one hand, people (myself, my friends whom I have consulted) have the intuition that this additional requirement is reasonable. For this reason, they are troubled by the idea that it is permissible, in case (a''), to take the life of the man in r_1. On the other hand, this additional requirement is totally unreasonable. After all, if the whole

justification for taking a human life in these cases is that nothing is lost by doing so and no one is, therefore, being treated unfairly, then it should be permissible to take that life whenever nothing is lost and no one is treated unfairly. That
seems to be the case whenever the person in question will die anyway in the
very near future,[13] so why should we be concerned with the nature of the cause
of his death if we do nothing? I conclude, therefore, that we should adopt (I'),
following here our rationale and not our intuitions.

There are, however, serious problems even with (I'). Consider a case in
which both A and B will die in a relatively short time if nothing is done, taking
B's life is the only way to save A's life, and taking A's life is the only way to
save B's life. According to (I'), it would be permissible for anyone to take B's life
in order to save A's life. This, however, seems wrong. Why should B's life be sacrificed to save A's life instead of A's life being sacrificed to save B's? Similarly,
according to (I'), it would be permissible for anyone to take A's life in order to
save B's. This, too, seems wrong. Why should A's life be sacrificed to save B's
life rather than B's life being sacrificed to save A's?

The simplest solution to this problem would be to replace (I') with:

(I''') It is permissible to take B's life to save A's life if B is going to die
anyway in a relatively short time, taking B's life is the only way of saving A's life, and taking A's life (or doing anything else) will not save B's
life. This, however, will not do, for (I''') does not allow us, in the case
we are considering, to save either A or B. We must let them both die
since the situation does not favor one over the other. This type of Buri-
dan's Ass conclusion makes (I''') unattractive.

It would seem far better to replace (I') with:

(I'''') It is permissible to take B's life to save A's life if B is going to die
anyway in a relatively short time, taking B's life is the only way of saving A's life and either (i) taking A's life (or doing anything else) will not
save B's life or (ii) taking A's life (or doing anything else) will save B's
life but one has, by a fair random method, determined that one should
save A's life rather than B's life.

Notice that (I'''') entails that, in the case we are now considering, one should
not, because it is not permissible to, simply take the life of one to save the life
of the other. Rather, one should choose whose life is to be saved and whose life
is to be sacrificed by a fair random method. The rationale for this is pretty
straightforward. When (i) is not the case, we face a choice as to whom we should

---

[13] This point helps to shed light upon what is meant by "in a relatively short time." The
important thing is that B should not suffer any significant losses (in terms of unrealized
potentialities for the period between the time we take his life and the time at which he
would have died anyway) because of the taking of his life. Consequently, we must attend
to his expectations for that period as well as to its length. It may, after all, be permissible
to take B's life even if, had we done nothing, he would have lived for five years so long
as he would live them in a coma. In the case of a person with normal expectations, however, five years would certainly be too long.

save and whose life we should take (and we clearly should take one to save the other), so the only way that we can avoid being unfair is to use a random device to choose for us.

How do these modifications in our original principle, (I), affect the issue of abortion? Well, since (I'''') places even stronger restrictions on the taking of a human life than does (I), it certainly does not allow as permissible any abortions that were not allowed as permissible under (I). But there are some abortions that are, according to (I), permissible but which are not according to (I''''). According to (I), an abortion is always permissible if both the foetus and mother will die if nothing is done and the only way to save the mother is to abort the foetus. According to (I''''), an abortion is permissible only if, in addition to the satisfaction of those conditions, it is the case that the foetus will die in a relatively short time if nothing is done and either there is no way to save the foetus or there is a way but, by a fair random procedure, we have determined that we should save the mother and not the foetus.

I conclude, therefore, that if the foetus is a human being having the same right to life as does any other human being, then the fact that the mother would die otherwise does not justify an abortion unless the very stringent requirements laid down in (I'''') are met.

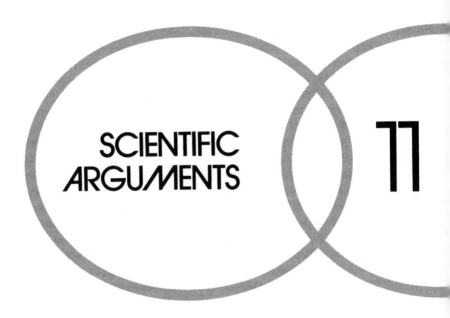

SCIENTIFIC ARGUMENTS

11

When scientists praise each other's work, they sometimes say that the analysis of some phenomenon is *elegant, beautiful,* or even *tasteful.* It may seem strange to call a piece of scientific research *tasteful,* but this only shows a misunderstanding of the character of scientific thought. It is a parody of the scientific enterprise to think that it consists simply of amassing huge quantities of data to prove or disprove some hypothesis. Of course, experimental data are the final court of appeal in scientific research, but the point of scientific theory is to make sense out of nature, to explain it, to make it more intelligible. It is in its explanatory power that a theory can be elegant, beautiful, or even tasteful.

The Law of Buoyancy

Our first example of a scientific argument is drawn from the ancient world. It has a famous story attached to it. The ruler of Syracuse was worried that a crown he had purchased was not made of pure gold, but he could think of no way of testing whether baser metals had been mixed with the gold. He turned to the mathematician Archimedes for help. Sitting in the public bath—so the story goes—Archimedes was able to solve this problem by deriving the Law of Buoyancy. He was so excited by this discovery that he went bounding through the streets of Syracuse in his nothing-at-all shouting "Eureka!"—which, by the way, does not mean *"Yippee,"* but *"I have found it."*

The proof itself is a model of elegant scientific reasoning. It not only proves the Law of Buoyancy; it also makes sense out of it, and does so in a very simple way. The proof exploits two fundamental propositions:

(1) The surface of a liquid in a vessel is part of the surface of a sphere with the center of the earth as its center. (Proven as Proposition 1.)

(2) The liquid in two sides of a vessel acts like two sides of a lever. (From Postulate 1.)

You may have to think for a moment to see that this first proposition is true. Think about the surface of a tub of water. It conforms perfectly to the surface of the earth and since the surface of the earth is the surface of a sphere, the surface of the water in the tub is also part of the surface of a sphere. (Notice, by the way, that Archimedes simply takes it as an established fact that the earth is spherical. Contrary to popular belief today, this was well known in the ancient world.) The second proposition depends upon the common sense observation that an object immersed in a liquid exerts a force on that liquid. When an object floats, this force must be balanced by some opposite force. The genius of Archimedes' proof was to look at the problem in terms of these two propositions. After that, everything follows from the most simple geometry.

On Floating Bodies
ARCHIMEDES

POSTULATE 1.

"Let it be supposed that a fluid is of such a character that, its parts lying evenly and being continuous, that part which is thrust the less is driven along by that which is thrust the more; and that each of its parts is thrust by the fluid which is above it in a perpendicular direction if the fluid be sunk in anything and compressed by anything else."

Proposition 1.

If a surface be cut by a plane always passing through a certain point, and if the section be always a circumference [of a circle] whose centre is the aforesaid point, the surface is that of a sphere.

For, if not, there will be some two lines drawn from the point to the surface which are not equal.

* T. L. Heath, ed., *The Works of Archimedes* (New York: Dover Publications, 1953), pp. 253–59.

Suppose O to be the fixed point, and A, B to be two points on the surface such that OA, OB are unequal. Let the surface be cut by a plane passing through OA, OB. Then the section is, by hypothesis, a circle whose centre is O.

Thus $OA = OB$; which is contrary to the assumption. Therefore the surface cannot but be a sphere.

Proposition 2.

The surface of any fluid at rest is the surface of a sphere whose centre is the same as that of the earth.

Suppose the surface of the fluid cut by a plane through O, the centre of the earth, in the curve $ABCD$.

$ABCD$ shall be the circumference of a circle.

For, if not, some of the lines drawn from O to the curve will be unequal. Take one of them, OB, such that OB is greater than some of the lines from O to the curve and less than others. Draw a circle with OB as a radius. Let it be EBF, which will therefore fall partly within and partly without the surface of the fluid.

Draw OGH making with OB an angle equal to the angle EOB, and meeting the surface in H and the circle in G. Draw also in the plane an arc of a circle PQR with centre O and within the fluid.

Then the parts of the fluid along PQR are uniform and continuous, and the part PQ is compressed by the part between it and AB, while the part QR is compressed by the part between QR and BH. Therefore the parts along PQ, QR will be unequally compressed, and the part which is compressed the less will be set in motion by that which is compressed the more.

Therefore there will not be rest; which is contrary to the hypothesis.

Hence the section of the surface will be the circumference of a circle whose centre is O; and so will all other sections by planes through O.

Therefore the surface is that of a sphere with centre O.

Proposition 3.

Of solids those which, size for size, are of equal weight with a fluid will, if let down into the fluid, be immersed so that they do not project above the surface but do not sink lower.

If possible, let a certain solid $EFHG$ of equal weight, volume for volume, with the fluid remain immersed in it so that part of it, $EBCF$, projects above the surface.

Draw through O, the centre of the earth, and through the solid a plane cutting the surface of the fluid in the circle $ABCD$.

Conceive a pyramid with vertex O and base a parallelogram at the surface of the fluid, such that it includes the immersed portion of the solid. Let this pyramid be cut by the plane of $ABCD$ in OL, OM. Also let a sphere within the fluid and below GH be described with centre O, and let the plane of $ABCD$ cut this sphere in PQR.

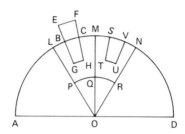

Conceive also another pyramid in the fluid with vertex O, continuous with the former pyramid and equal and similar to it. Let the pyramid so described be cut in OM, ON by the plane of $ABCD$.

Lastly, let $STUV$ be a part of the fluid within the second pyramid equal and similar to the part $BGHC$ of the solid, and let SV be at the surface of the fluid.

Then the pressures on PQ, QR are unequal, that on PQ being the greater. Hence the part at QR will be set in motion by that at PQ, and the fluid will not be at rest; which is contrary to the hypothesis.

Therefore the solid will not stand out above the surface.

Nor will it sink further, because all the parts of the fluid will be under the same pressure.

Proposition 4.

A solid lighter than a fluid will, if immersed in it, not be completely submerged, but part of it will project above the surface.

In this case, after the manner of the previous proposition, we assume the solid, if possible, to be completely submerged and the fluid to be at rest in that position, and we conceive (1) a pyramid with its vertex at O, the centre of the earth, including the solid, (2) another pyramid continuous with the former and equal and similar to it, with the same vertex O, (3) a portion of the fluid within this latter pyramid equal to the immersed solid in the other pyramid, (4) a sphere with centre O whose surface is below the immersed solid and the part of the fluid in the second pyramid corresponding thereto. We suppose a plane to be drawn through the centre O cutting the surface of the fluid in the circle ABC, the solid in S, the first pyramid in OA, OB, the second pyramid in OB, OC, the portion of the fluid in the second pyramid in K, and the inner sphere in PQR.

Then the pressures on the parts of the fluid at PQ, QR are unequal, since

S is lighter than *K*. Hence there will not be rest; which is contrary to the hypothesis.

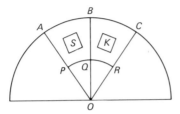

Therefore the solid *S* cannot, in a condition of rest, be completely submerged.

Proposition 5.

Any solid lighter than a fluid will, if placed in the fluid, be so far immersed that the weight of the solid will be equal to the weight of the fluid displaced.

For let the solid be *EGHF*, and let *BGHC* be the portion of it immersed when the fluid is at rest. As in Prop. 3, conceive a pyramid with vertex *O* including the solid, and another pyramid with the same vertex continuous with the former and equal and similar to it. Suppose a portion of the fluid *STUV* at the base of the second pyramid to be equal and similar to the immersed portion of the solid; and let the construction be the same as in Prop. 3.

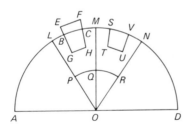

Then, since the pressure on the parts of the fluid at *PQ*, *QR* must be equal in order that the fluid may be at rest, it follows that the weight of the portion *STUV* of the fluid must be equal to the weight of the solid *EGHF*. And the former is equal to the weight of the fluid displaced by the immersed portion of the solid *BGHC*.

Proposition 6.

If a solid lighter than a fluid be forcibly immersed in it, the solid will be driven upwards by a force equal to the difference between its weight and the weight of the fluid displaced.

For let *A* be completely immersed in the fluid, and let *G* represent the weight of *A*, and (*G* + *H*) the weight of an equal volume of the fluid. Take a solid D, whose weight is H and add it to A. Then the weight of $(A + D)$ is less than that of an equal volume of the fluid; and, if $(A + D)$ is immersed in the fluid, it will project so that its weight will be equal to the weight of the fluid displaced. But its weight is $(G + H)$.

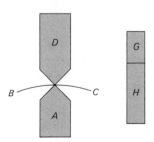

Therefore the weight of the fluid displaced is $(G + H)$, and hence the volume of the fluid displaced is the volume of the solid A. There will accordingly be rest with A immersed and D projecting.

Thus the weight of D balances the upward force exerted by the fluid on A, and therefore the latter force is equal to H, which is the difference between the weight of A and the weight of the fluid which A displaces.

Proposition 7.

A solid heavier than a fluid will, if placed in it, descend to the bottom of the fluid, and the solid will, when weighed in the fluid, be lighter than its true weight by the weight of the fluid displaced.

(1) The first part of the proposition is obvious, since the part of the fluid under the solid will be under greater pressure, and therefore the other parts will give way until the solid reaches the bottom.

(2) Let A be a solid heavier than the same volume of the fluid, and let $(G + H)$ represent its weight, while G represents the weight of the same volume of the fluid.

Take a solid B lighter than the same volume of the fluid, and such that the weight of B is G, while the weight of the same volume of the fluid is $(G + H)$.

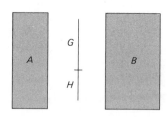

Let A and B be now combined into one solid and immersed. Then, since $(A + B)$ will be of the same weight as the same volume of fluid, both weights being equal to $(G + H) + G$, it follows that $(A + B)$ will remain stationary in the fluid.

Therefore the force which causes A by itself to sink must be equal to the upward force exerted by the fluid on B by itself. This latter is equal to the difference between $(G + H)$ and G [Prop. 6]. Hence A is depressed by a force equal to H, i.e. its weight in the fluid is H, or the difference between $(G + H)$ and G.

Conflicting Scientific Interpretations

Archimedes' derivation of the Law of Buoyancy turns upon the insight that the laws of the lever can be applied to what seems a totally different area. This ability to *extend* a theory through seeing such connections is characteristic of scientific progress. Another type of scientific development is more radical—knowledge is not simply extended, but, instead, one scientific framework is replaced (or largely replaced) by another. In biology, the Germ Theory of Disease and the Theory of Evolution Through Natural Selection are examples of such revolutionary developments. Einstein's Theory of Relativity and the rise of Quantum Mechanics are also revolutionary developments. Indeed, every branch of science has undergone at least one such revolutionary change during the past few centuries.

There are some important differences between scientific progress within a framework and the replacement of one framework by another.[1] In the first place, such changes in framework usually meet with strong resistance. A new conceptual framework will be unfamiliar and hard to understand, and may even seem absurd or unintelligible. Even today, for example, the thought that the earth is spinning on its axis and revolving around the sun seems completely counter to our common-sense view of the world. Also, arguments on behalf of a new framework will be very different from arguments that occur *within* a framework. Disputes over conceptual frameworks cannot be settled by a straightforward appeal to facts. The long debate between Albert Einstein and Niels Bohr concerning Quantum Theory did not turn upon matters of fact, but upon their interpretation. Einstein could not accept the indeterminacy involved in the Quantum Theory's interpretation of the world, and he worked until the end of his life to find some alternative to it. At present, almost no scientist shares Einstein's reservations.

The selection given below illustrates a clash between two such scientific frameworks. It is taken from Galileo's *Dialogue Concerning the Two World Systems—Ptolemaic and Copernican*. The interlocutors are Salviati, Sagredo, and Simplicio. Salviati represents the Copernican system; Simplicio, the Ptolemaic system; Sagredo acts as a moderator, forcing the other two participants in the dialogue to clarify and defend their positions. In attacking the Copernican system, Simplicio lists various

---

[1] Thomas Kuhn gives prominence to this difference in his important work, *The Structure of Scientific Revolutions*, 2nd ed. (Chicago: University of Chicago Press, 1970).

arguments from Aristotle that are supposed to show that the earth does not move. Some of these arguments are taken, he says:

> from experiments with heavy bodies which, falling from a height, go perpendicularly to the surface of the earth. Similarly, projectiles thrown vertically upward come down again perpendicularly by the same line, even though they have been thrown to immense height. These arguments are necessary proofs that their motion is toward the center of the earth, which, without moving in the least, awaits and receives them.[2]

Salviati replies that these phenomena do not show that the Ptolemaic system is correct and the Copernican system incorrect, since they can be explained in either world system. More generally, Salviati argues that no terrestrial phenomenon—that is, no phenomenon observable on the earth—can be cited to show that one of these systems is true and the other false. For that matter, no celestial phenomena will settle this issue either, since both world systems provide interpretations of the notions of heavenly bodies. That proponents of each of these systems can agree on particular facts yet disagree profoundly on their correct interpretation shows that we are dealing with a conflict between general frameworks, or general world systems. Arguments of this kind are very different from those that take place within a given scientific framework. This is evident at once if we compare Salviati's reply to Simplicio with Archimedes' derivation of the Law of Buoyancy.

Dialogue Concerning the Two World Systems— Ptolemaic and Copernican
GALILEO GALILEI

SALVIATI: Aristotle says, then, that a most certain proof of the earth's being motionless is that things projected perpendicularly upward are seen to return by the same line to the same place from which they were thrown, even though the movement is extremely high. This, he argues, could not happen if the earth moved, since in the time during which the projectile is moving upward and then downward it is separated from the earth, and the place from which the projectile began its motion would go a long way toward the east, thanks to the revolving of the earth, and the falling projectile would strike the earth that distance away from the place in question. Thus we can accommodate here the argument of the

[2] Galileo Galilei, *Dialogue Concerning the Two World Systems—Ptolemaic and Copernican,* Stillman Drake, trans. (Berkeley: University of California Press, 1953), p. 125.
* Galileo Galilei, *Dialogue Concerning the Two World Systems—Ptolemaic and Copernican,* Stillman Drake, trans. (Berkeley: University of California Press, 1953), pp. 139–49.

cannon ball as well as the other argument, used by Aristotle and Ptolemy, of seeing heavy bodies falling from great heights along a straight line perpendicular to the surface of the earth. Now, in order to begin to untie these knots, I ask Simplicio by what means he would prove that freely falling bodies go along straight and perpendicular lines directed toward the center, should anyone refuse to grant this to Aristotle and Ptolemy.

SIMPLICIO: By means of the senses, which assure us that the tower is straight and perpendicular, and which show us that a falling stone goes along grazing it, without deviating a hairsbreadth to one side or the other, and strikes at the foot of the tower exactly under the place from which it was dropped.

SALV: But if it happened that the earth rotated, and consequently carried along the tower, and if the falling stone were seen to graze the side of the tower just the same, what would its motion then have to be?

SIMP: In that case one would have to say "its motions," for there would be one with which it went from top to bottom, and another one needed for following the path of the tower.

SALV: The motion would then be a compound of two motions; the one with which it measures the tower, and the other with which it follows it. From this compounding it would follow that the rock would no longer describe that simple straight perpendicular line, but a slanting one, and perhaps not straight.

SIMP: I don't know about its not being straight, but I understand well enough that it would have to be slanting, and different from the straight perpendicular line it would describe with the earth motionless.

SALV: Hence just from seeing the falling stone graze the tower, you could not say for sure that it described a straight and perpendicular line, unless you first assumed the earth to stand still.

SIMP: Exactly so; for if the earth were moving, the motion of the stone would be slanting and not perpendicular.

SALV: Then here, clear and evident, is the paralogism of Aristotle and of Ptolemy, discovered by you yourself. They take as known that which is intended to be proved.

SIMP: In what way? It looks to me like a syllogism in proper form, and not a *petitio principii.*

SALV: In this way: Does he not, in his proof, take the conclusion as unknown?

SIMP: Unknown, for otherwise it would be superfluous to prove it.

SALV: And the middle term; does he not require that to be known?

SIMP: Of course; [otherwise it would be an attempt to prove *ignotum per aeque ignotum.*]

SALV: Our conclusion, which is unknown and is to be proved; is this not the motionlessness of the earth?

SIMP: That is what it is.

SALV: Is not the middle term, which must be known, the straight and perpendicular fall of the stone?

SIMP: That is the middle term.

SALV: But wasn't it concluded a little while ago that we could not have any knowledge of this fall being straight and perpendicular unless it was first known that the earth stood still? Therefore in your syllogism, the certainty of the middle term is drawn from the uncertainty of the conclusion. Thus you see how, and how badly, it is a paralogism.

SAGREDO: On behalf of Simplicio I should like, if possible, to defend Aristotle, or at least to be better persuaded as to the force of your deduction. You say that seeing the stone graze the tower is not enough to assure us that the motion of the rock is perpendicular (and this is the middle term of the syllogism) unless one assumes the earth to stand still (which is the conclusion to be proved). For if the tower moved along with the earth and the rock grazed it, the motion of the rock would be slanting, and not perpendicular. But I reply that if the tower were moving, it would be impossible for the rock to fall grazing it; therefore, from the scraping fall is inferred the stability of the earth.

SIMP: So it is. For to expect the rock to go grazing the tower if that were carried along by the earth would be requiring the rock to have two natural motions; that is, a straight one toward the center, and a circular one about the center, which is impossible.

SALV: So Aristotle's defense consists in its being impossible, or at least in his having considered it impossible, that the rock might move with a motion mixed of straight and circular. For if he had not held it to be impossible that the stone might move both toward and around the center at the same time, he would have understood how it could happen that the falling rock might go grazing the tower whether that was moving or was standing still, and consequently he would have been able to perceive that this grazing could imply nothing as to the motion or rest of the earth.

Nevertheless this does not excuse Aristotle, not only because if he did have this idea he ought to have said so, it being such an important point in the argu-

ment, but also, and more so, because it cannot be said either that such an effect
is impossible or that Aristotle considered it impossible. The former cannot be
said because, as I shall shortly prove to you, this is not only possible but necessary; and the latter cannot be said either, because Aristotle himself admits that
fire moves naturally upward in a straight line and also turns in the diurnal motion which is imparted by the sky to all the element of fire and to the greater
part of the air. Therefore if he saw no impossibility in the mixing of straight-up-
ward with circular motion, as communicated to fire and to the air up as far as
the moon's orbit, no more should he deem this impossible with regard to the
rock's straight-downward motion and the circular motion natural to the entire
globe of the earth, of which the rock is a part.

SIMP: It does not look that way to me at all. If the element of fire goes around
together with the air, this is a very easy and even a necessary thing for a particle
of fire, which, rising high from the earth, receives that very motion in passing
through the moving air, being so tenuous and light a body and so easily moved.
But it is quite incredible that a very heavy rock or a cannon ball which is
dropped without restraint should let itself be budged by the air or by anything
else. Besides which, there is the very appropriate experiment of the stone
dropped from the top of the mast of a ship, which falls to the foot of the mast
when the ship is standing still, but falls as far from that same point when the
ship is sailing as the ship is perceived to have advanced during the time of the
fall, this being several yards when the ship's course is rapid. . . .

SALV: Tell me, Simplicio: Do you feel convinced that the experiment on the ship
squares so well with our purpose that one may reasonably believe that whatever
is seen to occur there must also take place on the terrestrial globe?

SIMP: So far, yes; . . .

SALV: Rather, I hope that you will stick to it, and firmly insist that the result
on the earth must correspond to that on the ship, so that when the latter is perceived to be prejudicial to your case you will not be tempted to change your
mind.
   You say, then, that since when the ship stands still the rock falls to the foot
of the mast, and when the ship is in motion it falls apart from there, then conversely, from the falling of the rock at the foot it is inferred that the ship stands
still, and from its falling away it may be deduced that the ship is moving. And
since what happens on the ship must likewise happen on the land, from the falling of the rock at the foot of the tower one necessarily infers the immobility of
the terrestrial globe. Is that your argument?

SIMP: That is exactly it, briefly stated, which makes it easy to understand.

SALV: Now tell me: If the stone dropped from the top of the mast when the ship
was sailing rapidly fell in exactly the same place on the ship to which it fell

when the ship was standing still, what use could you make of this falling with regard to determining whether the vessel stood still or moved?

SIMP: Absolutely none; just as by the beating of the pulse, for instance, you cannot know whether a person is asleep or awake, since the pulse beats in the same manner in sleeping as in waking.

SALV: Very good. Now, have you ever made this experiment of the ship?

SIMP: I have never made it, but I certainly believe that the authorities who adduced it had carefully observed it. Besides, the cause of the difference is so exactly known that there is no room for doubt.

SALV: You yourself are sufficient evidence that those authorities may have offered it without having performed it, for you take it as certain without having done it, and commit yourself to the good faith of their dictum. Similarly it not only may be, but must be that they did the same thing too—I mean, put faith in their predecessors, right on back without ever arriving at anyone who had performed it. For anyone who does will find that the experiment shows exactly the opposite of what is written; that is, it will show that the stone always falls in the same place on the ship, whether the ship is standing still or moving with any speed you please. Therefore, the same cause holding good on the earth as on the ship, nothing can be inferred about the earth's motion or rest from the stone falling always perpendicularly to the foot of the tower.

SIMP: If you had referred me to any other agency than experiment, I think that our dispute would not soon come to an end; for this appears to me to be a thing so remote from human reason that there is no place in it for credulity or probability.

SALV: For me there is, just the same.

SIMP: So you have not made a hundred tests, or even one? And yet you so freely declare it to be certain? I shall retain my incredulity, and my own confidence that the experiment has been made by the most important authors who make use of it, and that it shows what they say it does.

SALV: Without experiment, I am sure that the effect will happen as I tell you, because it must happen that way; and I might add that you yourself also know that it cannot happen otherwise, no matter how you may pretend not to know it—or give that impression. But I am so handy at picking people's brains that I shall make you confess this in spite of yourself. . . .

Now tell me: Suppose you have a plane surface as smooth as a mirror and made of some hard material like steel. This is not parallel to the horizon, but somewhat inclined, and upon it you have placed a ball which is perfectly spherical and of some hard and heavy material like bronze. What do you believe this will do when released? Do you not think, as I do, that it will remain still?

SIMP: If that surface is tilted?

SALV: Yes, that is what was assumed.

SIMP: I do not believe that it would stay still at all; rather, I am sure that it would spontaneously roll down. . . .

SALV: Now how long would the ball continue to roll, and how fast? Remember that I said a perfectly round ball and a highly polished surface, in order to remove all external and accidental impediments. Similarly I want you to take away any impediment of the air caused by its resistance to separation, and all other accidental obstacles, if there are any.

SIMP: I completely understood you, and to your question I reply that the ball would continue to move indefinitely, as far as the slope of the surface extended, and with a continually accelerated motion. For such is the nature of heavy bodies, which *vires acquirunt eundo;* and the greater the slope, the greater would be the velocity.

SALV: But if one wanted the ball to move upward on this same surface, do you think it would go?

SIMP: Not spontaneously, no; but drawn or thrown forcibly, it would.

SALV: And if it were thrust along with some impetus impressed forcibly upon it, what would its motion be, and how great?

SIMP: The motion would constantly slow down and be retarded, being contrary to nature, and would be of longer or shorter duration according to the greater or lesser impulse and the lesser or greater slope upward.

SALV: Very well; up to this point you have explained to me the events of motion upon two different planes. On the downward inclined plane, the heavy moving body spontaneously descends and continually accelerates, and to keep it at rest requires the use of force. On the upward slope, force is needed to thrust it along or even to hold it still, and motion which is impressed upon it continually diminishes until it is entirely annihilated. You say also that a difference in the two instances arises from the greater or lesser upward or downward slope of the plane, so that from a greater slope downward there follows a greater speed, while on the contrary upon the upward slope a given movable body thrown with a given force moves farther according as the slope is less.

Now tell me what would happen to the same movable body placed upon a surface with no slope upward or downward.

SIMP: Here I must think a moment about my reply. There being no downward slope, there can be no natural tendency toward motion; and there being no upward slope, there can be no resistance to being moved, so there would be an indifference between the propensity and the resistance to motion. Therefore it seems to me that it ought naturally to remain stable. But I forgot; it was not so very long ago that Sagredo gave me to understand that this is what would happen.

SALV: I believe it would do so if one set the ball down firmly. But what would happen if it were given an impetus in any direction?

SIMP: It must follow that it would move in that direction.

SALV: But with what sort of movement? One continually accelerated, as on the downward plane, or increasingly retarded as on the upward one?

SIMP: I cannot see any cause for acceleration or deceleration, there being no slope upward or downward.

SALV: Exactly so. But if there is no cause for the ball's retardation, there ought to be still less for its coming to rest; so how far would you have the ball continue to move?

SIMP: As far as the extension of the surface continued without rising or falling.

SALV: Then if such a space were unbounded, the motion on it would likewise be boundless? That is, perpetual?

SIMP: It seems so to me, if the movable body were of durable material.

SALV: That is of course assumed, since we said that all external and accidental impediments were to be removed, and any fragility on the part of the moving body would in this case be one of the accidental impediments.

Now tell me, what do you consider to be the cause of the ball moving spontaneously on the downward inclined plane, but only by force on the one tilted upward?

SIMP: That the tendency of heavy bodies is to move toward the center of the earth, and to move upward from its circumference only with force; now the downward surface is that which gets closer to the center, while the upward one gets farther away.

SALV: Then in order for a surface to be neither downward nor upward, all its parts must be equally distant from the center. Are there any such surfaces in the world?

SIMP: Plenty of them; such would be the surface of our terrestrial globe if it were smooth, and not rough and mountainous as it is. But there is that of the water, when it is placid and tranquil.

SALV: Then a ship, when it moves over a calm sea, is one of these movables which courses over a surface that is tilted neither up nor down, and if all external and accidental obstacles were removed, it would thus be disposed to move incessantly and uniformly from an impulse once received?

SIMP: It seems that it ought to be.

SALV: Now as to that stone which is on top of the mast; does it not move, carried by the ship, both of them going along the circumference of a circle about its center? And consequently is there not in it an ineradicable motion, all external impediments being removed? And is not this motion as fast as that of the ship?

SIMP: All this is true, but what next?

SALV: Go on and draw the final consequence by yourself, if by yourself you have known all the premises.

SIMP: By the final conclusion you mean that the stone, moving with an indelibly impressed motion, is not going to leave the ship, but will follow it, and finally will fall at the same place where it fell when the ship remained motionless. And I, too, say that this would follow if there were no external impediments to disturb the motion of the stone after it was set free. But there are two such impediments; one is the inability of the movable body to split the air with its own impetus alone, once it has lost the force from the oars which it shared as part of the ship while it was on the mast; the other is the new motion of falling downward, which must impede its other, forward, motion.

SALV: As for the impediment of the air, I do not deny that to you, and if the falling body were of very light material, like a feather or a tuft of wool, the retardation would be quite considerable. But in a heavy stone it is insignificant, and if, as you yourself just said a little while ago, the force of the wildest wind is not enough to move a large stone from its place, just imagine how much the quiet air could accomplish upon meeting a rock which moved no faster than the ship! All the same, as I said, I concede to you the small effect which may depend upon such an impediment, just as I know you will concede to me that if the air were moving at the same speed as the ship and the rock, this impediment would be absolutely nil.

As for the other, the supervening motion downward, in the first place it is obvious that these two motions (I mean the circular around the center and the straight motion toward the center) are not contraries, nor are they destructive of one another, nor incompatible. As to the moving body, it has no resistance whatever to such a motion, for you yourself have already granted the resistance to be against motion which increases the distance from the center, and the tendency to be toward motion which approaches the center. From this it follows necessarily that the moving body has neither a resistance nor a propensity to

motion which does not approach toward or depart from the center, and in consequence no cause for diminution in the property impressed upon it. Hence the
cause of motion is not a single one which must be weakened by the new action,
but there exist two distinct causes. Of these, heaviness attends only to the drawing of the movable body toward the center, and impressed force only to its being
led around the center, so no occasion remains for any impediment.

The Orgone Theory of Wilhelm Reich

The following selection is drawn from the work of the controversial figure Wilhelm Reich. Although parts of Reich's clinical research continue
to attract serious and sympathetic attention, his work on orgone is almost universally rejected. For Reich, orgone was a primal life energy
that pervades the universe. He claimed that this radiation could charge
organic substances and that concentrated in a device called an orgone
accumulator it could be used therapeutically to charge the tissues, particularly the blood, and increase the bioenergetic level of the organism.
The Food and Drug Administration denied the validity of this claim and
obtained (by default) a sweeping injunction against Reich's work. Reich
was later charged with violating this injunction, prosecuted, found
guilty, and jailed. He died in Lewisburg Penitentiary in 1957.

Reich insisted that his position was based upon solid scientific evidence that had never been fairly evaluated. Part of his central argument
for the existence of orgone radiation is given below. It is useful to compare this argument first with the one we have cited from Archimedes,
and then with Galileo's position as stated by Salviati.

The Objective Demonstration of Orgone Radiation
WILHELM REICH

1. Are There Subjective Impressions of Light?

When we were children the light phenomena we saw with our eyes shut were
a constant source of fascination. Small dots, blue-violet in color, would appear
from nowhere, floating back and forth slowly, changing their course with every
movement of the eyes. They floated quite slowly in gentle curves, looping periodically into spirals, in a path somewhat as follows:

* From Wilhelm Reich, *The Cancer Biopathy*, Volume II of *The Discovery of the Orgone*,
translated by Andrew White with Mary Higgins and Chester M. Raphael, M.D. (New
York: Farrar, Straus & Giroux, Inc., 1973), pp. 96–103.

It was a delightful game to change the shape and track of the light dots by rubbing the eyes through our closed lids; we could influence even the color of the dots, the blue becoming red, green, or yellow. Part of the fun was to open the eyes suddenly, look into the bright light of a lamp, then close the eyes again and see the after-images. With a little imagination we could turn these forms into all kinds of things: rainbows, balloons, animal heads, human figures.

But such childish pleasures lost their interest as we grew up and studied physics, mathematics, and biology. We had to learn that such subjective optical phenomena were "unreal," something to be distinguished from objectively measurable, physical manifestations of light and its seven colors. In time, our concern for what could actually be measured and weighed obliterated the strong impressions of our sense organs. We no longer took them seriously. The practical everyday world demanded concentration on concrete details exclusively; fantasy only interfered. But the subjective light impressions remain, and the question must nag at many whether such clear phenomena as light impressions observed with the eyes closed do not, after all, represent a reality. The illusionary nature of these optical sensations is not so obvious as it appears.

We were educated to regard such things as these light impressions as "purely subjective" and therefore "not real." They could be of no concern to scientific research and were relegated to the realm of "human fantasy." Man's fantasy life, of course, is far removed from reality, being inspired by subjective desires and, moreover, unstable—which is why scientific research had to develop an objective, realistic foundation through experiment. The ideal experiment makes judgment independent of subjective fantasies, illusions, and wishes. To put it succinctly, man has no confidence in his faculties of perception. He prefers, with good reason, to rely on the photographic plate, the microscope, or the electroscope when examining phenomena.

Yet in spite of the progress made by turning from subjective experience to objective observation, an important quality of research has been lost. What we observe objectively may well exist in reality, but it is dead. In the interest of scientific objectivity, we kill what is alive before making any statements about it. The result is necessarily a mechanistic, machine-like image of life, from which life's most essential quality, its specific aliveness, is missing—an aliveness uncomfortably reminiscent of the intense organ sensations experienced in childhood. Every kind of mysticism—yoga, the fascist "surging of the blood," the receptivity of the spiritualist medium, or the ecstatic, divine epiphany of the dervish—is grounded upon these subjective organ sensations. Mysticism claims the existence of forces and processes that natural science denies or disdains. One moment of sharp deliberation tells us that *man cannot feel or imagine anything that has no real, objective existence in one form or another, for human sense perceptions are only functions of objective natural processes within the organism.* Could it not be that behind the "subjective" light impressions of our closed eyes there exists a reality after all? Is it not possible that through our subjective ocular sensations we perceive biological energy of our own organism? This thought seems strange, daring. But let us see!

To dismiss these subjective light impressions as simple "fantasy" is incorrect. Fantasy is an active property of an organism governed by certain natural laws and must therefore be "real." Not so long ago medicine rejected all functional and nervous ailments as unreal and imagined, because it did not understand them. But headache is headache, and light impression is light impression, whether we understand it or not.

Naturally we reject mystical claims based on *misinterpretation* of organ sensations. But that is not to deny the existence of these sensations. We must also reject a mechanistically fragmented natural science, because it separates organ sensations from the vital processes of the organs. *Self-perception is an essential part of the life process.* It is not a case of nerves being here, muscles there, and organ sensations somewhere else. The processes within the tissues, and our perception of them, form an indivisible *functional unity.* This must be one of the essential, experimentally documented, theoretical guidelines of our therapeutic work. Pleasure and anxiety express a particular state of functioning of the total organism. It is therefore important to make a clear distinction between functional thinking and mechanistically fragmented thinking, which can never penetrate to the essentials of the life process. Let us note four important principles of a *functional* view of nature:

1. Every living organism is a self-contained, functional unit, not merely a mechanical sum of organs. The fundamental biological function controls the total organism just as it governs each individual organ.

2. Every living organism is a part of surrounding nature and is functionally identical with it.

3. Every perception is based upon the correspondence of a function within the organism with a function in the external world, i.e., upon orgonotic harmony.

4. Every self-perception is the immediate expression of objective processes within the organism (psychophysical identity).

Little can be expected from philosophical speculations on the reality of our sensations if they exclude the principle that the observing, perceiving ego (subject) and the observed, perceived object together form a functional unity. Mechanistic research divides this unity into a duality. In its total rejection of sensation, contemporary mechanistic empiricism is beyond redemption. *Every important discovery originates in the subjective sensation or experience of an objective fact, i.e., in orgonotic harmony.* What is required is to objectivize the subjective sensation, separating it from its stimulus and comprehending the origin of the stimulus. As orgone therapists, we do this every hour of every day when we try to understand the bodily expressions of the patient by identifying ourselves with the patient and his functions. Once we comprehend these expressions emotionally, we let our intellect work and objectivize the phenomenon.

Now, with this understanding of orgonotic harmony, let us return to our childhood fantasies and impressions of light. How can we establish *objectively* whether these impressions "seen" with our eyes closed correspond to real processes?

2. Flickering in the Sky Made Objective (the Orgonoscope)

First of all we try to determine whether similar phenomena can be perceived with *open* eyes in broad daylight. If we observe carefully for a sufficient length of time, we discover that they can. We gaze at a screen, a wall, or a white door. *We observe a flickering.* The impression is of shadows or foggy vapors traveling more or less rapidly and rhythmically over the surface of things. Rather than disregarding this observation as a mere "subjective ocular impression," we resolve to establish *objectively* whether this flickering is taking place merely in our eyes or all around us.

Devising a method of differentiating is not easy, however. We begin by closing our eyes. Instantly the flickering seems to change into a movement of small dots, shapes, and colors. We open and close our eyes repeatedly until we are convinced that the phenomena we perceive with our eyes closed are *different* from those we observed while looking at the wall opposite us.

We look into the blue sky, as though gazing into the far distance. At first we see nothing. But if we continue to observe, we discover, to our surprise, a rhythmical, wave-like flickering, clearly perceptible across the blue sky. *Does this flickering exist merely in our eyes, or is it in the sky?* We continue to observe the phenomena over several days, under varying weather conditions and at different times of the day. It is striking that the flickering in the sky varies a great deal in kind and in intensity. Next we experiment at night. Since our observations are now unhampered by diffused daylight the wave-like flickering is even *more distinct.* Here and there we believe we catch a glimpse of a lightning flash in the form of a streak or dots. The flickering and delicate flashings are also to be observed in dark clouds, where they are more intense. As we observe the sky over a period of weeks, we notice that the flickering of the stars varies in intensity. On some nights, the stars shine clearly and calmly; on others their flickering is subdued; on still others, it is extraordinarily vivid. Astronomers ascribe the flickering of the stars to diffuse light. There was a time when we accepted this explanation unquestioningly. However, now that the actual existence of a flickering in the sky has become a crucial question for us, we must ask ourselves whether the flickering of stars may be related to the flickering in the sky *between* the stars. If so, we have taken the first step toward demonstrating the objective existence of an unknown something in the atmosphere. The flickering of the stars is certainly no subjective ocular phenomenon; observatories are built on high mountains in order to eliminate it. The unknown something that makes the stars flicker must therefore be moving close to the surface of the earth. But it is certainly not diffuse light; otherwise the flickering would not vary in intensity as it does. Such "explanations" only obscure facts. Let us defer the answer.

The longer and more precisely we observe the flickering in the sky and across the surface of objects, the more imperative it becomes to delineate a limited field. We construct a metal tube 1 to 3 feet long and 1 to 2 inches in diameter, with a dull black interior. We look through it at the walls in the day time and the sky at night. The tube isolates a circle which appears *brighter* than the area around it. Keeping both eyes open and looking through the tube with one eye, we see a dark-blue night sky within which is a disk of brighter blue. Within the disk itself we perceive, first of all, a flickering movement, then, unmistakably, delicate dots and streaks of light appearing and disappearing. The phenomenon becomes less distinct in the immediate vicinity of the moon; the darker the atmosphere in the background, the clearer the phenomenon.

Are we perhaps this time victims of an illusion? To find out we insert a plano-convex eyepiece with a magnification of approximately 5x in the viewing end of the tube and look through. The bright circular field is now broader; the dots and streaks of light appear larger and more distinct. *It is impossible to magnify subjective light impressions; therefore, the phenomenon must be objective.* Moreover, no flickering is perceptible along the dark interior walls of the tube; the flickering is confined strictly to the bright section of the disk, and therefore cannot be "subjective" sensation. We have isolated a limited area and are now in a position to examine the phenomenon carefully under conditions that eliminate diffuse light from the atmosphere as a factor. But first we shall make some improvements in the primitive orgonoscope we have improvised:

C: cellulose disk, exterior surface dull
WM: wire mesh, on both sides of disk
M: metal cylinder, about 4" long, 2" wide
L: biconvex lens, about 10x, focused on disk
T: telescopic tube, 1' to 2' long, about 2"wide
EP: eyepiece, 5x, for additional magnification

Orgonoscope

We point our tube toward the dark night sky in front of the mirror of a good microscope equipped with apochromatic lenses. We use a 10x object lens and a 5x eyepiece. Our eyes need to be accustomed to the dark for about twenty-five minutes. The microscope reflects the light phenomena in the sky with total clarity. Every single flash of light is clearly discernible. We remove the eyepiece from the tube. Now the flickering is seen in smaller scale, but it is more intense; we are no longer able to distinguish individual flashes of light.

Can the phenomena be ascribed to the haze in the atmosphere? Let us try observing the phenomenon on foggy or hazy nights. It does not take long to see that the phenomena are either very weak or have disappeared completely. *Fog or haze does not cause flickering in the circular field. The movement of light particles in the field of the microscope has nothing to do with the movement of fog.*

By careful observation, we are able to establish that the light and wave phenomena extend across the entire sky and become weaker only when close to stars or the moon because of the stronger light. They are at their most intense on clear nights and when humidity is relatively low. When the humidity rises above 50 percent, the radiation phenomena decrease in intensity. In other words, *humidity absorbs the radiation in the atmosphere*, just as it absorbs the SAPA radiation.

At night we direct our tube at various places—on the ground, the pavement, loose earth, a lawn, walls, etc. We see the same movements of light particles. They are more pronounced on soil than, on asphalt. We point the tube at thick shrubs from a distance of about 10 cm., moving the tube slowly away from the foliage and then back to it. Without doubt, the phenomena are more intense at the leaves than in the surroundings. They seem to come from the leaves themselves. We look at a variety of flower blossoms. The radiation phenomena are more intense close to the blossom than at the stalk.

Earth, walls, bushes, grass, animals, the atmosphere, all show the same phenomena. The conclusion to be drawn from these findings is inescapable: *The radiation phenomena are present everywhere, with variations only in the density and intensity of the energy.* Perhaps we would have wished to find them present in some places and not in others. Then, the discovery would not have been so overwhelming. But we have to stay with the facts, however strange they now begin to appear.

A THEOLOGICAL DEBATE

12

The Problem of Evil and the Nature of God

One of the most difficult questions in Christian theology is to reconcile the perfection of God with the appearance of evil in the world. The two selections given below are serious and important discussions of this issue. The first is drawn from David Hume's *Dialogues Concerning Natural Religion*. The general issue in this dialogue is whether religion can be based upon rational and natural (rather than *super*natural) principles. A believer in natural religion holds that we can prove the existence of God and discover God's nature only through inferences that start from the character of the natural world. The basic argument has the following form: the order and regularity in the world allows us to infer the existence of an intelligent and benevolent being as its creator. Three figures take part in Hume's dialogue: Demea, a representative of orthodox religion, Cleanthes, a defender of natural religion, and Philo, a skeptic. Cleanthes is under constant attack from two sides: from Demea, who is appalled by Cleanthes' rejection of faith and revelation in his defense of religion, and by Philo, who finds Cleanthes' naturalistic arguments unconvincing. In the tenth dialogue, they turn to the problem of evil. Philo and Demea attempt to outdo each other in pointing out the great quantity of evil in the world, saying such things as this:

> Were a stranger to drop on a sudden into this world, I would show
> him, as a specimen of its ills, an hospital full of diseases, a prison

crowded with malefactors and debtors, a field of battle strewed with carcases, a fleet foundering in the ocean, a nation languishing under tyranny, famine, or pestilence. To turn the gay side of life to him and give him a notion of its pleasures—whither should I conduct him? To a ball, to an opera, to court? He might justly think that I was only showing him a diversity of distress and sorrow.

Philo, having agreed with Demea about the vast extent of evil in the world, now challenges Cleanthes to justify his claim that the creator of this world is perfect. How, that is, can we infer the existence of a perfect being from the character of a creation which is itself less than perfect?

Dialogues Concerning Natural Religion
DAVID HUME

And is it possible, Cleanthes, said Philo, that after all these reflections, and infinitely more which might be suggested, you can still persevere in your anthropomorphism, and assert the moral attributes of the Deity, his justice, benevolence, mercy, and rectitude, to be of the same nature with these virtues in human creatures? His power, we allow, is infinite; whatever he wills is executed; but neither man nor any other animal is happy; therefore, he does not will their happiness. His wisdom is infinite; he is never mistaken in choosing the means to any end; but the course of nature tends not to human or animal felicity; therefore, it is not established for that purpose. Through the whole compass of human knowledge there are no inferences more certain and infallible than these. In what respect, then, do his benevolence and mercy resemble the benevolence and mercy of men?

Epicurus' old questions are yet unanswered.

Is he willing to prevent evil, but not able? then is he impotent. Is he able, but not willing? then is he malevolent. Is he both able and willing? whence then is evil?

You ascribe, Cleanthes, (and I believe justly) a purpose and intention to nature. But what, I beseech you, is the object of that curious artifice and machinery which she has displayed in all animals—the preservation alone of individuals, and propagation of the species? It seems enough for her purpose, if such a rank be barely upheld in the universe, without any care or concern for the happiness of the members that compose it. No resource for this purpose: no machinery in order merely to give pleasure or ease; no fund of pure joy and contentment; no indulgence without some want or necessity accompanying it. At least, the few

* Norman Kemp Smith, ed., *Hume's Dialogues Concerning Natural Religion*, 2nd ed. (London: 1947).

phenomena of this nature are overbalanced by opposite phenomena of still greater importance.

Our sense of music, harmony, and indeed beauty of all kinds, gives satisfaction, without being absolutely necessary to the preservation and propagation of the species. But what racking pains, on the other hand, arise from gouts, gravels, megrims, toothaches, rheumatisms, where the injury to the animal machinery is either small or incurable? Mirth, laughter, play, frolic seem gratuitous satisfactions which have no further tendency; spleen, melancholy, discontent, superstition are pains of the same nature. How then does the Divine benevolence display itself, in the sense of you anthropomorphites? None but we mystics, as you were pleased to call us, can account for this strange mixture of phenomena, by deriving it from attributes infinitely perfect but incomprehensible.

And have you, at last, said Cleanthes smiling, betrayed your intentions, Philo? Your long agreement with Demea did indeed a little surprise me, but I find you were all the while erecting a concealed battery against me. And I must confess that you have now fallen upon a subject worthy of your noble spirit of opposition and controversy. If you can make out the present point, and prove mankind to be unhappy or corrupted, there is an end at once of all religion. For to what purpose establish the natural attributes of the Deity, while the moral are still doubtful and uncertain?

You take umbrage very easily, replied Demea, at opinions the most innocent and the most generally received, even amongst the religious and devout themselves; and nothing can be more surprising than to find a topic like this— concerning the wickedness and misery of man—charged with no less than atheism and profaneness. Have not all pious divines and preachers who have indulged their rhetoric on so fertile a subject, have they not easily, I say, given a solution of any difficulties which may attend it? This world is but a point in comparison of the universe; this life but a moment in comparison of eternity. The present evil phenomena, therefore, are rectified in other regions, and in some future period of existence. And the eyes of men, being then opened to larger views of things, see the whole connection of general laws, and trace, with adoration, the benevolence of rectitude of the Deity through all the mazes and intricacies of his providence.

No! replied Cleanthes, no! These arbitrary suppositions can never be admitted, contrary to matter of fact, visible and uncontroverted. Whence can any cause be known but from its known effects? Whence can any hypothesis be proved but from the apparent phenomena? To establish one hypothesis upon another is building entirely in the air; and the utmost we ever attain by these conjectures and fictions is to ascertain the bare possibility of our opinion, but never can we, upon such terms, establish its reality.

The only method of supporting Divine benevolence—and it is what I willingly embrace—is to deny absolutely the misery and wickedness of man. Your representations are exaggerated; your melancholy views mostly fictitious; your inferences contrary to fact and experience. Health is more common than sickness; pleasure than pain; happiness than misery. And for one vexation which we meet with, we attain, upon computation, a hundred enjoyments.

Admitting your position, replied Philo, which yet is extremely doubtful, you must at the same time allow that, if pain be less frequent than pleasure, it is infinitely more violent and durable. One hour of it is often able to outweigh a day, a week, a month of our common insipid enjoyments; and how many days, weeks, and months are passed by several in the most acute torments? Pleasure, scarcely in one instance, is ever able to reach ecstasy and rapture; and in no one instance can it continue for any time at its highest pitch and altitude. The spirits evaporate, the nerves relax, the fabric is disordered, and the enjoyment quickly degenerates into fatigue and uneasiness. But pain often, good God, how often! rises to torture and agony; and the longer it continues, it becomes still more genuine agony and torture. Patience is exhausted, courage languishes, melancholy seizes us, and nothing terminates our misery but the removal of its cause or another event which is the sole cure of all evil, but which, from our natural folly, we regard with still greater horror and consternation.

But not to insist upon these topics, continued Philo, though most obvious, certain, and important, I must use the freedom to admonish you, Cleanthes, that you have put the controversy upon a most dangerous issue, and are unawares introducing a total scepticism into the most essential articles of natural and revealed theology. What! no method of fixing a just foundation for religion unless we allow the happiness of human life, and maintain a continued existence even in this world, with all our present pains, infirmities, vexations, and follies, to be eligible and desirable! But this is contrary to everyone's feeling and experience; it is contrary to an authority so established as nothing can subvert. No decisive proofs can ever be produced against this authority; nor is it possible for you to compute, estimate, and compare all the pains and all the pleasures in the lives of all men and of all animals; and thus, by your resting the whole system of religion on a point which, from its very nature, must for ever be uncertain, you tacitly confess that that system is equally uncertain.

But allowing you what never will be believed, at least, what you never possibly can prove, that animal or, at least, human happiness in this life exceeds its misery, you have yet done nothing; for this is not, by any means, what we expect from infinite power, infinite wisdom, and infinite goodness. Why is there any misery at all in the world? Not by chance, surely. From some cause then. Is it from the intention of the Deity? But he is perfectly benevolent. Is it contrary to his intention? But he is almighty. Nothing can shake the solidity of this reasoning, so short, so clear, so decisive, except we assert that these subjects exceed all human capacity, and that our common measures of truth and falsehood are not applicable to them—a topic which I have all along insisted on, but which you have, from the beginning, rejected with scorn and indignation.

But I will be contented to retire still from this intrenchment, for I deny that you can ever force me in it. I will allow that pain or misery in man is *compatible* with infinite power and goodness in the Deity, even in your sense of these attributes: what are you advanced by all these concessions? A mere possible compatibility is not sufficient. You must *prove* these pure, unmixt, and uncontrollable attributes from the present mixed and confused phenomena, and from these alone. A hopeful undertaking! Were the phenomena ever so pure and unmixed, yet, being finite, they would be insufficient for that purpose. How much more, where they are also so jarring and discordant!

Here, Cleanthes, I find myself at ease in my argument. Here I triumph.

The Perfection of God and the Problem of Evil

The next selection comes from Book VII of St. Augustine's *Confessions*. This is a difficult passage, and commentators disagree about its correct interpretation. It is important to keep a number of things in mind when analyzing this argument. First, the issue at hand is not to prove the existence of God or to establish that God is a perfect being. For Augustine these matters are derived from faith and revelation. Therefore, Philo's arguments, so effective against Cleanthes, do not touch Augustine's position. Philo does not argue that this world, with evil in it, *could not* have been created by a perfect being. On the contrary, he says, "I will acknowledge that pain or misery is compatible with infinite power and goodness in the Diety." He only objects to attempts to prove that God is a perfect being on the basis of the character of this world which, with its evil, gives no evidence of a perfect creator. St. Augustine's problem has a different form from that of Cleanthes: he is not trying to justify the claim that God is perfect, he is trying to explain the existence of evil in a world created by a perfect being. He wants to explain *how* God's perfection and the existence of evil are compatible.

Second, St. Augustine sets high standards for understanding the appearance of evil in a world created by an omnipotent and perfect God. He does not simply shrug his shoulders and say, "The ways of God are not the ways of man." Nor is he willing to settle for an unconvincing explanation. The passage begins with St. Augustine rejecting some traditional explanations of the source of evil.

Finally, in the middle part of this selection, St. Augustine suggests that a proper understanding of the source of evil demands a proper understanding of the nature of God's *infinity*. The explicit argument that begins in Section 11 must be understood within this framework.

Confessions
SAINT AUGUSTINE

3

But although I declared and firmly believed that you, our Lord God, the true God who made not only our souls but also our bodies and not only our souls and bod-

* St. Augustine, *Confessions*, Book VII, R. S. Pine-Coffin, trans. (Harmondsworth, England: Penguin Books, 1961), pp. 136–49.

ies but all things, living and inanimate, as well, although I believed that you were free from corruption or mutation or any degree of change, I still could not find a clear explanation, without complications, of the cause of evil. Whatever the cause might be, I saw that it was not to be found in any theory that would oblige me to believe that the immutable God was mutable. If I believed this, I should myself become a cause of evil, the very thing which I was trying to discover. So I continued the search with some sense of relief, because I was quite sure that the theories of the Manichees were wrong. I repudiated these people with all my heart, because I could see that while they were inquiring into the origin of evil they were full of evil themselves, since they preferred to think that yours was a substance that could suffer evil rather than that theirs was capable of committing it.

I was told that we do evil because we choose to do so of our own free will, and suffer it because your justice rightly demands that we should. I did my best to understand this, but I could not see it clearly. I tried to raise my mental perceptions out of the abyss which engulfed them, but I sank back into it once more. Again and again I tried, but always I sank back. One thing lifted me up into the light of your day. It was that I knew that I had a will, as surely as I knew that there was life in me. When I chose to do something or not to do it, I was quite certain that it was my own self, and not some other person, who made this act of will, so that I was on the point of understanding that herein lay the cause of my sin. If I did anything against my will, it seemed to me to be something which happened to me rather than something which I did, and I looked upon it not as a fault, but as a punishment. And because I thought of you as a just God, I admitted at once that your punishments were not unjust.

But then I would ask myself once more: "Who made me? Surely it was my God, who is not only good but Goodness itself. How, then, do I come to possess a will that can choose to do wrong and refuse to do good, thereby providing a just reason why I should be punished? Who put this will into me? Who sowed this seed of bitterness in me, when all that I am was made by my God, who is Sweetness itself? If it was the devil who put it there, who made the devil? If he was a good angel who became a devil because of his own wicked will, how did he come to possess the wicked will which made him a devil, when the Creator, who is entirely good, made him a good angel and nothing else?"

These thoughts swept me back again into the gulf where I was being stifled. But I did not sink as far as that hell of error where no one confesses to you his own guilt, choosing to believe that you suffer evil rather than that man does it.

4

Now that I had realized that what is incorruptible is better than that which is not, I took this as the basis for further research and acknowledged that, whatever your nature might be, you must be incorruptible. For no soul has ever been, or ever will be, able to conceive of anything better than you, who are the supreme, the perfect Good. And since, as I now believed, there could be no possible doubt that the incorruptible is better than the corruptible, it followed that you must be incorruptible; otherwise I should be able to think of something that was better than my God. So, once I had seen that the incorruptible is superior to the corruptible, I had to search for you in the light of this truth and make it the starting point of my inquiry into the origin of evil, that is, the origin of corruption, by which your substance cannot possibly be violated. For there is no means whatsoever by which corruption can injure our God, whether by an act of will, by necessity, or by chance. This is because he is God and what he wills is good and he is himself that same Good: whereas to be corrupted is not good. And you are never compelled, my God, to do or suffer anything against your will, because your will is not greater than your power. It would be greater only if you were greater than yourself, for the will and power of God are God himself. Neither can anything unforeseen happen to you, because you know all things and nothing, whatever its nature, exists except by reason of the very fact that you know it. Need I say more to prove that the substance which is God cannot be corruptible since, if it were, it would not be God?

5

I was trying to find the origin of evil, but I was quite blind to the evil in my own method of research. In my mind's eye I pictured the whole of creation, both the things which are visible to us, such as the earth and the sea, the air and the stars, the trees and the animals which live their lives and die, and the things which we cannot see, such as the firmament of Heaven above, with all its angels and everything in it that is spiritual—for I thought of spiritual things, too, as material bodies, each in its allotted place. I imagined the whole of your creation as a vast mass made up of different kinds of bodies, some of them real, some of them only the bodies which in my imagination took the place of spirits. I thought of this mass as something huge. I could not, of course, know how big it really was, but I made it as large as need be, though finite in all directions. I pictured you, O Lord, as encompassing this mass on all sides and penetrating it in every part, yet yourself infinite in every dimension. It was as though there were sea everywhere, nothing but an immense, an infinite sea, and somewhere within it a sponge, as large as might be but not infinite, filled through and through with the water of this boundless sea. In some such way as this I imagined that your creation, which was finite, was filled by you, who were infinite. I said to myself, "Here is God, and here is what he has created. God is good, utterly and entirely better than the things which he has made. But, since he is good, the things that he has made are also good. This is how he contains them all in himself and fills them all with his presence.

"Where then is evil? What is its origin? How did it steal into the world? What is the root or seed from which it grew? Can it be that there simply is no evil? If so, why do we fear and guard against something which is not there? If our fear is unfounded, it is itself an evil, because it stabs and wrings our hearts for nothing. In fact the evil is all the greater if we are afraid when there is nothing to fear. Therefore, either there is evil and we fear it, or the fear itself is evil.

"Where then does evil come from, if God made all things and, because he is good, made them good too? It is true that he is the supreme Good, that he is himself a greater Good than these lesser goods which he created. But the Creator and all his creation are both good. Where then does evil come from?

"Can it be that there was something evil in the matter from which he made the universe? When he shaped this matter and fitted it to his purpose, did he leave in it some part which he did not convert to good? But why should he have done this? Are we to believe that, although he is omnipotent, he had not the power to convert the whole of this matter to good and change it so that no evil remained in it? Why, indeed, did he will to make anything of it at all? Why did he not instead, by this same omnipotence, destroy it utterly and entirely? Could it have existed against his will? If it had existed from eternity, why did he allow it to exist in that state through the infinite ages of the past and then, after so long a time, decide to make something of it? If he suddenly determined to act, would it not be more likely that he would use his almighty power to abolish this evil matter, so that nothing should exist besides himself, the total, true, supreme, and infinite Good? Or, if it was not good that a God who was good should not also create and establish something good, could he not have removed and annihilated the evil matter and replaced it with good, of which he could create all things? For he would not be omnipotent if he could not create something good without the help of matter which he had not created himself."

These were the thoughts which I turned over and over in my unhappy mind, and my anxiety was all the more galling for the fear that death might come before I had found the truth. But my heart clung firmly to the faith in Christ your Son, our Lord and Saviour, which it had received in the Catholic Church. There were many questions on which my beliefs were still indefinite and wavered from the strict rule of doctrine, yet my mind never relinquished the faith but drank it in more deeply day by day.

10

... Under your guidance I entered into the depths of my soul, and this I was able to do because *your aid befriended me.* I entered, and with the eye of my soul, such as it was, I saw the Light that never changes casting its rays over the same eye of my soul, over my mind. It was not the common light of day that is seen by the eye of every living thing of flesh and blood, nor was it some more spacious light of the same sort, as if the light of day were to shine far, far brighter than it does and fill all space with a vast brilliance. What I saw was something quite, quite different from any light we know on earth. It shone above my mind, but not in the way that oil floats above water or the sky hangs over the earth. It was above me because it was itself the Light that made me, and I was below because I was made by it. All who know the truth know this Light, and all who know this Light know eternity. It is the Light that charity knows.

Eternal Truth, true Love, beloved Eternity—all this, my God, you are, and it is to you that I sigh by night and day. When first I knew you, you raised me up so that I could see that there was something to be seen, but also that I was not yet able to see it. I gazed on you with eyes too weak to resist the dazzle of your splendour. Your light shone upon me in its brilliance, and I thrilled with love and dread alike. I realized that I was far away from you. It was as though I were in a land where all is different from your own and I heard your voice calling from on high, saying "I am the food of full-grown men. Grow and you shall feed on me. But you shall not change me into your own substance, as you do with the food of your body. Instead you shall be changed into me." I realized too that you have chastened man for his sins; you made my life melt away like gossamer, and I asked myself "Is truth then nothing at all, simply because it has no extension in space, with or without limits?" And, far off, I heard your voice saying *I am the God who IS*. I heard your voice, as we hear voices that speak to our hearts, and at once I had no cause to doubt. I might more easily have doubted that I was alive than that Truth had being. For we catch sight of the Truth, as he is known through his creation.

11

Also I considered all the other things that are of a lower order than yourself, and I saw that they have not absolute being in themselves, nor are they entirely without being. They are real in so far as they have their being from you, but unreal in the sense that they are not what you are. For it is only that which remains in being without change that truly is. As for me, *I know no other content but clinging to God*, because unless my being remains in him, it cannot remain in me. But *himself ever unchanged, he makes all things new. I own him as my God; he has no need of aught that is mine*.

12

It was made clear to me also that even those things which are subject to decay are good. If they were of the supreme order of goodness, they could not become corrupt; but neither could they become corrupt unless they were in some way good. For if they were supremely good, it would not be possible for them to be corrupted. On the other hand, if they were entirely without good, there would be nothing in them that could become corrupt. For corruption is harmful, but unless it diminished what is good, it could do no harm. The conclusion then must be either that corruption does no harm—which is not possible; or that everything which is corrupted is deprived of good—which is beyond doubt. But if they are deprived of all good, they will not exist at all. For if they still exist but can no longer be corrupted, they will be better than they were before, because they now continue their existence in an incorruptible state. But could anything be more preposterous than to say that things are made better by being deprived of all good?

So we must conclude that if things are deprived of all good, they cease altogether to be; and this means that as long as they are, they are good. Therefore, whatever is, is good; and evil, the origin of which I was trying to find, is not a substance, because if it were a substance, it would be good. For either it would be an incorruptible substance of the supreme order of goodness, or it would be a corruptible substance which would not be corruptible unless it were good. So it became obvious to me that all that you have made is good, and that there are no substances whatsoever that were not made by you. And because you did not make them all equal, each single thing is good and collectively they are very good, for our God made his whole creation *very good*.

13

For you evil does not exist, and not only for you but for the whole of your creation as well, because there is nothing outside it which could invade it and break down the order which you have imposed on it. Yet in the separate parts of your creation there are some things which we think of as evil because they are at variance with other things. But there are other things again with which they are in accord, and then they are good. In themselves, too, they are good. And all these things which are at variance with one another are in accord with the lower part of creation which we call the earth. The sky, which is cloudy and windy, suits the earth to which it belongs. So it would be wrong for me to wish that these earthly things did not exist, for even if I saw nothing but them, I might wish for something better, but still I ought to praise you for them alone. For all things *give praise to the Lord on earth, monsters of the sea and all its depths; fire and hail, snow and mist, and the storm-wind that executes his decree; all you mountains and hills, all you fruit trees and cedars; all you wild beasts and cattle, creeping things and birds that fly in air; all you kings and peoples of the world, all you that are princes and judges on earth; young men and maids, old men and boys together; let them all give praise to the Lord's name.* The heavens, too, ring with your praises, O God, for you are the God of us all. *Give praise to the Lord in heaven; praise him, all that dwells on high. Praise him, all you angels of his, praise him, all his armies. Praise him, sun and moon; praise him, every star that shines. Praise him, you highest heavens, you waters beyond the heavens. Let all these praise the Lord.* And since this is so, I no longer wished for a better world, because I was thinking of the whole of creation, and in the light of this clearer discernment I had come to see that though the higher things are better than the lower, the sum of all creation is better than the higher things alone.

PHILOSOPHICAL ARGUMENTS 13

It is not easy to explain the character of philosophical reasoning. Indeed, the nature of philosophical reasoning is itself a philosophical problem. We can, however, get some sense of the character of philosophical thought by comparing it with reasoning as it occurs in daily life. In the opening chapters of this book we noticed that in our everyday discussions, much is taken for granted and left unsaid. In general, there is no need to state things that are already a matter of common agreement. In contrast, philosophers usually try to make these underlying assumptions *explicit* and then subject them to criticism. To take an extreme example, in our daily life we simply take it for granted that a world exists outside of our minds. Virtually everything we say and do rests upon this assumption. A person who seriously doubts this is considered insane. It is, however, typical of philosophy to bring this assumption to the surface, ask what it really amounts to, and inquire into the evidence for it.

Another feature of everyday thinking and speaking is that it is controlled by various practical considerations. If I tell friends that I will meet them tomorrow, I do not first take into account everything that might make my statement false. If there is an earthquake, a declaration of war, or an unexpected chance to meet the Queen of England, then, in all likelihood, I will not meet them tomorrow. In fact, there are endlessly many things that might prevent me from meeting my friends tomorrow or make it unreasonable for me to do so. Yet, when I say without qualification that I will meet them tomorrow, I have not been dishonest or even careless, for my remark is implicitly qualified by all kinds of practical reservations that we understand and take for granted. In contrast, philosophers have traditionally tried to find propositions that are true in an *unqualified* way. They have not been content to make claims that are true simply for all practical purposes.

Connected with the idea that philosophers seek unqualified truth is the notion that they seek *fundamental truths*. Fundamental truths, if there are any, cannot be derived from other truths. Traditionally, philosophers have searched for the underlying principles of knowledge, morality, and the structure of the universe. When coordinated, a set of such principles forms a *philosophical system*.

The Search for a Foundation

The first example of philosophical reasoning illustrates the features of traditional philosophical thought. The material comes from René Descartes' *Meditations on First Philosophy*. In these meditations, Descartes undertakes a critical survey of all that he has believed in order, first, to clear his mind of errors, and, second, to find some unqualified truth that will serve as the foundation for a secure philosophical system. In order to achieve these ends, Descartes begins by subjecting his previous opinions to a radical philosophical doubt; he rejects (as if false) any opinion for which there can be the slightest possibility that it is mistaken. This radical doubt undercuts virtually all of our beliefs of common life and of science as well. Descartes does, however, discover one truth that is not subject to such doubt: that he exists as a thinking thing. This is something he cannot doubt, for even to try doubting it confirms it. This knowledge of himself as a thinking thing becomes the starting point for Descartes' philosophy. The material below comes from the first two of Descartes' six meditations.

Meditations on First Philosophy
RENÉ DESCARTES

MEDITATION I

Of the Things of Which We May Doubt

Several years have now elapsed since I first became aware that I had accepted, even from my youth, many false opinions for true, and that conse-

---

* René Descartes, *Meditations on First Philosophy*, John Veitch, trans. (Edinburgh: W. Blackwell, 1873).

quently what I afterwards based on such principles was highly doubtful; and from that time I was convinced of the necessity of undertaking once in my life to rid myself of all the opinions I had adopted, and of commencing anew the work of building from the foundation, if I desired to establish a firm and abiding superstructure in the sciences. But as this enterprise appeared to me to be one of great magnitude, I waited until I had attained an age so mature as to leave me no hope that at any stage of life more advanced I should be better able to execute my design. On this account, I have delayed so long that I should henceforth consider I was doing wrong were I still to consume in deliberation any of the time that now remains for action. To-day, then, since I have opportunely freed my mind from all cares, [and am happily disturbed by no passions], and since I am in the secure possession of leisure in a peaceable retirement, I will at length apply myself earnestly and freely to the general overthrow of all my former opinions. But, to this end, it will not be necessary for me to show that the whole of these are false—a point, perhaps, which I shall never reach; but as even now my reason convinces me that I ought not the less carefully to withhold belief from what is not entirely certain and indubitable, than from what is manifestly false, it will be sufficient to justify the rejection of the whole if I shall find in each some ground for doubt. Nor for this purpose will it be necessary even to deal with each belief individually, which would be truly an endless labour; but, as the removal from below of the foundation necessarily involves the downfall of the whole edifice, I will at once approach the criticism of the principles on which all my former beliefs rested.

All that I have, up to this moment, accepted as possessed of the highest truth and certainty, I received either from or through the senses. I observed, however, that these sometimes misled us; and it is the part of prudence not to place absolute confidence in that by which we have even once been deceived.

But it may be said, perhaps, that, although the senses occasionally mislead us respecting minute objects, and such as are so far removed from us as to be beyond the reach of close observation, there are yet many other of their informations (presentations), of the truth of which it is manifestly impossible to doubt; as for example, that I am in this place, seated by the fire, clothed in a winter dressing-gown, that I hold in my hands this piece of paper, with other intimations of the same nature. But how could I deny that I possess these hands and this body, and withal escape being classed with persons in a state of insanity, whose brains are so disordered and clouded by dark bilious vapours as to cause them pertinaciously to assert that they are monarchs when they are in the greatest poverty; or clothed [in gold] and purple when destitute of any covering; or that their head is made of clay, their body of glass, or that they are gourds? I should certainly be not less insane than they, were I to regulate my procedure according to examples so extravagant.

Though this be true, I must nevertheless here consider that I am a man, and that, consequently, I am in the habit of sleeping, and representing to myself in dreams those same things, or even sometimes others less probable, which the insane think are presented to them in their waking moments. How often have I dreamt that I was in these familiar circumstances,—that I was dressed, and occupied this place by the fire, when I was lying undressed in bed? At the present moment, however, I certainly look upon this paper with eyes wide awake; the head which I now move is not asleep; I extend this hand consciously and with express purpose, and I perceive it; the occurrences in sleep are not so distinct as all this. But I cannot forget that, at other times, I have been deceived in sleep by similar illusions; and, attentively considering those cases, I perceive so clearly that there exist no certain marks by which the state of waking can ever be distinguished from sleep, that I feel greatly astonished; and in amazement I almost persuade myself that I am now dreaming.

Let us suppose, then, that we are dreaming, and that all these particulars—namely, the opening of the eyes, the motion of the head, the forth-putting of the hands—are merely illusions; and even that we really possess neither an entire body nor hands such as we see. Nevertheless, it must be admitted at least that the objects which appear to us in sleep are, as it were, painted representations which could not have been formed unless in the likeness of realities; and, therefore, that those general objects, at all events,—namely, eyes, a head, hands, and an entire body—are not simply imaginary, but really existent. For, in truth, painters themselves, even when they study to represent sirens and satyrs by forms the most fantastic and extraordinary, cannot bestow upon them natures absolutely new, but can only make a certain medley of the members of different animals; or if they chance to imagine something so novel that nothing at all similar has ever been seen before, and such as is, therefore, purely fictitious and absolutely false, it is at least certain that the colours of which this is composed are real.

And on the same principle, although these general objects, viz. [a body], eyes, a head, hands, and the like, be imaginary, we are nevertheless absolutely necessitated to admit the reality at least of some other objects still more simple and universal than these, of which, just as of certain real colours, all those images of things, whether true and real, or false and fantastic, that are found in our consciousness, are formed.

To this class of objects seem to belong corporeal nature in general and its extension; the figure of extended things, their quantity or magnitude, and their number, as also the place in, and the time during, which they exist, and other things of the same sort. We will not, therefore, perhaps reason illegitimately if we conclude from this that Physics, Astronomy, Medicine, and all the other sciences that have for their end the consideration of composite objects, are indeed of a doubtful character; but that Arithmetic, Geometry, and the other sciences of the same class, which regard merely the simplest and most general objects, and scarcely inquire whether or not these are really existent, contain somewhat that is certain and indubitable: for whether I am awake or dreaming, it remains true that two and three make five, and that a square has but four sides; nor does it seem possible that truths so apparent can ever fall under a suspicion of falsity [or incertitude].

Nevertheless, the belief that there is a God who is all-powerful, and who created me, such as I am, has, for a long time, obtained steady possession of my mind. How, then, do I know that he has not arranged that there should be neither earth, nor sky, nor any extended thing, nor figure, nor magnitude, nor place, providing at the same time, however, for [the rise in me of the perceptions of all these objects, and] the persuasion that these do not exist otherwise than as I perceive them? And further, as I sometimes think that others are in error respecting matters of which they believe themselves to possess a perfect knowledge, how do I know that I am not also deceived each time I add together two and three, or number the sides of a square, or form some judgment still more simple, if more simple indeed can be imagined? But perhaps Deity has not been willing that I should be thus deceived, for He is said to be supremely good. If, however, it were repugnant to the goodness of Deity to have created me subject to constant deception, it would seem likewise to be contrary to his goodness to allow me to be occasionally deceived; and yet it is clear that this is permitted. Some, indeed, might perhaps be found who would be disposed rather to deny the existence of a Being so powerful than to believe that there is nothing certain. But let us for the present refrain from opposing this opinion, and grant that all which is here said of a Deity is fabulous: nevertheless in whatever way it be supposed that I reached the state in which I exist, whether by fate, or chance, or by an endless series of antecedents and consequents, or by any other means, it is clear (since to be deceived and to err is a certain defect) that the probability of my being so imperfect as to be the constant victim of deception, will be increased exactly in proportion as the power possessed by the cause, to which they assign my origin, is lessened. To these reasonings I have assuredly nothing to reply, but am constrained at last to avow that there is nothing of all that I formerly believed to be true of which it is impossible to doubt, and that not through thoughtlessness or levity, but from cogent and maturely considered reasons; so that henceforward, if I desire to discover anything certain, I ought not the less carefully to refrain from assenting to those same opinions than to what might be shown to be manifestly false.

But it is not sufficient to have made these observations; care must be taken likewise to keep them in remembrance. For those old and customary opinions perpetually recur—long and familiar usage giving them the right of occupying my mind, even almost against my will, and subduing my belief; nor will I lose the habit of deferring to them and confiding in them so long as I shall consider them to be what in truth they are, viz., opinions to some extent doubtful, as I have already shown, but still highly probable, and such as it is much more reasonable to believe than deny. It is for this reason I am persuaded that I shall not be doing wrong, if, taking an opposite judgment of deliberate design, I become my own deceiver, by supposing, for a time, that all those opinions are entirely false and imaginary, until at length, having thus balanced my old by my new prejudices, my judgment shall no longer be turned aside by perverted usage from the path that may conduct to the perception of truth. For I am assured that, meanwhile, there will arise neither peril nor error from this course, and that I cannot for the present yield too much to distrust, since the end I now seek is not action but knowledge.

I will suppose, then, not that Deity, who is sovereignly good and the fountain of truth, but that some malignant demon, who is at once exceedingly potent and deceitful, has employed all his artifice to deceive me; I will suppose that the sky, the air, the earth, colours, figures, sounds, and all external things, are nothing better than the illusions of dreams, by means of which this being has laid snares for my credulity; I will consider myself as without hands, eyes, flesh, blood, or any of the senses, and as falsely believing that I am possessed of these; I will continue resolutely fixed in this belief, and if indeed by this means it be not in my power to arrive at the knowledge of truth, I shall at least do what is in my power, viz., [suspend my judgment], and guard with settled purpose against giving my assent to what is false, and being imposed upon by this deceiver, whatever be his power and artifice.

But this undertaking is arduous, and a certain indolence insensibly leads me back to my ordinary course of life; and just as the captive, who, perchance, was enjoying in his dreams an imaginary liberty, when he begins to suspect that it is but a vision, dreads awakening, and conspires with the agreeable illusions that the deception may be prolonged; so I, of my own accord, fall back into the train of my former beliefs, and fear to arouse myself from my slumber, lest the time of laborious wakefulness that would succeed this quiet rest, in place of bringing any light of day, should prove inadequate to dispel the darkness that will arise from the difficulties that have now been raised.

MEDITATION II

Of the Nature of the Human Mind; and That It Is More Easily Known Than the Body

The Meditation of yesterday has filled my mind with so many doubts, that it is no longer in my power to forget them. Nor do I see, meanwhile, any principle on which they can be resolved; and, just as if I had fallen all of a sudden into very deep water, I am so greatly disconcerted as to be unable either to plant my feet firmly on the bottom or sustain myself by swimming on the surface. I will, nevertheless, make an effort, and try anew the same path on which I had entered yesterday, that is, proceed by casting aside all that admits of the slightest doubt, not less than if I had discovered it to be absolutely false; and I will continue always in this track until I shall find something that is certain, or at least, if I can do nothing more, until I shall know with certainty that there is nothing certain. Archimedes, that he might transport the entire globe from the place it occupied to another, demanded only a point that was firm and immovable; so also, I shall be entitled to entertain the highest expectations, if I am fortunate enough to discover only one thing that is certain and indubitable.

I suppose, accordingly, that all the things which I see are false (fictitious); I believe that none of those objects which my fallacious memory represents ever existed; I suppose that I possess no senses; I believe that body, figure, extension, motion, and place are merely fictions of my mind. What is there, then, that can be esteemed true? Perhaps this only, that there is absolutely nothing certain.

But how do I know that there is not something different altogether from the objects I have now enumerated, of which it is impossible to entertain the slightest doubt? Is there not a God, or some being, by whatever name I may designate him, who causes these thoughts to arise in my mind? But why suppose such a being, for it may be I myself am capable of producing them? Am I, then, at least not something? But I before denied that I possessed senses or a body; I hesitate, however, for what follows from that? Am I so dependent on the body and the senses that without these I cannot exist? But I had the persuasion that there was absolutely nothing in the world, that there was no sky and no earth, neither minds nor bodies; was I not, therefore, at the same time, persuaded that I did not exist? Far from it; I assuredly existed, since I was persuaded. But there is I know not what being, who is possessed at once of the highest power and the deepest cunning, who is constantly employing all his ingenuity in deceiving me. Doubtless, then, I exist, since I am deceived; and, let him deceive me as he may, he can never bring it about that I am nothing, so long as I shall be conscious that I am something. So that it must, in fine, be maintained, all things being maturely and carefully considered, that this proposition I am, I exist, is necessarily true each time it is expressed by me, or conceived in my mind. . . .

Skepticism Unanswered

We have seen that Descartes begins his *Meditations* by calling into question virtually every belief of common life. There is a purpose to his skepticism, however. It provides him with a test for knowledge of the highest order. The following specimen of philosophical reasoning, by Hume, is also skeptical, but this time the skeptical doubts go unanswered. Indeed, at the end of the discussion the claim is made that there is no answer to the doubts that have been raised.

Hume notices what is obvious enough, that many of our beliefs go beyond present experience. In particular, we hold a great many beliefs concerning the future. In the first place, our practical life would be impossible without a great many such beliefs. When we eat a piece of bread, we assume that it will nourish us rather than poison us, that it will not explode when we pick it up, that it will not turn into a kangaroo. If asked why we hold these beliefs the natural answer is that we have learned such things from experience. Hume agrees, but then goes on to ask a deeper question: how can experience give a *rational* basis for beliefs concerning the future? His remarkable answer is that no rational argument can justify our reliance upon past experience in forming beliefs about the future. If we do base our beliefs about the future on past experience, this is a matter of brute instinct rather than reasoning.

Hume's argument—it is usually referred to as his *skepticism concerning induction*—has attracted attention for more than two centuries. It is an elegant argument that is surprisingly simple in form, yet very difficult to answer. After sketching the main pattern of the argument, you can get some appreciation of its depth by trying some answers of your own. In general, answers to Hume's skepticism concerning induction have suffered from the common flaw of assuming the very point at issue: that past experience is a *rational* guide to the future.

Skeptical Doubts Concerning the Operations of the Understanding
DAVID HUME

PART I

All the objects of human reason or inquiry may naturally be divided into two kinds, to wit, *relations of ideas,* and *matters of fact.* Of the first kind are the sciences of geometry, algebra, and arithmetic; and in short, every affirmation which is either intuitively or demonstratively certain. *That the square of the hypothenuse is equal to the squares of the two sides,* is a proposition which expresses a relation between these figures. *That three times five is equal to the half of thirty,* expresses a relation between these numbers. Propositions of this kind are discoverable by the mere operation of thought, without dependence on what is anywhere existent in the universe. Though there never was a circle or triangle in nature, the truths demonstrated by Euclid would for ever retain their certainty and evidence.

Matters of fact, which are the second objects of human reason, are not ascertained in the same manner; nor is our evidence of their truth, however great, of a like nature with the foregoing. The contrary of every matter of fact is still possible; because it can never imply a contradiction, and is conceived by the mind with the same facility and distinctness, as if ever so comfortable to reality. *That the sun will not rise tomorrow* is no less intelligible a proposition, and implies no more contradition than the affirmation, *that it will rise.* We should in vain, therefore, attempt to demonstrate its falsehood. Were it demonstratively false, it would imply a contradiction, and could never be distinctly conceived by the mind.

It may, therefore, be a subject worthy of curiosity, to inquire what is the nature of that evidence which assures us of any real existence and matter of fact, beyond the present testimony of our senses, or the records of our memory. This part of philosophy, it is observable, has been little cultivated, either by the ancients or moderns; and therefore our doubts and errors, in the prosecution of so important an inquiry, may be the more excusable; while we march through such difficult paths without any guide or direction. They may even prove useful, by exciting curiosity, and destroying that implicit faith and security, which is the bane of all reasoning and free inquiry. The discovery of defects in the common philosophy, if any such there be, will not, I presume, be a discouragement, but

* David Hume, *Enquiry Concerning Human Understanding* (Edinburgh: Kincaid, 1741).

rather an incitement, as is usual, to attempt something more full and satisfactory than has yet been proposed to the public.

All reasonings concerning matter of fact seem to be founded on the relation of *cause and effect.* By means of that relation alone we can go beyond the evidence of our memory and senses. If you were to ask a man, why he believes any matter of fact, which is absent; for instance, that his friend is in the country, or in France; he would give you a reason; and this reason would be some other fact; as a letter received from him, or the knowledge of his former resolutions and promises. A man finding a watch or any other machine in a desert island, would conclude that there had once been men in that island. All our reasonings concerning fact are of the same nature. And here it is constantly supposed that there is a connection between the present fact and that which is inferred from it. Were there nothing to bind them together, the inference would be entirely precarious. The hearing of an articulate voice and rational discourse in the dark assures us of the presence of some person: Why? because these are the effects of the human make and fabric, and closely connected with it. If we anatomize all the other reasonings of this nature, we shall find that they are founded on the relation of cause and effect, and that this relation is either near or remote, direct or collateral. Heat and light are collateral effects of fire, and the one effect may justly be inferred from the other.

If we would satisfy ourselves, therefore, concerning the nature of that evidence, which assures us of matters of fact, we must inquire how we arrive at the knowledge of cause and effect.

I shall venture to affirm, as a general proposition, which admits of no exception, that the knowledge of this relation is not, in any instance, attained by reasonings a priori; but arises entirely from experience, when we find that any particular objects are constantly conjoined with each other. Let an object be presented to a man of ever so strong natural reason and abilities; if that object be entirely new to him, he will not be able, by the most accurate examination of its sensible qualities, to discover any of its causes or effects. Adam, though his rational faculties be supposed, at the very first, entirely perfect, could not have inferred from the fluidity and transparency of water that it would suffocate him, or from the light and warmth of fire that it would consume him. No object ever discovers, by the qualities which appear to the senses, either the causes which produced it, or the effects which will arise from it; nor can our reason, unassisted by experience, ever draw any inference concerning real existence and matter of fact.

This proposition, *that causes and effects are discoverable, not by reason but by experience,* will readily be admitted with regard to such objects, as we remember to have once been altogether unknown to us; since we must be conscious of the utter inability, which we then lay under, of foretelling what would arise from them. Present two smooth pieces of marble to a man who has no tincture of natural philosophy; he will never discover that they will adhere together in such a manner as to require great force to separate them in a direct line, while they make so small a resistance to a lateral pressure. Such events, as bear little analogy to the common course of nature, are also readily confessed to be known only by experience; nor does any man imagine that the explosion of gunpowder, or the attraction of a loadstone, could ever be discovered by arguments *a priori*. In like manner, when an effect is supposed to depend upon an intricate machinery or secret structure of parts, we make no difficulty in attributing all our knowledge of it to experience. Who will assert that he can give the ultimate reason, why milk or bread is proper nourishment for a man, not for a lion or a tiger?

But the same truth may not appear, at first sight, to have the same evidence with regard to events, which have become familiar to us from our first appearance in the world, which bear a close analogy to the whole course of nature, and which are supposed to depend on the simple qualities of objects, without any secret structure of parts. We are apt to imagine that we could discover these effects by the mere operation of our reason, without experience. We fancy, that were we brought on a sudden into this world, we could at first have inferred that one billiard ball would communicate motion to another upon impulse; and that we needed not to have waited for the event, in order to pronounce with certainty concerning it. Such is the influence of custom, that, where it is strongest, it not only covers ·our natural ignorance, but even conceals itself, and seems not to take place, merely because it is found in the highest degree.

But to convince us that all the laws of nature, and all the operations of bodies without exception, are known only by experience, the following reflections may, perhaps, suffice. Were any object presented to us, and were we required to pronounce concerning the effect, which will result from it, without consulting past observation; after what manner, I beseech you, must the mind proceed in this operation? It must invent or imagine some event, which it ascribes to the object as its effect; and it is plain that this invention must be entirely arbitrary. The mind can never possibly find the effect in the supposed cause, by the most accurate scrutiny and examination. For the effect is totally different from the cause, and consequently can never be discovered in it. Motion in the second billiard ball is a quite distinct event from motion in the first: nor is there anything in the one to suggest the smallest hint of the other. A stone or piece of metal raised into the air, and left without any support, immediately falls: but to consider the matter *a priori*, is there anything we discover in this situation which can beget the idea of a downward, rather than an upward, or any other motion, in the stone or metal?

And as the first imagination or invention of a particular effect, in all natural operations, is arbitrary, where we consult not experience; so must we also esteem the supposed tie or connection between the cause and effect, which binds them together, and renders it impossible that any other effect could result from the operation of that cause. When I see, for instance, a billiard ball moving in a straight line towards another; even suppose motion in the second ball should by accident be suggested to me, as the result of their contact or impulse; may I not conceive, that a hundred different events might as well follow from that cause? May not both these balls remain at absolute rest? May not the first ball return in a straight line, or leap off from the second in any line or direction? All these suppositions are consistent and conceivable. Why then should we give the preference to one, which is no more consistent or conceivable than the rest?

All our reasonings *a priori* will never be able to show us any foundation for this preference.

In a word, then, every effect is a distinct event from its cause. It could not, therefore, be discovered in the cause, and the first invention or conception of it, *a priori*, must be entirely arbitrary. And even after it is suggested, the conjunction of it with the cause must appear equally arbitrary; since there are always many other effects, which, to reason, must seem fully as consistent and natural. In vain, therefore, should we pretend to determine any single event, or infer any cause or effect, without the assistance of observation and experience.

Hence we may discover the reason why no philosopher, who is rational and modest, has ever pretended to assign the ultimate cause of any natural operation, or to show distinctly the action of that power, which produces any single effect in the universe. It is confessed, that the utmost effort of human reason is to reduce the principles, productive of natural phenomena, to a greater simplicity, and to resolve the many particular effects into a few general causes, by means of reasonings from analogy, experience, and observation. But as to the causes of these general causes, we should in vain attempt their discovery; nor shall we ever be able to satisfy ourselves, by any particular explication of them. These ultimate springs and principles are totally shut up from human curiosity and inquiry. Elasticity, gravity, cohesion of parts, communication of motion by impulse; these are probably the ultimate causes and principles which we ever discover in nature; and we may esteem ourselves sufficiently happy, if, by accurate inquiry and reasoning, we can trace up the particular phenomena to, or near to, these general principles. The most perfect philosophy of the natural kind only staves off our ignorance a little longer; as perhaps the most perfect philosophy of the moral or metaphysical kind serves only to discover larger portions of it. Thus the observation of human blindness and weakness is the result of all philosophy, and meets us at every turn, in spite of our endeavors to elude or avoid it.

Nor is geometry, when taken into the assistance of natural philosophy, ever able to remedy this defect, or lead us into the knowledge of ultimate causes, by all that accuracy of reasoning for which it is so justly celebrated. Every part of mixed mathematics proceeds upon the supposition that certain laws are established by nature in her operations; and abstract reasonings are employed, either to assist experience in the discovery of these laws, or to determine their influence in particular instances, where it depends upon any precise degree of distance and quantity. Thus, it is a law of motion, discovered by experience, that the moment or force of any body in motion is in the compound ratio or proportion of its solid contents and its velocity; and consequently, that a small force may remove the greatest obstacle or raise the greatest weight, if, by any contrivance or machinery, we can increase the velocity of that force, so as to make it an overmatch for its antagonist. Geometry assists us in the application of this law, by giving us the just dimensions of all the parts and figures which can enter into any species of machine; but still the discovery of the law itself is owing merely to experience, and all the abstract reasonings in the world could never lead us one step towards the knowledge of it. When we reason *a priori*, and consider merely any object or cause, as it appears to the mind, independent of all observation, it never could suggest to us the notion of any distinct object, such as its effect; much less, show us the inseparable and inviolable connection between them. A man must be very sagacious who could discover by reasoning that crystal is the effect of heat, and ice of cold, without being previously acquainted with the operation of these qualities.

Part II

But we have not yet attained any tolerable satisfaction with regard to the question first proposed. Each solution still gives rise to a new question as difficult as the foregoing, and leads us on to farther inquiries. When it is asked, *What is the nature of all our reasonings concerning matter of fact?* the proper answer seems to be, that they are founded on the relation of cause and effect. When again it is asked, *What is the foundation of all our reasonings and conclusions concerning that relation?* it may be replied in one word, *experience.* But if we still carry on our sifting humor, and ask, *What is the foundation of all conclusions from experience?* this implies a new question, which may be of more difficult solution and explication. Philosophers, that give themselves airs of superior wisdom and sufficiency, have a hard task when they encounter persons of inquisitive dispositions, who push them from every corner to which they retreat, and who are sure at last to bring them to some dangerous dilemma. The best expedient to prevent this confusion, is to be modest in our pretensions: and even to discover the difficulty ourselves before it is objected to us. By this means, we may make a kind of merit of our very ignorance.

I shall content myself, in this section, with an easy task, and shall pretend only to give a negative answer to the question here proposed. I say then, that, even after we have experience of the operations of cause and effect, our conclusions from that experience are *not* founded on reasoning, or any process of the understanding. This answer we must endeavor both to explain and to defend.

It must certainly be allowed, that nature has kept us at a great distance from all her secrets, and has afforded us only the knowledge of a few superficial qualities of objects; while she conceals from us those powers and principles on which the influence of those objects entirely depends. Our senses inform us of the color, weight, and consistence of bread; but neither sense nor reason can ever inform us of those qualities which fit it for the nourishment and support of a human body. Sight or feeling conveys an idea of the actual motion of bodies; but as to that wonderful force or power, which would carry on a moving body for ever in a continued change of place, and which bodies never lose but by communicating it to others; of this we cannot form the most distant conception. But notwithstanding this ignorance of natural powers and principles, we always presume, when we see like sensible qualities, that they have like secret powers, and expect that effects, similar to those which we have experienced, will follow from them. If a body of like color and consistence with that bread, which we have formerly eat, be presented to us, we make no scruple of repeating the experiment, and foresee, with certainty, like nourishment and support. Now this is a process of the mind or thought, of which I would willingly know the foundation. It is allowed on all hands that there is no known connection between the sensible qualities and the secret powers; and consequently, that the mind is not led to form such a conclusion concerning their constant and regular conjunction, by anything which it knows of their nature. As to past *experience*, it can be allowed to give *direct* and *certain* information of those precise objects only, and that precise period of time, which fell under its cognizance: but why this experience should be extended to future times, and to other objects, which, for aught we know, may be only in appearance similar; this is the main question on which I would insist. The bread, which I formerly eat, nourished me; that is, a body of such sensible qualities was, at that time, endued with such secret powers: but does it follow, that other bread must also nourish me at another time, and that like sensible qualities must always be attended with like secret powers? The consequence seems no wise necessary. At least, it must be acknowledged that there is here a consequence drawn by the mind; that there is a certain step taken; a process of thought, and an inference, which wants to be explained. These two propositions are far from being the same, *I have found that such an object has always been attended with such an effect*, and *I forsee, that other objects, which are, in appearance, similar, will be attended with similar effects*. I shall allow, if you please, that the one proposition may justly be inferred from the other; I know, in fact, that it always is inferred. But if you insist that the inference is made by a chain of reasoning, I desire you to produce that reasoning. The connection between these propositions is not intuitive. There is required a medium, which may enable the mind to draw such an inference, if indeed it be drawn by reasoning and argument. What that medium is, I must confess, passes my comprehension; and it is incumbent on those to produce it, who assert that it really exists, and is the origin of all our conclusions concerning matter of fact.

This negative argument must certainly, in process of time, become altogether convincing, if many penetrating and able philosophers shall turn their inquiries this way and no one be ever able to discover any connecting proposition or intermediate step, which supports the understanding in this conclusion. But as the question is yet new, every reader may not trust so far to his own penetration, as to conclude, because an argument escapes his inquiry, that therefore it does not really exist. For this reason it may be requisite to venture upon a more difficult task; and enumerating all the branches of human knowledge, endeavor to show that none of them can afford such an argument.

All reasonings may be divided into two kinds, namely demonstrative reasoning, or that concerning relations of ideas, and moral reasoning, or that concerning matter of fact and existence. That there are no demonstrative arguments in the case seems evident; since it implies no contradiction that the course of nature may change, and that an object, seemingly like those which we have experienced, may be attended with different or contrary effects. May I not clearly and distinctly conceive that a body, falling from the clouds, and which, in all other respects, resembles snow, has yet the taste of salt or feeling of fire? Is there any more intelligible proposition than to affirm, that all the trees will flourish in December and January, and decay in May and June? Now whatever is intelligible, and can be distinctly conceived, implies no contradiction, and can never be proved false by any demonstrative argument or abstract reasoning *a priori.*

If we be, therefore, engaged by arguments to put trust in past experience, and make it the standard of our future judgment, these arguments must be probable only, or such as regard matter of fact and real existence, according to the division above mentioned. But that there is no argument of this kind, must appear, if our explication of that species of reasoning be admitted as solid and satisfactory. We have said that all arguments concerning existence are founded on the relation of cause and effect; that our knowledge of that relation is derived entirely from experience; and that all our experimental conclusions proceed upon the supposition that the future will be conformable to the past. To endeavor, therefore, the proof of this last supposition by probable arguments, or arguments regarding existence, must be evidently going in a circle, and taking that for granted, which is the very point in question.

In reality, all arguments from experience are founded on the similarity which we discover among natural objects, and by which we are induced to expect effects similar to those which we have found to follow from such objects. And though none but a fool or madman will ever pretend to dispute the authority of experience, or to reject that great guide of human life, it may surely be allowed a philosopher to have so much curiosity at least as to examine the principle of human nature, which gives this mighty authority to experience, and makes us draw advantage from that similarity which nature has placed among different objects. From causes which appear *similar* we expect similar effects. This is the sum of all our experimental conclusions. Now it seems evident that, if this conclusion were formed by reason, it would be as perfect at first, and upon one instance, as after ever so long a course of experience. But the case is far otherwise. Nothing so like as eggs; yet no one, on account of this appearing similarity, expects the same taste and relish in all of them. It is only after a long course of uniform experiments in any kind, that we attain a firm reliance and security with regard to a particular event. Now where is that process of reasoning which, from one instance, draws a conclusion, so different from that which it infers from a hundred instances that are nowise different from that single one? This question I propose as much for the sake of information, as with an intention of raising difficulties. I cannot find, I cannot imagine any such reasoning. But I keep my mind still open to instruction, if anyone will vouchsafe to bestow it on me.

Should it be said that, from a number of uniform experiments, we *infer* a connection between the sensible qualities and the secret powers; this, I must confess, seems the same difficulty, couched in different terms. The question still recurs, on what process of argument this *inference* is founded? Where is the medium, the interposing ideas, which join propositions so very wide of each other? It is confessed that the color, consistence, and other sensible qualities of bread appear not, of themselves, to have any connection with the secret powers of nourishment and support. For otherwise we could infer these secret powers from the first appearance of these sensible qualities, without the aid of experience;

contrary to the sentiment of all philosophers, and contrary to plain matter of fact. Here, then, is our natural state of ignorance with regard to the powers and influence of all objects. How is this remedied by experience? It only shows us a number of uniform effects, resulting from certain objects, and teaches us that those particular objects, at that particular time, were endowed with such powers and forces. When a new object, endowed with similar sensible qualities, is produced, we expect similar powers and forces, and look for a like effect. From a body of like color and consistence with bread we expect like nourishment and support. But this surely is a step or progress of the mind, which wants to be explained. When a man says, *I have found, in all past instances, such sensible qualities conjoined with such secret powers:* And when he says, *Similar sensible qualities will always be conjoined with similar secret powers,* he is not guilty of a tautology, nor are these propositions in any respect the same. You say that the one proposition is an inference from the other. But you must confess that the inference is not intuitive; neither is it demonstrative: Of what nature is it, then? To say it is experimental, is begging the question. For all inferences from experience suppose, as their foundation, that the future will resemble the past, and that similar powers will be conjoined with similar sensible qualities. If there be any suspicion that the course of nature may change, and that the past may be no rule for the future, all experience becomes useless, and can give rise to no inference or conclusion. It is impossible, therefore, that any arguments from experience can prove this resemblance of the past to the future; since all these arguments are founded on the supposition of that resemblance. Let the course of things be allowed hitherto ever so regular; that alone, without some new argument or inference, proves not that, for the future, it will continue so. In vain do you pretend to have learned the nature of bodies from your past experience. Their secret nature, and consequently all their effects and influence, may change, without any change in their sensible qualities. This happens sometimes, and with regard to some objects: Why may it not happen always, and with regard to all objects? What logic, what process of argument secures you against this supposition? My practice, you say, refutes my doubts. But you mistake the purport of my question. As an agent, I am quite satisfied in the point; but as a philosopher, who has some share of curiosity, I will not say scepticism, I want to learn the foundation of this inference. No reading, no inquiry has yet been able to remove my difficulty, or give me satisfaction in a matter of such importance. Can I do better than propose the difficulty to the public, even though, perhaps, I have small hopes of obtaining a solution? We shall, at least, by this means, be sensible of our ignorance, if we do not augment our knowledge.

I must confess that a man is guilty of unpardonable arrogance who concludes, because an argument has escaped his own investigation, that therefore it does not really exist. I must also confess that, though all the learned, for several ages, should have employed themselves in fruitless search upon any subject, it may still, perhaps, be rash to conclude positively that the subject must, therefore, pass all human comprehension. Even though we examine all the sources of our knowledge, and conclude them unfit for such a subject, there may still remain a suspicion, that the enumeration is not complete, or the examination not accurate. But with regard to the present subject, there are some considerations which seem to remove all this accusation of arrogance or suspicion of mistake.

It is certain that the most ignorant and stupid peasants—nay infants, nay even brute beasts—improve by experience, and learn the qualities of natural objects, by observing the effects which result from them. When a child has felt the sensation of pain from touching the flame of a candle, he will be careful not to put his hand near any candle; but will expect a similar effect from a cause which is similar in its sensible qualities and appearance. If you assert, therefore, that the understanding of the child is led into this conclusion by any process of argument or ratiocination, I may justly require you to produce that argument; nor have you any pretense to refuse so equitable a demand. You cannot say that the argument is abstruse, and may possibly escape your inquiry; since you confess that it is obvious to the capacity of a mere infant. If you hesitate, therefore, a moment, or if, after reflection, you produce any intricate or profound argument, you, in a manner, give up the question, and confess that it is not reasoning which engages us to suppose the past resembling the future, and to expect similar effects from causes which are, to appearance, similar. This is the proposition which I intended to enforce in the present section. If I be right, I pretend not to have made any mighty discovery. And if I be wrong, I must acknowledge myself to be indeed a very backward scholar; since I cannot now discover an argument which, it seems, was perfectly familiar to me long before I was out of my cradle.

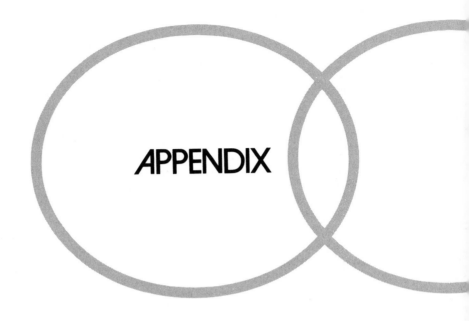

APPENDIX

The two essays reprinted here have served as the background for the basic ideas of Part I. They are included in their entirety for those students who wish to pursue topics in informal analysis at a more advanced level.

Performative Utterances

J. L. AUSTIN

I

You are more than entitled not to know what the word "performative" means. It is a new word and an ugly word, and perhaps it does not mean anything very much. But at any rate there is one thing in its favour, it is not a profound word. I remember once when I had been talking on this subject that somebody afterwards said: "You know, I haven't the least idea what he means, unless it could be that he simply means what he says". Well, that is what I should like to mean.

Let us consider first how this affair arises. We have not got to go very far back in the history of philosophy to find philosophers assuming more or less as a matter of course that the sole business, the sole interesting business, of any

* J. L. Austin, "Performative Utterances," *Philosophical Papers*, 2nd ed., J. O. Urmson and G. J. Warnock, eds. (Oxford: Clarendon Press, 1970), pp. 233–52.

utterance—that is, of anything we say—is to be true or at least false. Of course they had always known that there are other kinds of things which we say— things like imperatives, the expressions of wishes, and exclamations—some of which had even been classified by grammarians, though it wasn't perhaps too easy to tell always which was which. But still philosophers have assumed that the only things that they are interested in are utterances which report facts or which describe situations truly or falsely. In recent times this kind of approach has been questioned—in two stages, I think. First of all people began to say: "Well, if these things are true or false it ought to be possible to decide which they are, and if we can't decide which they are they aren't any good but are, in short, nonsense". And this new approach did a great deal of good; a great many things which probably are nonsense were found to be such. It is not the case, I think, that all kinds of nonsense have been adequately classified yet, and perhaps some things have been dismissed as nonsense which really are not; but still this movement, the verification movement, was, in its way, excellent.

However, we then come to the second stage. After all, we set some limits to the amount of nonsense that we talk, or at least the amount of nonsense that we are prepared to admit we talk; and so people began to ask whether after all some of those things which, treated as statements, were in danger of being dismissed as nonsense did after all really set out to be statements at all. Mightn't they perhaps be intended not to report facts but to influence people in this way or that, or to let off steam in this way or that? Or perhaps at any rate some elements in these utterances performed such functions, or, for example, drew attention in some way (without actually reporting it) to some important feature of the circumstances in which the utterance was being made. On these lines people have now adopted a new slogan, the slogan of the "different uses of language". The old approach, the old statemental approach, is sometimes called even a fallacy, the descriptive fallacy.

Certainly there are a great many uses of language. It's rather a pity that people are apt to invoke a new use of language whenever they feel so inclined, to help them out of this, that, or the other well-known philosophical tangle; we need more of a framework in which to discuss these uses of language; and also I think we should not despair too easily and talk, as people are apt to do, about the *infinite* uses of language. Philosophers will do this when they have listed as many, let us say, as seventeen; but even if there were something like ten thousand uses of language, surely we could list them all in time. This, after all, is no larger than the number of species of beetle that entomologists have taken the pains to list. But whatever the defects of either of these movements—the "verification" movement or the "use of language" movement—at any rate they have effected, nobody could deny, a great revolution in philosophy and, many would say, the most salutary in its history. (Not, if you come to think of it, a very immodest claim.)

Now it is one such sort of use of language that I want to examine here. I want to discuss a kind of utterance which looks like a statement and grammatically, I suppose, would be classed as a statement, which is not nonsensical, and yet is not true or false. These are not going to be utterances which contain curious verbs like "could" or "might", or curious words like "good", which many philosophers regard nowadays simply as danger signals. They will be perfectly straightforward utterances, with ordinary verbs in the first person singular present indicative active, and yet we shall see at once that they couldn't possibly be true or false. Furthermore, if a person makes an utterance of this sort we should say that he is *doing* something rather than merely *saying* something. This may sound a little odd, but the examples I shall give will in fact not be odd at all, and may even seem decidedly dull. Here are three or four. Suppose, for example, that in the course of a marriage ceremony I say, as people will, "I do"—(sc. take this woman to be my lawful wedded wife). Or again, suppose that I tread on your toe and say "I apologize". Or again, suppose that I have the bottle of champagne in my hand and say "I name this ship the *Queen Elizabeth*". Or suppose I say "I bet you sixpence it will rain tomorrow". In all these cases it would be absurd to regard the thing that I say as a report of the performance of the action which is undoubtedly done—the action of betting, or christening, or apologizing. We should say rather that, in saying what I do, I actually perform that action. When I say "I name this ship the *Queen Elizabeth*" I do not describe the christening ceremony, I actually perform the christening; and when I say "I do" (sc. take this woman to be my lawful wedded wife), I am not reporting on a marriage, I am indulging in it.

Now these kinds of utterance are the ones that we call *performative* utterances. This is rather an ugly word, and a new word, but there seems to be no word already in existence to do the job. The nearest approach that I can think of is the word "operative", as used by lawyers. Lawyers when talking about legal instruments will distinguish between the preamble, which recites the circumstances in which a transaction is effected, and on the other hand the operative part—the part of it which actually performs the legal act which it is the purpose of the instrument to perform. So the word "operative" is very near to what we want. "I give and bequeath my watch to my brother" would be an operative clause and is a performative utterance. However, the word "operative" has other uses, and it seems preferable to have a word specially designed for the use we want.

Now at this point one might protest, perhaps even with some alarm, that I seem to be suggesting that marrying is simply saying a few words, that just saying a few words *is* marrying. Well, that certainly is not the case. The words have to be said in the appropriate circumstances, and this is a matter that will come up again later. But the one thing we must not suppose is that what is needed in addition to the saying of the words in such cases is the performance of some internal spiritual act, of which the words then are to be the report. It's very easy to slip into this view at least in difficult, portentous cases, though perhaps not so easy in simple cases like apologizing. In the case of promising—for example, "I promise to be there tomorrow"—it's very easy to think that the utterance is simply the outward and visible (that is, verbal) sign of the performance of some inward spiritual act of promising, and this view has certainly been expressed in many classic places. There is the case of Euripides' Hippolytus, who said "My tongue swore to, but my heart did not"—perhaps it should be "mind" or "spirit" rather than "heart", but at any rate some kind of backstage artiste. Now it is clear from this sort of example that, if we slip into thinking that such utterances are reports, true or false, of the performance of inward and spiritual acts, we open a loophole to perjurers and welshers and bigamists and so on, so that there are disadvantages in being excessively solemn in this way. It is better, perhaps, to stick to the old saying that our word is our bond.

However, although these utterances do not themselves report facts and are not themselves true or false, saying these things does very often *imply* that certain things are true and not false, in some sense at least of that rather woolly word "imply". For example, when I say "I do take this woman to be my lawful wedded wife", or some other formula in the marriage ceremony, I do imply that I'm not already married, with wife living, sane, undivorced, and the rest of it. But still it is very important to realize that to imply that something or other is true, is not at all the same as saying something which is true itself.

These performative utterances are not true or false, then. But they do suffer from certain disabilities of their own. They can fail to come off in special ways, and that is what I want to consider next. The various ways in which a performative utterance may be unsatisfactory we call, for the sake of a name, the infelicities; and an infelicity arises—that is to say, the utterance is unhappy—if certain rules, transparently simple rules, are broken. I will mention some of these rules and then give examples of some infringements.

First of all, it is obvious that the conventional procedure which by our utterance we are purporting to use must actually exist. In the examples given here this procedure will be a verbal one, a verbal procedure for marrying or giving or whatever it may be; but it should be borne in mind that there are many non-verbal procedures by which we can perform exactly the same acts as we perform by these verbal means. It's worth remembering too that a great many of the things we do are at least in part of this conventional kind. Philosophers at least are too apt to assume that an action is always in the last resort the making of a physical movement, whereas it's usually, at least in part, a matter of convention.

The first rule is, then, that the convention invoked must exist and be accepted. And the second rule, also a very obvious one, is that the circumstances in which we purport to invoke this procedure must be appropriate for its invocation. If this is not observed, then the act that we purport to perform would not come off—it will be, one might say, a misfire. This will also be the case if, for example, we do not carry through the procedure—whatever it may be—correctly and completely, without a flaw and without a hitch. If any of these rules are not observed, we say that the act which we purported to perform is void, without effect. If, for example, the purported act was an act of marrying, then we should say that we "went through a form" of marriage, but we did not actually succeed in marrying.

Here are some examples of this kind of misfire. Suppose that, living in a country like our own, we wish to divorce our wife. We may try standing her in front of us squarely in the room and saying, in a voice loud enough for all to hear, "I divorce you". Now this procedure is not accepted. We shall not thereby have succeeded in divorcing our wife, at least in this country and others like it. This is a case where the convention, we should say, does not exist or is not accepted. Again, suppose that, picking sides at a children's party, I say "I pick George". But George turns red in the face and says "Not playing". In that case I plainly, for some reason or another, have not picked George—whether because there is no convention that you can pick people who aren't playing, or because George in the circumstances is an inappropriate object for the procedure of picking. Or consider the case in which I say "I appoint you Consul", and it turns out that you have been appointed already—or perhaps it may even transpire that you are a horse; here again we have the infelicity of inappropriate circumstances, inappropriate objects, or what not. Examples of flaws and hitches are perhaps scarcely necessary—one party in the marriage ceremony says "I will", the other says "I won't"; I say "I bet sixpence", but nobody says "Done", nobody takes up the offer. In all these and other such cases, the act which we purport to perform, or set out to perform is not achieved.

But there is another and a rather different way in which this kind of utterance may go wrong. A good many of these verbal procedures are designed for use by people who hold certain beliefs or have certain feelings or intentions. And if you use one of these formulae when you do not have the requisite thoughts or feelings or intentions then there is an abuse of the procedure, there is insincerity. Take, for example, the expression, "I congratulate you". This is designed for use by people who are glad that the person addressed has achieved a certain feat, believe that he was personally responsible for the success, and so on. If I say "I congratulate you" when I'm not pleased or when I don't believe that the credit was yours, then there is insincerity. Likewise if I say I promise to do something, without having the least intention of doing it or without believing it feasible. In these cases there is something wrong certainly, but it is not like a misfire. We should not say that I didn't in fact promise, but rather that I did promise but promised insincerely; I did congratulate you but the congratulations were hollow. And there may be an infelicity of a somewhat similar kind when the performative utterance commits the speaker to future conduct of a certain description and then in the future he does not in fact behave in the expected way. This is very obvious, of course, if I promise to do something and then break my promise, but there are many kinds of commitment of a rather less tangible form than that in the case of promising. For instance, I may say "I welcome you", bidding you welcome to my home or wherever it may be, but then I proceed to treat you as though you were exceedingly unwelcome. In this case the procedure of saying "I welcome you" has been abused in a way rather different from that of simple insincerity.

Now we might ask whether this list of infelicities is complete, whether the kinds of infelicity are mutually exclusive, and so forth. Well, it is not complete, and they are not mutually exclusive; they never are. Suppose that you are just about to name the ship, you have been appointed to name it, and you are just about to bang the bottle against the stem; but at that very moment some low type comes up, snatches the bottle out of your hand, breaks it on the stem, shouts out "I name this ship the *Generalissimo Stalin*", and then for good measure kicks away the chocks. Well, we agree of course on several things. We agree that the ship certainly isn't now named the *Generalissimo Stalin,* and we agree that it's an infernal shame and so on and so forth. But we may not agree as to how we should classify the particular infelicity in this case. We might say that here is a case of a perfectly legitimate and agreed procedure which, however, has been invoked in the wrong circumstances, namely by the wrong person, this low type instead of the person appointed to do it. But on the other hand we might look at it differently and say that this is a case where the procedure has not as a whole been gone through correctly, because part of the procedure for naming a ship is that you should first of all get yourself appointed as the person to do the naming and that's what this fellow did not do. Thus the way we should classify infelicities in different cases will be perhaps rather a difficult matter, and may even in the last resort be a bit arbitrary. But of course lawyers, who have to deal very much with this kind of thing, have invented all kinds of technical terms and have made numerous rules about different kinds of cases, which enable them to classify fairly rapidly what in particular is wrong in any given case.

As for whether this list is complete, it certainly is not. One further way in which things may go wrong is, for example, through what in general may be called misunderstanding. You may not hear what I say, or you may understand me to refer to something different from what I intended to refer to, and so on. And apart from further additions which we might make to the list, there is the general over-riding consideration that, as we are performing an act when we issue these performative utterances, we may of course be doing so under duress or in some other circumstances which make us not entirely responsible for doing what we are doing. That would certainly be an unhappiness of a kind—any kind of nonresponsibility might be called an unhappiness; but of course it is a quite different kind of thing from what we have been talking about. And I might mention that, quite differently again, we could be issuing any of these utterances, as we can issue an utterance of any kind whatsoever, in the course, for example, of acting a play or making a joke or writing a poem—in which case of course it would not be seriously meant and we shall not be able to say that we seriously performed the act concerned. If the poet says "Go and catch a falling star" or whatever it may be, he doesn't seriously issue an order. Considerations of this kind apply to any utterance at all, not merely to performatives.

That, then, is perhaps enough to be going on with. We have discussed the performative utterance and its infelicities. That equips us, we may suppose, with two shining new tools to crack the crib of reality maybe. It also equips us—it always does—with two shining new skids under our metaphysical feet. The question is how we use them.

II

So far we have been going firmly ahead, feeling the firm ground of prejudice glide away beneath our feet which is always rather exhilarating, but what next? You will be waiting for the bit when we bog down, the bit where we take it all back, and sure enough that's going to come but it will take time. First of all let us ask a rather simple question. How can we be sure, how can we tell, whether any utterance is to be classed as a performative or not? Surely, we feel, we ought to be able to do that. And we should obviously very much like to be able to say that there is a grammatical criterion for this, some grammatical means of deciding whether an utterance is performative. All the examples I have given hitherto do in fact have the same grammatical form; they all of them begin with the verb in the first person singular present indicative active—not just any kind of verb of course, but still they all are in fact of that form. Furthermore, with these verbs that I have used there is a typical asymmetry between the use of this person and tense of the verb and the use of the same verb in other persons and other tenses, and this asymmetry is rather an important clue.

For example, when we say "I promise that . . .", the case is very different from when we say "He promises that . . .", or in the past tense "I promised that . . .". For when we say "I promise that . . ." we do perform an act of promising—we give a promise. What we do *not* do is to report on somebody's performing an act of promising—in particular, we do not report on somebody's use of the expression "I promise". We actually do use it and do the promising. But if I say "He promises", or in the past tense "I promised", I precisely do report on an act of promising, that is to say an act of using this formula "I promise"—I report on a present act of promising by him, or on a past act of my own. There is thus a clear difference between our first person singular present indicative active, and other persons and tenses. This is brought out by the typical incident of little Willie whose uncle says he'll give him half-a-crown if he promises never to smoke till he's 55. Little Willie's anxious parent will say "Of course he promises, don't you, Willie?" giving him a nudge, and little Willie just doesn't vouchsafe. The point here is that he must do the promising himself by saying "I promise", and his parent is going too fast in saying he promises.

That, then, is a bit of a test for whether an utterance is performative or not, but it would not do to suppose that every performative utterance has to take this standard form. There is at least one other standard form, every bit as common as this one, where the verb is in the passive voice and in the second or third person, not in the first. The sort of case I mean is that of a notice inscribed "Passengers are warned to cross the line by the bridge only", or of a document reading "You are hereby authorized" to do so-and-so. These are undoubtedly performative, and in fact a signature is often required in order to show who it is that is doing the act of warning, or authorizing, or whatever it may be. Very typical of this kind of performative—especially liable to occur in written documents of course—is that the little word "hereby" either actually occurs or might naturally be inserted.

Unfortunately, however, we still can't possibly suggest that every utterance which is to be classed as a performative has to take one or another of these two, as we might call them, standard forms. After all it would be a very typical performative utterance to say "I order you to shut the door". This satisfies all the criteria. It is performing the act of ordering you to shut the door, and it is not true or false. But in the appropriate circumstances surely we could perform exactly the same act by simply saying "Shut the door", in the imperative. Or again, suppose that somebody sticks up a notice "This bull is dangerous", or simply "Dangerous bull", or simply "Bull". Does this necessarily differ from sticking up a notice, appropriately signed, saying "You are hereby warned that this bull is dangerous"? It seems that the simple notice "Bull" can do just the same job as the more elaborate formula. Of course the difference is that if we just stick up "Bull" it would not be quite clear that it is a warning; it might be there just for interest or information, like "Wallaby" on the cage at the zoo, or "Ancient Monument". No doubt we should know from the nature of the case that it was a warning, but it would not be explicit.

Well, in view of this break-down of grammatical criteria, what we should like to suppose—and there is a good deal in this—is that any utterance which is performative could be reduced or expanded or analysed into one of these two standard forms beginning "I . . ." so and so or beginning "You (or he) hereby . . ." so and so. If there was any justification for this hope, as to some extent there is, then we might hope to make a list of all the verbs which can appear in these standard forms, and then we might classify the kinds of acts that can be performed by performative utterances. We might do this with the aid of a dictionary, using such a test as that already mentioned—whether there is the characteristic asymmetry between the first person singular present indicative active and the other persons and tenses—in order to decide whether a verb is to go into our list or not. Now if we make such a list of verbs we do in fact find that they fall into certain fairly well-marked classes. There is the class of cases where we deliver verdicts and make estimates and appraisals of various kinds. There is the class where we give undertakings, commit ourselves in various ways by saying something. There is the class where by saying something we exercise various rights and powers, such as appointing and voting and so on. And there are one or two other fairly well-marked classes.

Suppose this task accomplished. Then we could call these verbs in our list explicit performative verbs, and any utterance that was reduced to one or the other of our standard forms we could call an explicit performative utterance. "I order you to shut the door" would be an explicit performative utterance, whereas "Shut the door" would not—that is simply a "primary" performative utterance or whatever we like to call it. In using the imperative we may be ordering you to shut the door, but it just isn't made clear whether we are ordering you or entreating you or imploring you or beseeching you or inciting you or tempting you, or one or another of many other subtly different acts which, in an unsophisticated primitive language, are very likely not yet discriminated. But we need not overestimate the unsophistication of primitive languages. There are a great many devices that can be used for making clear, even at the primitive level, what act it is we are performing when we say something—the tone of voice, cadence, gesture—and above all we can rely upon the nature of the circumstances, the context in which the utterance is issued. This very often makes it quite unmistakable whether it is an order that is being given or whether, say, I am simply urging you or entreating you. We may, for instance, say something like this: "Coming from him I was bound to take it as an order". Still, in spite of all these devices, there is an unfortunate amount of ambiguity and lack of discrimination in default of our explicit performative verbs. If I say something like

"I shall be there", it may not be certain whether it is a promise, or an expression of intention, or perhaps even a forecast of my future behaviour, of what is going to happen to me; and it may matter a good deal, at least in developed societies, precisely which of these things it is. And that is why the explicit performative verb is evolved—to make clear exactly which it is, how far it commits me and in what way, and so forth.

This is just one way in which language develops in tune with the society of which it is the language. The social habits of the society may considerably affect the question of which performative verbs are evolved and which, sometimes for rather irrelevant reasons, are not. For example, if I say "You are a poltroon", it might be that I am censuring you or it might be that I am insulting you. Now since apparently society approves of censuring or reprimanding, we have here evolved a formula "I reprimand you", or "I censure you", which enables us expeditiously to get this desirable business over. But on the other hand, since apparently we don't approve of insulting, we have not evolved a simple formula "I insult you", which might have done just as well.

By means of these explicit performative verbs and some other devices, then, we make explicit what precise act it is that we are performing when we issue our utterance. But here I would like to put in a word of warning. We must distinguish between the function of making explicit what act it is we are performing, and the quite different matter of *stating* what act it is we are performing. In issuing an explicit performative utterance we are not stating what act it is, we are showing or making explicit what act it is. We can draw a helpful parallel here with another case in which the act, the conventional act that we perform, is not a speech-act but a physical performance. Suppose I appear before you one day and bow deeply from the waist. Well, this is ambiguous. I may be simply observing the local flora, tying my shoe-lace, something of that kind; on the other hand, conceivably I might be doing obeisance to you. Well, to clear up this ambiguity we have some device such as raising the hat, saying "Salaam", or something of that kind, to make it quite plain that the act being performed is the conventional one of doing obeisance rather than some other act. Now nobody would want to say that lifting your hat was stating that you were performing an act of obeisance; it certainly is not, but it does make it quite plain that you are. And so in the same way to say "I warn you that . . ." or "I order you to . . ." or "I promise that . . ." is not to state that you are doing something, but makes it plain that you are—it does constitute your verbal performance, a performance of a particular kind.

So far we have been going along as though there was a quite clear difference between our performative utterances and what we have contrasted them with, statements or reports or descriptions. But now we begin to find that this distinction is not as clear as it might be. It's now that we begin to sink in a little. In the first place, of course, we may feel doubts as to how widely our performatives extend. If we think up some odd kinds of expression we use in odd cases, we might very well wonder whether or not they satisfy our rather vague criteria for being performative utterances. Suppose, for example, somebody says 'Hurrah'. Well, not true or false; he is performing the act of cheering. Does that make it a performative utterance in our sense or not? Or suppose he says "Damn"; he is performing the act of swearing, and it is not true or false. Does that make it performative? We feel that in a way it does and yet it's rather different. Again, consider cases of "suiting the action to the words"; these too may make us wonder whether perhaps the utterance should be classed as performative. Or sometimes, if somebody says "I am sorry", we wonder whether this is just the same as "I apologize"—in which case of course we have said it's a performative utterance—or whether perhaps it's to be taken as a description, true or false, of the state of his feelings. If he had said "I feel perfectly awful about it", then we should think it must be meant to be a description of the state of his feelings. If he had said "I apologize", we should feel this was clearly a performative utterance, going through the ritual of apologizing. But if he says "I am sorry" there is an unfortunate hovering between the two. This phenomenon is quite common. We often find cases in which there is an obvious pure performative utterance and obvious other utterances connected with it which are not performative but descriptive, but on the other hand a good many in between where we're not quite sure which they are. On some occasions of course they are obviously used the one way, on some occasions the other way, but on some occasions they seem positively to revel in ambiguity.

Again, consider the case of the umpire when he says "Out" or "Over", or the jury's utterance when they say that they find the prisoner guilty. Of course, we say, these are cases of giving verdicts, performing the act of appraising and so forth, but still in a way they have some connexion with the facts. They seem to have something like the duty to be true or false, and seem not to be so very remote from statements. If the umpire says "Over", this surely has at least something to do with six balls in fact having been delivered rather than seven, and so on. In fact in general we may remind ourselves that "I state that . . ." does not look so very different from "I warn you that . . ." or "I promise to . . .". It makes clear surely that the act that we are performing is an act of stating, and so functions just like "I warn" or "I order". So isn't "I state that . . ." a performative utterance? But then one may feel that utterances beginning "I state that . . ." do have to be true or false, that they *are* statements.

Considerations of this sort, then, may well make us feel pretty unhappy. If we look back for a moment at our contrast between statements and performative utterances, we realize that we were taking statements very much on trust from, as we said, the traditional treatment. Statements, we had it, were to be true or false; performative utterances on the other hand were to be felicitous or infelicitous. They were the doing of something, whereas for all we said making statements was not doing something. Now this contrast surely, if we look back at it, is unsatisfactory. Of course statements are liable to be assessed in this matter of their correspondence or failure to correspond with the facts, that is, being true or false. But they are also liable to infelicity every bit as much as are performative utterances. In fact some troubles that have arisen in the study of statements recently can be shown to be simply troubles of infelicity. For example, it has been pointed out that there is something very odd about saying something like this: "The cat is on the mat but I don't believe it is". Now this is an outrageous thing to say, but it is not self-contradictory. There is no reason why the cat shouldn't be on the mat without my believing that it is. So how are we to classify what's wrong with this peculiar statement? If we remember now the doctrine of infelicity we shall see that the person who makes this remark about the cat is in much the same position as somebody who says something like this: "I promise that I shall be there, but I haven't the least intention of being there." Once again you can of course perfectly well promise to be there without having the least intention of being there, but there is something outrageous about saying it, about actually avowing the insincerity of the promise you give. In the same way there is insincerity in the case of the person who says "The cat is on the mat but I don't believe it is", and he is actually avowing that insincerity—which makes a peculiar kind of nonsense.

A second case that has come to light is the one about John's children—the case where somebody is supposed to say "All John's children are bald but John hasn't got any children". Or perhaps somebody says "All John's children are bald", when as a matter of fact—he doesn't say so—John has no children. Now those who study statements have worried about this; ought they to say that the statement "All John's children are bald" is meaningless in this case? Well, if it is, it is not a bit like a great many other more standard kinds of meaningless-ness; and we see, if we look back at our list of infelicities, that what is going wrong here is much the same as what goes wrong in, say, the case of a contract for the sale of a piece of land when the piece of land referred to does not exist. Now what we say in the case of this sale of land, which of course would be effected by a performative utterance, is that the sale is void—void for lack of reference or ambiguity of reference; and so we can see that the statement about all John's children is likewise void for lack of reference. And if the man actually says that John has no children in the same breath as saying they're all bald, he is making the same kind of outrageous utterance as the man who says "The cat is on the mat and I don't believe it is", or the man who says "I promise to but I don't intend to".

In this way, then, ills that have been found to afflict statements can be precisely paralleled with ills that are characteristic of performative utterances. And after all when we state something or describe something or report something, we do perform an act which is every bit as much an act as an act of ordering or warning. There seems no good reason why stating should be given a specially unique position. Of course philosophers have been wont to talk as though you or I or anybody could just go round stating anything about anything and that would be perfectly in order, only there's just a little question: is it true or false? But besides the little question, is it true or false, there is surely the question: *is* it in order? Can you go round just making statements about anything? Suppose for example you say to me "I'm feeling pretty mouldy this morning". Well, I say to you "You're not"; and you say "What the devil do you mean, I'm not?" I say "Oh nothing—I'm just stating you're not, is it true or false?" And you say "Wait a bit about whether it's true or false, the question is what did you mean by making statements about somebody else's feelings? I told you I'm feeling pretty mouldy. You're just not in a position to say, to state that I'm not". This brings out that you can't just make statements about other people's feelings (though you can make guesses if you like); and there are very many things which, having no knowledge of, not being in a posiiton to pronounce about, you just can't state. What we need to do for the case of stating, and by the same token describing and reporting, is to take them a bit off their pedestal, to realize that they are speech-acts no less than all these other speech-acts that we have been mentioning and talking about as performative.

Then let us look for a moment at our original contrast between the performative and the statement from the other side. In handling performatives we have been putting it all the time as though the only thing that a performative utterance had to do was to be felicitous, to come off, not to be a misfire, not to be an abuse. Yes, but that's not the end of the matter. At least in the case of many utterances which, on what we have said, we should have to class as performative—cases where we say "I warn you to . . .", "I advise you to . . ." and so on—there will be other questions besides simply: was it in order, was it all right, as a piece of advice or a warning, did it come off? After that surely there will be the question: was it good or sound advice? Was it a justified warning? Or in the case, let us say, of a verdict or an estimate: was it a good estimate, or a sound verdict? And these are questions that can only be decided by considering how the content of the verdict or estimate is related in some way to fact, or to evidence available about the facts. This is to say that we do require to assess at least a great many performative utterances in a general dimension of correspondence with fact. It may still be said, of course, that this does not make them *very* like statements because still they are not true or false, and that's a little black and white speciality that distinguishes statements as a class apart. But actually—though it would take too long to go on about this—the more you think about truth and falsity the more you find that very few statements that we ever utter are just true or just false. Usually there is the question are they fair or are they not fair, are they adequate or not adequate, are they exaggerated or not exaggerated? Are they too rough, or are they perfectly precise, accurate, and so on? "True" and "false" are just general labels for a whole dimension of different appraisals which have something or other to do with the relation between what we say and the facts. If, then, we loosen up our ideas of truth and falsity we shall see that statements, when assessed in relation to the facts, are not so very different after all from pieces of advice, warnings, verdicts, and so on.

We see then that stating something is performing an act just as much as is giving an order or giving a warning; and we see, on the other hand, that, when we give an order or a warning or a piece of advice, there is a question about how this is related to fact which is not perhaps so very different from the kind of question that arises when we discuss how a statement is related to fact. Well, this seems to mean that in its original form our distinction between the performative and the statement is considerably weakened, and indeed breaks down. I will just make a suggestion as to how to handle this matter. We need to go very much farther back, to consider all the ways and senses in which saying anything at all is doing this or that—because of course it is always doing a good many different things. And one thing that emerges when we do do this is that, besides the question that has been very much studied in the past as to what a certain utterance *means*, there is a further question distinct from this as to what was the *force*, as we may call it, of the utterance. We may be quite clear what "Shut the door" means, but not yet at all clear on the further point as to whether as uttered at a certain time it was an order, an entreaty or whatnot. What we need besides the old doctrine about meanings is a new doctrine about all the possible forces of utterances, towards the discovery of which our proposed list of explicit performative verbs would be a very great help; and then, going on from there, an investigation of the various terms of appraisal that we use in discussing speech-acts of this, that, or the other precise kind—orders, warnings, and the like.

The notions that we have considered then, are the performative, the infelicity, the explicit performative, and lastly, rather hurriedly, the notion of the forces of utterances. I dare say that all this seems a little unremunerative, a little complicated. Well, I suppose in some ways it is unremunerative, and I suppose it ought to be remunerative. At least, though, I think that if we pay attention to these matters we can clear up some mistakes in philosophy; and after all philosophy is used as a scapegoat, it parades mistakes which are really the mistakes of everybody. We might even clear up some mistakes in grammar, which perhaps is a little more respectable.

And is it complicated? Well, it is complicated a bit; but life and truth and things do tend to be complicated. It's not things, it's philosophers that are simple. You will have heard it said, I expect, that over-simplification is the occupational disease of philosophers, and in a way one might agree with that. But for a sneaking suspicion that it's their occupation.

Logic and Conversation
H. P. GRICE

It is a commonplace of philosophical logic that there are, or appear to be, divergences in meaning between, on the one hand, at least some of what I shall call the *formal* devices '$\sim$', '$\cdot$', '$\vee$', '$\supset$', '(x)', '$(\exists x)$', '$(\imath x)$' (when these are given a standard two-valued interpretation), and, on the other, what are taken to be their analogues or counter parts in natural language, such expressions are 'not', 'or', 'if', 'all', 'some' (or 'at least one'), 'the'. Some logicians may at some time have wanted to claim that there are in fact no such divergences; but such claims, if made at all, have been somewhat rashly made, and those suspected of making them have been subjected to some pretty rough handling.

Those who concede that such divergences exist adhere, in the main, to one or other of two rival groups, which for the purposes of this article I shall call the

* H. P. Grice, "Logic and Conversation," in *The Logic of Grammar*, Donald Davidson and Gilbert Harman, eds. (Encino, California: Dickinson Publishing Co., 1975), pp. 64–153.

formalists and the informalist groups. An outline of a not uncharacteristic formalist position may be given as follows: In so far as logicians are concerned with the formulation of very general patterns of valid inference, the formal devices possess a decisive advantage over their natural counterparts. For it will be possible to construct in terms of the formal devices a system of very general formulas, a considerable number of which can be regarded as, or are closely related to, patterns of inferences, the expression of which involves some or all of the devices. Such a system may consist of a certain set of simple formulas which must be acceptable if the devices have the meaning which has been assigned to them, and an indefinite number of further formulas, many of them less obviously acceptable, each of which can be shown to be acceptable if the members of the original set are acceptable. We have thus a way of handling dubiously acceptable patterns of inference, and if, as is sometimes possible, we can apply a decision procedure, we have an even better way. Furthermore, from a philosophical point of view, the possession by the natural counterparts of those elements in their meaning, which they do not share with the corresponding formal devices, is to be regarded as an imperfection of natural languages; the elements in question are undesirable excrescences. For the presence of these elements has the result that the concepts within which they appear cannot be precisely and clearly defined, and that at least some statements involving them cannot, in some circumstances, be assigned a definite truth-value. The indefiniteness of these concepts is not only objectionable in itself but leaves open the way to metaphysics; we cannot be certain that none of these natural language expressions is metaphysically 'loaded'. For these reasons the expressions, as used in natural speech, cannot be regarded as finally acceptable, and may turn out to be, finally, not fully intelligible. The proper course is to conceive and begin to construct an ideal language, incorporating the formal devices, the sentences of which will be clear, determinate in truth-value, and certifiably free from metaphysical implications; the foundations of science will now be philosophically secure, since the statements of the scientist will be expressible (though not necessarily actually expressed) within this ideal language. (I do not wish to suggest that all formalists would accept the whole of this outline, but I think that all would accept at least some part of it.)

To this, an informalist might reply in the following vein. The philosophical demand for an ideal language rests on certain assumptions which should not be conceded; these are, that the primary yardstick by which to judge the adequacy of a language is its ability to serve the needs of science, that an expression cannot be guaranteed as fully intelligible unless an explication or analysis of its meaning has been provided, and that every explication or analysis must take the form of a precise definition which is the expression or assertion of a logical equivalence. Language serves many important purposes besides those of scientific inquiry. We can know perfectly well what an expression means (and so *a fortiori* that it is intelligible) without knowing its analysis, and the provision of an analysis may (and usually does) consist in the specification, as generalized as possible, of the conditions which count for or against the applicability of the expression being analyzed. Moreover, while it is no doubt true that the formal devices are specially amenable to systematic treatment by the logician, it remains the case that there are very many inferences and arguments, expressed in natural language and not in terms of these devices, which are nevertheless recognizably valid. So there must be a place for an unsimplified, and so more or less unsystematic, logic of the natural counterparts of those devices. This logic may be aided and guided by the simplified logic of the formal devices, but cannot be supplanted by it. Indeed, not only do the two logics differ, but sometimes they come into conflict: rules which hold for a formal device may not hold for its natural counterpart.

Now on the general question of the place in philosophy of the reformation of natural language, I shall, in this article, have nothing to say. I shall confine myself to the dispute in its relation to the alleged divergences mentioned at the outset. I have moreover no intention of entering the fray on behalf of either contestant. I wish, rather, to maintain that the common assumption of the contestants that the divergences do in fact exist is (broadly speaking) a common mistake, and that the mistake arises from an inadequate attention to the nature and importance of the conditions governing conversation. I shall, therefore, proceed at once to inquire into the general conditions which, in one way or another, apply to conversation as such irrespective of its subject matter.

IMPLICATURE

Suppose that A and B are talking about a mutual friend C, who is now working in a bank. A asks B how C is getting on in his job, and B replies, "Oh quite well, I think; he likes his colleagues, and he hasn't been to prison yet." At this point A might well inquire what B was implying, what he was suggesting, or even what he meant by saying that C had not yet been to prison. The answer might be any one of such things as that C is the sort of person likely to yield to the temptation provided by his occupation, that C's colleagues are really very unpleasant and treacherous people, and so forth. It might of course be quite unnecessary for A to make such an inquiry of B, the answer to it being, in the context, clear in advance. I think it is clear that whatever B implied, suggested, or meant, in this example is distinct from what B said, which was simply that C had not been to prison yet. I wish to introduce, as a term of art, the verb 'implicate', the related nouns 'implicature' (cf. 'implying') and 'implicatum' (cf. 'what is implied'). The point of this maneuver is to avoid having, on each occasion, to choose between this or that member of the family of verbs for which 'implicate' is to do general duty. I shall, for the time being at least, have to assume to a considerable extent an intuitive understanding of the meaning of 'say' in such contexts, and an ability to recognize particular verbs as members of the family with which 'implicate' is associated. I can, however, make one or two remarks which may help to clarify the more problematic of these assumptions, namely that connected with the meaning of the word 'say'.

(1) In the sense in which I am using the word 'say', I intend what someone has said to be closely related to the conventional meaning of the words (the sentence) which he has uttered. Suppose someone to have uttered the sentence "He

is in the grip of a vice." Given a knowledge of the English language, but no knowledge of the circumstances of the utterance, one would know something about what the speaker had said, on the assumption that he was speaking standard English, and speaking literally. One would know that he had said, about some particular male person or animal X, that at the time of the utterance (whatever that was) either (i) that X was unable to rid himself of a certain kind of bad character trait, or (ii) that some part of X's person was caught in a certain kind of tool or instrument. (This is an approximate account, of course.) But for a full identification of what the speaker had said, one would need to know (a) the identity of X, (b) the time of utterance, (c) the meaning, on the particular occasion of utterance, of the phrase "in the grip of a vice" (a decision between (i) and (ii)). This brief indication of my use of 'say' leaves it open whether a man who says (today) "Harold Wilson is a great man" and another who says (also today) "The British Prime Minister is a great man" would, if each knew that the two singular terms had the same reference, have said the same thing. But whatever decision is made about this question, the apparatus I am about to provide will be capable of accounting for any implicatures that might depend on the presence of one rather than another of these singular terms in the sentence uttered. Such implicatures would merely be related to different maxims.

(2) In some cases the conventional meaning of the words used will determine what is implicated, besides helping to determine what is said: If I say (smugly) "He is an Englishman; he is, therefore, brave," I have certainly committed myself by virtue of the meaning of my words, to its being true that his being brave is a consequence of (follows from) his being an Englishman. But while I have said that he is an Englishman, and said that he is brave, I do not want to say that I have *said* (in the favored sense) that it follows from his being an Englishman that he is brave, though I have certainly indicated, and so implicated, that this is so. I do not want to say that my utterance of this sentence would be, *strictly speaking,* false should the consequence in question fail to hold. So *some* implicatures are conventional, unlike the one with which I introduced this discussion of implicature.

I wish to represent a certain subclass of nonconventional implicatures, which I shall call *conversational* implicatures, as being essentially connected with certain general features of discourse; so my next step is to try to say what these features are.

The following may provide a first approximation to a general principle. Our talk exchanges do not normally consist of a succession of disconnected remarks, and would not be rational if they did. They are, characteristically, to some degree at least cooperative efforts. Each participant recognizes in them, to some extent, a common purpose or set of purposes, or at least a mutually accepted direction. This purpose or direction may be fixed from the start (e.g., by an initial proposal of a question for discussion), or it may evolve during the exchange; it may be fairly definite, or it may be so indefinite as to leave very considerable latitude to the participants (as in a casual conversation). But at each stage, *some* possible conversational moves would be excluded as conversationally unsuitable. We might then formulate a rough general principle which participants will be expected (ceteris paribus) to observe, viz: "Make your conversational contribution such as is required, at the stage at which it occurs, by the accepted purpose or direction of the talk exchange in which you are engaged." One might label this the Cooperative Principle (CP).

On the assumption that some such general principle as the above is acceptable, one may perhaps distinguish four categories under one or other of which will fall certain more specific maxims and submaxims, the following of which will in general yield results in accordance with the Cooperation Principle. Echoing Kant, I call these categories Quantity, Quality, Relation, and Manner. The category of *Quantity* relates to the quantity of information to be provided and under it fall the maxims

(1) "Make your contribution as informative as is required (for the current purposes of the exchange),"

and possibly

(2) "Do not make your contribution more informative than is required."

(The second maxim is disputable; it might be said that to be overinformative is not a transgression of the CP but merely a waste of time. However, it might be answered that such overinformativeness may be confusing in that it is liable to raise side issues; and there may also be an indirect effect, in that the hearers may be misled, as a result of thinking that there is some particular *point* in the provision of excess information. However this may be, there is perhaps a different reason for doubt about the admission of this second maxim, namely, that its effect will be secured by a later maxim, which concerns relevance.)

Under the category of *Quality* falls a supermaxim: "Try to make your contribution one that is true," and two more specific maxims:

(1) "Do not say what you believe to be false."
(2) "Do not say that for which you lack adequate evidence."

Under the category of *Relation* I place a single maxim, namely, "Be relevant." Though the maxim itself is terse, its formulation conceals a number of problems which exercise me a good deal; questions about what different kinds and foci of relevance there may be, how these shift in the course of a talk exchange, how to allow for the fact that subjects of conversation are legitimately changed, and so on. I find the treatment of such questions exceedingly difficult, and I hope to revert to them in a later lecture [not included here].

Finally under the category of *Manner*, which I understand as relating, not (like the previous categories) to what is said, but rather to how what is said is to be said, I include the supermaxim: "Be perspicuous" and various maxims such as

(1) "Avoid obscurity of expression"
(2) "Avoid ambiguity"
(3) "Be brief (avoid unnecessary prolixity)"
(4) "Be orderly"

And one might need others.

It is obvious that the observance of some of these maxims is a matter of lesser urgency than is the observance of others; a man who has expressed himself with undue prolixity would, in general, be open to milder comment than would a man who had said something which he believes to be false. Indeed it might be felt that the importance of at least the first maxim of Quality is such that it should not be included in a scheme of the kind which I am constructing; other maxims only come into operation on the assumption that this maxim of Quality is satisfied. While this may be correct, so far as the generation of implicatures is concerned it seems to play a role not totally different from the other maxims; and it will be convenient, for the present at least, to treat it as a member of the list of maxims.

There are of course all sorts of other maxims (aesthetic, social, or moral in character) such as "Be polite," which are also normally observed by participants in talk exchanges, and these may also generate nonconventional implicatures. The conversational maxims, however, and the conversational implicatures connected with them, are specially connected (I hope) with the particular purposes which talk (and so talk exchange) is adapted to serve and is primarily employed to serve. I have stated my maxims as if this purpose were a maximally effective exchange of information; this specification is of course too narrow, and the scheme needs to be generalized to allow for such general purposes as influencing or directing the actions of others.

As one of my avowed aims is to see talking as a special case or variety of purposive, indeed rational, behavior, it may be worth noting that the specific expectations or presumptions connected with at least some of the foregoing maxims have their analogues in the sphere of transactions which are not talk exchanges. I list briefly one such analogue for each conversational category.

I *Quantity.* If you are assisting me to mend a car, I expect your contribution to be neither more nor less than is required; if for example, at a particular stage I need four screws, I expect you to hand me four, rather than two or six.

II *Quality.* I expect your contributions to be genuine and not spurious. If I need sugar as an ingredient in the cake you are helping me bake, I do not expect you to hand me salt; if I need a spoon, I do not expect a trick spoon made of rubber.

III *Relation.* I expect a partner's contribution to be appropriate to immediate needs at each stage of the transaction; if I am mixing ingredients for a cake, I do not expect to be handed a good book, or even a pot-holder (though this might be an appropriate contribution at a later stage).

IV *Manner.* I expect a partner to make it clear what contribution he is making, and to execute his performance with reasonable dispatch.

These analogies are relevant to what I regard as a fundamental question about the CP and its attendant maxims, namely, what the basis is for the assumption which we seem to make, and on which (I hope) it will appear that a great range of implicatures depend, that talkers will in general (ceteris paribus and in the absence of indications to the contrary) proceed in the manner which these principles prescribe. A dull but no doubt at a certain level adequate answer is that it is just a well-recognized empirical fact that people *do* behave in these ways; they have learned to do so in childhood, and have not lost the habit of doing so; and indeed it would involve a good deal of effort to make a radical departure from the habit. It is much easier, for example, to tell the truth than to invent lies.

I am, however, enough of a rationalist to want to find a basis which underlies these facts, undeniable though they may be; I would like to be able to think of the standard type of conversational practice not merely as something which all or most do *in fact* follow, but as something which it is *reasonable* for us to follow, which we *should not* abandon. For a time I was attracted by the idea that observance of the CP and the maxims, in a talk exchange, could be thought of as a quasi-contractual matter, with parallels outside the realm of discourse. If you pass by when I am struggling with my stranded car, I no doubt have some degree of expectation that you will offer help; but once you join me in tinkering under the hood, my expectations become stronger and take more specific forms (in the absence of indications that you are merely an incompetent meddler). Likewise, talk exchanges seem to me to exhibit, characteristically, certain features which jointly distinguish cooperative transactions: (1) that the participants have some common immediate aim, like getting a car mended (Their ultimate aims may of course be independent and even in conflict; each may want to get the car mended in order to drive off leaving the other stranded. In characteristic talk exchanges there is a common aim even if, as in an over-the-wall chat, it is a second-order one, namely, that each party should for the time being identify himself with the transitory conversational interests of the other.); (2) that the contributions of the participants should be dovetailed, mutually dependent; (3) that there is some sort of understanding (which may be explicit but which is often tacit) that, other things being equal, the transaction should continue in appropriate style unless both parties agree it should terminate. You don't just shove off, or start doing something else.

But while some such quasi-contractual basis as this may apply to some cases, there are too many types of exchange, like quarreling and letter writing, which it fails to fit comfortably. In any case one feels that the talker who is irrelevant or obscure has primarily let down not his audience but himself. So I would like to be able to show that observance of the CP and maxims is reasonable (rational) along the following lines: that any one who cares about the goals that are central to conversation/communication (such as giving and receiving information, influencing and being influenced by others) must be expected to have an interest, given suitable circumstances, in participation in talk exchanges which will be profitable only on the assumption that they are conducted in general accordance with the CP and the maxims. Whether any such conclusion can be reached, I am uncertain; in any case I am fairly sure I cannot reach it until I am a good deal clearer about the nature of relevance and of the circumstances in which it is required.

It is now time to show the connection between the CP and maxims on the one hand, and conversational implicature on the other.

A participant in a talk exchange may fail to fulfill a maxim in various ways which include the following:

(1) He may quietly and unostentatiously *violate* a maxim; if so, in some cases he will be liable to mislead.

(2) He may *opt out* from the operation both of the maxim and of the CP; he may say, indicate, or allow it to become plain that he is unwilling to cooperate in the way in which the maxim requires. He may say, for example, "I cannot say more, my lips are sealed."

(3) He may be faced by a *clash:* he may be unable, for example, to fulfill the first maxim of Quantity ("Be as informative as required") without violating the second maxim of Quality ("Have adequate evidence for what you say").

(4) He may *flout* a maxim; that is, he may *blatantly* fail to fulfill it. On the assumption that the speaker is able to fulfill the maxim and do so without violating another maxim (because of a clash), is not opting out, and is not in view of the blatancy of his performance, trying to mislead, the hearer is faced with a minor problem: how can his saying what he did say be reconciled with the supposition that he is observing the overall CP? This situation is one which characteristically gives rise to a conversational implicature; and when a conversational implicature is generated in this way, I shall say that a maxim is being *exploited.*

I am now in a position to characterize the notion of conversational implicature, a man who, by (in when) saying (or making as if to say) that *p* has implicated that *q,* may be said to have conversationally implicated that *q, provided that:* (1) he is to be presumed to be observing the conversational maxims, or at least the cooperative principle; (2) the supposition that he is aware that, or thinks that *q,* is required in order to make his saying or making as if to say *p* (or doing so in *those* terms) consistent with this presumption; and (3) that the speaker thinks (and would expect the hearer to think that the speaker thinks) that it is within the competence of the hearer to work out, or grasp intuitively, that the supposition mentioned in (2) *is* required. Apply this to my initial example, to B's remark that C has not yet been to prison. In a suitable setting A might reason as follows: "(1) B has apparently violated the maxim 'Be relevant' and so may be regarded as having flouted one of the maxims conjoining perspicuity; yet I have no reason to suppose that he is opting out from the operation of the CP; (2) given the circumstances I can regard his irrelevance as only apparent if and only if I suppose him to think that C is potentially dishonest; (3) B knows that I am capable of working out step (2). So B implicates that C is potentially dishonest."

The presence of a conversational implicature must be capable of being worked out; for even if it can in fact be intuitively grasped, unless the intuition is replaceable by an argument, the implicature (if present at all) will not count as a *conversational* implicature; it will be a *conventional* implicature. To work out that a particular conversational implicature is present, the hearer will rely on the following data: (1) the conventional meaning of the words used, together with the identity of any references which may be involved; (2) the CP and its maxims; (3) the context linguistic or otherwise of the utterance; (4) other items of background knowledge; (5) the fact (or supposed fact) that all relevant items falling under the previous heading are available to both participants, and that both participants know or assume this to be so. A general pattern for the working out of a conversational implicature might be given as follows: "He has said that p; there is no reason to suppose that he is not observing the maxims, or at least the CP; he could not be doing this unless he thought that q; he knows (and knows that I know that he knows) that I can see that the supposition that he thinks that q is required; he has done nothing to stop me thinking that q; therefore he intends me to think, or is at least willing to allow me to think, that q; and so he has implicated that q."

I shall now offer a number of examples which I shall divide into three groups.

Group A: Examples in which no maxim is violated, or at least in which it is not clear that any maxim is violated.

(1) A is standing by an obviously immobilized car and is approached by B, and the following exchange takes place:

A: "I am out of petrol."
B: "There is a garage round the corner."

(*Gloss*: B would be infringing the maxim "Be relevant" unless he thinks, or thinks it possible, that the garage is open, and had petrol to sell; so he implicated that the garage is, or at least may be, open, and so on.)

In this example, unlike the case of the remark "He hasn't been to prison yet," the unstated connection between B's remark and A's remark is so obvious that, even if one interprets the supermaxim of Manner, "Be perspicuous," as applying not only to the expression of what is said, but also to the connection of what is said, with adjacent remarks, there seems to be no case for regarding that supermaxim as infringed in this example. The next example is perhaps a little less clear in this respect.

(2) A: "Smith doesn't seem to have a girl friend these days."
B: "He has been paying a lot of visits to New York lately."

B implicates that Smith has, or may have, a girl friend in New York. Gloss is unnecessary in view of that given for the previous example.

In both examples the speaker implicates that which he must be assumed to believe in order to preserve the assumption that he is observing the maxim of relation.

Group B: An example in which a maxim is violated, but its violation is to be explained by the supposition of a clash with another maxim. A is planning with B an itinerary for a holiday in France. Both know that A wants to see his friend C if to do so would not involve too great a prolongation of his journey:

A: "Where does C live?"
B: "Somewhere in the South of France."

(*Gloss*: There is no reason to suppose that B is opting out; his answer is, as he well knows, less informative than is required to meet A's needs; this infringement of the first maxim of Quantity can only be explained by the supposition that B is aware that to be more informative would be to say something which infringed the maxim of Quality, "Don't say what you lack adequate evidence for," so B implicates that he does not know in which town C lives.)

Group C: Examples which involve exploitation, that is, a procedure by which a maxim is flouted for the purpose of getting in a conversational implicature by means of something of the nature of a figure of speech. In these examples, though some maxim is violated at the level of what is said, the hearer is entitled to assume that that maxim, or at least the overall Cooperative Principle, is observed at the level of what is implicated.

(1a) (A flouting of the first maxim of Quantity): A is writing a testimonial about a pupil who is a candidate for a philosophy job, and his letter reads as follows: "Dear Sir, Mr. X's command of English is excellent, and his attendance at tutorials has been regular, Yours, etc." (*Gloss:* A cannot be opting out, since if he wished to be uncooperative, why write at all? He cannot be unable, through ignorance, to say more, since the man is his pupil; moreover, he knows that more information than this is wanted. He must, therefore, be wishing to impart information which he is reluctant to write down. This supposition is only tenable on the assumption that he thinks that Mr. X is no good at philosophy. This, then, is what he is implicating.)

Extreme examples of a flouting of the first maxim of Quantity are provided by utterances of patent tautologies like "Women are women," "War is war." I would wish to maintain that at the level of what is said, in my favored sense, such remarks are totally noninformative and so, at that level, cannot but infringe the first maxim of Quantity in any conversational context. They are, of course, informative at the level of what is implicated, and the hearer's identification of their informative content at this level is dependent on his ability to explain the speaker's selection of this *particular* patent tautology.

(1b) (An infringement of the second maxim of Quantity: "Do not give more information than is required" on the assumption that the existence of such a maxim should be admitted.) A wants to know whether p; and B volunteers not only the information that p, but information to the effect that it is certain that p, and that the evidence for its being true that p is so-and-so and such-and-such.

B's volubility may be undesigned, and if it is so regarded by A, it may raise in A's mind a doubt whether B is as certain as he says he is ("Methinks the lady doth protest too much"). But if it is thought of as designed, it would be an oblique way of conveying that it is to some degree controversial whether or not p. It is however arguable that such an implicature could be explained by reference to the maxim of Relation without invoking an alleged second maxim of Quantity.

(2a) Examples in which the first maxim of Quality is flouted.

Irony. X, with whom till now A has been on close terms, has betrayed a secret of A's to a business rival. A and his audience both know this. A says "X is a fine friend." (*Gloss:* It is perfectly obvious to A and his audience that what A has said or has made as if to say is something which he does not believe, and the audience knows that A knows that this is obvious to the audience. So, unless A's utterance is entirely pointless, A must be trying to get across some proposition other than the one he purports to be putting forward. This must be some obviously related proposition; the most obviously related proposition is the contradictory of the one he purports to be putting forward.)

Metaphor. For example, "You are the cream in my coffee." Such examples characteristically involve categorical falsity, so the contradictory of what the speaker has made as if to say will, strictly speaking, be a truism; so it cannot be *that* that such a speaker is trying to get across. The most likely supposition is that the speaker is attributing to his audience some feature or features in respect of which the audience resembles (more or less fancifully) the mentioned substance.

It is possible to combine metaphor and irony by imposing on the hearer two stages of interpretation. I say "You are the cream in my coffee," intending the hearer to reach first the metaphor interpretant "You are my pride and joy," and then the irony interpretant "You are my bane."

Meiosis. Of a man to have broken up all the furniture, one says "He was a little intoxicated."

Hyperbole. "Every nice girl loves a sailor."

(2b) Examples in which the second maxim of Quality "Do not say that for which you lack adequate evidence" is flouted are perhaps not easy to find, but the following seems to be a specimen. I say of X's wife, "She is probably deceiving him this evening." In a suitable context, or with a suitable gesture or tone of voice, it may be clear that I have no adequate reason for supposing this to be so. My partner, to preserve the assumption that the conversational game is still being played, assumes that I am getting at some related proposition for the acceptance of which I *do* have a reasonable basis. The related proposition might well be that she is given to deceiving her husband, or possibly that she is the sort of person who wouldn't stop short of such conduct.

(3) Examples in which an implicature is achieved by real as distinct from apparent violation of the maxim of Relation are perhaps rare, but the following seems to be a good candidate. At a genteel tea party A says "Mrs. X is an old bag." There is a moment of appalled silence, then B says "The weather has been quite delightful this summer, hasn't it?" B has blatantly refused to make what *he* says relevant to A's preceding remark. He thereby implicates that A's remark should not be discussed, and perhaps more specifically, that A has committed a social gaffe.

(4) Examples in which various maxims falling under the supermaxim "Be perspicuous" are flouted.

(a) *Ambiguity.* We must remember that we are only concerned with ambiguity that is deliberate, and which the speaker intends or expects to be recognized by his hearer. The problem the hearer has to solve is why a speaker should, when still playing the conversational game, go out of his way to choose an ambiguous utterance. There are two types of case:

(i) Examples in which there is no difference, or no striking difference, between two interpretations of an utterance in respect of straightforwardness; neither interpretation is notably more sophisticated, less standard, more recondite or more farfetched than the other. We might consider Blake's lines: "Never seek to tell thy love, Love that never told can be." To avoid the complications introduced by the presence of the imperative mood, I shall consider the related sentence, "I sought to tell my love, love that never told can be." There may be a double ambiguity here. "My love" may refer to either a state of emotion or an object of emotion, and "Love that never told can be" may mean either "Love that cannot be told" or "Love that if told cannot continue to exist." Partly because of the sophistication of the poet and partly because of internal evidence (that the ambiguity is kept up), there seems to be no alternative to supposing that the ambiguities are deliberate and that the poet is conveying both what he would be saying if one interpretation were intended rather than the other, and vice versa; though no doubt the poet is not explicitly *saying* any of these things, but only conveying or suggesting them (cf. "Since she [nature] pricked thee out for women's pleasure, mine be thy love, and thy love's use their treasure.")

(ii) Examples in which one interpretation is notably less straightforward than another. Take the complex example of the British General who captured the town of Sind and sent back the message "Peccavi." The ambiguity involved ("I have Sind"—"I have sinned") is phonemic not morphemic; and the expression actually used is unambiguous; but since it is in a language foreign to speaker and hearer, translation is called for, and the ambiguity resides in the standard translation into native English.

Whether or not the straightforward interpretant ("I have sinned") is being conveyed, it seems that the nonstraightforward must be. There might be stylistic reasons for conveying by a sentence merely its nonstraightforward interpretant, but it would be pointless, and perhaps also stylistically objectionable, to go to the trouble of finding an expression which nonstraightforwardly conveys that p, thus imposing on an audience the effort involved in finding this interpretant, if this interpretant were otiose so far as communication was concerned. Whether the straightforward interpretant is also being conveyed seems to depend on whether such a supposition would conflict with other conversational requirements; for example, would it be relevant, would it be something that the speaker could be supposed to accept, and so on. If such requirements are not satisfied, then the straightforward interpretant is not being conveyed. If they are, it is. If the author of "Peccavi" could naturally be supposed to think that he had committed some kind of transgression, for example, had disobeyed his orders in capturing Sind, and if reference to such a transgression would be relevant to the presumed interests of the audience, then he would have been conveying both interpretations; otherwise he would be conveying only the one.

(b) *Obscurity.* How do I exploit, for the purposes of communication, a deliberate and overt violation of the requirement that I should avoid obscurity? Obviously, if the Cooperative Principle is to operate, I must intend my partner to understand what I am saying despite the obscurity which I import into my utterance. Suppose that A and B are having a conversation in the presence of a third party, for example, a child; then A might be deliberately obscure, though not too obscure, in the hope that B would understand and that the third party would not. Furthermore, if A expects B to see that A is being deliberately obscure, it seems reasonable to suppose that, in making his conversational contribution in this way, A is implicating that the contents of his communication should not be imparted to the third party.

(c) *Failure to be brief or succinct.* Compare the remarks

(1) "Miss X sang 'Home sweet home.' "
(2) "Miss X produced a series of sounds which corresponded closely with the score of 'Home sweet home.' "

Suppose that a reviewer has chosen to utter (2) rather than (1). (*Gloss:* Why has he selected that rigmarole in place of the concise and nearly synonymous "sang"? Presumably to indicate some striking difference between Miss X's performance and those to which the word "singing" is usually applied. The most obvious supposition is that Miss X's performance suffered from some hideous defect. The reviewer knows that this supposition is what is likely to spring to mind; so that is what he is implicating.)

I have so far considered only cases of what I might call particularized conversational implicature; that is to say, cases in which an implicature is carried by saying that *p* on a particular occasion, in virtue of special features of the context; cases in which there is no room for the idea that an implicature of this sort is *normally* carried by saying that *p*. But there are cases of generalized conversational implicature. Sometimes one can say that the use of a certain form of words in an utterance would normally (in the *absence* of special circumstances) carry such-and-such an implicature or type of implicature. Noncontroversial examples are perhaps hard to find, since it is all too easy to treat a generalized conversational implicature as if it were a conventional implicature. I offer an example which I hope may be fairly noncontroversial.

Anyone who uses a sentence of the form "X is meeting a woman this evening" would normally implicate that the person to be met was someone other than X's wife, mother, sister, or perhaps even close platonic friend. Similarly, if I were to say "X went into a house yesterday and found a tortoise inside the front door," my hearer would normally be surprised if some time later I revealed that the house was X's own. I could produce similar linguistic phenomena involving the expression "a garden", "a car", "a college", and so on. Sometimes, however, there would normally be no such implicature ("I have been sitting in a car all morning"), and sometimes a reverse implicature ("I broke a finger yesterday"). I am inclined to think that one would not lend a sympathetic ear to a philosopher who suggested that there are three senses of the form of expression "an X": one in which it means roughly "something which satisfies the conditions defining the word X"; another in which it means approximately "an X (in the first sense) which is only remotely related in a certain way to some person indicated by the context"; and yet another in which it means "an X (in the first sense) which is closely related in a certain way to some person indicated by the context." Would we not much prefer an account on the following lines (which of course may be incorrect in detail)? When someone by using the form of expression "an X" implicates that the X does not belong to or is not otherwise closely connected with some identifiable person, the implicature is present because the speaker has failed to be specific in a way in which he might have been expected to be specific, with the consequence that it is likely to be assumed that he is not in a position to be specific. This is a familiar implicature situation, and is classifiable as a failure, for one reason or another, to fulfill the first maxim of Quantity. The only difficult question is why it should, in certain cases, be presumed, independently of information about particular contexts of utterance, that specification of the closeness or remoteness of the connection between a particular person or object and a further person who is mentioned or indicated by the utterance should be likely to be of interest. The answer must lie in the following region: transactions between a person and other persons or things closely connected with him are liable to be very different as regards their concomitants and results from the same sort of transactions involving only remotely connected persons or things; the concomitants and results, for instance, of my finding a hole in *my* roof are likely to be very different from the concomitants and results of my finding a hole in someone else's roof. Information, like money, is often given without the giver knowing to just what use the recipient will want to put it. If someone to whom a transaction is mentioned gives it further consideration, he is likely to find himself wanting the answers to further questions which the speaker may not be able to identify in advance; if the appropriate specification will be likely to enable the hearer to answer a considerable variety of such questions for himself, then there is a presumption that the speaker should include it in his remark; if not, then there is no such presumption.

Finally, we can now show that, conversational implicature being what it is, it must possess certain features.

(1) Since to assume the presence of a conversational implicature we must assume that at least the Cooperative Principle is being observed, and since it is possible to opt out of the observation of this principle, it follows that a generalized conversational implicature can be canceled in a particular case. It may be explicitly canceled, by the addition of a clause which states or implies that the speaker has opted out, or it may be contextually canceled, if the form of utterance which usually carries it is used in a context which makes it clear that the speaker *is* opting out.

(2) In so far as the calculation that a particular conversational implicature is present requires, besides contextual and background information, only a knowledge of what has been said (or of the conventional commitment of the utterance), and in so far as the manner of expression plays no role in the calculation, it will not be possible to find another way of saying the same thing, which simply lacks the implicature in question, except where some special feature of the substituted version is itself relevant to the determination of an implicature (in virtue of one of the maxims of manner). If we call this feature "nondetachability," one may expect a generalized conversational implicature which is carried by a familiar, nonspecial locution to have a high degree of nondetachability.

(3) To speak approximately, since the calculation of the presence of a conversational implicature presupposes an initial knowledge of the conventional force of the expression the utterance of which carries the implicature, a conver-

sational implicatum will be a condition which is not included in the original specification of the expression's conventional force. Though it may not be impossible for what starts life, so to speak, as a conversational implicature to become conventionalized, to suppose that this is so in a given case would require special justification. So, initially at least, conversational implicata are not part of the meaning of the expressions to the employment of which they attach.

(4) Since the truth of a conversational implicatum is not required by the truth of what is said (what is said may be true, what is implicated may be false), the implicature is not carried by what is said, but only by the saying of what is said or by "putting it that way."

(5) Since to calculate a conversational implicature is to calculate what has to be supposed in order to preserve the supposition that the Cooperative Principle is being observed, and since there may be various possible specific explanations, a list of which may be open, the conversational implication in such cases will be a disjunction of such specific explanations; and if the list of these is open, the implicatum will have just the kind of indeterminacy which many actual implicata do in fact seem to possess.

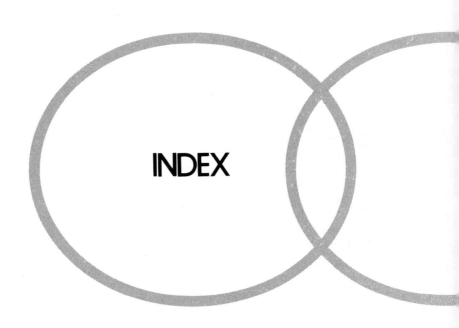

INDEX